CLASS AND POWER IN THE NEW DEAL

CLASS AND POWER IN THE NEW DEAL

Corporate Moderates, Southern Democrats, and the Liberal-Labor Coalition

G. William Domhoff and Michael J. Webber

STANFORD UNIVERSITY PRESS
STANFORD, CALIFORNIA

Stanford University Press
Stanford, California

Printed in the United States of America on acid-free,
archival-quality paper.

Library of Congress Cataloging-in-Publication Data
Domhoff, G. William, author.
    Class and power in the New Deal : corporate moderates,
southern Democrats, and the liberal-labor coalition /
G. William Domhoff and Michael J. Webber.
        pages cm
    Includes bibliographical references and index.
    ISBN 978-0-8047-7452-9 (cloth : alk. paper)—
ISBN 978-0-8047-7453-6 (pbk. : alk. paper)
    1. New Deal, 1933–1939. 2. United States—Politics and
government—1933–1945. 3. United States—Economic
policy—1933–1945. 4. United States—Social policy.
I. Webber, Michael J. author. II. Title.
E806. D66 2011
973.917—dc22
                                        2011004556

Typeset by Classic Typography in 10/13 Sabon

CONTENTS

AAA	Agricultural Adjustment Administration
AALL	American Association for Labor Legislation
AFL	American Federation of Labor
BAC	Business Advisory Council
BAE	Bureau of Agricultural Economics
CES	Committee on Economic Security
CIO	Congress of Industrial Organizations
CP	Communist Party
FSA	Farm Security Administration
IRC	Industrial Relations Counselors, Inc.
NAM	National Association of Manufacturers
NCF	National Civic Federation
NCL	National Consumers' League
NICB	National Industrial Conference Board
NLRB	National Labor Relations Board
NRA	National Recovery Administration (1933–1935)
PWA	Public Works Administration
SSRC	Social Science Research Council
WPA	Works Progress Administration

ACKNOWLEDGMENTS

Many thanks to Walter L. Goldfrank and Ira Katznelson for detailed readings of an earlier draft of the manuscript, which saved us from many errors and led to several changes in style and emphasis. Many thanks also to Sanford Jacoby for important suggestions on reorganizing the final chapter and to Michael Mann for his assurances that we had presented the best possible substantive case. We also thank Peter Swenson for comments on specific aspects of the manuscript relating to his own research on American labor history and on the Social Security Act. A special thanks to Harvey Klehr for his patient and extremely helpful answers to our many questions about the role of the Communist Party during the New Deal, and to Judith Stepan-Norris for her reassuring and informative comments on the section on the Communist Party in the second chapter. We are grateful to Dan Clawson and Howard Kimeldorf for their thoughts on the factors leading to success in unionization struggles, with an extra thanks to Kimeldorf for allowing us to draw on his new ideas concerning this difficult question and for his suggestions to improve Chapter 2.

We also are extremely appreciative of the very perceptive suggestions and critiques provided by two anonymous reviewers for Stanford University Press, whose comments motivated us to make it a much better book than it originally was. Finally, we are very grateful to Bruce Kaufmann for providing us with copies of the memorandums sent to clients by Industrial Relations Counselors, Inc., during 1934 and 1935, which gave us a unique new window into the very different ways in which moderate conservatives in the corporate community regarded the Social Security Act and the National Labor Relations Act.

CLASS AND POWER IN THE NEW DEAL

Introduction

It was a balmy, slightly damp evening on June 27, 1936, as nearly a hundred thousand people jammed into the stands and playing surface at Franklin Field in Philadelphia. The huge crowd had gathered in eager anticipation of President Franklin D. Roosevelt's acceptance speech to the Democratic National Convention, which would launch his bid for a second term, and millions more across the country were waiting to listen on the radio. The light rain stopped and the skies cleared only minutes before Roosevelt rode onto the field in his presidential limousine, and then the spotlights that had been sweeping back and forth across the darkened stadium focused on the president as he crossed the covered stage and approached the podium. Basking in the acclaim for having steered many major pieces of reform legislation through Congress in his first term and optimistic about his prospects for re-election with the economy recovering from its low point in March 1933, Roosevelt was in a triumphal mood as he riveted the crowd with one of the most inspirational and defiant speeches in American presidential history.

Pressing home his political advantage, Roosevelt revisited one of the enduring themes of his New Deal, namely the perfidious and selfish nature of the business community. As usual, he was careful to distinguish the rapacious few from the good citizenship of the many. But his speech nonetheless excoriated the "economic royalists" whose power was based upon a "concentration of control over material things." They had tried to create a new despotism "wrapped in the robes of legal sanction," and now they were reaching out for control of the government itself. The political liberties won during the American Revolution might become meaningless, he warned, in the face of a small group that had "almost complete control over other people's property, other people's money, other people's labor—over other people's lives." There now existed a "new industrial dictatorship" that limited opportunity through monopoly and crushed individual initiative in "the cogs of a great machine" in which "privileged enterprise had replaced free enterprise."

The economic royalists complain that "we seek to overthrow the institutions of America," Roosevelt thundered, but "what they really complain of is that we seek to take away their power. Our allegiance to American institutions requires the overthrow of this kind of power." Modern governments, Roosevelt insisted, had "inescapable obligations to their citizens," including the protection of homes and families, the establishment of economic opportunity, and assistance to those in need. The fight against economic tyranny was "a war for the survival of democracy" that would move forward despite business opposition, he promised, because the current generation of Americans had a "rendezvous with destiny" (Roosevelt 1938, pp. 230–236). (For a sense of the crowd at Franklin Field before Roosevelt's speech, a brief excerpt from his speech, and footage of him shortly after the speech ended, see videos 65675036466, 65675036463, and 65675036467 at http://www.criticalpast.com.)

When the ballots were counted that November, Roosevelt had beaten Republican Alfred M. Landon in a landslide. He captured 60.8 percent of the popular vote, won the Electoral College by 523 to 8, and had healthy majorities in the Senate (75-16) and House (331-88). He won 76 percent of lower-income voters but only 42 percent of upper-income voters. More striking, only 18 percent of the business executives who made campaign donations gave anything to Roosevelt, and only a handful of that small minority came from the large financial institutions and industrial corporations that had been the object of Roosevelt's all-out challenge (Webber 2000, pp. 12–15).

And yet, despite all the acrimonious rhetoric and mutual invective between Roosevelt and the economic royalists, some of the richest and most powerful corporate leaders of that era had played a major role in the formulation of the ideas underlying the three most important, controversial, and enduring policies that emerged during the New Deal—the Agricultural Adjustment Act of 1933, the National Labor Relations Act of 1935, and the Social Security Act of 1935. But why would they help draft key elements of the New Deal and then do everything they could to defeat Roosevelt's bid for a second term?

The purpose of this book is to demonstrate that many of the wealthiest and best-organized corporate owners and executives were heavily involved in policy formulation even while opposing the liberal and labor political figures who became increasingly visible and important within the Democratic Party in the first few years of the New Deal. In the process, we seek to demonstrate the superiority of our theory of class dominance, tailored specifically for the United States, over other theoretical perspectives in explaining these three policy initiatives. In particular, we focus our critical attention on three rival theories widely used in sociological and political analyses of the New Deal—historical institutionalism, Marxism, and protest-disruption theory. Although we share some general assumptions and agreements with each of these theories, we show how they are more often wrong than right in their own separate ways when it comes to the key issues concerning the New Deal.

To be more specific, the book describes how Northern corporate moderates, representing some of the largest fortunes and biggest companies of that era, proposed all three of the major policy innovations that today define the New Deal, sometimes in reaction to pressures from the leaders of organized labor or disruptive efforts by grassroots leftist activists. It also explains how Southern Democrats shaped these proposals to fit the needs of plantation capitalists and large agricultural interests throughout the country before they allowed any of them to pass. As for the ultraconservatives in the corporate community, who were most likely the main "economic royalists" that Roosevelt had in mind in his convention speech, they uniformly opposed these New Deal initiatives, but they did not have any impact because there were so few conservative Republicans in Congress.

In sum, corporate moderates proposed, corporate ultraconservatives opposed, and Southern Democrats disposed in a context in which organized labor and the Communist Party were able to apply pressure through work stoppages, strikes, and demonstrations. In addition, urban liberals, concerned with ameliorating the uncertainties of the marketplace and mitigating the worst effects of unfair business and labor practices for ordinary Americans, had an impact on the National Labor Relations Act and Social Security Act as members of the New Deal coalition and as allies of organized labor.

POLICY AND POLITICS

Although corporate moderates originated all three of the policies mentioned earlier, which demonstrates that they continued to control the policy agenda even in the face of a major loss of public confidence in business, they did not do so by themselves. They had the help of the many experts they employed in their foundations, consulting firms, and think tanks. The corporate moderates and the experts, working together within what we show to be a closely knit policy-planning network, had a continuing impact in part because the nascent liberal-labor coalition could provide no workable policy alternatives in the first year or two of the New Deal, and in part because government agencies were understaffed and did not have the ability to generate new policies. The corporate moderates also retained their access to many elected officials because they were among the primary financial backers of their successful campaigns. Although most newly elected officials did not have any firm policy positions, they had a crucial role because they were open to new initiatives; if they had not been elected, it is far less likely that any of the policies we discuss would have been enacted. Politicians also decided on the timing for the introduction of these measures and sometimes provided the popular phraseology in which the policies were debated.

The distinction between policy and politics emphasized in this book is embodied in the person and presidential style of Franklin D. Roosevelt, who is considered by most historians to be the greatest president of the twentieth century. Roosevelt was a consummate politician whose skills have been detailed in many sources. He was a master of timing, synthesis, compromise, phrasing, ambiguity, reassurance, and symbolism. He knew the strengths, weaknesses, and interests of all the groups he had to deal with and was always looking for the compromises that would lead to enduring policy outcomes (Swenson 2002). After running a cautious centrist campaign in 1932, with vague mentions of a "New Deal" but no specifics, he spoke in moving terms at his inauguration about including everyone and balancing the pursuit of wealth with other important values. He told people there was nothing to fear but fear itself and made himself the champion of the common person. He came to use the term *liberal* to characterize his views while at the same time saying that he was no more than a Christian and a Democrat when it came to philosophies. Nonetheless, he only cautiously accepted the main thrusts of modern-day urban liberalism on some issues.

In fact, the distinction between policy and politics is, in the words of one of his biographers, "pure Roosevelt" (Smith 2007, p. 281). He had one set of people for political strategy and another set for policy suggestions. While relations between the two groups were cordial, their roles were strictly differentiated and carefully observed. At the same time, Roosevelt had to carry out a delicate balancing act in obtaining legislation from Congress, even though there were large Democratic majorities in both the House and the Senate. He needed to assuage the powerful Northern conservative leaders in his own party, who were sometimes part of major Wall Street financial networks, while at the same time being sensitive to the special needs of the Southern Democrats, who had played a crucial role in securing the Democratic nomination for him in 1932 and in any case controlled all the key committees he had to deal with in Congress due to the seniority system.

However, the same sources that spell out Roosevelt's virtues as a political leader, often in vivid and enjoyable portraits of how he operated, also suggest that he had no sure grasp of policy details or much interest in them (for one excellent example, see Cohen 2009). For instance, his close advisors were never sure he understood the agricultural subsidy program, and New Deal historian Arthur Schlesinger (1958, p. 38) concludes that Roosevelt "knew little first hand about the problems of grain and cotton surpluses." Another historian, Frank Freidel (1973, pp. 89–90), argues that Roosevelt's "eclecticism" in encouraging the inclusion of different plans within the Agricultural Adjustment Act was due at least in part to the fact that he "had little real understanding of the proposed mechanisms" and that eventually "his ignorance created embarrassment." Still another historian, James E. Sargent (1981, pp. 161–162), uses some of Roosevelt's own statements to show that he "did not understand his complex farm program in detail."

On the issue of old-age social insurance, now popularly known as "social security," he knew he wanted its tax base separate from the usual tax sources, and that both employers and employees should contribute, as advocated by insurance companies and corporate experts, but little more. On the issue of unemployment compensation, the most detailed account of how the policy developed concludes that Roosevelt did not have a good understanding of its key provisions (Nelson 1969). Roosevelt revealed his inability to understand economic policy when he insisted in early 1937 that budget deficits should be eliminated because unemployment was declining and the economy therefore could grow on its own. In combination with an inadvertent tightening of the money supply by the Federal Reserve Board and major cutbacks in government employment programs, the result was a sharp slowdown in the economy and the increase in unemployment that his Keynesian economic advisors had warned him would happen. This economic downturn weakened unions just as they were having some success in organizing unskilled industrial workers. It also contributed to Republicans' gains in the Senate and the House that allowed a conservative voting coalition—defined as a majority of Southern Democrats and Northern Republicans voting together on an issue in opposition to a majority of non-Southern Democrats—to defeat any further reforms (Smith 2007, pp. 395–397).

As we explain in Chapters 2 and 3, the main links between Roosevelt and the policy-planning network during the presidential campaign and in the first months of the New Deal came through his "Brain Trust," a trio of Columbia University professors that he recruited to give him policy advice. In effect, they packaged the alternatives suggested by the corporate moderates and their policy experts into memos that Roosevelt could use in planning his political strategies and crafting his speeches. For the social insurance policies developed in the last six or seven months of 1934, his main liaison was Secretary of Labor Frances Perkins, a longtime advocate of laws governing working conditions, minimum wages, and social insurance stretching back to the Progressive Era. When it came to the formulation of the National Labor Relations Act, Roosevelt kept the issue at an arm's length and had no direct hand in shaping it, or even in working out the strategy for turning it into legislation, until after it had been passed overwhelmingly by the Senate in the spring of 1935.

Although our primary purpose is to demonstrate the scholarly usefulness of our version of a class-domination theory, the book also may be of more general interest because it challenges current conventional wisdom on the origins of the programs it analyzes. For example, the agricultural support system that now costs $15–20 billion each year was not created by farmers, although the approval of agricultural interests—especially Southern agricultural interests—was necessary to pass it. In fact, the basic ideas in the plan were opposed by many farmers outside the South until late 1932 and early 1933; the plan had to be sold to them by the agricultural economists and corporate leaders who perfected it at the instigation of the policy-oriented foundation executive who first proposed it.

As for the Social Security Act, it was not the work of liberals and labor leaders, as currently believed due to the fact that they defend it and conservatives dislike it. Instead, it was created by industrial relations experts who worked for foundations, consulting firms, and think tanks funded by several of the largest corporations of the 1930s, including some of those that also backed the subsidy program for agricultural interests. True enough, the Social Security Act was opposed in testimony before Congress by a wide range of ultraconservative corporate leaders, but their objections on this particular issue primarily reflected their growing animosity toward Roosevelt for some of the New Deal's other policies, particularly in relation to unions and collective bargaining, not substantive objections to the plans for social security created by the moderate conservatives of the corporate world.

Even the National Labor Relations Act, which gave life and hope to trade unions and made them important power actors for the next forty years, was in part the result of a series of institutional innovations in 1933 that emerged from proposals made by the same corporate moderates who fashioned the Social Security Act. However, this case is more complicated than the first two because militant union leaders and Communists created the strikes and work stoppages that started the ball rolling (see, for example, Levine 1988). Then liberal corporate lawyers and law school professors, who were employed temporarily at the National Labor Relations Board between 1934 and late 1935, crafted a new set of regulations based on what had been learned in the last six months of 1933 by an earlier incarnation of the labor board. The revised formulations of the labor board's composition, duties, and powers carried the program several steps beyond what the corporate moderates would accept, causing them to join their ultraconservative colleagues in opposition to legislation for which their earlier ideas had provided legitimacy. Despite this united corporate opposition, the act passed because Southern plantation capitalists deserted the corporate community in a rare act of class disloyalty on a labor issue, which was made possible by the liberal-labor coalition's willingness to exclude agricultural and domestic labor from the provisions of the act.

The fact that we claim there were different outcomes on the three policy struggles suggests that our analysis closely follows the archival record and that our theory does not inevitably lead to the same conclusion for each and every case. Instead, divisions among owners of large income-producing properties—in this case, divisions between Northern corporate owners and Southern plantation owners—can provide openings for significant victories for liberals and organized labor when they are united. But these victories can be reversed—as proved to be the case for the National Labor Relations Act—when the Northern and Southern segments of the ownership class united and the union movement was divided by rivalries between its craft and unskilled segments, rivalries that were intensified in 1937 and 1938 by tensions over the role of Communists in several industrial unions and at the National Labor Relations Board. The result was the Taft-Hartley Act of 1947, which made it much easier for employers to resist unionization (Gross 1981).

A GENERAL PERSPECTIVE ON CLASS DOMINANCE

Our version of class-domination theory starts with the work of sociologists C. Wright Mills (1956, 1962) and Michael Mann (1986) in assuming that there are political, military, and religious bases of power in addition to the economic base that is given primacy in Marxist theory. (Mann [1986, p. 22] uses the term *ideological* to describe the organizations concerned with generating norms, ritual practices, and answers to questions about the meaning and purpose of life, but we prefer the term *religious* because most of these organizations are religious in nature.)

We begin with Mann's view that power, defined as the ability to achieve desired social outcomes, has both collective and distributive dimensions. Collective power, the capacity of a group, class, or nation to be effective and productive, concerns the degree to which a collectivity has the technological resources, organizational forms, and social morale to achieve its general goals. As important as collective power is for societal growth and productivity, our focus in this book is on distributive power, the ability of a group, class, or nation to be successful in conflicts with other groups, classes, or nations on issues of concern to it.

In this view, both collective and distributive power emerge from the same organizational bases, with organizations defined as sets of rules, roles, and routines developed so that a human group can accomplish specific purposes. Although people have a vast array of purposes that have led to a large number of organizations, the historical record shows that only economic, political, military, and religious organizations weigh heavily in terms of generating societal power.

The four organizational bases are conceptualized as "overlapping and intersecting sociospatial networks of power" that have widely varying extensions in physical space at different times in Western history. For example, economic networks were very small in early Western history compared to political and military networks, but political networks, which provide the basis for the state in any society beyond the size of tribes and chiefdoms, were comparatively smaller in the Middle Ages, when economic networks were becoming more extensive and autonomous (Mann 1986, pp. 1, 390–397). Because these networks are ways of attaining human goals, the theory's focus is on the logistics of power, which are constantly changing with the development of new technologies and the emergence of new organizational forms and religious beliefs. Due to the emphasis on social networks, the notion of a "bounded society" or "social system" is abandoned, along with traditional arguments over "levels," "dimensions," and "agency versus structure" (Mann 1986, Chapter 1).

When the level of development reaches a large enough scale within any organization, a permanent division of labor emerges within it that further increases its collective power due to a specialization of function. In addition, it usually leads to a hierarchical distribution of power within the organization because "those who occupy supervisory and coordinating positions have an immense organizational superiority over the others" (Mann 1986, pp. 6–7). As theorists of varying persuasions have noted, those who supervise and coordinate can then turn the organization into a power base for themselves due to the information and material resources they come to control, their ability to reshape the structure of the organization, their power to hire and fire underlings, and their opportunities to make alliances with other organizational leaders. The interorganizational alliances then generate a more general power structure that uses its combined resources to develop barriers that make it difficult for people outside or on the bottom of these organizations to participate in the governance of the society in general. Put in other terms, those who supervise and coordinate end up "at the top"; they become the leadership group, the "power elite," within any historically specific power structure.

As the four main organizational networks become further intertwined, they have even more potential to greatly increase collective power. This is most directly observed historically through the way in which political and military networks, by then closely intertwined in a new institutional form, the state, aided in the development of economic networks. For example, they increased the collective power of economic networks through activities as varied as protecting trade routes and making it possible to employ coerced or slave labor. This point also can be seen in the ways in which religious networks intensify social cohesion and provide the normative values that property owners within economic networks sometimes use to intensify their demands for greater labor productivity from non-owning classes.

However, and very critical in terms of understanding power in nation-states, the mobilization of greater collective power comes to depend on the resolution of prior questions about distributive power within organizations. Who has power over whom has to be settled within and between the four main organizational networks before collective power can be exercised in any sustained way. Given the investment of time, energy, and identity that people put into the organizations they belong to, the battle over distributive power is an ongoing and often deadly one that is front and center in most historical accounts even while collective power is often slowly accumulating in the background.

According to this four-network theory of social power, no one network came first historically or is more basic than the others: each one always has presupposed the existence of the others. It is therefore not possible to reduce power to one primary form, as Bertrand Russell (1938, pp. 10–11) concluded decades ago, and as sociologist Dennis Wrong (1995) confirmed in his analysis of the social science literature nearly sixty years later. In keeping with this conclusion, the four networks are foreshadowed in egalitarian hunting and gathering societies when hunting parties are organized (economic networks, with meat shared equally among all members of the society); when communal gatherings are called in an attempt to defuse interpersonal disputes that threaten to rip apart the whole group (political organization, which is fundamentally about regulating human interactions within a specific territory); when the men band together to do battle with rival groups or clans (military organization); and when rituals of social solidarity and expiation are performed in an attempt to control the anxiety, guilt, and fear of death that have been part of daily existence for most individuals since the dawn of humanity (religious organization).

The fact that all four networks have always existed does not mean that they are of necessity equal in terms of their social power in any given time or place. For a variety of reasons, including logistical and organizational advances in one or another network, different networks have been ascendant in different times and places, as seen, for example, in the military empires that dominated Western civilization for several thousand years after the rise of the first city-states. To add further complexity, one kind of organizational power can be turned into any one of the others. As a consequence of these many contingent outcomes, generalizations from society to society or historical epoch to historical epoch are of limited value (Mann 1986). Even within Western societies, comparative studies are of limited value, so Mann (1986, p. 503) emphasizes that "historical, not comparative, sociology" has been the principal method in his work, and we follow his lead in that regard in this book. Put another way, every country is distinctive enough that fine-grained historical analyses are necessary on the type of policy issues we want to examine here.

Within this general context, Mann (1986, p. 23) defines classes as "groups with differential power over the social organization of the extraction, transformation, distribution, and consumption of the objects of nature." In most of the economic networks that have arisen in the course of world history, and obviously in a capitalist system, there is an "ownership class" that holds legal possession of the entities that do the mining, producing, distributing, and retailing of the goods and services available in the society. However, the ownership class is not inevitably a dominant or ruling class because leaders within the political, military, or religious networks may have greater power. A dominant class such as we think exists in the United States is therefore defined as "an economic class that has successfully monopolized other power sources to dominate a state-centered society at large" (Mann 1986, p. 25). In other words, a dominant economic class is one that has overcome the potential autonomy of the state while at the same time subordinating the military and religious networks. Thus our stress is on the fact that class domination is not inevitable but highly dependent on many historical factors.

Nor is class conflict always the primary reason for social change at all points in Western history. It has been important only at certain periods in history, such as ancient Greece, early Rome, and the capitalist era. Most of the time in most places, the non-owning classes have been too spatially fragmented and without the means to communicate and organize across places to have any sustained impact. Put more generally, people are "embedded" within organizational networks that are controlled by the organizational leaders, which leaves the vast majority, the non-owners who work in fields and factories, with little room to maneuver (Mann 1986, p. 7).

For several reasons, then, many of the major conflicts that lead to social change have been among the leaders of the four main power networks, with state officials, military leaders, or religious leaders taking the dominant role until the gradual growth and extension of economic networks in the past several hundred years made it possible for property owners to rise in importance. The "arms race," for example, has been a motor of social change in Western society since the fourteenth century, and major wars between nation-states have reshaped Western civilization for the past several hundred years. We therefore place importance on politics in and of itself in present-day societies, both as an arena in which the struggles over power take place and as a means of satisfying ideological and material interests.

Although leaders within economic networks have become major power actors in many countries in recent centuries, we think they have been extremely powerful in the United States since its inception for a number of reasons that are made more apparent by very generalized historical comparisons with European countries. First, the absence of a feudal economic elite based in the exploitation of peasant agricultural production meant that the newly forming American capitalist class had no economic rivals that it had to fend off or assimilate, a dramatic contrast with the situation facing the nascent capitalist classes in several large European countries, which did not replace landlords as the main political force until the twentieth century (Guttsman 1969; Richard Hamilton 1991; Mayer 1981).

Second, the pre-revolutionary history of the United States as a set of separate colonial territories outside the context of the European multistate system led to a federal form of government easily dominated by local and regional economic elites because many government functions were located at the state and local levels. Even when the Founding Fathers, overwhelmingly members of the economic elite of their era, created a more centralized government in 1789, potentially powerful government leaders were circumscribed by the well-known system of checks and balances, and were further hampered by the fact that they could not play off one strong economic class against another in an attempt to gain autonomy from the merchant, industrial, and plantation capitalists.

Third, the absence of any dangerous rival states on American borders, along with the protection the British navy provided against continental European states throughout most of the nineteenth century, meant that the country did not have a large standing army until World War II and thereafter. The relatively small armies that played a large role historically in taking territory from Native Americans and Mexico were never big enough to be major rivals to economic elites, although a few famous generals did become presidents. By the time the United States developed into a world military power, civilian traditions of military control were well established.

Finally, the United States does not have one established church, such as existed in most European countries at one time, which means that there is no large-scale ideology network that can rival corporate leaders for power. That is, the potential power of churches is limited by the separation of church and state, which reflects both the weak nature of the church network at the time of the Constitutional Convention and the Founders' own secular tendencies. We agree that Protestant churches had a big role in shaping American morality and culture, but we also note that their constant splintering into new denominations, and then further schisms within the dominations, has limited them as a source of distributive social power.

This quick overview of what gives the United States its particular distinctiveness from a power-network point of view, which in our opinion justifies Mann's (1986) emphasis on historically oriented studies such as this one, is supplemented by another historically rare factor, an electoral system that leads inexorably to two political parties for two reasons (Rae 1971; Rosenstone, Behr, and Lazarus 1996). First, the election of senators and representatives from specific states and districts that require only a plurality of the vote, not a majority, called a single-member-district plurality system, has led to two-party systems in most countries where it is utilized, although strong ethnic or regional third parties sometimes persist (Lipset and Marks 2000). Second, the election of a president is in essence a strong version of the single-member-district plurality system, with the country as a whole serving as the only district. Due to the great power of the presidency, especially since the beginning of the twentieth century, the pull toward two parties that exists in any single-member-district electoral system is even stronger in the United States. As a result of these two factors, a vote for a candidate from a leftist or rightist third party is tantamount to a vote for the voter's least favored candidate on the other side of the political fence. Groups with at least some views in common therefore attempt to form the largest possible pre-electoral coalitions even though numerous policy preferences may have to be jettisoned or trimmed back.

A two-party system, or any form of a party system, for that matter, was neither foreseen nor desired by the Founding Fathers (Hofstadter 1969). However, the slightly differing interests of the Southern plantation capitalists and Northern industrial and banking interests soon led to two rival parties, the Democratic Republicans and the Federalists, which then searched for allies with somewhat similar interests. For the Southerners, this meant a land-merchant-banking faction in New York that opposed Federalist bank plans, Irish merchants who disliked the Federalists for their English origins and sympathies, and shipping and merchant businesses with ties to the South (Hammond 1957, Chapter 5, Young 1967, Chapter 10; Goodman 1964). For the Federalists, this meant Northern farmers eager for industrialization to increase their urban markets (Genovese 1965, p. 162). We develop these points in relation to the Democrats in Chapter 1; see Domhoff (1990, pp. 235–246) for a summary of the early history of the two-party system.

Moreover, as we also demonstrate in Chapter 1, American economic networks became even more powerful with the rise of corporations in the second half of the nineteenth century, and by the early twentieth century the owners and managers of these corporations, along with the owners of plantations and agribusinesses, had the necessary economic and political connections among themselves to create a constantly evolving policy-planning network at the national level. This nonprofit organizational network, consisting of foundations, think tanks, and discussion groups, helped the owners of these large income-producing properties in reaching some degree of consensus on the new policy issues that suddenly faced them in the

1930s. Cohesion, consensus seeking, and open and direct involvement in government policymaking are therefore our watchwords when it comes to understanding the power of the corporate rich—the core of the ownership class from the 1870s onward—during the New Deal.

More generally, we demonstrate in this book that the ownership class wins far more often than it loses on the issues of concern to it—everything from building and shaping government institutions to obtaining the subsidies some industries need. These successes add up to class dominance in an ongoing class conflict over a wide range of familiar issues. Class conflict as we conceive of it starts with grievances, strikes, and demonstrations and sometimes leads to bargaining over hourly wages, the length and intensity of the working day, and working conditions. It occasionally broadens to include policy battles over the way in which the labor process is controlled and organized and over the degree to which government will regulate business on a wide range of issues. Only rarely does it widen to include the issues that are raised by socialists, such as control over investment in new plant and equipment and the degree to which enterprises are to be privately or publicly owned.

With these comments on our general theory of class dominance in the United States as a backdrop, we can present a brief synopsis of our explanations for why moderate conservatives in the corporate community reacted as they did to the three major policy issues generated by the Great Depression. In the case of the Agricultural Adjustment Act, its main policy provisions created harmony within the ownership class by providing financial subsidies for agricultural interests without causing the tariff battles over manufactured goods that would follow from many farmers' desire to sell surplus production overseas at a discount. Attempts by agricultural workers to take advantage of this act, with the help of Communist and Socialist party organizers, were easily defeated, so the problem of class conflict did not arise in the process of implementing the act.

As for the National Labor Relations Act, corporate moderates suggested an early version of the act in a vain attempt to reduce strikes by convincing workers to join corporate-sponsored employee representation plans or to reach bargains with employers through a handful of small craft unions. But they then abandoned those goals when experience soon showed that craft workers and industrial workers were more united than in the past and more willing to join independent unions, which greatly increased the possibility of class conflict and the development of an independent union movement by corporate employees.

In the case of the Social Security Act, on the other hand, corporate executives had been working on ways to retire superannuated workers on private pensions for over a decade preceding the New Deal in order to improve productivity and efficiency. However, they slowly came to see in the 1930s that this policy could be carried out more effectively—and less expensively—through a government program that would at the same time deal with the fact that many of the private pension funds were in danger of failing due to the depth of the depression.

Historical institutionalism, like all of the several variants of institutionalist theory, starts with a very general definition of an institution as the norms and customs, whether formal or informal, that shape social relationships. In other words, institutions are patterned and repeated ways of doing things that are widely accepted within the society. Historical institutionalists stress that larger and more formal institutions develop in a step-by-step way in response to the specific issues that confront them, which means that institutional arrangements are different from issue to issue, place to place, and time to time.

However, the wide range of possible institutional arrangements does not mean that such arrangements are easily changed. To the contrary, historical institutionalists strongly emphasize that each policy decision influences and places limits on what can take place at a later time. Policymaking becomes "path dependent" in the sense that it continues in directions that provide positive feedback based on the first steps that were taken. As organizations develop vested interests, institutional pathways become even more self-reinforcing.

Historical institutionalists also join other institutionalists in emphasizing that institutions develop in relation to each other and take each other's actions and likely reactions into account when they contemplate any changes in their own strategies for stability or expansion. Drawing on the new institutionalism within organizational sociology, historical institutionalists utilize the concept of "institutional fields," which are networks of institutions that recognize each other as working on similar issues, even if they disagree strongly among themselves (see, for example, Powell and DiMaggio 1991). The net result is an institutional framework that further shapes and constrains the options for policy responses to new developments.

The fact that institutions develop in distinct ways and are embedded in institutional fields means that societies usually change very slowly and reluctantly. Institutional leaders build on previous policy decisions when they think about creating new policies. The emphasis on precedent and custom gives rise to institutional inertia, which is the product of both formal rules and informal understandings. The need for legitimacy for new policy options also contributes to institutional inertia. Given all this, it takes extraordinary upheavals, such as wars or depressions, or highly creative social movements such as the Civil Rights Movement, to significantly change the ways in which institutions operate and relate to each other.

For us, these ideas can explain much of the daily routine in a stable social order once power relations are fully established. However, we think they fall far short of a fully satisfactory theory because they are not encased within a larger and more dynamic theory that analyzes the driving forces that make every institutional arrangement first and foremost a power structure. As organizational theorist Charles Perrow (2002, p. 19) notes, institutional theory "de-emphasizes power and conflict" and instead "emphasizes routines, imitation, unreflective responses, custom and normative practices, and convergence of organizational forms." One goal of this book is to show that our theory provides the larger and more dynamic framework that is needed. What historical institutionalists sometimes explain in terms of commonsense concepts such as norms, paths, and inertia, we see more often as a stalemate—perhaps temporary—in the constant jockeying for dominance among rival power networks.

Perhaps the most distinctive feature of historical institutionalism is its emphasis on the potential autonomy of "the state," a concept that encompasses the formal and generally recognized political institutions of a large-scale society (Skocpol 1979, 1980). *State* is a term that can have many varied and subtle meanings, but for purposes of this book it will be used interchangeably with the more familiar general term *government* so that we can be sure we are being clear when we mean the state level of American government (such as Arkansas or Ohio) as compared to the more abstract concept of "the state" or "the government" as a general governing and administrative apparatus whose unique and indispensable function is regulating the myriad activities that occur within its territory. More generally, historical institutionalists see states as "crucial causal forces in politics" whose leaders are "potentially key players in political outcomes given their functions and mandate to carry out state policy" (Amenta 2005, p. 101).

When it comes to the New Deal, historical institutionalists have four main contentions, all of which relate to their belief that the American government is in general far more independent of other societal forces than any alternative theorists realize. First, government officials were independent and important in creating the new policies we discuss in this book. Second, government officials built new state institutions—for example, departments and agencies—that gave government more "capacity," which in turn gave government officials more independence and autonomy. Put in terms of one of the historical institutionalists' key phrases, state officials were "state-builders." Third, many independent private-sector experts and consultants are important in understanding power during the New Deal because they had new ideas for solving the problems the government faced and they often helped government officials enhance their institutional capacity. Fourth, the leaders of the capitalist class—a term we use interchangeably with *ownership class* in this book—were not very important when it came to policymaking during the New Deal. Business suffered a loss of power following the Great Depression, which led to a change in the balance of forces in relation to other societal groups and government. Furthermore, the owners and managers of corporations were too narrowly focused on their own particular business concerns due to the pressures of market competition, did not have the breadth of vision to formulate general policies, often disagreed among themselves, and in any event did not have the institutional capacity to generate policy alternatives or the clout with government officials that is often attributed to them by "society-oriented" theorists (see Manza 2000, pp. 305–307, for a concise statement of historical institutionalists' main concerns relating to the New Deal).

Although the non-Marxian power analysts who stress the large role business plays in American society always have agreed that governments are potentially autonomous (see, for example, Domhoff 1967; Mills 1956; Mann 1993), we come to nearly the opposite conclusion in the case of the United States even though some of the disagreements are of course a matter of degree. To begin with, on the basis of our analysis in the previous section of the long-standing nature of business dominance in the United States, we doubt the historical institutionalist claim that large financial institutions and corporations quickly lost power in the face of the Great Depression due to the public's loss of confidence in business. Instead, we demonstrate that corporate groping for ways to cope with the consequences of an unexpected economic catastrophe of huge proportions, along with disagreements between the Northern and Southern segments of the ownership class on labor issues, account for the outcomes during the New Deal that are stressed by historical institutionalists.

Due to the existence of the policy-planning network discussed in the previous section, we disagree that the main nongovernment experts involved in policymaking during the New Deal were independent in the way that historical institutionalists claim. We agree that experts were important because they introduced new ideas that mattered, and that many experts were independent of either the corporate community or the government. However, most of the experts who influenced public policy on the key issues we discuss in this book were employees of the corporate moderates in a policy-planning network that grew gradually over the first three decades of the twentieth century, with its main organizations fully developed and in place shortly before the New Deal began. Here we are referring to foundations such as the

Carnegie Corporation and the Rockefeller Foundation; think tanks such as The Brookings Institution, the National Bureau for Economic Research, the Social Science Research Council, and Industrial Relations Counselors, Inc.; and discussion groups such as the National Industrial Conference Board and committees of the National Association of Manufacturers and the Chamber of Commerce of the United States (now called the U.S. Chamber of Commerce, the name we use in this book for simplicity's sake). Historical institutionalists deny that the foundations and think tanks in this network are as closely linked to the corporate rich as we think they are, so the evidence we present throughout the book for our claims on this issue is especially important in a comparison of our views with theirs (see, for example, Amenta 1998; Hacker 2002; Hacker and Pierson 2002; Orloff 1993).

We also show, in disagreement with the historical institutionalists, that the state-building before and during the New Deal was carried out in large part by the corporate moderates with the help of their policy-planning network, as first seen in the twentieth century with the formation of the Federal Trade Commission (Kolko 1963; Weinstein 1968, Chapter 3) and the Bureau of the Budget (now called the Office of Management and Budget to reflect its expanded powers) (Domhoff 1970, p. 180; Kahn 1997). The importance of this corporate-financed policy-planning network in shaping the American government will be demonstrated once again in this book. In fact, the creation of the Agricultural Adjustment Administration and the Social Security Administration can be fairly characterized as state-building by the capitalist class and the policy-planning network rather than as state-building by government officials.

Contrary to historical institutionalists, we also argue that most elected officials were not independent of the moderate conservatives and ultraconservatives in the corporate community, who provided the lion's share of their financial support in the twentieth century, including the New Deal era (Alexander 1992; Heard 1960; Overacker 1932, 1933; Webber 2000). In fact, it was not until 1936 that organized labor and liberal governmental appointees provided an appreciable amount of money to the Democratic Party (Webber 2000, pp. 107–126; Overacker 1937, pp. 489–490).

Finally, we raise questions about the reputed independence of the American federal government due to the fact that most of the appointed officials in government agencies come from corporations and the policy-planning network, once again including the New Deal era (Burch 1980, 1981a, 1981b; Mintz 1975; Salzman and Domhoff 1980). This point holds very strongly for the Agricultural Adjustment Administration and the Social Security Administration, but the National Labor Relations Board provides a major exception from 1935 to 1939 (Gross 1974, 1981).

MARXISM AND THE NEW DEAL

Marxists begin with several unique concepts that make their theory distinctive and at odds with our own starting point. These concepts are familiar to most social scientists and therefore need not be discussed in detail: historical materialism, the dialectical theory of history, the labor theory of value, the inevitable collapse of capitalism due to its internal contradictions, the eventual triumph of a united working class, and the creation of a non-market planned economy called socialism. In this view, the technologies and social arrangements (the means and mode of production) within which the economic system functions are the starting point for understanding history and social structure, which is what is meant by "historical materialism." Marxists claim that the political and ideological dimensions of societies are implied by this concept, but non-Marxian social scientists, including Mills (1962) and Mann (1986), believe that it leads to an overemphasis of economic networks that is not supported by the historical record. For example, Marxists traditionally claim that the state arose to protect the institution of private property from the non-owning classes, but we do not think archeological, anthropological, or historical findings support that conclusion.

The overemphasis on economic networks in Marxist theory is also seen in the idea that the engine of history is class struggle, an inevitable emergence of the inner dynamics of the battle between property owners and non-owners, beginning with slaveholders versus slaves, followed by feudal landowners versus peasants, and then capitalists versus wage workers. The labor theory of value, the idea that commodities have value in so far as human labor power has been used to produce them, is a central feature of this historical process. For most Marxists, the struggle over the appropriation of *surplus* value (whatever workers produce over and above their own subsistence needs) is intrinsic to all societies. Although the extraction of this surplus is transparent in slave and feudal societies, in which it is often violent and brutal, in capitalist societies the expropriation of profit is said to be disguised by the operation of free markets (the idea of a fair day's pay for fair day's work masks the power capitalists exercise in markets) and veiled by political and religious ideology. These economic relationships are the basis upon which political power is organized and distributed and thus, for most Marxists, economic and political power become closely, if not inseparably, linked. Once this economically reductionist framework is in place, other ideas, such as the inevitable collapse of capitalism through internal contradictions, the eventual triumph of a united working class, and the creation of a socialist society, are deduced as part of the inexorable march of history.

Our only agreement with Marxism at a theoretical level is that classes and class conflict are the starting point for an understanding of the American power structure due to the historical absence of four power bases that existed in most European countries: feudalism, a strong centralized state, a large standing army, and an established church.

We think many Marxists underestimate the resiliency of capitalism and that most of them overestimate the strength and militancy of the working class. Moreover, and more important in terms of the concerns of this book, we have specific disagreements with Marxists in the case of the New Deal that are different from our disagreements with the historical institutionalists. We conclude they are wrong in believing that a significant number of corporate leaders, or even any corporate leaders, instituted reforms out of fear of working-class militancy or of the Communist Party. Instead, we see labor activism and disruption as one of several factors in the passage of the reform that all members of the corporate world opposed, the National Labor Relations Act, and we argue that pressures from union leaders or leftist activists had little or nothing to do with the passage of the Agricultural Adjustment Act and the Social Security Act.

PROTEST-DISRUPTION THEORY AND THE NEW DEAL

Protest-disruption theory begins with the idea that power first and foremost resides in the "interdependent" nature of social relationships, that is, in the cooperative relations in which people are involved due to the nature of group life. The institutionalized networks of cooperation that emerge in any large-scale society, which we have discussed in terms of collective power, mean that everyone has potential power within these networks. Interdependent relations therefore become sites of contention as people attempt to advance their interests, which we have described earlier as a battle over distributive power. While the emphasis in most historical accounts, including ours, is usually on the power of landlords, capitalists, state leaders, or priests, the protest-disruption theorists stress that peasants, workers, citizens, and congregants also have potential power because of their "ability to exert power over others by withdrawing or threatening to withdraw from social cooperation" (Piven 2008, p. 5). The term *disruption* is therefore used to refer to a "power strategy that rests on withdrawing cooperation in social relations" (Piven 2006, p. 23). Although the theory is sometimes referred to as the "theory of disruptive power" or "disruptive-power" theory, we think that the name "protest-disruption" theory best captures its essence: popular protest causes disruptions in the power structure that make social change possible.

However, not all forms of interdependent power have the same potential for generating social change. The most crucial interdependencies are those based "in the cooperative activities that generate the material bases of social life, and that sustain the force and authority of the state" (Piven 2006, p. 22). Thus the economic interdependencies around class and class power that characterize capitalist societies loom large in this analysis, which gives it a commonality with Marxism. Social movements are also of enormous significance because they have the potential for mobilizing the disruptive power of subordinated people through such activities as strikes, boycotts, strategic nonviolence, and organized violence. In other words, social change only occurs when average people find ways to disrupt the everyday functioning of the social system—to break the rules that specify the terms of their subordination—in such a way that elites on the top, whether capitalists or government officials or military leaders or clergy, cannot carry out their everyday routines (Piven and Cloward 2003, for the most detailed theoretical statement of this theory).

In stressing the importance of protest and disruption, protest-disruption theorists tend to downplay the role of organizations in social change because those within organizations, and especially their leaders, usually come to be more concerned with organizational survival than with promoting the militancy that generates reform. Leaders of organizations make contributions only to the degree that they help a protest movement win as much as it can at the present moment instead of worrying about the future of their organizations. More often than not, though, building an organization simply increases the likelihood that it will be co-opted by leaders in the current power structure. For example, protest-disruption theorists believe, as do many Marxists, that unions inhibited and limited the influence of protest movements during the 1930s, usually by limiting strikes rather than trying to escalate them (Piven and Cloward 1977, Chapter 3).

We think protest-disruption theory provides new insights concerning the way in which the protest and disruption generated by the Great Depression led to welfare, relief payments, and government jobs programs, which were very similar to the policies used to control the unruly unemployed since the beginnings of capitalism, and then to the dismantling of these programs once a semblance of order was restored (Piven and Cloward [1971] 1993). However, we draw on earlier critiques of protest-disruption theorists' analysis, as well as the history of the Communist Party, to suggest that in this case the disruption was generated from an organized power center, the Communist Party, to a far greater extent than protest-disruption theorists claim (Kerbo and Shaffer 1992; Klehr 1984; Valocchi 1990, 1993). In addition, we argue that pressures and letter-writing campaigns by elderly citizens who subscribed to the Townsend Plan as well as other groups in 1935 had nothing to do with the creation of a cabinet committee to oversee the drafting of provisions for unemployment and old-age insurance. Nor did the Townsend Plan proponents or the other pressure groups generating media headlines have much if any impact on the passage of the act in the summer of 1935, as archival research by sociologist Edwin Amenta (2006) demonstrates. We also think that the role of disruption is overemphasized in protest-disruption theorists' explanation of the passage of the National Labor Relations Act; disruption was a key ingredient, but there were other factors as well.

THE NEGLECT OF CLASS DOMINANCE DURING THE NEW DEAL

If the historical accounts and archival documents we draw upon in this book are as clear as we think they are in supporting our claims for a class-dominance perspective in relation to the three key policy initiatives of the New Deal, why have so few social scientists given much credence to such claims in the past? This question is especially intriguing to us because by our reading of newspaper articles and memoirs from that era, the views we present would not come as a complete surprise to knowledgeable political observers who experienced and lived the New Deal firsthand. They knew that a few hundred large companies sat astride the economy and that plantation capitalists ruled the South—and had veto power over any initiatives put forth by the Democratic Party. Ordinary citizens were familiar with the lead role taken by specific corporate leaders and the experts they employed because they often spoke over the radio and were interviewed by the main newspapers and magazines. However, for several reasons, the story we tell has been lost from sight by the social scientists that theorize about the New Deal.

First, as already suggested, the formulation of policies is one thing in the United States, the politics of passing them another, and now we add that sustaining a newly created policy into the future (implementation and institutionalization) is still another. The policies created by the corporate moderates became Roosevelt's policies once they entered the legislative process and subsequently were framed as liberal Democratic policies by both friend and foe alike, even though the liberals and leftists of that era were usually less than pleased with them. At the same time, ultraconservative Republicans and highly conservative business executives excoriated these policies. Very soon, neither liberal Democrats nor conservative Republicans had any political incentive to give any policy credit to corporate moderates, most of whom were moderate Republicans or centrist Democrats.

Second, Supreme Court rulings in 1935 striking down key New Deal measures forced Democrats to craft new rationales for these programs that did not fully reflect their origins or main purposes. To take the most important example, the policy justification for the Social Security Act had to be changed at the last minute because a Supreme Court ruling in early May 1935 undermined the original arguments for the new legislation and endangered its constitutionality. In a case concerning a new government retirement program for railroad employees, the court ruled that pensions that would make it possible for railroad workers to enjoy their declining years are not "proper objects" of legislation under the constitution. Nor are the alleged positive effects of pensions on the efficiency and morale of younger members of the workforce an acceptable rationale. The new preamble therefore emphasized that such legislation would contribute to the "general welfare" of the country, which is permissible under the Constitution. In other words, an ideology based in social welfare had to be constructed that stressed "needs," not efficiency and control of labor markets (Graebner 1980). This change in justification caused the labor-market and industrial relations bases of the plan to be lost from sight and contributed to the belief—strongly held by most historical institutionalists—that social workers and liberal experts created the Social Security Act (for example, Orloff 1993), a belief that we show in Chapter 4 to be inaccurate and then critique in more detail in the concluding chapter.

Third, there is a general impression in the historical literature that corporate leaders uniformly opposed every aspect of the New Deal. Ultraconservative business executives of the day did testify against the Social Security Act, a fact that is used by historical institutionalists as evidence that big business in general opposed the act (Hacker and Pierson 2002). In addition, all but a few corporate leaders strongly opposed the final version of the National Labor Relations Act. But these examples obscure a much more nuanced story of corporate involvement in policy formulation in the New Deal.

Fourth, previous accounts are lacking because some of the most important archival material necessary for a more complete analysis did not become available until the second half of the 1980s or even later, after most of the theorists we are criticizing turned their attention to other topics. In particular, the Rockefeller Archive Center proved to be a crucial new source in the 1980s, as did the General Electric Archives in the 2000s, which as far as we know have not been utilized in analyses of major New Deal policies. Furthermore, the private memoranda sent to its corporate clients by a key consulting organization of that era, Industrial Relations Counselors, Inc., whose expertise played a big role in shaping both the National Labor Relations Act and the Social Security Act, were not available until early in this century (Kaufman 2003). With one or two exceptions, more recent scholarship on the New Deal has not made use of these sources because that scholarship does not focus on big corporations, major policies, or the federal government. Instead, most new historical studies since the late 1980s tend to examine the local effects of the New Deal, such as the effects of the Work Projects Administration on the arts or agriculture in a particular region, or the effects of federal programs on women, African Americans, Latinos, and Native Americans.

One important exception to this general picture is new scholarship, based on newly opened archival sources, revealing that Roosevelt's court-packing plan of 1937, which he sprung on his disappointed loyalists shortly after his overwhelming victory in the 1936 elections, was not a spur-of-the-moment proposal. Discussions concerning ways to cope with the conservative majority on the Supreme Court in fact began early in the New Deal, but became more serious in January 1935 when the Supreme Court declared the "hot oil" provisions of the National Recovery Act unconstitutional, leading Roosevelt to instruct his attorney general to look into the possibility of appointing additional justices to the court. A string of anti–New Deal decisions later in the year reinforced his resolve (Leuchtenburg 1995, pp. 85–96; Smith 2007, pp. 377–389; Shesol 2010). We find this work of great consequence because it shows that new findings and interpretations concerning the New Deal are still possible.

Even with these new archival sources, it should be noted, the record is not as complete as it could be on the policies that concern us because key figures in these events, such as the presidents of General Electric and Standard Oil of New Jersey, did not leave detailed personal records behind. Moreover, the records of most of the large corporations involved in these issues, with the important exception of large life insurance companies involved in the Social Security Act (Klein 2003), are not yet available, if they ever will be. The story therefore has to be pieced together from a variety of archives, which means that both sides of a correspondence are not always available. As a result, the history of these issues is often written from the point of view of those who maintained the most meticulous records or made themselves accessible to historians for after-the-fact interviews.

Finally, we would note that most of the exhaustive studies of the New Deal by historians, which are the basis for most social science theorizing, are focused on the politics of the era, not the origins of policies. They look at who sponsored new legislation and the strategies that were used to pass it or defeat it. In particular, they examine the critical role of the president in pulling together coalitions of interest groups, concerned citizens, and legislators on each issue. In fact, most of these books are biographies of Roosevelt. The ways in which policies arrived to the president or members of Congress are usually a secondary matter that does not extend beyond the role of their staffs in these politically oriented books.

OTHER NEW DEAL LEGISLATION

To avoid misunderstandings, we want to reiterate why we are not looking at the other innovative New Deal legislation that was important to the functioning of the economic system or that made many people's lives better.

Some of it was confined to narrow sectors of the economy, although there was intensive conflict between moderate conservatives and ultraconservatives in these sectors. Other pieces of legislation were not generally controversial, and still others did not endure after they fulfilled their short-term function. To begin with, the Emergency Banking Act of 1933, passed very early in Roosevelt's presidency, was certainly important for a number of reasons, but this act was in large part written by the bankers and Treasury Department officials in the Hoover Administration, which is a good example of the New Deal receiving credit for a "reform" that it did not create (Freidel 1973, Chapter 13).

In fact, Roosevelt opposed one crucial element of banking reform, government insurance of bank deposits, as did the top executives in the largest New York banks, which held 25 percent of the nation's deposits and would have to provide a large portion of a government insurance fund. However, the idea was heartily endorsed by the owners of smaller banks in states and Congressional districts in the South and West that were represented by Democrats, who had the support of Vice President John Nance Garner (who also owned a small bank in Uvalde, Texas) and Jesse Jones, a Houston multimillionaire with lumber, real estate, publishing, and banking interests. (Jones was in charge of the New Deal's Reconstruction Finance Corporation, which eventually ended up recapitalizing most of the country's insolvent banks (Jones 1951; Olson 1988).) Roosevelt only reluctantly agreed to deposit insurance up to $2,500 three months later (that's $42,000 in 2010 dollars) when it was added to the Banking Act of 1933 by Garner and Jones with the help of a Republican leader in the Senate, and it was increased to $5,000 (the equivalent of $82,000 in 2010 dollars) when the law went into effect on July 1, 1934 (Freidel 1973, pp. 235–236, 441–443; Leuchtenburg 1963, p. 31).

The same Banking Act of 1933 also included a provision, suggested as early as December 1929 by President Herbert Hoover, that had a major impact on the structure of the American financial system. It forced the powerful private banking houses that dominated Wall Street into choosing between commercial banking (taking in deposits and making loans) and investment banking (marketing corporate stocks and bonds ["securities"] and advising corporations on mergers and acquisitions). The idea had been championed for several years by leaders in the Senate and House with central roles on banking and currency committees, which had accumulated damning evidence through hearings that several Wall Street firms that comingled commercial and investment banking were fleecing customers in many ways, such as using their deposits to make speculative gambles in the stock market and loans to their own officers (see, for example, Carosso 1970 Chapter 16, for a full and colorful discussion of the startling revelations from the various Congressional investigations that began in March 1932 and continued through the early months of 1934). Most Wall Street leaders opposed this division, although it already had been called for and put into practice in March 1933 by the chairman of the world's largest bank at the time, Chase National Bank, which was controlled by the family of John D. Rockefeller Sr. (Carosso 1970, p. 347). (The Rockefeller family's control of this bank is mentioned further in Chapter 1 as one part of a larger discussion of the breadth of the family's vast economic interests.) The Banking Act of 1933 passed in the Senate without a single dissenting vote (Leuchtenburg 1963, p. 60).

Congress also built on its investigations of Wall Street overreach and wrongdoing to create the Securities Act of 1933, which is often called the "Truth in Securities Act" because its primary focus was on the full disclosure of all relevant information related to stock and bond offerings, along with restriction on insider dealings. Leading financiers insisted that they agreed with the basic ideas in principle and reacted with cautious optimism to two weak measures that were written at Roosevelt's request by a former chair of the Federal Trade Commission and a Wall Street lawyer who had been an advocate of reforms since he was involved with Congressional investigations of Wall Street twenty years earlier. However, Congressional Democrats from the South and West, who knew that stronger controls were necessary, commissioned a more stringent and tightly written set of regulations, to be overseen by the already established Federal Trade Commission. These regulations were written for them by a trio of "New Deal" lawyers who had taught securities regulation at Harvard Law School in one case, graduated from Harvard Law School and worked for five years on corporate reorganizations for a Wall Street law firm in another case, and graduated from the University of Chicago Law School and specialized in corporate reorganizations at a Wall Street law firm for eleven years in the third case (Parrish 1970, pp. 59–60).

But many Wall Street leaders objected deeply to the new regulatory proposals, sometimes claiming that none was really needed in any case. They were most upset by the liability provisions, along with the damages imposed, because the law said that each underwriter was "liable for the entire amount of the issue, regardless of the size of his participation" (Carosso 1970, p. 359). They claimed that they should only be liable for that portion of the entire offering that they had agreed to underwrite. Among other things, they also did not like the fact that there was a twenty-day post-registration waiting period before the stocks could be sold to the public. Nevertheless, only slight alterations were made before the law passed.

Once the rules for commercial and investment banking were revised, Congress turned its attention in early 1934 to the many self-serving and often illegal activities carried out by the New York Stock Exchange itself, which led angry business leaders in many parts of the country to join Roosevelt in calling for tighter regulation of the stock market by an independent government agency. The leaders of the stock exchange quickly established some minor efforts at self-regulation in an attempt to fend off government action, but the weakness of the regulations only reinforced the determination of corporate moderates and New Dealers to create effective regulation through the legislative craftmanship of the same team of legislative drafters that had written the "Truth in Securities Act" a year earlier.

The result was a strengthening of the disclosure and transparency laws through the Securities Exchange Act of 1934, but the act also contained "many provisions that had been endorsed by investment bankers," including a five-member Securities and Exchange Commission to replace the Federal Trade Commission as the regulatory agency for investment banks (Carosso 1970, p. 379). In addition, the new regulatory agency was given a wide degree of discretion in setting standards and thus was rendered more susceptible in the long run to control by the industry itself (Carosso 1970, p. 379). Just as significant, the new law relaxed the strong liability standards in the Securities Act of 1933 vigorously opposed by investment bankers; henceforth, an individual investment firm was only responsible for the part of a new stock offering it had agreed to finance and market.

Taken together, the Banking Act of 1933, the Securities Act of 1933, and the Securities Exchange Act of 1934 protected predatory financiers from each other and saved middle-class investors who didn't know any better from the worst sharks, but most of all, these three acts protected the corporate system from destructive practices that undermined many corporations as well as public acceptance of the economic system. As the author of the most detailed archival account of the two securities acts concludes, "the Securities and Exchange Commission, utilizing full disclosure, investigations, stop orders, stock exchange surveillance, and participation in utility reorganization, only reduced opportunities for corporate theft and restricted the methods by which individuals, while inflicting pecuniary damage on each other, could derange the entire economy" (Parrish 1970, p. 232). And, as the most detailed history of American investment banking concludes in relation to the Securities Act of 1933, "Despite the bitter controversy it inspired, the Securities Act did not alter significantly the role and function of the investment banker, nor did it change materially the way he conducted his business" (Carosso 1970, p. 363).

The breakup of financial firms that practiced both commercial and investment banking, which notably included the most powerful banking house in the United States from the 1890s until the 1930s, J. P. Morgan & Company, turned out to have very little impact on their overall power. For example, most partners in J. P. Morgan & Company stayed on to create a commercial bank, but a few of them left to form the investment banking firm of Morgan Stanley, with the help of $6.6 million in nonvoting preferred stock from J. P. Morgan & Company, and often worked with their former partners on deals that involved long-standing Morgan-oriented corporations. Other firms took similar steps (Carosso 1970, pp. 372–374). (As of 2010, JPMorgan Chase and Morgan Stanley were still among the five most important financial firms in New York, although the government had to allow Morgan Stanley to become a commercial bank on one-day notice in December, 2008, to rescue it from possible bankruptcy during the financial meltdown.) As for the twenty-day waiting period after registering a new stock offering, it was by and large circumvented with "preliminary" written announcements and informal oral understandings (Carosso 1970, p. 366).

The creation of the Tennessee Valley Authority (TVA) in 1933 was a major government project that was vigorously opposed by Wall Street and the utility company empires it controlled because it could generate and transmit electrical power that would compete directly with private utilities in order to provide a "yardstick" and keep their pricing honest. However, Southern politicians welcomed the TVA because they felt the "Yankees" on Wall Street who controlled the utilities in the South exploited them. They also knew they needed the fertilizer, flood control, and small industries that might grow up along a 652-mile river that flows through northern Alabama and western Kentucky as well as Tennessee. Progressive Republicans in the Great Plains and Western states supported the project as a possible harbinger of similar plans in their states. Although no other plans with the scope of the Tennessee Valley Authority were passed, landowners in the arid West, rabid opponents of the federal government in recent decades, were eager for the smaller and more focused, but nonetheless extremely important, projects that inserted the federal government into the areas of flood control, electric power, and soil and water conservation, which greatly increased land values for the conservative and ultraconservative benefactors (for example, Lowitt 1984, p. 218).

The New Deal also passed legislation, the National Housing Act of 1934, that made home ownership easier, but moderates within the real estate industry created that legislation in order to revive the housing industry (see, for example, Gotham 2000, 2002). Then, too, the Home Owners Loan Act of 1933, which made it possible for the government to purchase the mortgages of people falling behind in their payments, certainly saved millions of home owners from losing their homes (20 percent of all mortgages were soon owned by the agency created by this act). But the legislation was also eagerly sought by the financial institutions that held a huge percentage of these worthless mortgages and benefited greatly when they were able to convert them into government bonds (Leuchtenburg 1963, pp. 297–298; Schlesinger 1958, p. 53; Smith 2007, pp. 325–326).

As for the Civilian Conservation Corps, the Public Works Administration, and the Works Progress Administration, they were indeed liberal projects that put many people to work, and they left an enduring legacy of dams, parks, public buildings, and new forests that is all but forgotten, as recent accounts have reminded readers in dramatic detail (Smith 2006; Taylor 2008). Nevertheless, it is still the case that in June 1937 Roosevelt "ordered a drastic cut in WPA [Works Progress Administration] work-relief rolls and virtually ended PWA [Public Works Administration] construction operations as the first steps in a concerted drive to make good his often-repeated promise to bring the budget into balance" (Huthmacher 1973, p. 153). These monies were soon restored in the face of a dramatic rise in unemployment, but they were cut off again a few years later by the conservative voting coalition as its price for supporting the industrial conversion for defense (Waddell 2001). For the most part, then, these agencies are a classic example of "regulating the poor" in the way first described by protest-disruption theorists, that is, providing the unemployed with food, work, or both to quell social disruption, then closing down the programs once disruption subsided in order to maintain the private labor market (Piven and Cloward [1971] 1993). They therefore do not fit with the historical institutionalist claim that once government bureaucracies are established they take on a life of their own and are difficult to dismantle.

There is one general piece of legislation that mattered and endured, but is not discussed in this book, the Fair Labor Standards Act of 1938. The act prohibited child labor, set maximum hours at forty-four per week, and established a wage floor of twenty-five cents per hour that would rise in steps of five cents per year to a limit of forty cents. As economic historian Gavin Wright (1986, p. 219) has observed, the act "was clearly passed by Congress with its eye on the South," since comparatively few employers outside the region were affected by the new minimum wage rates. Almost 20 percent of Southern industrial workers earned below the new minimum as compared to fewer than 3 percent in the rest of the country, and the new law affected 44 percent of Southern textile workers but only 6 percent in the North. Many Northern industrialists supported the act in the belief that it would protect them from cheap labor competition from the South, and organized labor also supported the act, largely because of worries that low Southern wage rates might begin to undermine their relatively successful efforts to raise wages in the North (see, for example, Biles 1994, p. 100; Kennedy 1999, pp. 344–346).

Southern conservatives, emboldened by their successes in defeating an anti-lynching bill, the Court-packing plan, executive reorganization, and regional planning authorities ("the seven little TVA's") in 1937 and early 1938, led the vigorous opposition to the law. Southern business leaders, especially the lumber interests that spent $200,000 annually lobbying against wages and hours legislation, also opposed the act. In the opinion of Southern elites, low wages were an article of faith and constituted one of the few advantages the South held in its competition with Northern industry. Nonetheless, after a bruising political fight in both the House and the Senate, the act passed and Roosevelt signed it into law on June 25, 1938. The final legislation was riddled with exemptions and exclusions, particularly for agricultural workers and women workers; 22.8 percent of male workers, including many nonwhite workers, were excluded, along with 42.2 percent of the female workforce (see Biles 1994, p. 100; Mettler 2002, p. 248). Moreover, Congress kept for itself the power to adjust minimum wages rather than giving it to the secretary of labor, as the draft legislation proposed. The result was that Congress has allowed the minimum wage to decline in real dollars during many decades, including a long downward slide since a high point in 1968 that has been only partially arrested from time to time.

Even with its limitations, the Fair Labor Standards Act was a major accomplishment, a fulfillment of policies that were first incorporated into federal legislation in 1933 as part of one of the New Deal's failed experiments, the National Recovery Administration, a government agency we discuss in Chapter 3. But the Fair Labor Standards Act nonetheless came in the wake of the three key acts discussed in this book. It was a mop-up operation, the last hurrah of the New Deal before the conservative voting coalition solidified its emerging dominance due to the Republican resurgence in the 1938 elections. Thus it is not nearly as controversial or theoretically important as the Agricultural Adjustment Act, the National Labor Relations Act, and the Social Security Act, which is why we feel comfortable in leaving it out of our discussion (Leuchtenburg 1963, pp. 261–263; Smith 2007, pp. 408–409).

For all the many improvements in everyday life delivered to average and lower-income Americans by the several pieces of innovative legislation we have just briefly discussed, it is the three major policy innovations analyzed in this book that had the greatest long-run impact on the overall functioning of American capitalism and on average people's lives. In addition, they provide the acid test for any theory that claims to understand power, conflict, and social change in the United States.

SUMMARY

In drawing this introduction to a close, it is important to emphasize once again that we are putting the politics of legislating these policies into the background even though we agree that politicians and the political process are an essential part of the overall picture. For example, the fact that the Democrats went from a small minority party to strong majorities in the Senate and the

House, thanks to the 1930 and 1932 elections, was one of the preconditions for the passage of the Agricultural Adjustment Act in 1933, as was Roosevelt's victory over President Herbert Hoover in 1932. In addition, the further unexpected gains for the Democrats in the House and the Senate in 1934 set the stage psychologically and politically for the passage of the Social Security Act and National Labor Relations Act in 1935.

However, to repeat an earlier point, it was not these new Democratic office holders who created the specific policies that we discuss. They certainly wanted "something to be done," and fast, but the policies that were enacted came from the network of large corporations, foundations, and think tanks mentioned earlier in this chapter and discussed in more detail in the next. Policy proposals put forth by liberal and leftist experts were pushed aside easily, except in the case of the National Labor Relations Act, when liberal corporate lawyers and law professors were able to carry the original corporate plans beyond what the moderate conservatives envisioned due to the strength of the liberal-labor coalition in Congress on this issue by early 1935. As this example shows, we will only discuss the political side of the equation to the degree that it is necessary to understand why these particular policies won out over the liberal and left alternatives that were available.

CHAPTER ONE

The Power Actors

Six recognizable networks of power participated in the conflicts concerning the origins, aftermath, and implementation of policies during the New Deal. Three of them—corporate moderates, ultraconservatives, and plantation and agribusiness owners—were segments of an ownership class that was dominant in terms of its power to defeat other power networks and shape government policy to its liking. At the same time, the three segments often had disagreements among themselves even while they agreed wholeheartedly on one crucial issue: for them to maintain class power and high profits, their opponents on the other side of the class divide—primarily the trade unionists and the liberals, but also the Communist Party and other leftist groups—had to be thwarted on all their main policy suggestions.

As it turned out, the trade unionists and liberals had even more disagreements and antagonisms among themselves than did the ownership class at the onset of the Roosevelt Administration. Their differences made it all the more difficult for them to gain any traction against an ownership class that entered into the conflicts with many advantages provided to it by previous generations of wealthy land and business owners, who already had shaped the Constitution for their benefit. Earlier generations of property owners also had passed federal legislation that furthered the interests of private property in general and corporations in particular, and obtained rulings from the Supreme Court—which consisted in large measure of corporate lawyers—that made any attempt to challenge the status quo seem all but impossible (see, for example, Burch 1981a, 1981b; Carp and Stidham 1998, for information on Supreme Court justices).

This chapter focuses mostly on the corporate moderates and the plantation capitalists because they had the most fully developed organizational bases and played the major role in originating—or resisting—the policies that we analyze. Organized labor and the small band of liberals are discussed less fully because their separate histories and their relationship are more brief and less complex. Moreover, their coalition did not develop until the New Deal was under way, which means the story of their relationship is best told in the context of the New Deal itself.

Our consideration later in the chapter of the role of the Communist Party may come as a surprise to many readers, but we think the new information that emerged in the 1990s from previously secret Soviet and American files about its large-scale financial support and extensive union involvements provides support for political scientist Harvey Klehr's (1984, p. ix) earlier contention that the party played "a supporting role" in some of the major conflicts of that era. The Communists possessed a combination of ideological, organizational, and financial resources that gave them the potential to have a significant impact. Moreover, they had a larger hand in the disruption during the 1930s than is emphasized by protest-disruption theorists, who stress the threat of grassroots upheaval in explaining New Deal policies. In the final analysis, though, the party had little or no impact beyond, first, its highly organized demonstrations in the early 1930s that contributed to a growing mood of protest and, second, its substantial contribution to the creation of industrial unions in the late 1930s. The Communists' deference to instructions from the Soviet Union on many key policy issues—but not on joining forces with the new industrial union movement, in which the American leaders took the initiative—and their derisive attitude toward liberals and union leaders made them a very unwelcome ally. The exception to this generalization concerned the union-building efforts after 1935, when the anti-Communist leaders of the industrial unions entered into a secret bargain with Communist officials in order to make use of many dozens of the party's union organizers (Haynes, Klehr, and Anderson 1998, pp. 52–68). As the most exhaustive and convincing study of the complex role of Communists in the union movement in the 1930s concludes, they were the strongest expression of working-class radicalism in the United States "despite the supine and craven obedience" of the party's leaders to the political dictates of Soviet leaders (Stepan-Norris and Zeitlin 2003, p. 1).

THE CORPORATE COMMUNITY: MODERATES AND ULTRACONSERVATIVES

The appearance of a reasonably cohesive group of corporate moderates just as the twentieth century began was due to two loosely related developments in the last three decades of the nineteenth century, a period in which major technological and transportation advances and the rise of a factory system transformed the economic landscape. First, there were several intensely violent conflicts between workers and their employees that began in 1877 and erupted periodically thereafter. It was an era characterized by several waves of strikes and work stoppages by workers, fierce resistance to unions by almost all employers, and repressive action against labor militancy by all levels of government and corporate-financed detective agencies.

Second, there was a gradual adoption of the corporate form of ownership by business owners in order to raise more capital, limit liability, and allow businesses to continue after the deaths of their founding owners (Roy 1997). The corporatization process started with textile companies and railroads in the early nineteenth century, then spread to coal and telegraph companies after mid-century, and finally to industrial companies in the late 1880s, leading to the creation of dozens of new manufacturing corporations starting in the 1890s (see, for example, Bunting 1987; Roy 1983). At the same time, commercial and investment banks on Wall Street had an integrative role in these developments through their ability to raise capital in Great Britain, France, and Germany; they also contributed to the general leadership of the corporate community and provided large campaign donations to candidates in both political parties (see, for example, Alexander 1992; Carosso 1970; Overacker 1932). Between 1897 and 1904 alone, $6 billion worth of corporations were organized, six times the worth of all incorporations in the previous eighteen years, leading to a situation in which the top 4 percent of companies produced 57 percent of the industrial output: "By any standard of measurement," concludes historian James Weinstein (1968, p. 63), "large corporations had come to dominate the American economy by 1904" (compare with Roy 1997). The result was the emergence of a corporate community that is defined by overlapping ownership patterns, interlocking boards of directors, a shared concern to limit the power of employees, and a common desire to keep the role of government at a necessary minimum (see Bunting 1983; Roy 1983; Mizruchi 1982; Mizruchi and Bunting 1981 for network analyses of the emerging corporate community).

In this context of continuing labor strife and corporatization, along with the return of prosperity in the late 1890s after three years of depression, an "era of good feelings" began to emerge in the nation's factories that encouraged moderate conservatives in some of the new corporations to differentiate themselves from their ultraconservative colleagues. They did so by indicating to union leaders that they might be willing to make bargains with them as a possible way to reduce industrial strife. Then, too, some smaller businesses, especially in bituminous coal mining, thought that unions that could insist on a minimum wage might be one way to limit the vicious wage competition that plagued their industries (Colin Gordon 1994; Ramirez 1978). Moreover, companies were urged by some of the expert advisors of the day to organize themselves into employer associations so they could enter into the multi-employer collective bargaining agreements that are essential in highly competitive industries if unions are going to be useful in helping to stabilize an industry (Swenson 2002).

On the other side of this class warfare, leaders within the most important labor organization of that era, the American Federation of Labor (a federation of craft unions created in 1886), had decided on the basis of several failed efforts that unions could not defeat the burgeoning industrial corporations through ill-timed strikes and spontaneous work stoppages. They also had given up any hope that elected officials or judges might aid them because they saw political entanglements as divisive and were convinced moreover that the new corporate titans dominated government at all levels. They therefore decided it might make sense to react positively to the overtures from corporate moderates. In addition, a few trade union leaders were among the voices encouraging employers to form their own organizations, on the grounds that such organizations would make cooperation and multi-employer bargaining between corporations and labor much easier (Brody 1980, pp. 23–24).

The most visible organization to develop in this changed atmosphere was the National Civic Federation (hereafter usually called the NCF). Formed in 1900 and composed of leaders from both big corporations and major trade unions, it also included well-known leaders from the worlds of finance, academia, and government. Building on this cross-section of leaders, it was the first national-level policy-discussion group formed by the newly emerging corporate community. It therefore has been studied extensively from several different angles (for example, Cyphers 2002; Green 1956; Jensen 1956; Weinstein 1968). The explicit goal of the federation was to develop means to harmonize capital-labor relations, and its chosen instrument for this task was the trade union agreement, or what is now called collective bargaining. The hope for the NCF rested on the fact that some of its corporate leaders stated publicly that the right kind of trade unions could play a constructive part in reducing labor strife and in helping American business sell its products overseas.

In particular, the first president of the NCF, Senator Mark Hanna of Ohio, a mining magnate and Republican kingmaker who had a major role in the election of Republican President William McKinley in 1896 and 1900, was respected by labor leaders for the way he had dealt with striking miners on some of his properties. He also worked to convince his colleagues that the improved productivity and efficiency that would follow from good labor relations would make it possible for American products to compete more effectively in overseas markets because the finished goods would be of both a higher quality and a lower price. In exchange, labor would be able to benefit through employment security and the higher wages that would come with increased productivity and sales (Weinstein 1968, Chapter 1). In terms of present-day theorizing, Hanna and the NCF were trying to create a cross-class coalition or alliance that would be beneficial for both parties (Swenson 2002, pp. 143–144).

Nor did the NCF hesitate to seek the advice of experts, including some who were considered reformers or even liberals, which is another reason for thinking that the corporate moderates were somewhat different from ultraconservatives. The most famous of these reform-oriented experts, who figures in the story of unemployment compensation in Chapter 4, was an atypical economist, John R. Commons, who had been part of many reform efforts in the previous decade. Commons became a researcher and strike mediator for the NCF while managing its New York office from 1902 to 1904. He adopted the NCF emphasis on collective bargaining and championed the concept ever afterward. When he left for a position at the University of Wisconsin, where he trained several of the economists who later worked on the Social Security Act, half of his salary was paid by moderate conservatives in the NCF who admired his efforts. Commons later claimed that his two years with the NCF were among the "five big years" of his life (Commons 1934, p. 133).

At first glance the NCF focus on collective bargaining may seem to reflect the corporate moderate's acceptance of an equal relation between capital and labor in a pluralistic American context, which would not fit with our theory of corporate dominance. In our view, however, collective bargaining is the outcome of a power struggle that reflects the underlying balance of power in favor of the corporations. From the corporate point of view, a focus on collective bargaining involved a narrowing of demands by skilled workers to a manageable level. It held out the potential for satisfying most of them at the expense of the unskilled workers and socialists in the workforce, meaning that it decreased the possibility of a challenge to the capitalist system itself. However farfetched in hindsight, the possibility of such a challenge seemed to have some validity in the early twentieth century due to the volatility of capitalism, the seeming plausibility of at least some aspects of Marx's theory of inevitable capitalist collapse, and the strong socialist sentiments of a growing minority of intellectuals and workers. In this context, it is understandable that moderate conservatives in the corporate community preferred unions for skilled workers to periodic disruption by frustrated workers or constant political challenges from socialists, who won an increasing number of city and state elections in the first twelve years after they founded a new political party in 1901 (see, for example, Weinstein 1967).

From the labor standpoint, collective bargaining over wages, hours, and working conditions seemed to be the best that it could do at that juncture. Despite the growing agitation by socialists, most workers apparently did not think it was worth the costs to organize a political challenge to capitalism, or even to continue to attempt to organize unions that included both skilled and unskilled workers, as some activists had tried to do between 1869 and 1886. They therefore decided to fight for what their power to disrupt forced the corporate leaders to concede in principle; this strategic decision to work toward unions based on bargaining for better wages, hours, and working conditions was embraced even by the committed socialists who predominated in a handful of unions, including the Brewery Workers Union and the International Association of Machinists (Laslett 1970). More generally, sociologist Howard Kimeldorf (1999, p. 149) has shown that both the leftist and apolitical unions that often fought each other very vigorously "relied on labor solidarity, mass mobilization, and unrestricted direct action to find their way across what was still a largely uncharted organizational landscape."

Thus, from our perspective, the process and content of collective bargaining is actually a complicated power relationship that embodies the strengths and weaknesses of both sides. Its existence reveals the power of labor, but the narrowness of the unions and the substance of what is bargained about reflect the power of capital. Collective bargaining is "both a result of labor's power as well as a vehicle to control workers' struggles and channel them in a path compatible with capitalist development" (Ramirez 1978, p. 215).

Drawing on a new formulation by Kimeldorf (2010, p. 1), we would generalize Ramirez's point to say that unionization is possible when workers in any given industry can find "forms of disruptive potential that threaten employer profits." More specifically:

> The industries that organized earliest and most completely in the United States typically displayed a high disruptive capacity rooted in the difficulty of finding replacement workers ("scabs") in the event of a strike or less formal job action. In turn, the difficulty of finding scabs can be a result of skill barriers to entering the trade (e.g., construction workers, machinists, typographers), the importance of a fast turn-around in services rendered that makes the search for replacement workers too time consuming and costly (e.g., shipping and railroads), or simply the inability to recruit strikebreakers due to the geographic isolation of the workplace (e.g., mining, logging, and other extractive industries) or the fear of violence that keeps scabs away (Kimeldorf 2010, p. 1).

According to this perspective, violence may play a role in organizing a union, but primarily as a means of keeping replacement workers from entering job sites, not as the main strategy. Most of this violence is between strikers and scabs or police and strikers, with destruction of equipment and other forms of sabotage relatively rare even though it is sometimes threatened.

However, it is important to add that the unionization and collective bargaining that sometimes developed in industries in which workers had disruptive potential is not quite a standoff with both sides having the same amount of power. They are close to equal when it comes to collective bargaining once the ability of workers to organize and disrupt has been demonstrated, but it is also the case that it is very difficult to sustain most unions if the legal or coercive power of government is employed to support employers in their refusal to recognize unions or in their use of physical violence to disperse striking workers and their sympathizers. Thus political power has to be added to the collective bargaining equation and can serve as the tipping point if and when collective bargaining fails and one or both sides of an open class struggle resorts to disruption or organized violence. In this context, the matter of who controls key government offices, starting with the presidency, becomes critical, contrary to the structural Marxists of the 1970s, who were extremely critical of a non-Marxian class dominance perspective (for example, Gold, Lo, and Wright 1975; Mollenkopf 1975).

Once again, we stress that the unionism the NCF leaders were willing to support was a narrow one such as was represented by the American Federation of Labor (AFL), focused almost exclusively on skilled or craft workers, to the exclusion of the unskilled industrial workers in mass-production industries. (The most important exception was the coal-mining industry, in which all coal company workers were organized into one "industrial" union, that is, a union that included coal workers with different types and levels of skills.) Furthermore, the corporation leaders in the NCF objected to any "coercion" of nonunion workers by union members and to any laws that might "force" employers to negotiate. Everything was to be strictly voluntary, although government could be called in to mediate when both sides agreed to arbitration. Indeed, there was precedent for such voluntary arbitration in federal legislation passed in 1898 that allowed for mediation between interstate railroads and those unionized employees who worked on the trains themselves (such as engineers, brakemen, and conductors).

Within this limited framework, the NCF and other corporate moderates seemed to be having at least some success in their first two years. Leaders in the new employers' associations not only signed agreements with their workers but spoke favorably of the NCF and its work. None was in a major mass-production industry, however, and the new era did not last very long. As membership grew and unions began making more demands, the employers' dislike of unions resurfaced accordingly. In other words, class conflict once again emerged, which soon led to organized opposition to unions within the very same employer associations that had been created to encourage trade agreements. This sequence of events reveals the difficulties of maintaining cross-class coalitions, which were to break down more often than not in future decades as well. Either the workers try to impose conditions that employers find unreasonable, or else some employers, known as "chiselers" in that era, try to gain market share or earn higher profits by undercutting the terms of the agreement. It is for these reasons that we think collective bargaining agreements are more often the result of power deadlocks than cross-class alliances. By our reading, the potential benefits of cross-class alliances are less often the basis for collective bargaining agreements than political scientist Peter Swenson (2002) suggests, at least for the United States.

This usual sequence of events was most dramatically demonstrated when the National Metal Trades Association, which included a wide range of manufacturers who made use of metal in their production processes, broke its agreement with the International Association of Machinists only thirteen months after signing it in May 1900. The turnabout occurred when the machinists tried to place limits on the number of apprentices in a shop and resisted piece rates and doubling up on machines (Swenson 2002, pp. 49–52). The angry employers announced in a "Declaration of Principles" "we will not admit of any interference with the management of our business" (Brody 1980, p. 25). The failure of cross-class alliances is also demonstrated by the refusal of steel unions even to consider the terms offered in 1901 by J. P. Morgan, the most powerful financier of the day, for his acceptance of already established unions in subsidiaries of his newly organized behemoth, U.S. Steel. Instead, the union actually "called a general strike against the corporation to force immediate agreements on its entire tin plate, sheet steel, and steel hoop operations, thus breaking current agreements in some of them" (Swenson 2002, p. 51). The corporation then crushed the strike and the union. Other labor disputes soon followed in a variety of other industries. Between 1902 and 1904, at least 198 people were killed and 1,966 were injured in such disputes (Archer 2007, p. 121). Nevertheless, union membership grew an average of two percent a year from 1904 to 1915 despite the renewed warfare (Nelson 1997, pp. 92–93; Zieger and Gall 2002, pp. 18–19).

The individual employer associations were reinforced in their anti-union efforts when the industry-wide National Association of Manufacturers (NAM) moved into their ranks. Founded in 1896 to encourage the marketing of American products overseas, its first president was also an early member of the NCF and tried to avoid any discussion of management-labor issues within NAM. However, when anti-union employers took over the association in late 1902 in a three-way race for the presidency, it quickly turned into the largest and most visible opponent of trade unions in the United States. It thereby became the core organization for the ultraconservatives in the corporate community, a role it has played ever since, but always buttressed by the organizations established by specific industries, such as the Iron and Steel Institute and the American Automobile Manufacturers Association. That is, both the moderate conservatives and the ultraconservatives had an identifiable organizational focus in that era that makes it possible to analyze any changes in their policy positions.

The rise of the anti-union movement caused the NCF to draw back from its collective bargaining emphasis, but it continued to endorse collective bargaining as a principle even though it no longer pushed for it. At the same time, though, the organization began to put greater emphasis on urging employers to pay good wages and install welfare programs of the kind that had been tried by a few corporations in earlier decades in an attempt to mollify workers. "After 1905," says Weinstein (1968, p. 18), "welfare work increasingly was seen as a substitute for the recognition of unions." These widespread efforts were successful in many large corporations and were an important forerunner of the welfare-capitalism strategy to combat unions emphasized during the 1920s. In fact, the Welfare Department within the National Civic Federation played a large role in disseminating this perspective (Cyphers 2002). In present-day theorizing, these large-scale employers, many of them using advanced production technologies, were paying "efficiency wages" in an effort to increase profits through enhanced productivity and at the same time protect themselves against disruption, sabotage, and the destruction of equipment:

> Employers enjoying some sort of monopoly in technology, product patents, customer loyalty, or other sources of economic rent, were those most likely to be able to afford high money wages as well as benefits. Efficiency wages were probably also well advised to protect high returns on their expensive investments in advanced machinery from the inexperience, indifference, indiscipline, and ill-will of footloose and disloyal workers (Swenson 2002, p. 57).

The National Civic Federation also expressed its differences with the ultraconservatives in the corporate community through its role in creating the Federal Trade Commission in 1913 to deal with several different problems of concern to it, such as cutthroat competition in some business sectors, variations in business regulation from state to state, and continuing criticism from reformers and socialists over the lack of adequate federal government supervision of corporations. After losing in Congress in 1908 to the NAM and middle-sized business associations on an earlier regulatory bill, the NCF formed a private committee in 1912 that included corporate members and economists, and enjoyed the full-time assistance of the legal counsel of the Iron and Steel Institute (Weinstein 1968, p. 87). The draft bill created by the new working group was sent to a senator who was also a member of NCF as well as to a leading member of the House of Representatives, the Commissioner of Corporations, and President Woodrow Wilson. Although Congress and the executive branch received other suggestions on how to regulate corporations, the NCF version "was almost a model for the final legislation" except that there were no federal licensing provisions for inter-state businesses and two fewer commissioners than the NCF recommended (Weinstein 1968, p. 89). In this early effort at state-building by members of the corporate community, NCF members were clearly reacting to outside pressures, and readily said so at the time. The important issue from their point of view was that the reforms did not interfere with the growth and profitability of large corporations.

The NCF also showed its willingness to compromise through its advocacy of workmen's compensation beginning in 1908, an issue we discuss more fully in Chapter 4. Here the essential point is that the moderate conservatives were able to work with progressives and reformers on the issue, including some advocates who became important figures in the New Deal.

On the basis of the corporate moderates' willingness to accept some degree of business regulation and unionization for workers, Weinstein (1968, pp. xi–xiii), in his seminal original research in National Civic Federation archives, calls the NCF's members "corporate liberals" because they talked in terms of cooperation and social responsibility, and were willing to have government supervise some kinds of corporate activity rather than adhering to the single-minded classical liberal goal of removing all government controls from private enterprise. However, his use of that phrase raised the hackles of his fellow Marxists in the 1970s because they did not like the idea that a corporate capitalist could be called a liberal at any level of abstraction (for example, Gold, Lo, and Wright 1975). Moreover, it does go too far to say that corporate leaders themselves were involved in the creation of modern liberalism or favored the degree of worker inclusion and government welfare advocated by American liberals by the late 1920s (see, for example, Starr 2007 for a good account of the rise of modern liberalism and its main tenets). We therefore emphasize that "corporate liberalism" is not a concept we have ever employed (see Domhoff 1990, pp. 40–44 for a history of the use of the phrase). Nor do we employ it in this book, which demonstrates the limits of the moderation of the corporate moderates. However, it is still critical to emphasize that the gap between the corporate moderates and the New Deal liberals was not as wide on some issues as is often assumed by theorists of all stripes. In terms of the cases discussed in later chapters, the gap was wide when it came to unions and collective bargaining, but it was narrow on the issues of unemployment compensation and old-age pensions.

THE AMERICAN ASSOCIATION FOR LABOR LEGISLATION

The creation of the National Civic Federation gave renewed hope to the reformers and progressives in economics, political science, and sociology because they had been working for changes in the American business system since the 1880s with little success. Thanks in part to being included in National Civic Federation discussions, and in consultative work with business leaders on the local level, several of them came together in 1906 to form a small group, the American Association for Labor Legislation, to promote "uniform progressive state and local labor laws and, where possible, national labor legislation" (Eakins 1966, p. 59). They did so by doing careful research, writing model legislation, and encouraging discussion of labor issues in the journal they created, the *American Labor Legislation Review*. They also served as a clearinghouse that answered questions from all levels of government across the country and did educational outreach work with professionals, government officials, and party leaders through speeches, conferences, books, press releases, and legislative testimony. It was a small expert group that in no way reached the general public. The reformist political economists who formed the American Economic Association in 1886 took the lead role on most issues.

The American Association for Labor Legislation (hereafter usually AALL) had several overlaps in leadership and financing with the NCF, but it also included reformers and even a few socialists who were not invited to take part in NCF deliberations. In addition, progressive women reformers from the settlement house movement, the National Consumers' League, and the Women's Trade Union League (who are discussed in more detail in the section on the development of liberalism) served on its advisory board. As a consequence, the AALL worked closely with other reformist organizations located in New York City, all of which had offices in the same building. "What's this bunch calling itself today?" a magazine editor asked one of the women reformers when he poked his head in a conference room one day (Goldmark 1953, pp. 68–69). The organizations were financed by a small number of wealthy individuals, including some of the political economists and women activists who came from well-to-do family backgrounds (Domhoff 1970, pp. 172–173). In other words, being an economist, a liberal, or a socialist and being wealthy were not mutually exclusive categories in that era. There are reformers and socialists who figure in this history who grew up in the social upper class and then inherited wealth that they used to work for social change. All that said, the AALL was more independent of the corporate community than any other expert group or think tank we discuss in this chapter.

Commons, the former NCF employee, who was not from a wealthy background, played a key role in the American Association for Labor Legislation from its outset and served as its secretary from 1907 to 1909, even though he was by then at the University of Wisconsin. He was succeeded as secretary by one of his Wisconsin students, John B. Andrews, who directed the AALL and organized most of its activities from that point until his death in 1943, when the organization became inactive and disbanded soon thereafter. Many of Commons's other students worked on projects for the AALL over the next several decades. On the basis of his experience dealing with businessmen and convinced that the secret to reform was to appeal to the profit motive, Commons and his students decided to build reform measures on business principles and concentrate on the state level. These preferences were reinforced by the AALL's many defeats at the federal level between 1906 and 1925 (Moss 1996). By the late 1920s, the AALL was focused even more on the state level because of its fear that the Supreme Court would rule federal labor legislation unconstitutional.

The AALL also had the support of one of the most brilliant and persuasive minds of the early twentieth century, Louis Brandeis, a corporate lawyer turned reformer who was appointed to the Supreme Court in 1916 and became a powerful behind-the-scenes player in Washington in the 1930s. Born into wealth in 1856 and a graduate of Harvard Law School, Brandeis worked as a conventional corporate lawyer from 1879 until the late 1890s, when he became a critic of the "curse of bigness" and legal counsel for the National Consumers' League, of which his sisters-in-law, Josephine and Pauline Goldmark, were top leaders (Baltzell 1964, pp. 188–192; Linda Gordon 1994, pp. 83–84). He also joined the AALL's Advisory Council and in 1911 wrote draft legislation for unemployment insurance that contained an incentive feature meant to induce employers to minimize unemployment; the proposed bill lowered the required premiums for businesses if they did not lay off workers.

During its nearly forty years of existence the AALL worked on a wide variety of labor legislation that ranged from accident insurance to health insurance to unemployment insurance to old-age pensions, with varying degrees of success. It had a strong impact on the health of workers through the legislation it helped write to combat industrial diseases (Pierce 1953, pp. 27–34; Domhoff 1970, pp. 174–175). However, there is one labor issue it did not include on its agenda, support for unions, which is a major reason why it could attract the financial support and participation of some corporate moderates as well as include reformers and socialists in its discussions. In terms of understanding why it took so long for a liberal-labor coalition to emerge in the United States, it is also noteworthy that the AALL's legislative approach did not attract much support from the AFL until the New Deal era because of the AFL's general wariness toward government (Skocpol 1992, pp. 208–209). In an argument over one issue in 1916, Gompers resigned from the organization and called it an association for the assassination of labor (Domhoff 1970, pp. 170–178, for a more detailed account of the AALL that includes its relationship with organized labor).

In fact, right up to the Great Depression, the AFL's philosophy of "voluntarism," which in practice meant an emphasis on winning concessions from employers directly through strikes, slowdowns, and other "job actions," led it to oppose social welfare programs on the grounds that workers should rely only on their own efforts to improve their situation. Government-inspired "welfare" only invited state interference into labor's affairs and would ultimately lead to outside domination of the labor movement (Brody 1980, p. 27; Kimeldorf 1999, p. 13). While wariness toward government intentions was the major factor in AFL attitudes toward social legislation, its leaders were also concerned that state-sponsored welfare programs would undermine the mutual aid funds that craft unions had used so successfully both to attract new members and to maintain their allegiance to the cause (Lubove 1968, pp. 15–18).

THE RISE OF THE POLICY-PLANNING NETWORK

After having a big part in the creation of the Federal Trade Commission and workmen's compensation insurance in the first fourteen years of its existence, the National Civic Federation declined in importance during and after World War I, partly because it had fulfilled much of its mild reformist agenda and lost interest in making a strong push for collective bargaining, but also because the top staff member (whose name had become synonymous with the organization itself) became vehement in his opposition to any reformers or socialists who disagreed with him. In addition, many of the NCF's business members no longer wanted to be in an organization with union leaders and the handful of strong reformers who were among its expert advisors. They came to prefer organizations of their own.

As a result of this confluence of factors, the NCF was replaced by a new set of organizations that tried to influence policy at all levels of government, starting with the U.S. Chamber of Commerce, which was founded in 1912 (see, for example, Colin Gordon 1994, pp. 144–145). The NCF continued as a meeting ground for aging corporate leaders and conservative union leaders in the 1920s, and even included future president Franklin D. Roosevelt and his wife among its attendees for a time, but by then it was a ghost of its former self. In the 1930s the few remaining members were opposed to the New Deal and obsessed with fighting communism.

Corporate leaders also created new think tanks and policy-discussion groups modeled after the AALL and NCF in most respects. They were funded by several of the then-new philanthropic foundations that by now are an integral part of the American organizational landscape, including the Carnegie Corporation (1911) and Rockefeller Foundation (1913), both of which had several corporate leaders among their trustees. Taken together, these interlocked foundations, think tanks, and policy-discussion organizations gradually became a policy-planning network with close financial and trustee ties to the corporate community. The network also drew on university researchers, especially for the policy-discussion groups in which business leaders, experts from think tanks, and government officials gathered to discuss policy options relating to specific issues ranging from agriculture to municipal government to economics to foreign affairs (Domhoff 1979, Chapter 3; McGann 2007; Rich 2004).

The first of the think tanks at the national level, the Institute of Government Research, was formed in Washington in 1916 with money from a wealthy St. Louis merchant, Robert Brookings, and the Carnegie Corporation. Its goal was efficient government through practical research. Its most immediate and major success was the creation of a Bureau of the Budget in 1919 that would help the executive branch better manage the government as a whole (Domhoff 1970, p. 180; Kahn 1997). In 1922 the Carnegie Corporation financed the establishment of a companion think tank, the Institute of Economic Research, and in 1923 Robert Brookings and the Carnegie Corporation provided money for the Brookings Graduate School of Economics, where applied researchers interested in working for the federal government, or already working for it, could earn a Ph.D. In 1927 these three organizations were merged as The Brookings Institution. It has been a presence in Washington ever since, sometimes drifting rightward, sometimes mildly left of center, depending on the leanings of the corporate community, but never deserving of the label now used by the *New York Times* and the *Washington Post* to describe it—"liberal." It is an organization founded and still directed by corporate moderates, but it employs a few liberal experts from time to time in the context of a cautious group of centrists (Domhoff 1970, pp. 182–183; 2010, Chapter 4).

The National Industrial Conference Board, now named simply the Conference Board, was created in 1916 with the backing of several trade associations, primarily as an organization to gather information on prices, family budgets, hours of work, and other relevant economic statistics. However, it also served to some extent as a discussion and conference group as well. Just below the surface, its founders were reacting to what they saw as overly liberal tendencies in some parts of the corporate community (Eakins 1966, Chapter 3; Colin Gordon 1994, pp. 147–150). The National Bureau of Economic Research, which overshadowed the National Industrial Conference Board and rivaled The Brookings Institution in its first few decades, was founded in 1919 as a continuation of statistical research conducted by a Harvard Business School professor, a Columbia University economist, and a moderate business leader when they worked together for the War Industries

Board during World War I. With primary funding from the Carnegie Corporation, the organization avoided partisan disputes and stressed fact gathering as a way to generate support for necessary reforms (Domhoff 1970, pp. 180–182). It carried out research for the Republican secretary of commerce and future president, Herbert Hoover, in the 1920s, and later became a primary recruiting grounds for members of the Council of Economic Advisors, created in 1946 (Domhoff 1987).

THE ROCKEFELLER INFLUENCE

The policy-planning network was aided and supplemented by the efforts of John D. Rockefeller Jr., who had the help of almost a dozen lawyers, policy experts, and former business executives who were on his personal payroll. Although the name Rockefeller is now synonymous with wealth and power, the full scope of Rockefeller wealth and the massive role of the family's foundations, advisory groups, and charities is not fully appreciated today because the family is no longer involved in any large corporations and includes many liberal and environmentally concerned members. In the early 1920s the descendants of John D. Rockefeller Sr. were worth an estimated $2.5 billion, which was two-and-a-half times as much as their nearest rivals, the Fords, Mellons, and du Ponts (Lundberg 1937, pp. 26–27). Not only were John D. Rockefeller Sr. and his family far and away the richest family of that era, but Rockefeller Sr. may have been the richest man in American history, far surpassing the wealth of even a Bill Gates of Microsoft if both fortunes are compared as a percentage of the Gross National Product for their respective eras (Klepper and Gunther 1996). Although Rockefeller Sr. lived to 1937, when he was ninety-seven years old, most of his fortune was inherited or controlled by Rockefeller Jr. by 1915, and most of the rest of it was managed by Rockefeller Jr. and his employees for his sisters and their families. For this reason, Rockefeller Jr. is the central figure in terms of Rockefeller influence on the policy-planning network during the New Deal. (From this point on in the book, we will call John D. Rockefeller Jr. simply "John D. Rockefeller" or "Rockefeller," and refer to his father as "John D. Rockefeller Sr." on the few occasions that his name appears.)

The Rockefeller fortune was based primarily in five of the oil companies created in 1911 out of the original Standard Oil when it was broken up by antitrust action. In the 1920s and 1930s the Rockefellers held the largest blocks of stock in these companies and had great influence on their management. Four of the five were in the top eleven corporations in terms of their assets in 1933, with Standard Oil of New Jersey at No. 2, Standard Oil of New York at No. 4, Standard Oil of Indiana at No. 6, and Standard Oil of California at No. 11 (Burch 1980, p. 14). Standard Oil of New Jersey was by far the most politically involved of these companies. Rockefeller had his offices in its headquarters building and was close to the senior management throughout the 1920s and 1930s, especially the president during these years, Walter C. Teagle. A grandson of one of John D. Rockefeller Sr.'s original partners, Teagle worked as an executive for various Standard Oil companies for fifteen years before heading Standard Oil of New Jersey from late 1917 until his retirement in 1937. By the 1930s he was a director of White Motors in Cleveland and Coca Cola in Atlanta due to personal friendships with their top officers. He served on the Petroleum War Service Board in World War I and chaired a Share-the-Work campaign for Hoover in 1932, making dozens of speeches across the country (Wall and Gibb 1974, Chapter 15). He also figured prominently in the development of the National Labor Relations Act and the Social Security Act.

Despite the huge amount of wealth the Rockefellers retained in the Standard Oil companies, they had diversified their holdings. Most important, by the early 1930s they controlled the largest bank in the country, Chase National Bank, chaired by Rockefeller's brother-in-law, Winthrop Aldrich, who took the lead on Wall Street in calling for the separation of commercial and investment banking in early 1933. In addition, they owned a major coal company, Consolidation Coal, and several minor railroads. The family also diversified into real estate in the early 1930s by building Rockefeller Center in New York City with the help of a large loan from Metropolitan Life Insurance, a company with which Rockefeller enjoyed a close relationship, including the placement of one of his personal employees on its board of directors. The largest development of its kind up until that time, Rockefeller Center opened in the early 1930s and lost money for many years thereafter (Fitch 1993; Okrent 2003). By the 1970s, however, it was at the center of the Rockefeller fortune, with any involvement in the oil companies long in the past. Similarly, involvement in Chase National Bank (which became Chase Manhattan Bank in 1955 and merged into JP Morgan Chase in 2000) ceased in the mid-1980s with the retirement of David Rockefeller, Rockefeller's fifth and youngest son, after many years as either its president or chairman.

Most fatefully in terms of the development of American labor relations, the Rockefellers owned Colorado Fuel and Iron, a mining company, with Rockefeller serving as a member of its board of directors, along with several of his personal employees. The company and Rockefeller became infamous because they played the central role in a prolonged and deadly labor dispute in 1913–1914 that came to be known as the Ludlow Massacre when twenty people died in a daylong battle between the Colorado National Guard and striking miners. The total included ten women and two children who were burned to death after machine gun fire ignited the makeshift tent city in which they were living after having been evicted from company housing by the company management. More generally, over sixty-six people died in the open warfare between labor and mine operators in Colorado between May and September of 1914; the violence only ended when President Wilson sent federal troops to the area (Zieger and Gall 2002, p. 23). Rockefeller's reaction to this disaster reshaped corporate-moderate policy thinking about labor relations over the next fifteen years, and had a direct impact on labor policy in the early New Deal, as we show in Chapter 3.

In addition to his corporate involvement and great personal wealth, Rockefeller also controlled three foundations, the General Education Fund, the Rockefeller Foundation, and the Laura Spelman Rockefeller Memorial Fund. Although he did not take a direct role in all of the foundations, he had an executive committee, made up of his main employees from each of them, who met with him to determine whether he should give his own money directly to a project or if the project should be assigned to a foundation. However, he did chair the board of the Rockefeller Foundation, which had its offices in the Standard Oil of New Jersey Building from its founding in 1913 until 1933. Rockefeller and his foundations supported a wide array of think tanks and policy-discussion organizations within the larger context of massive financial donations for medical research, education, national parks, ecumenical Protestant organizations, and museums (Schenkel 1995). He spent far more money on one of his favorite personal projects, the restoration of Colonial Williamsburg, than he did on think tanks and policy-discussion groups, but the relatively small amounts of money he contributed to organizations in the policy-planning network nonetheless had a major impact on the Agricultural Adjustment Act, the National Labor Relations Act, and the Social Security Act.

The general importance of the three Rockefeller foundations can be seen through figures on assets and donations in 1933–1934. At a time when a mere twenty foundations held 88 percent of the assets held by all foundations, the assets of the three Rockefeller Foundations (which were the largest, second-largest, and seventh-largest on the list) were more than the combined assets of the other seventeen foundations (Lundberg 1937, p. 324). As another indication of how concentrated foundation giving was at the outset of the New Deal, three Rockefeller-related and four Carnegie-related foundations accounted for well over half of the donations in 1934. To give a sense of proportion, the most liberal and socially oriented foundation of the 1930s, the Russell Sage Foundation, was the thirteenth largest donor in 1934, with just over $267,000 in donations. By comparison, the Rockefeller Foundation alone gave $11.8 million, forty-four times as much. In addition, the Rosenwald Fund, tenth on the list in terms of assets, worked closely with the Rockefeller group; the donor for the foundation, Julius Rosenwald, one of the three original owners and officers of Sears, Roebuck, and its top executive in the early decades of the twentieth century, joined the board of the Rockefeller Foundation in 1917, the same year he created the Rosenwald Fund. Thereafter he often coordinated his donations with the Rockefeller philanthropies on specific projects until his death in 1932, including several that aided education for African Americans in the South (see, for example, Werner 1939, pp. 120–122, 132–134, 334–336). Moreover, most of the other foundations in the top twenty were not concerned with public policy; they gave donations to local charities, educational institutions, libraries, and museums.

The first Rockefeller-created philanthropy, the General Education Board, founded in 1902 to support education projects, had an unexpected indirect impact on the American power structure through its role in financing the county farm agent system in 1905–1906, which soon evolved into the Extension Service within the Department of Agriculture. With further financial support from the Rosenwalds' Sears, Roebuck company starting in 1912, which gave $1,000 to eleven counties in the Midwest to hire county agents, the Extension Service in turn became an important basis for organizing plantation capitalists and the most prosperous farmers outside the South into a new association, the American Farm Bureau Federation (usually called the Farm Bureau). These donations set the stage for federal appropriations for county agents (see, for example, Werner 1939, pp. 62–63 for the role of Rosenwald and Sears, Roebuck). The Farm Bureau in effect became the representative of the agriculture segment of the American ownership class in the 1920s. The Farm Bureau is of major significance for our analysis because it had a hand in refining and lobbying for the Agricultural Adjustment Act, as we explain in Chapter 2.

After an attempt to gain a federal charter through the U.S. Senate failed in 1910 because of concerns over how the foundation would be used by its founders, the Rockefeller Foundation was established in the state of New York in 1913 with a very broad mandate to benefit humankind everywhere (Chernow 1998, pp. 563–566, for background on its creation). Through a series of donations from the Rockefeller family that soon totaled $250 million, which is the equivalent of $5.5 billion in 2010 dollars, the foundation was twice the size of the Carnegie Corporation established two years earlier (Lagemann 1989, for the history of the Carnegie Corporation). Rockefeller took over as chair in 1917 and served in that position until 1939. It was through this position that he had his most direct involvement in the events of the 1930s.

The Laura Spelman Rockefeller Memorial Fund, known at the time simply as "the Memorial," was created as a charitable foundation in 1918 in remembrance of the recently deceased Mrs. John D. Rockefeller Sr. but it was transformed into an ambitious fund for the advancement of the social sciences in 1921. At that juncture Rockefeller hired a twenty-seven-year-old statistician and psychologist, Beardsley Ruml, who had been working as an assistant to the president of the Carnegie Corporation, to become its new director (Harr and Johnson 1988, pp. 187–192, for an overview of the Memorial's early years from the Rockefeller perspective; Reagan 1999, Chapter 6, for an account of Ruml's work in the 1920s and the early New Deal). Under Ruml's guidance the Memorial supported basic research in the social sciences at levels that had never been heard of before, creating what is sometimes called "the golden age of the social sciences" while at the same time providing more modest sums to create or support policy-planning organizations (Bulmer and Bulmer 1981, for a detailed account of the Memorial's work; Lagemann 1989, pp. 69–70). In 1928–1929 the Memorial was folded into the Division of the Social Sciences of the Rockefeller Foundation after making a $10 million grant to a new foundation headed by Ruml, the Spelman Fund, which concentrated on the funding of research and organizations having to do with public administration.

Regarding Rockefeller philanthropic involvement in the policy-planning network, the Rockefeller Foundation supported the founding of the Institute of Government Research in 1916 and gave it money for specific projects in the 1920s (Saunders 1966, pp. 14–16, 25, 49). Two of Rockefeller's personal employees sat on its board of directors as well. Between 1924 and 1927, the Memorial gave $2.8 million to Brookings-related organizations (Bulmer and Bulmer 1981, p. 387). The Memorial also gave the National Bureau of Economic Research between 14 percent and 16 percent of its income from 1923 to 1928, and Rockefeller philanthropies in general gave the organization over 60 percent of its income in 1932 and 1933 (Bulmer and Bulmer 1981, p. 393). Overall, the Rockefeller Foundation and the Memorial were the National Bureau of Economic Research's largest single contributors in its first thirty years (Alchon 1985, pp. 117, 157, 165, 217–232; Fosdick 1952, p. 213).

Rockefeller philanthropies were also the major financial backers of a new coordinating and grant-giving organization for social science research founded in 1923, the Social Science Research Council (SSRC). The SSRC quickly became an important source of policy expertise for the next fifteen years through committees set up to discuss policies related to agriculture, unemployment insurance, and industrial relations. As discussed in Chapters 2 and 4, the advisors who served on these committees had a part in the creation of the Agricultural Adjustment Act and the Social Security Act. Over 90 percent of the SSRC's funding in its first ten years came from Rockefeller foundations, a pattern of support that continued into the 1940s. Nominally governed by a thirty-two-person board whose members were suggested by the professional associations for each social science, the organization was run in practice from 1925 on by the six-member Policy Planning Committee and the president. The Policy Planning Committee was a self-perpetuating body whose members often were selected by Rockefeller advisors from within other organizations founded or funded by Rockefeller philanthropies (Fisher 1993, p. 49). Among the original six members of the Policy Planning Committee were one of the founders of the National Bureau of Economic Research and an economist who worked for the Institute of Economics and then became the first president of The Brookings Institution in 1927.

The Rockefeller group also involved itself in policy planning at the urban level, providing donations to bureaus of municipal research early in the century that gradually created an array of organizations encompassing every aspect of city government and public administration (Domhoff 1978, pp. 163–167; Roberts 1994). In conjunction with a political scientist at the University of Chicago (itself a product of endowments by the Rockefeller family, starting in 1890), Ruml helped create a new coordinating organization for the nascent urban policy-planning network, the Public Administration Clearing House, in 1930–1931 (see Schenkel 1995, pp. 219–220, 223–225, for Rockefeller family involvement in the University of Chicago, including Rockefeller's service as a trustee for several years soon after he graduated from college). Shortly after the Clearing House was established, virtually every municipal, public administration, and social welfare organization in the country moved its headquarters to a building not far from the University of Chicago, where the Clearing House had its headquarters, and then developed in their scope and importance with the help of Rockefeller philanthropies, especially the new Spelman Fund (Brownlow 1958, Chapters 22–24; Karl 1974; Roberts 1994).

The leaders of the Public Administration Clearing House had an influential role in convincing the newly elected President Roosevelt in 1933 that local private and public relief agencies could not deal with the growing unemployment and unrest, urging him to transfer this increasingly expensive operation to the federal government. The process started with a three-day meeting in Chicago in late November 1932, called by the American Social Welfare Association, which included about eighty participants from a wide variety of groups, with the chair of the Public Administration Clearing House presiding over the discussions. At the meeting, "principles were enunciated and standards defined which set the keynote for the Congressional hearings during the early months of 1933, and which forecast the terms of the Federal Emergency Relief Agency and the subsequent policies of and methods of FERA" (Brown 1940, p. 135). As the director of the Public Administration Clearing House later put it in his autobiography, the five resolutions that were adopted have "determined the federal, state, and local administration of public welfare, as far as relief is concerned, since that time" (Brownlow 1958, p. 274). The organizations involved in the conference, especially the American Public Welfare Association, then assisted in the creation and administration of the new relief programs.

Three years later, the SSRC gave President Roosevelt a memorandum that suggested establishing the Committee on Administrative Management under its auspices to make recommendations for augmenting and reorganizing the president's White House staff. The president altered the proposal by making the committee a governmental one to give him more control over the process and to ensure that the study was not "associated with the Rockefeller name" (Fisher 1993, p. 142; Brownlow 1958, p. 333). Then Roosevelt appointed the director of the Public Administration Clearing House, the director of the Institute of Public Administration, and the University of Chicago political scientist involved in the founding of the SSRC to serve as the three-person committee. The result was a report that was strongly resisted by Congress because it seemingly gave too much power to the president. After many wrangles and delays in gaining Congressional approval of a revised plan, the report did lead to some strengthening of the White House staff in 1939, laying the groundwork for the enlarged staff that helped give the White House increasing dominance over Congress after World War II (Karl 1963, 1974; Polenberg 1966).

For all that Rockefeller and his employees and foundations did to aid in the general development of the policy-planning network, their most direct contribution to the New Deal was the hiring of experts and creation of policies that were financed in reaction to the violent labor conflicts in two Rockefeller companies between 1913 and 1916. As explained earlier in this section, Rockefeller's personal concern with new policies for dealing with labor strife began unexpectedly when the Colorado Fuel and Iron Company became involved in a murderous labor struggle with striking miners in 1913. As the tensions and violence escalated, Rockefeller resisted appeals to intervene because he firmly believed the company's managers were protecting an inviolate principle he shared with his father: employees should have the right to resist joining a union when they are being pressured by outside agitators who want to exploit both the men and the companies (Gitelman 1988, Chapter 1). In essence, Rockefeller claimed that union leaders run a protection racket.

After first denying any direct involvement in the events leading to the Ludlow Massacre, Rockefeller then endured grueling appearances before the temporary presidential commission on industrial relations (discussed in the labor section of this chapter) that released many damaging and incriminating documents about his involvement in key decisions leading to the confrontation (for example, Weinstein 1968, pp. 191–198). The most detailed historical account of Ludlow and its aftermath, based on documents at the Rockefeller Archive Center, proved that Rockefeller had no information on the actual working conditions at the company and had no interest in examining independent reports that were offered to him (Gitelman 1988). In fact, his first step in the midst of the crisis was to hire a famous public relations expert, Ivy Lee, who worked for Rockefeller from then until his death many years later. His next step, well after the massacre occurred, was to hire a Canadian labor relations expert, MacKenzie King, who had worked for twelve years in his country's Ministry of Labor. (Following his graduation from the University of Toronto, King did graduate work at the University of Chicago and Harvard.) After several long discussions between King and Rockefeller that led to a deep personal relationship that lasted for the rest of their lives, King then served as one of Rockefeller's closest advisors until he became Prime Minister of Canada after leading the Liberal Party to victory in 1921.

Rockefeller's original idea was to hire King to direct a new department of industrial relations within the Rockefeller Foundation, an idea that was immediately criticized by reformers and journalists as a blatant misuse of nontaxable family money to further the interests of the corporate community. The proposal was quickly abandoned, and Rockefeller hired King out of his own pocket, a practice he continued with his future efforts in managing class conflict, as we shall soon see. The incident also sensitized Rockefeller to avoid funding other controversial issues through his foundations.

Once King's employment status was settled, he proceeded to acquaint Rockefeller with the basic tenets of welfare capitalism and to convince him to foster "employee representation plans," whereby workers within a plant could elect their own representatives to talk with management periodically on company time about their grievances. This plan was based on the theory that there is a potential "harmony of interests" between the social classes if employers and workers begin to think of each other as human beings working together on a common endeavor that has mutual, although admittedly differential, rewards. The stress was on "human relations" in industry. According to most analysts, employee representation plans, called "company unions" by their critics, were designed as a way to avoid industry-wide labor unions, although Rockefeller and virtually everyone who ever worked for him always insisted otherwise.

King and Rockefeller were not the first to propose employee representation plans as a way to deal with labor conflict in the United States. In a discussion of several similar efforts in small American companies well before King came on the scene, historian Daniel Nelson (1982) concludes that the origins of the idea go back at least to 1905 when the liberal Filene family, owners of William Filene & Sons, a major department store in Boston, offered their employees a way to discuss the management of the store even though there was no labor conflict with their primarily female workforce. However, King and Rockefeller were the first to develop a systematic plan, publicize it widely, and install it in major corporations. When workers at Colorado Fuel and Iron voted for the plan and it seemed to work, Rockefeller received considerable praise in the media as a statesman and reformer. He then urged its adoption at the other companies where he had major stock interests. (Shortly thereafter, Colorado Fuel and Iron endured the first of four strikes by the United Mine Workers over a period of fifteen years before it was unionized in 1933.)

However, the plan did not come soon enough at Standard Oil of New Jersey, where major violence ripped through the company's main plant in Bayonne, New Jersey, in July 1915, in a strike over wage levels after the company refused any arbitration and blamed the strike on outside agitators. Several days of fighting led to the death of six workers and a score of injuries, many at the hands of a detective agency the company hired to protect the refineries (Gibb and Knowlton 1956, Chapter 6; Gitelman 1988, p. 159). Once the men agreed to return to work, they received a pay increase and shorter hours, as they had demanded. Just over a year later another strike in Bayonne resulted in the deaths of three people and thirty serious injuries during a week of fires and rioting (Gibb and Knowlton 1956, p. 152). Rockefeller then asked the company's board of directors to consider the adoption of his new approach to labor relations, which was a more difficult request to make than it might seem for the son of the founder and a major stockholder. Revealing once again the divisions among owners about how to deal with workers, the board had rejected his efforts to change labor policy a few years earlier, leading him to resign from the board (Gitelman 1988, p. 217). But this time the board agreed.

To implement the program, Rockefeller brought in Clarence J. Hicks, a former YMCA employee turned industrial advisor at, first, International Harvester, chaired by another one of Rockefeller's brothers-in-law, Cyrus McCormick Jr., and then Colorado Fuel and Iron. Hicks became the vice president of industrial relations at Standard Oil of New Jersey in 1917, where he served until his retirement in 1933. He reported directly to Teagle, which put him at the center of the Rockefeller industrial relations network.

After pushing for the installation of employee representation plans at several other companies in which he had an ownership interest, Rockefeller used Standard Oil of New Jersey as a launching pad for creating what came to be called the Special Conference Committee, an informal and secret group made up of the presidents and industrial relations vice presidents for ten of the largest companies in the country and one bank: U.S. Steel, General Motors, General Electric, DuPont, Bethlehem Steel, International Harvester, Standard Oil of New Jersey, U.S. Rubber, Goodyear, Westinghouse, and Irving Trust (AT&T was added in 1925) (see, for example, Colin Gordon 1994, pp. 152–155; Scheinberg 1986, pp. 152–158). The main purpose of the committee was to exchange information and ideas on labor relations. Eight of the ten original companies in the Special Conference Committee had adopted employee representation plans by 1925 (Sass 1997, p. 45). However, they did so with varying degrees of enthusiasm and diligence. Hicks served as chairman of the Special Conference Committee from its inception until 1936.

The industrial relations executives from the individual companies within the Special Conference Committee met with each other several times a year and once a year with the presidents also present. Between meetings they were kept informed of ongoing developments in the field of labor relations by an executive secretary, Edward S. Cowdrick, a former journalist from Colorado hired by Rockefeller as a personal public relations employee after he wrote a favorable magazine article in 1915 on company representation plans (Gitelman 1988, p. 185). In addition to his efforts for the Special Conference Committee, Cowdrick worked on several projects with industrial relations experts who were part of the Rockefeller circle. He was deeply involved in battles over labor legislation during the New Deal.

In 1921, at the urging of King and one of Rockefeller's most trusted personal employees, lawyer Raymond Fosdick, Rockefeller formed an industrial consulting group, Industrial Relations Counselors, Inc. (usually called IRC at the time and in the remainder of this book), in order to generalize the results of the experiences within the Rockefeller-influenced companies and develop a program of research on industrial relations. The new consulting firm, the first of its kind according to labor historian Irving Bernstein (1960), began as a subgroup of Fosdick's law firm, which was on a retainer to Rockefeller. In 1926 it became an independent entity with a little over twenty employees, financed almost entirely by Rockefeller's personal fortune at the cost of about $1.2 million a year in 2010 dollars (Gitelman 1988, pp. 33ff). The group was soon doing highly detailed studies of labor relations in Rockefeller-related companies, providing reports (available through the Rockefeller Archive Center) that clearly stated any faults its investigators found and included suggestions to improve working conditions and labor relations. It strongly advocated employee representation plans and identified those foremen and executives who treated workers harshly (see Kaufman 2009, for a detailed analysis of IRC reports on companies and for its general impact on how managers treated employees in the workplace). In 1926 this work led to the employment of the first of two social insurance experts who will be at the center of our discussion of the origins of the Social Security Act in Chapter 4.

The trustees for IRC at the time of its formal incorporation in 1926—three corporate leaders, two Rockefeller employees, and the president of Dartmouth College—provide a good sense of how well the Rockefeller group was integrated into both the corporate community and the policy-planning network. One of the most noted corporate executives of the era, Owen D. Young, was the chairman of General Electric and a Democrat; he sat on the boards of General Motors, RCA, NBC, and the National Bureau of Economic Research. Also from the corporate community was one of Rockefeller's brothers-in-law mentioned earlier, Cyrus McCormick Jr., who was a director of National City Bank of New York and a trustee of Princeton University in addition to being the chairman of International Harvester. Like Young, he was a Democrat and in addition had been a strong backer of Woodrow Wilson's presidential candidacy in 1912. The third business member, Henry Dennison, president of the Dennison Manufacturing Company in Boston, was a highly visible corporate moderate and a co-founder of a new foundation, the Twentieth Century Fund, in 1919.

The two Rockefeller employees, Arthur Woods, a Republican and friend of Herbert Hoover, and Raymond Fosdick, a Democrat and acquaintance of Franklin D. Roosevelt, served as directors of corporations, foundations, and think tanks for Rockefeller. Woods was a vice president at Colorado Fuel and Iron; a director of Bankers Trust and Consolidation Coal; and a trustee of the General Education Board, the Rockefeller Foundation, and the Laura Spelman Rockefeller Memorial Fund. Fosdick, one of Rockefeller's lawyers since 1912, sat on the boards of Consolidation Coal, Davis Coal, and Western Maryland Railroad, and was a trustee of the Institute of Public Administration, the Rockefeller Foundation, the General Education Board, the Laura Spelman Rockefeller Memorial Fund, and the Rockefeller Institute for Medical Research. He served as the president of the Rockefeller Foundation from 1936 to 1948 and wrote a history of the foundation (Fosdick 1952). As one of Rockefeller's two or three closest advisors on labor relations, along with Teagle and Hicks, Fosdick figures in our account of Rockefeller involvement in labor relations during the New Deal. As for the sixth and final IRC trustee, Ernest Hopkins, the president of Dartmouth College, he also served as a trustee for the Laura Spelman Rockefeller Memorial Fund at the time.

Over and beyond the applied work by the IRC employees, Rockefeller and his aides started industrial relations institutes at major universities in order to develop the expertise needed to bring about harmonious labor relations. The first grant supported a new Department of Industrial Relations within the Wharton School of Business at the University of Pennsylvania, chaired by Joseph Willits, who became involved in the work of the Social Science Research Council shortly thereafter. He then served on many committees related to Rockefeller projects, had a hand in fashioning the administration of the Social Security Board, and in 1939 became director of the Rockefeller Foundation's Division of Social Sciences (Fisher 1993, pp. 54–55,

121, 183). Their second initiative involved the formation of an industrial relations section in the Department of Economics at Princeton, starting with direct overtures from Rockefeller and Fosdick (Fosdick was a graduate of Princeton, and John D. Rockefeller III was then a student there). This project was developed under the guidance of Hicks from his post at Standard Oil of New Jersey. Shortly thereafter, industrial relations institutes were created at several other universities, including MIT, the University of Michigan, and Stanford, and in the late 1930s another one was developed at the California Institute of Technology (Gitelman 1984, p. 24).

More generally, the Rockefeller foundations began to fund studies relating to human relations in industry. For example, they took an interest in the work of an Australian immigrant, Elton Mayo, whose grandiose claims about the importance of psychology in work relations greatly intrigued Hicks and his colleagues, who funded his research and helped him to obtain a position at the new Harvard Business School. He is best known for his "Hawthorne Studies" at General Electric, which were in fact very poorly done and inaccurate, but which nonetheless gave a major boost to human relations studies before the inadequacy of the research was fully understood (Hoopes 2003, Chapter 5; Jacoby 1997, pp. 221–228).

The creation of employee representation plans and support for the new academic field of industrial relations made Rockefeller a leading figure among the moderate conservatives within the corporate community, with ultraconservative business leaders openly criticizing him for his efforts. However, his policy prescriptions were a step backward from the positions taken by the National Civic Federation at the beginning of the twentieth century because his insistence that conflict could be eliminated through good human relations practices undercut the legitimacy of unions and collective bargaining. Few members of the National Civic Federation had gone so far as to think that government should enforce any worker rights to collective bargaining, but some of them understood that conflict between capital and labor might be inevitable and that collective bargaining was the best practical way of regulating that conflict. The Rockefeller group's unwillingness to accept this lesson led to a major defeat for it during the New Deal, but only after it had laid the groundwork for the first National Labor Board in 1933.

There were other corporate moderates who came to prominence in the 1920s. Several of them were based in Boston and worked through its Chamber of Commerce. In particular, Henry I. Harriman, a utility company executive in that city, became involved in the U.S. Chamber of Commerce in the late 1920s. He was elected chamber president in 1932, which led to his participation in the formulation of the Agricultural Adjustment Act and the National Industrial Recovery Act. Two other corporate moderates, both directors of the AALL, figure in our later account on the Social Security Act.

Morris Leeds, an electrical engineer, was a founder of Leeds & Northrup, which manufactured electrical measuring and control devices in Philadelphia, and a member of the SSRC's Committee on Industry as well. Sam A. Lewisohn, the scion of a German-Jewish mining and investment banking fortune, and the vice president of the family's Miami Copper Company, also wrote books concerning the responsibilities of management. Like the Rockefeller group, all the corporate moderates discussed in this paragraph opposed unions in the name of employee representation plans.

PLANTATION CAPITALISTS AND OTHER BIG AGRICULTURAL INTERESTS

The Southern plantation capitalists were a separate segment of the ownership class from the inception of the Republic until well after the New Deal due to their reliance on a narrowly based agricultural export economy, predominantly in cotton, tobacco, sugar, and rice. Initially rooted in one of the most extensive, harsh, and lucrative slave systems in human history, the plantation capitalists were able to use a combination of terrorism, politics, and help from allies in the North to reestablish their dominance over the freedmen after the Civil War. This time their dominance was based on two other highly exploitative systems, tenant farming and sharecropping, in which the former slaveholders acted as landlords who provided the former slaves with varying degrees of financial backing and equipment in exchange for a share of the crop. These systems are best understood as the point at which the freedmen had the power to resist complete subjugation (Schwartz 1976).

Even in the years from 1790 to 1860, when the slaveowners had greater wealth than their Northern counterparts and provided nine of the first fifteen presidents, they considered themselves to be on the defensive because they were agrarians in an industrializing society and slaveholders in a land of free labor and free soil (see Wright 1978, p. 35, for the conclusion that "Slaveholders constituted the wealthiest class in the country by far"). Their fears were sharply increased by the rise of the Abolitionists; the success of the underground railroad, which helped somewhere between thirty thousand and a hundred thousand slaves to escape from bondage between 1810 and 1850; and perhaps even more by the concern that Southern states would lose power as the nation expanded westward (Marx 1998, p. 61; Piven 2006, Chapter 2).

In combination with lynching, farm burning, and other brutal and illegal methods, the remnants of the slaveholding class, in conjunction with upwardly mobile whites from both the North and the South, used complete allegiance to the Democratic Party to gradually undo Republican attempts at reconstruction (Billings 1979; Foner 2006; Woodward 1951). As individual

Southern states were gradually released from federal control on the assurance that the rights of the freedmen would be respected, their white leaders quickly elected Democrats to Congress in large numbers; more than 90 percent of them had served in the Confederate government or army (Foner 2006). The increasing power of the white Democrats, in conjunction with the flagging support for Reconstruction in the North due to its own problems and racial biases, set the stage for a new power-sharing relationship between the Northern and Southern rich, both of which had their own distinctive political parties by this point. It began when the 1876 presidential election led to a massive Democratic victory nationwide in the popular vote but a virtual deadlock in the electoral college (185 for the Republican candidate, 184 for the Democrat) because Republicans controlled the vote count in three Southern states where the Democrat most likely won—Florida, Louisiana, and South Carolina.

The result was months of threats and bargaining after Democrats challenged the electoral count in those three states. Finally, secret negotiators representing both parties reached a complicated bargain called the Compromise of 1877. The Republicans were awarded the presidency in exchange for (1) the removal of the remaining federal troops from the South, (2) the appointment of a Southern Democrat to the cabinet in the patronage-rich position of postmaster general, and (3) the promise of continuing government subsidies for rebuilding the South. The bargain also was supposed to include a gradual switch to the Republican Party on the part of the Southern white rich. However, they quickly realized that they needed to remain Democrats to make it impossible for a low-income black-white voting coalition to gain a toehold in the two-party system, a possibility that seemed especially fraught with danger by the early 1870s because populism had begun to develop in the areas dominated by white farmers with small holdings (Polakoff 1973; Woodward 1966, 1973). The Compromise of 1877 marked the end of Reconstruction in the South and paved the way for Democratic one-party rule (Foner 2006, pp. 197–198).

Still, it took time to completely undermine Reconstruction and deprive African Americans of the vote while at the same time forcing them into tenant farming and sharecropping. In 1880, for example, a majority of African American males voted in presidential elections in all Southern states except Georgia and Mississippi. Although terror and violence continued to be used to disenfranchise African Americans, plantation capitalists and their allies also turned to electoral fraud and legislative means to deprive them of their ability to vote, especially poll taxes and literacy requirements. As Northerners turned even more of a blind eye to the plight of African Americans in the former slave states, Southern states passed state constitutional amendments and various legal statutes to institute segregationist Jim Crow laws and eliminate the right of African Americans to vote (Perman 2001).

Although disenfranchisement was aimed primarily at African Americans, it also was used to eliminate as many low-income white voters as possible due to the political mobilization of poor whites that reoccurred as a result of their experiences in the Populist movement in the 1880s and 1890s. For example, the Populist Party won 45 percent of the vote in Georgia during the presidential election of 1894 and captured the governorship of North Carolina (with Republican help) in 1896, in a context of declining agricultural prices, high interest rates, and high railroad freight charges. Southern Democrats responded by invoking reminders of the Northern invasion of the Confederacy, white supremacy, and racial segregation while at the same time incorporating some of the reformist demands of the Populists (Goodwyn 1978; Grantham 1988; Woodward 1960).

Complete planter dominance through the Democratic Party was solidified by the "white primary" system introduced early in the twentieth century. This system maintained one-party white dominance while at the same time providing a semblance of political choice and electoral competition, thereby allowing the dominant planter class to continue to profess its allegiance to democratic principles. In effect, inter-party competition was replaced by intra-party competition among the decreasing percentage of whites that still had the right to vote. By 1915, all Southern states had adopted some form of the white primary (Key 1949, Chapter 2; Kousser 1974, pp. 72–82). It was at this point that the "Solid South" and low voter turnout that characterized the New Deal era came into full flower, giving the plantation capitalists compete control of their region on all the issues of concern to them (Key 1949). With all due allowance for the populist-oriented stem-winders within the Democratic Party, who talked of their love of the poor and the downtrodden in order to win office, this was the party of the Southern white rich, at whose core stood the plantation capitalists.

Although the Southern segment of the ownership class was clearly the junior partner to the corporation-dominated North after its defeat in the Civil War, it nonetheless had regained significant political power by the early twentieth century due to the nature of the American governmental and electoral systems. However, the major power role we assign to the Southern ownership class at the national level during this era is often lost from sight because of the narrow definition of the South—the eleven states that seceded from the union in 1860—that is increasingly adopted without regard to the historical reality and its segregationist legacy. Sometimes the region is shrunk even further by stressing some of the differences between the border states and the "Deep South" of South Carolina, Georgia, Alabama, Mississippi, and Louisiana, which become the only "bad guys" in the story. But in fact the South consisted of seventeen states during the era of our concern. These were the eleven slave states of the Confederacy (Alabama, Arkansas, Florida, Georgia, Louisiana, Mississippi, North Carolina, South Carolina, Tennessee, Texas, and Virginia), the non-secessionist slave states (Maryland, Delaware, Kentucky, and Missouri), West Virginia (which was part of the slave state of Virginia until it became a separate state in 1863), and Oklahoma (which became a state in November 1907 following the merger of what had been, prior to the Civil War, the slaveowning Oklahoma and Indian territories). In addition to being former slave states or territories, all seventeen of these states had state laws requiring school segregation until the *Brown* vs. *Board of Education* decision by the Supreme Court in 1954.

While there were some policy differences among the Congressional representatives of the Southern states in Congress, they shared three key points during the New Deal era: (1) all of them were Democrats, (2) all of them supported racial segregation, and (3) all but two of them were opponents of organized labor. At that juncture, the Southern Democrats had 35 percent of the seats in both the Senate and the House. Bitter memories of the Civil War, the years of Reconstruction, and the terrorist era led by the "Redeemers" still burned hot in the 1930s in many of these states. Any Southern members of Congress who were sixty or older at the onset of the New Deal were either "Redeemers" themselves in their youth or had relatives who had fought in the Civil War or taken part in the establishment of Jim Crow.

Given their numerical strength and extreme solidarity on key racial and class issues in Congress, the Southerners remained the dominant faction in the Democratic Party, as they had been even before the Civil War, when some well-to-do Southerners were not yet Democrats. Between 1896 and 1928, for example, 84.5 percent of the total Electoral College vote for all Democratic presidential candidates came from the South, with the exception of 1912, when Wilson carried many states outside the South because of the appearance of both Republican President William Howard Taft and former Republican President Theodore Roosevelt on the ballot (Potter 1972, p. 32). But the real strength of Southern Democrats can be seen in their mastery of Congress. In the six decades following the Civil War, Southerners were a majority in the Democratic Party in both the House and Senate. More important, because Southern members of Congress were virtually unopposed in elections, they had long tenure in office, which allowed them to build up an impressive amount of seniority when compared with legislators from other regions, giving them control of any congressional committee they wished to dominate when there was a Democratic majority because of the seniority system for picking chairs (Potter 1972, pp. 38, 45–66).

More pointedly in terms of the power structure during the New Deal, in March 1933, the seniority system in Congress meant that Southerners chaired nine of the fourteen most important committees in the Senate and twelve of seventeen in the House (Texas alone had nine chairmen of permanent committees). Roosevelt relied on Southerners to manage New Deal legislation on the floor of Congress: Joe Robinson (Arkansas), Pat Harrison (Mississippi), and James Byrnes (South Carolina) in the Senate and Joseph W. Byrns (Tennessee), William Bankhead (Alabama), Sam Rayburn (Texas), and Robert Lee Doughton (North Carolina) in the House. When they were not in control of committees, Southern Democrats were adept at utilizing various parliamentary devices, especially the filibuster, to obstruct legislation they deemed inimical to Southern interests.

Building from their base at the state and Congressional levels, plantation capitalists and their allies controlled the Democratic Party at the presidential level despite the growing influence of urban machine Democrats in the North, starting with the requirement that until 1936 any presidential nominee had to receive the support of two-thirds of the delegates at the party's nominating convention. But they also had long-standing economic and political ties with New York, the most important state in the North, through the many financiers and merchants in and around New York City who made their fortunes in good part through financing, shipping, and marketing Southern export crops. In fact, the rise of the port of New York itself can be attributed to its role in the cotton trade (Albion [1939] 1984; Foner 1941). Furthermore, antebellum New York merchants trading with the South were much more likely to support Democrats. Of the merchants who depended on Southern trade, 83 percent were Democrats; of those who conducted one-half of their business with the South, 75 percent were Democrats; and of those who did one-third of their business with the South, 39 percent were Democrats (Danforth 1974, pp. 163–165). On the eve of the Civil War, New York City was conducting business worth $200 million per year with the five deep South cotton states, and New York was pivotal in providing the South with finance on long-term credit and in supplying specialized merchandise (Foner 1941, pp. 7, 319–320). There was strong sympathy in these circles for allowing the Confederacy to go its own way, and even talk of secession by New York. Such an eventuality would have had a major impact on the federal government because at the outbreak of the Civil War the New York port provided 86 percent of federal revenues from tariffs on imports. However, sentiments swung decisively to the Northern side when shots were fired at Fort Sumter in April 1861, and cooler heads eventually prevailed, including the most important Democratic financial backer of that era, Wall Street banker August Belmont (Katz 1968).

These economic ties translated into a political alliance when it came to presidential politics. From 1876 to 1932, there were fifteen presidential elections, and Democrats nominated a New York governor six times (including Franklin D. Roosevelt in 1932, whose father at one time was president of a New York holding company that owned most Southern railroad lines), a New Jersey governor twice, another New Yorker or Pennsylvanian three times, and the Nebraska populist William Jennings Bryan three times (1896, 1900, and 1908). There were two overriding imperatives for Southern Democrats in this political calculation. First, any alliance with the West potentially exposed the South once again to Populism, which risked the revival of a Southern Populist movement that had been electorally contained and socially suppressed. Second, by nominating conservative Democrats for the White House, Southerners received some assurance that the nation's highest office would always be occupied by someone, whether a Republican or a Democrat, who would neither use federal power to intervene in Southern racial segregation nor appoint racially liberal justices to the Supreme Court (Hough 2006, pp. 30–35).

This New York-Southern alliance at the presidential level also had the support of many people in the southern halves of Ohio, Indiana, and Illinois, an area settled by immigrants from Virginia. It is for this reason that the Democratic presidential ticket most frequently started with a New Yorker and then included a vice presidential candidate from Indiana, Illinois, Ohio, or another border state to the South. Indeed, in the fifteen presidential elections from 1876 to 1932, every Democratic vice presidential candidate was from one of these areas with three exceptions, including Franklin D. Roosevelt in 1920, when a newspaper editor born and raised in southern Ohio, James W. Cox, was at the top of the ticket.

When it came to the Congressional level, however, the Southern Democrats often followed a different political strategy that reflected their agricultural base and their desire for government subsidies to develop the region. Here they forged alliances with Western Democrats and Western Republicans with common economic interests in agriculture and low tariffs against Northern Republicans and Northern Democrats. This alliance also supported programs to improve rivers and harbors, and as a consequence the South regularly received 40–50 percent of the federal appropriations for this purpose (Harris 1976, pp. 495–499). More generally, Southern Democrats were eager to attract Northern capital and therefore granted tax exemptions to railroads, utilities, and manufacturing companies as long as they accepted the plantation capitalists' conditions for the conservative industrialization and modernization of the region: it would be based on racial segregation, cheap labor, and low tariffs (Key 1949; Rae 1994, pp. 27–40; Wright 1986, pp. 62–64, 173). Put more generally, many Southern leaders came to believe in the early twentieth century that their ability to keep the region free of unions might prove to be a helpful factor in attracting unionized business sectors in the North, as first seen in the case of the textile industry.

The economic organizations developed by the Southern ownership class, most of which were agricultural associations that looked out for the specific interests of cotton, tobacco, sugar, or rice growers, were always standing right behind the Southern Democrats in terms of policy advice and financial support. The inclusion of banking and merchant interests within the agricultural associations meant that they were more than narrow interest groups for a specific crop; they were an interweaving of the main economic interests in the South (Saloutos 1960). In addition, the relative handful of industrialists in the South were banded together in the Southern States Industrial Council, which maintained close ties with the national-level National Association of Manufacturers as a bastion of the ultraconservative wing of the corporate community. At its heart were the iron and steel mills of Birmingham and the textile mills that were moving southward from New England to escape high labor costs and strike actions, presaging a process that happened in several other industries in the decades after the passage of the National Labor Relations Act.

On top of their involvement in their own regional organizations, the plantation capitalists had a central role in another organization of great importance to them, the American Farm Bureau Federation, the organization that spoke for the agricultural segment of the nationwide ownership class by the outset of the New Deal. As we explained earlier in discussing the influence of the Rockefeller philanthropies, the Farm Bureau is based on the county agent system that first developed in the South after 1906 when officers of the General Education Board became involved in a farm demonstration project in Texas supported by the Department of Agriculture. The General Education Board's agreement to fund educational programs as part of a federal government effort to exterminate the boll weevil led to a wider program of government education for farmers (General Education Board 1930). This program became the basis for the county agent system for connecting farmers to the federal government and land grant colleges, which began with startup funding from Rockefeller sources and their close ally, the Rosenwald Foundation; it gradually grew into a nationwide government extension service on the basis of joint funding by states and the federal government (McConnell 1953, pp. 24–30).

The most prosperous planters and commercial farmers then took advantage of the decentralized extension service to create the Farm Bureau, which became powerful because it had a strong local base and at the same time could lobby successfully at the national level. It had the help of local businesses, especially bankers, who had made a calculated decision to join with business-oriented farm groups early in the twentieth century as an antidote to the populism that had arisen in the 1880s and 1890s (McConnell 1953, pp. 20, 29–32; McCune 1956, Chapter 1). This alliance of large agricultural and banking interests helped to reinforce and increase class differences between large and small producers (McConnell 1953, pp. 170–172, 181). It also created one of the many overlapping private-public power structures that were discovered by political scientists in the 1950s and 1960s to be a crucial factor in understanding American corporate power, a point that is ignored by historical institutionalists when they claim considerable independence for the American government (see McConnell 1966 for the best summary and creative synthesis of this information).

The Farm Bureau had its informal beginnings in 1911 through the efforts of an extension agent in Binghamton, New York, who served as a representative for farmers within the local Chamber of Commerce, where the Lackawanna Railroad joined with the Department of Agriculture to finance his efforts (McCune 1956, Chapter 2). As the idea of farm agents with ties to business spread across the country, the Farm Bureau, independent of any local chambers of commerce, was founded in 1919. In the case of the South, the exceptionally close relationship that developed between the Farm Bureau, Southern Democrats, and local representatives of the Department of Agriculture served to make agricultural dominance of the Southern Democratic delegation in Congress an even more potent weapon because it reduced the possibility of any potential for the kind of conflict that sometimes develops between organized interest groups and political parties (Kirkendall 1966, pp. 92–93; McConnell 1953, p. 78).

Thanks to the rise of the Farm Bureau, the Southern planters were able to build a strong alliance with other large-scale farmers across the country by the late 1920s, especially the corn and hog farmers of the Midwest, who together with the Southern planters were the dominant farming interests in the nation in the years before 1930 (soon to be joined in the 1930s by the large agribusiness interests and ranchers in California). One of the key figures in forging the alliance and keeping it together was an Alabama cotton plantation owner, Edward A. O'Neal, who became president of the Farm Bureau in 1931 and shaped its policies throughout the New Deal era.

At the national level, Southern plantation owners, prosperous Midwestern farmers, and California agribusiness also used the Farm Bureau during the New Deal as a way to interact with corporate leaders in the National Association of Manufacturers and other organizations dominated by ultra-conservative corporate leaders (McCune 1956). However, these close interactions with the ultraconservatives did not keep the Farm Bureau from joining with the corporate moderates within the U.S. Chamber of Commerce to support the main tenets of the Agricultural Adjustment Act and then to take part in a successful class struggle against the liberals and Communists, who were trying to organize the tenant farmers, farm laborers, and unemployed rural people whose lives were thrown into turmoil by the Great Depression and the negative impacts of the Agricultural Adjustment Act. In short, the Farm Bureau, the National Association of Manufactures, the U.S. Chamber of Commerce, and the corporate moderates who operated through their policy-planning organizations had created an interlocked network that had the capacity to create classwide policies on issues of common concern.

TRADE UNIONS: THE STRUGGLE TO ORGANIZE

As was also the case in Western Europe, the early forms of labor organization in the United States were largely mutual aid societies or craft guilds that restricted entry into a craft and enforced workplace standards. Industrial development in the early nineteenth century slowly widened the gap between employers and skilled workers, who came to see the onset of industrial factories as a threat to both their wages and status. Workers soon formed fledgling craft unions in an attempt to resist wage cuts, longer working hours, and unsafe working conditions while also protecting their political, social, and economic rights. Most of these unions were local in scope, but as both labor and product markets became more national due to improvements in transportation and as employers began to decrease wages and de-skill jobs, workers came to believe that they would have to organize on a wider basis if they were to be effective. But they faced enormous resistance from employers and had little success until the late 1890s.

The first halting steps beyond separate craft guilds at the local level occurred between 1833 and 1837 when workers in a wide range of skilled jobs (including railroading, mining, canal building, and building construction) formed citywide labor organizations in and around Boston, New York, and Philadelphia to resist the longer hours and wage cuts that were being demanded by employers. Union leaders from these cities met yearly under the name General Trades' Union, but in fact there was little coordination beyond the city level. However, the new labor leaders did speak out against increasingly frequent claims by publicists of the day (building on the ideas of Adam Smith) that the new economic conditions were simply due to abstract and neutral economic laws (see, for example, Lambert 2005). Instead, they asserted that they had been dispossessed, which they cast as a threat to the United States as a republic because it stripped them of their rights and independence as free white male citizens. The defense of labor was thereby equated with the defense of American republican government (Voss 1993, pp. 29–36). Although there were strikes by carpenters, shoe binders, textile workers, and tailors in defense of what they claimed to be their republican rights, the attempts to organize in any important way ended abruptly with the onset of the nation's first industrial depression in 1837 and were not revived until after the Civil War. Many local craft organizations were disbanded.

But in the context of a post–Civil War boom in a rapidly industrializing economy, skilled workers revived old craft unions and started new ones, and for the first time seemed to be building a national labor organization that might have some staying power. The labor movement's main organizational focus until the mid-1880s soon became the Noble and Holy Order of the Knights of Labor, usually shortened to the Knights of Labor, which was founded in 1869 as a secret society by a handful of Philadelphia garment cutters who had given up on their own craft union. Their credo emphasized citizenship rights, action in support of general social progress, cooperative forms of organization for the society as a whole, and, significantly, the inclusion of workers of all crafts and races in one union for the first time (Voss 1993, pp. 73–82). They also started reading rooms, held parades, and supported local labor parties. The top leaders were ambivalent about strikes because strikes alienated both employers and the general public, so they tended to focus on education, persuasion, and legislative changes in the first decade. Although they emphasized their openness to unskilled as well as skilled workers, to women as well as men, and to African Americans as well as whites, they were in fact mostly white male craft workers as the union grew to a few thousand members nationwide between 1869 and 1877.

Four months after the Compromise of 1877 handed the Republicans the disputed presidential election, and just a few weeks after the last of the federal troops were removed from the secessionist states, labor relations suddenly took a violent turn that was to characterize the next several decades and shape the nature of the American union movement. The new era began when the Baltimore and Ohio Railroad announced in mid-July that it would impose an immediate 10 percent pay cut, the third for that year. In the face of an ongoing depression that had lingered since 1873, other railroads had already made draconian wage cuts without major protest, but in Martinsburg, West Virginia, the announcement by the Baltimore and Ohio led to a spontaneous strike in the company's rail yards that did not end quickly.

City officials called out the local militia, but its members were reluctant to use force against workers who were part of their own community. The governor asked for federal troops, leading to a clash in which workers stopped trains and destroyed railroad property. The strike rapidly spread to other nearby cities. The violence was especially extensive in Pittsburgh, already a growing industrial center based in the iron and steel industry. When militia brought in from Philadelphia fired into the demonstrators, killing several people, the angry mob burned down thirty-nine buildings and destroyed 104 locomotives and 1,245 freight and passenger cars. The strike became national in scope, drawing in nearly a hundred thousand workers and at one point stopping half the nation's rail freight from moving (Bruce 1959; Foner 1977). In all, governors in seven different states had to call out their militia.

By the time government troops, traveling from city to city via trains, finally quelled the uprising after two weeks of effort, over a hundred people had been killed and many more were imprisoned (see Stowell 1999 for the most recent account). Given the traditional, more tolerant responses to strikes, the extent of the violence came as a shock to both workers and employers. Up until that time, as already noted, strikes usually had been called in an effort to reduce the long working hours that increasingly had been imposed upon workers, and somewhat less often to protest sudden wage cuts. Americans generally viewed strikes as a legitimate form of action because employees had an independent stature that reflected both their valued work skills and their belief in republican values (Lambert 2005). Courts had sometimes condemned strikes as conspiracies or restraints of trade, but fines were usually small and there were no imprisonments, and in any case the Massachusetts Supreme Court had rejected the conspiracy and restraint of trade charges in 1854 (Dubofsky and Dulles 2004, pp. 59–61). The only previous known deaths from strike activity—two in number—had occurred in New York City in 1850 when police shot into the crowd to break up a strike by tailors who were protesting wage cuts (Lambert 2005, p. 22).

But after 1877 American labor relations were the most violent in the Western world with the exception of Russia (Mann 1993). It is one of those superficial paradoxes of history that the most democratic and the most despotic countries in the Western world would have the most violent labor clashes. It was the strongly held American belief in the right of business owners to have complete control over their property, along with capitalist dominance of both political parties and a history of violence in dealing with Native Americans and slaves, not to mention the horrendous casualty rate in the Civil War, that made the pitched labor battles as normal and expectable to most Americans as they were to Russians with their totally different history. Between 1877 and 1900, American presidents sent the U.S. Army into eleven strikes, governors mobilized the National Guard in somewhere between 118 and 160 labor disputes, and mayors called out the police on numerous occasions to maintain "public order" (Archer 2007, p. 120; Cooper 1980, pp. 13–16; Lambert 2005, p. 44).

In the aftermath of the summer of violence in 1877, a few railroad corporations began to consider the kind of employee benefits, such as accident insurance and old-age pensions, that are discussed in Chapter 4 as a precursor to the Social Security Act. Generally speaking, though, very little changed in terms of employer-employee relations. Instead, corporate leaders put their efforts into creating stronger military forces to control workers when necessary, starting with reorganized militias and fortified local armories. In addition, militia units were often directly funded and supplied by corporate leaders: Cyrus McCormick Sr., the founder of International Harvester, equipped an Illinois National Guard regiment, and five cavalry companies were funded by a group of Chicago businessmen (Smith 2003). The regular army also developed close ties to the corporate community. Three business leaders in Chicago, for example, provided the money for a military base just twenty miles north of their city (Archer 2007, pp. 121–122; Cooper 1980, pp. 85–86). The use of private security forces in labor disputes also grew. Corporate leaders paid and directed the activities of deputy sheriffs and deputy marshals, regularly employed Pinkerton Detective Agency strikebreakers (the company had thirty thousand regular and reserve agents in 1890), and attempted to establish and control their own police forces (Norwood 2002; Smith 2003).

The violence of 1877 also led to a change of strategy by many local affiliates of the Knights of Labor, who decided that the strikes had failed because they lacked the proper leadership and organization. Reflecting the changing circumstances as corporations grew in size and power, the Knights decided to drop their semi-secret ways and take a more active role in creating the kind of organizations that could counter employers and even challenge the new corporate system. They also emphasized again that their doors were open to membership by both skilled and unskilled workers as well as women and people of all racial and ethnic backgrounds. With the economy improving at the same time, the Knights claimed to have fifty thousand members in 1883.

It was at this point that the Knights seemed to be on the verge of major success due to highly publicized strikes by railroad shopmen in 1883 and 1884 against one of the most notorious Robber Barons of the day, railroad magnate Jay Gould. The successes involved only the restoration of wage cuts, but local activists saw them as evidence for the potential power of the union and the strike weapon:

> In its wake, thousands of workers—particularly semiskilled and unskilled workers—joined the Order. By the summer of 1885, membership had doubled and a local assembly [the Knights' term for a local chapter] had been established in nearly every city and mid-sized town in the country (Voss 1993, pp. 75–76).

Buoyed by their new hopes, many Knights assemblies decided to join a general strike to force employers to grant the eight-hour day, an action first advocated by another loose-knit national labor organization to which some of them also belonged, the Federation of Organized Trades and Labor Unions. The date was set for May 1, 1886. The top leader of the Knights opposed the idea, fearful that such a strike could not be won, but sociologist Kim Voss (1993, p. 77) concludes that large numbers of workers were taken with the idea that they could establish the eight-hour day on their own initiative, a step toward imposing their own work rules (compare with Lambert 2005, p. 56). As workers across the country prepared for the upcoming general strike, another Knights-affiliated union went on strike against another Gould railroad, this time in the Southwest, demanding a daily wage of $1.50 for unskilled workers and the reinstatement of a worker who had been fired for attending a union meeting. Workers across the country became members of the Knights out of sympathy for this strike, but Gould held firm this time.

As the railroad strike in the Southwest dragged on, the May 1 strike for the eight-hour day began with over fifteen hundred work stoppages throughout the country that involved several hundred thousand people. But the tide turned against them on May 3 when police in Chicago fired into a crowd of thirty thousand pro-strike demonstrators and killed two people, with several more wounded. At that point anarchists came into the picture by calling for a massive protest rally the next day, which attracted fifty thousand people to Haymarket Square. After two hours of speeches and many reminders that the event was to be nonviolent, and with the demonstrators starting to disperse, a bomb was thrown at the police when they suddenly started to break up the gathering, killing one policeman and wounding seventy others. The police then began shooting, killing one worker and wounding many more (Lambert 2005; Voss 1993).

The corporations and their allies in city governments across the country used what was quickly labeled as the Haymarket Riot as a pretext for a major counterattack by federal troops and private corporate armies. They now defined all union leaders as Communists, socialists, and, especially, anarchists. The result of the corporate and government repression was a complete defeat for the Knights of Labor on both the eight-hour day and the railroad strike. Moreover, the organization gradually collapsed over the next few years, losing 90 percent of its membership in four years (see, for example, Lambert 2005, p. 57). Four of the anarchists involved in organizing the Haymarket demonstration were hanged from the gallows in Chicago six months after the riot even though there was no evidence that any of them were involved in planting the bomb. A fifth committed suicide in his jail cell before he could be hanged.

Although various factors seem to have contributed to the decline of the Knights, including tensions between craft and unskilled workers, Voss (1993, pp. 186–204) uses cross-national comparisons with Great Britain and France, and a close look at the rise and decline of Knight assemblies in New Jersey, to argue that the most important factor was the unusual strength and cohesion of American employer associations, which displayed brutal determination in combating the growth of labor unions. In addition, she shows that the British and French governments in effect forced employers to compromise with workers (Voss 1993, pp. 238–239). For a combination of reasons, including the continuing power of land-based aristocrats and the greater strength of their national governments, the capitalist class did not dominate Britain or France (compare Guttsman 1969; Richard Hamilton 1991; Mann 1993). It is here that comparative studies and the emphasis on the variability of power structures from capitalist country to country stressed by historical institutionalists can be of some use, but they miss the significance of Voss's analysis when looking at the United States.

The repression of 1886 led to a rapid decline for the Knights of Labor, but the events of that year also gave rise to a very different kind of union movement, the American Federation of Labor, which took away several lessons from the failures of the Knights. These lessons eventually made it possible for the AFL to force corporate moderates to consider the possibility of collective bargaining as an acceptable compromise in the face of ongoing labor strife that ranged from slowdowns to strikes to sabotage and the destruction of equipment. The new federation was founded in early December 1886, a few months after the strikes of the spring and summer had ended in defeat. Convinced that previous forms of unionization were too diffuse and fragmented to withstand the violence that corporations could bring to bear against workers, its leaders organized as a federation of narrow, self-interested craft unions that included iron molders, miners, typographers, tailors, bakers, furniture workers, metal workers, carpenters, and cigar-makers. It was the separate unions, not the AFL itself, that conducted the main activities of organized labor (such as recruitment, bargaining, and strike calling) and the federation was always dependent upon its constituent organizations for finances. By 1892 the AFL included forty unions, most of them with a few thousand members. The carpenters (57,000), typographers (28,000), cigar makers (27,000), iron and steel workers (24,000), and iron molders (23,000) were the five largest (Foner 1955, p. 171).

Craft unions, with exclusive membership jurisdictions and high membership dues, were able to grow stronger than the Knights' assemblies because they used new organizational measures to survive the combined onslaught of employers and government authorities when they called strikes and could fend off replacement workers. To secure the long-term loyalty of their members, they first provided sickness, unemployment, and strike benefits in addition to the burial insurance that had been a staple of craft guilds since the colonial era. Second, craft unions became more centralized, such that authority for strike action had to come from the national-level leadership, thus reducing the potentially fatal consequences for a nationwide organization if there were independent anti-corporate initiatives by local affiliates (Shefter 1994, p. 153). Despite their considerable autonomy and independence however, the national-level craft leaders ceded some authority to speak for them on general policy issues to the leader of the federation, voted into office by delegates from each union for two-year terms at national meetings. Samuel Gompers, the federation's founding president, originally a leader of the cigar makers' union, served as president for all but two years from 1886 until his death in 1924.

With their organizational strategy in place, the craft unions then girded for the focused strike actions and boycotts they selectively employed in carrying out what the preamble to their original constitution described as a "struggle" that was going on "between the oppressors and the oppressed of all countries, a struggle between the capitalist and the laborer, which grows in intensity from year to year, and will work disastrous results to the toiling millions if they are not combined for mutual protection and benefit" (American Federation of Labor 1901, p. 3). This ringing general analysis of capitalism, which remained a part of the AFL's constitution into the 1930s, was used against the AFL for decades thereafter by editorial writers and conservatives, but at the same time the federation also adopted a more pragmatic and less politically threatening strategy toward employers and the government by emphasizing higher wages, shorter working hours, and better working conditions. This strategy, known as "pure and simple unionism," would be carried out through direct actions against individual companies or a single industrial sector.

As part of this confrontational but narrowly focused approach, the AFL tried to avoid involvement in broad-based political organizations, especially at the national level. Its leaders feared that political activity might divide their unions in a context in which the nation's electoral rules and the history of the two dominant political parties made it highly unlikely that workers could form their own political party. Believing that the political activism of the Knights of Labor, especially the frequent disagreements between craft unions and various groups of socialists within the organization, had contributed to its downfall, the AFL also kept anarchists and Marxists at a distance, and treated any claims they made with suspicion (Shefter 1994, p. 156). But employers nonetheless continued to resist the union pay scales, elaborate work rules, and apprenticeship limits that skilled craft workers wanted to retain in the workplace, which shows that full control of the workplace and the greatest possible profits, not simply concern about socialist ideas, was their primary concern. In addition, the employers increasingly sought to speed up the labor process with new forms of work organization (for example, Zieger and Gall 2002, pp. 27–28). They also employed growing numbers of unskilled immigrant laborers at lower wages in order to take advantage of the new machines and other technologies that were becoming available.

To counter these corporate initiatives, the craft unions within the AFL opposed the continuing influx of nonskilled industrial workers into the country because they saw the introduction of more workers and mass-production technologies as detrimental for their wages and social status. Instead of trying to fight corporations by joining with the growing number of unskilled workers, as many assemblies of the Knights of Labor had attempted to do, they decided that their best hope was in limiting the number of available workers in order to keep their wages as high as possible. That is, they knew that the control of labor markets is a key power issue in a capitalist social order. The fact that the newly arriving immigrants were mainly from Eastern and Southern Europe, and often from Catholic and Jewish backgrounds, only heightened the resolve of these white male craftsmen, who were overwhelmingly Protestants of Western and Northern European heritage. Over time, as political scientist Gwendolyn Mink (1986, p. 17) has argued, "ethnic differences and skill differences converged within an expanding labor market to precipitate organizational and nativist anxieties among skilled unionizing workers of older immigrant stock." As the craft unions' objections to immigrant industrial workers mounted, "ethnic exclusion solidified craft-based exclusion, stripping union economic action of its class-based potential" (Mink 1986, p. 72). The result was a political division in the working class, with immigrant industrial workers tending to support the pro-immigrant Republicans from 1896 to the late 1920s, while members of the AFL were more likely to vote Democratic because urban political machines were more tolerant of unions (Mink 1986, p. 155).

But pure and simple trade unionism for skilled workers organized into craft unions did not enjoy much success against big industrial corporations in the AFL's first decade. The problems are seen in the sudden collapse of the Amalgamated Association of Iron, Steel and Tin Workers, which provided the AFL with 10 percent of its members and had a contract with Andrew Carnegie's steel companies. When the union refused to accept the introduction of highly profitable new technology and changes in wage rates in 1892, Carnegie and his executives in effect forced a strike by cutting wages by nearly 18 percent at the Carnegie Steel Works in Homestead, Pennsylvania. The ensuing confrontation led to the deaths of ten workers and three of the three hundred armed Pinkerton Detective Agency guards who had been brought in to attack the strikers (Bernstein 1969, pp. 432–434; Scheinberg 1986, pp. 7–9). Eight thousand members of the Pennsylvania National Guard then occupied Homestead; the nationwide union was but a shell thereafter (see, for example, Dubofsky and Dulles 2004, pp. 153–170). In 1893–1894, when an estimated 150,000 workers in the railroad industry went on strike to protest wage cuts in the midst of a severe depression, roughly 32,000 state troopers were called out in twenty of the twenty-seven states affected, along with nearly 16,000 federal soldiers out of an available regular force of 20,000 (see, for example, Cooper 1980, pp. 144–164; Lambert 2005, pp. 58–63).

In the aftermath of these dramatic defeats, however, the AFL did make some headway outside the manufacturing sector, where the kinds of disruptive potential emphasized by Kimeldorf (1999) could be more effectively employed. For example, the newspaper industry had to accede to the unionization demands of printers, typographers, and pressmen's unions, and came to appreciate their businesslike attitude toward contract negotiations. Similarly, the building trade unions (such as carpenters, bricklayers, plasterers, and painters) grew from 67,000 in 1897 to 391,600 in 1904 because these skilled construction workers, who were not easily replaced by strikebreakers, could take advantage of their disruptive capacities due to the decentralized nature of the construction industry and their connections to the urban political machines (Brody 1980, p. 24; Zieger and Gall 2002, p. 22). It was in this context that the era of good feelings began in the late 1890s, encouraging some AFL leaders to accept the overtures from corporate moderates to enter into discussions of collective bargaining through the National Civic Federation. As we stated earlier in the chapter, it seemed at first as if more progress toward the acceptance of craft unions might be made at that point, but most employers were back to opposing unions by 1902, with a burst of violent confrontations over the next two years.

In spite of the efforts by the NCF and other corporate moderates to deal with labor conflict after 1904 through welfare and education programs instead of collective bargaining, there was another wave of industrial violence in 1911. Dynamite attacks at many construction sites across the country, and on the *Los Angeles Times*' entire building, by apolitical but militant members of the bridge and structural ironworkers' union were of particular surprise and concern. In reaction, President William Howard Taft sponsored legislation to create a commission on industrial relations to examine the causes of industrial unrest and labor sabotage, which resulted in further legitimation for the collective bargaining agreements sought by the AFL.

Although the National Civic Federation had abandoned its organizational emphasis on collective bargaining, several of its individual members nonetheless played the major role in the commission's deliberations. The nine-member commission, which was appointed by President Woodrow Wilson in 1913, consisted of three corporate leaders, all members of the NCF; three labor leaders, also members of the NCF; and three public members, two of whom, John R. Commons and a well-known socialite and reformer of the era, Mrs. Borden Harriman, were members of the NCF. The only non-NCF member was the chairman, Frank P. Walsh, an attorney, reformer, and advocate for the poor who led the commission into investigations, arguments, and pronouncements that angered the nonlabor members, including exposes relating to the Ludlow Massacre that were embarrassing to the Rockefeller family (Adams 1966; Weinstein 1968, Chapter 7).

The commissioners could not come to general agreement after hearing hundreds of hours of testimony and debating numerous legislative proposals, but the weight of their separate reports in 1915 favored greater use of the collective-bargaining mechanism. As Commons noted in a report that also was signed by Mrs. Harriman and the business members, but not the labor members, the important issue was "whether the labor movement should be directed towards politics or toward collective bargaining" (Weinstein 1968, p. 202). Commons went so far as to recommend new legislation empowering government advisory boards to mediate capital-labor relations and channel protest into collective bargaining, clearly foreshadowing the kinds of solutions that eventually were tried during the early New Deal.

The outbreak of World War I changed the power balance between business and organized labor. Supplies of new labor from Europe virtually dried up, the war fueled an economic boom, and the federal government expanded its role in the economy. Many AFL unions took advantage of the situation by calling strikes to gain union recognition, leading President Wilson to support the right of unions to exist and bargain collectively in exchange for a no-strike pledge. To ensure a smooth flow of production and secure the loyalty of workers in the face of the many socialist critics of the war, government officials, with the acquiescence of major corporate leaders, instituted the National War Labor Board in 1918 to mediate corporate-union conflicts. Composed of corporate and trade union leaders, it was co-chaired by former President Taft and Frank P. Walsh, the reformer who had served as chair of the recently disbanded commission on industrial relations. AFL membership increased from 2 million in 1916 to 3.2 million in 1919, mostly in unions that had existed since 1897, with the ten largest national unions accounting for nearly half the increase (Dubofsky and Dulles 2004, p. 191). While all this was going on, anti-war dissenters from radical unions and the Socialist Party were put in jail.

Leaders within the AFL were hopeful that this renewed harmony and success would continue after the war, but such was not to be the case. In 1919 nearly four million workers (21 percent of the workforce) took disruptive action in the face of employer reluctance to recognize or bargain with unions. There were major strikes in the nation's coalfields, among longshoremen in New York City, and among police in Boston, as well as a general strike in Seattle. The largest strike took place in the steel industry, when nearly 350,000 workers went on strike in an attempt to gain the right to bargain. Led by U.S. Steel, the biggest and most powerful manufacturing company in the country, the employers launched a strong counterattack, branding the strike leaders as foreign radical agitators, this time linking them to Bolshevism. They also employed thirty thousand African Americans as replacement workers, attacked picket lines, and broke up union meetings. With President Wilson appearing to favor steel executives, the defeat of the steel strike in December 1919 sealed the fate of collective bargaining in the ensuing decade (Zieger and Gall 2002, pp. 39–41).

During the 1920s, unions lost strike after strike as employer opposition to unions reversed many of the wartime advances by organized labor. Due in good part to a union-breaking campaign led by the NAM, union strength dropped from about 20 percent of the nonagricultural labor force in 1920 to less than 10 percent at the beginning of the New Deal. Over the course of these lean years for organized labor, union membership declined from five million in 1919 to just under three million in 1933 (Bernstein 1960, p. 84). Still, total union membership never fell below 1917 levels, no major union organizations disappeared, and there were some gains for the building trades, railroad brotherhoods, and the Teamsters (Nelson 1997, pp. 98–99). But the United Mine Workers, later to take the lead in organizing in the 1930s, fell from 500,000 in 1919 to under 80,000 in the early 1930s. The garment unions were also devastated—the Amalgamated Clothing Workers, another spearhead union in the 1930s, fell from 180,000 in 1920 to 60,000 in 1933 (with only 7,000 of those members paying dues) and the International Ladies' Garment Workers Union fell from 120,000 in 1920 to around 40,000 in 1933. The biggest unions were now in construction, transportation, entertainment, and printing (Zieger and Gall 2002, pp. 69–70). There were virtually no union members in mass production industries, which meant that manufacturers and other heavy industries did not even have to contemplate the adoption of the employee representation plans that Rockefeller and Industrial Relations Counselors, Inc., urged upon them as a way to limit unionization. Less than 4 percent of manufacturing companies with 10 to 250 employees had employee representation plans in 1929, and only 8.7 percent of the companies with over 250 employees had plans (Gitelman 1984, p. 38).

There were only two bright spots for organized labor in the twelve years of Republican rule from 1920 to 1932, starting with the Railway Labor Act of 1926, which proved to be an important precedent for the National Labor Relations Act nine years later. Setting the stage for this unusual outcome, railroad workers had gained strength during the war because the railroad owners were forced to accept collective bargaining and government regulation, as well as an eight-hour day at the same wages that workers had received previously for a ten-hour day. Furthermore, the federal government had to take over the railroads in 1917 because their owners could not make deliveries in a timely and efficient way, thereby hampering the war effort. As a result of this series of events, workers took the opportunity to organize and gained a greater role in railroad operations.

Railroads were returned to private ownership after the war, but both owners and workers were forced to accept the Railway Labor Board in 1920, which had the power to issue nonbinding proposals to resolve labor disputes (Nelson 1997, pp. 99–100). The result was several years of renewed conflict that led to a stalemate due to a combination of the skills of many rail workers and the vulnerability of expensive engines and train cars to sabotage and destruction. At that point corporate executives in the Association of Railway Executives and representatives of four railroad craft unions finally agreed in 1926 to accept a government mediation board that ended up dealing successfully with labor disputes in the industry. The new legislation passed against the wishes of the NAM and the Farm Bureau, who opposed it on principle because it contained "the first explicit congressional endorsement of the right of collective bargaining" (Zieger 1986, p. 34). At the same time, the law in effect permitted the continuation of attacks by the railroad corporations on organizing efforts by the unskilled labor force in the railroad yards and on track repair crews, reinforcing the cleavage between skilled and unskilled workers.

The second bright spot for organized labor prior to the New Deal, the Norris-LaGuardia Act of 1932, sponsored by progressive Republicans George Norris, a senator from Nebraska, and Fiorello LaGuardia, a congressman from New York City, had a number of important provisions agreed to by a temporary coalition of liberals and organized labor. It endorsed collective bargaining, prohibited employers from forcing new employees to forego union membership as a condition of employment, placed limits on the use of labor injunctions, and made it illegal to sue unions for the unlawful acts of individual members, except when there was clear proof that unions had taken part in or authorized the actions (O'Brien 1998, pp. 154–158). In essence, the act established unions as entities with rights and responsibilities, then provided them with a modicum of freedom to pursue those rights. But on the most important issue, collective bargaining, it did not provide any way to bring corporations to the bargaining table (O'Brien 1998, pp. 148–172).

Even with the Railway Labor Act and the Norris-LaGuardia Act on the law books, it did not seem likely that the weakened union movement would have any power to influence the New Deal. However, the AFL did have institutional legitimacy and a heritage of over forty-five years of labor organizing. Most of all, workers had the right to vote and the potential to disrupt production and destroy plants and equipment. The dynamiting of the *Los Angeles Times* building in 1911, the Ludlow Massacre in 1914, the deadly strikes at Standard Oil of New Jersey in 1915 and 1916, and the massive U.S. Steel strike in 1919 were only the most recent reminders of these disruptive capabilities.

There also was one new factor. The ongoing Depression led to changes in several policy positions at the AFL convention three months before the 1932 presidential election that proved to be pivotal. The AFL abandoned its opposition to national-level labor standards, unemployment insurance, and old-age pensions, although it continued to be hostile to minimum wage legislation. The labor federation was therefore positioned to try to influence the federal government to pass labor and social welfare laws favorable to workers. That meant it could become part of a liberal-labor coalition if the Democratic challenger to the incumbent Republican won the presidential election and included liberals in his governing coalition.

FROM PROGRESSIVE-ERA REFORMERS TO NEW DEAL LIBERALS

Modern liberalism gradually developed in the late nineteenth and early twentieth centuries as a reaction to corporate dominance of government on the one hand and a dislike for socialist solutions to corporate dominance on the other. The values and programs that gradually differentiated modern liberalism from classical liberalism first and foremost concerned the use of government, and especially the federal government, to regulate large corporations and restore some power to corporate employees. Modern liberalism also held that the provision of social services and financial support for low-income people, including previously excluded social groups, did not violate basic liberal principles. The early advocates defined themselves as "reformers" and "progressives," and they included both Republicans and Democrats. Even during the early New Deal, liberal Democrats and the Progressive Republicans in Congress were more likely to be called New Dealers than liberals. It was not until the late 1930s that all those who embraced the tenets and policies of modern liberalism were regularly called liberals (Starr 2007, Chapters 4–6 for the rise of modern liberalism).

The reformers of the Progressive Era had their strongest base in a variety of private organizations created to help workers and their families, including the settlement house movement, the National Consumers' League, the Women's Trade Union League, and a range of charitable and social service organizations. The settlement house movement also aided the emergence of social work as a profession by providing the new occupation with training grounds and new recruits. Some members of these groups were on university faculties or were leaders in church groups, with Quakerism contributing a disproportionate number of reformers. Some had independent incomes as members of upper-middle-class professions or from inherited wealth as members of upper-class families.

Jane Addams, the founder of the settlement house movement, and perhaps the most prominent reformer from 1890 until her death in 1935, was the daughter of one of the richest men in northern Illinois. She was a college graduate who had traveled widely in Europe. Her friends in Chicago, where she founded Hull House, the first American settlement house, were of the social elite, and she was a member of an exclusive club for women (Farrell 1967; Linn 1935). The situation is similar for many other leading names of the settlement house movement: Julia Lathrop, Mary McDowell, Alice Hamilton, Lillian Wald, and Mary Kingsbury Simkhovitch. For example, Simkhovitch, who married a Russian-born intellectual, was from an "old" family with varied connections. Her uncle had been in high management in the Pennsylvania Railroad and served on the Interstate Commerce Commission, and one of her cousins was at one point the chief executive of Standard Oil of California (Simkhovitch 1938).

The reformers received much of their financial support from wealthy friends. In the case of Hull House, the supporters included Anita McCormick of the International Harvester fortune and Rosenwald of Sears, Roebuck. Three of the regular large donors to the Henry Street Settlement in New York were Mrs. Solomon Loeb of a famous banking family, Jacob Schiff (a member of another famous banking family, and Mrs. Loeb's son-in-law as well), and John Crosby Brown, a leader of an investment bank (now Brown Brothers, Harriman) that had its start in the early nineteenth century. Other wealthy backers of reformist efforts included the daughters of super-rich power figures such as J. P. Morgan, E. H. Harriman, and Mark Hanna (Chambers 1963; Davis 1967; Wald 1934).

Several early foundations also were helpful to the reformers even though they were small by the standards of the Carnegie Corporation and the Rockefeller Foundation. The most important of them by far was the Russell Sage Foundation, which was started with a $10 million gift by Mrs. Russell Sage in 1907, a year after her husband died. This foundation played a leading role in the development of the social work profession, providing grants and office space for several organizations and financing various social work publications (Devine 1939; Glenn 1947). Since Russell Sage himself was one of the most ruthless and anti-union financiers of his era, with a large role in several railroad companies, the use of his money to fund programs that helped workers and their families was more than ironic (see Crocker 2006 for the story of Mrs. Sage's unusual life, which also serves as a window into the role of wealthy women in the Progressive Era). Donations from the Milbank Memorial Fund also were helpful to the early reformers. (Elizabeth Milbank Anderson, the founder of the Milbank Memorial Fund in 1905, was the daughter of a multi-millionaire financier. In addition, she gave $100,000 to the Henry Street Settlement in 1916 and joined its board of directors.) The Charity Organizing Services of New York, which contributed greatly to the creation of social work as a profession, was directed and financed by well-to-do New Yorkers (Chambers 1963; Devine 1939).

Two reform organizations established around the turn of the twentieth century demonstrate women's key role in the early reform movement. The first was the National Consumers' League (NCL), founded in 1898 to push for reform measures that would improve working conditions, especially for women, and abolish child labor. The organization was led by Florence Kelley, who is credited by many commentators as being second only to Jane Addams among progressive women. The daughter of an anti-slavery lawyer who abandoned his successful business career and served in the House of Representatives from Pennsylvania as a Radical Republican from 1861 until his death in 1890, she earned a B.A. degree from Cornell in 1892 and a law degree from Northwestern in 1894 while working at Hull House. In 1899 she joined the newly formed National Consumers' League and spent the remaining thirty-four years of her life working for minimum wage and maximum hour laws for working women. She also was part of the National Child Labor Committee that agitated for the creation of a Children's Bureau in the Department of Labor in 1912 and was among the founders of the National Association for the Advancement of Colored People (Chambers 1963; Storrs 2000).

The second new reform organization, the Women's Trade Union League, focused the energies of the most pro-union of the reformers (although most women reformers were sympathetic to the problems of labor, not all were convinced that unions were the answer). Created and directed by upper-class women, with the help of a few men, the league also included working-class women. Its most important leader from 1907 to 1921, Margaret Dreier Robbins, was the daughter of a wealthy Brooklyn businessman, a close friend of Florence Kelley, and a Republican (Boone 1942; Davis 1964). In addition to advocating laws protecting women in the workplace, some upper-class members joined in demonstrations and strike activities. Mrs. Franklin Roosevelt and her friend Mrs. Thomas Lamont, the wife of a famous investment banker with the J. P. Morgan firm, raised $30,000 for the organization's clubhouse in New York (Roosevelt and Hickok 1954, p. 262).

Although the breadth and depth of their impact should not be exaggerated, the progressive economic and social reforms of the early twentieth century did benefit some working people across the nation. Laws restricting child labor were adopted in thirty-eight states by 1912, and some legal protection was given to women working in the manufacturing sector in twenty-eight states. Public health and safety as well as maximum hours legislation was also passed, and the courts gradually came to a more liberal interpretation of such legislation (Dubofsky and Dulles 2004, pp. 188–189; McCammon 1995, 1996). But as we noted in our earlier discussion of the American Association for Labor legislation, many of those programs were opposed by organized labor due to its fear of government, making a strong alliance between reformers and trade unionists difficult.

Instead, the reformers found their closest allies in what may seem to be an unlikely place, the urban Democratic political machines. Machine Democrats were best known for seeking to control local government by hook or crook so they could give out patronage jobs and government construction contracts to their co-ethnics, but by the early twentieth century they were eager to gain the support of the growing number of urbanized workers, which they did through support for labor-oriented reforms. At the same time, the machines also maintained good relations with the AFL unions in their respective cities, which put them in the middle of a loose-knit coalition, with reformers on the one side and AFL leaders on the other. We demonstrate these points shortly when we highlight the careers of three reformers who went on to be important liberals during the New Deal.

However, we first want to emphasize that by no means did all, or even a majority, of the original progressives evolve into New Dealers, which is a useful point in underscoring the fact that modern liberalism went a step beyond previous reform efforts. A study of 105 early progressives who lived into the mid-1930s found that 60 of them opposed the New Deal, 40 supported it, and 5 were critical of it from a leftist perspective (Graham 1967). Those who opposed the New Deal were more likely to be Republicans or corporate lawyers. Their primary emphasis as progressives was on the modernization of government and the improvement of its efficiency, especially at the local level, where they heartily disliked the Democrats' political machines. At the national level they had accepted some regulation of corporations, including the Federal Trade Commission, as a way to deal with ruinous competition among corporations and some of the criticisms from populists and organized labor. But they regarded any government regulation of the relationship between business owners and their employees, such as setting minimum wages, as a dangerous government infringement on human freedom and the rights of private property. In other words, they were squarely on the side of employers when it came to class conflict.

Progressives who became New Dealers or leftists, on the other hand, were more likely to be involved in the settlement house movement, the National Consumers' League, the Women's Trade Union League, or the delivery of social services to low-income people, all of which brought their members into close contact with the problems facing urban workers and their families. Many women who began with a reformist or socialist orientation during the Progressive Era also became staunch New Dealers, including two activists in the National Consumers League, Mary Dewson, who was appointed to the first Social Security Board, and Josephine Roche, an assistant secretary of the Treasury. Roche was well prepared for this position because she had been president of the Rocky Mountain Fuel Company (1929–1934), which she inherited from her wealthy father, who had been part of the employer group, along with Rockefeller, that broke the Ludlow strike fifteen years earlier. By contrast, she invited the United Mine Workers to unionize the company and established good relations with the union leaders, later serving for twenty-three years as one of three advisors to its welfare and pension fund. It is also the case that men and women from the settlement house movement served in the New Deal, as did women from the National Consumers' League and the Women's Trade Union League (see Chambers 1963, pp. 254–257, for thumbnail sketches of a long list of other appointees and advisors who came from this tradition; see Linda Gordon 1994, for a detailed history of their activities and impact).

For our purposes, the rise of modern liberalism is embodied in the political careers of three of the central figures in the New Deal, Senator Robert F. Wagner of New York, who introduced several important pieces of New Deal legislation, Frances Perkins, who was appointed secretary of labor in 1933, and Harry Hopkins, who handled relief spending and government work projects for Roosevelt. Although we do not claim that any of the three provided major policy inputs into the three issues we discuss, we include their profiles here because they are three of the best examples there are of the new liberals. In addition, they did have a hand in bringing about passage of the National Labor Relations Act in the case of Wagner and the Social Security Act in the case of Perkins and Hopkins.

Wagner immigrated to the United States from Germany at the age of nine with his parents and siblings. His father worked as a janitor in tenement buildings before returning to Germany; an older brother who worked as a cook at the New York Athletic Club helped pay the future senator's way through City College of New York. Wagner then earned a two-year law degree at New York Law School in 1898 and in 1900 began his law practice with a law-school friend, who later did legal work for the AFL. Wagner joined the Democratic political machine at Tammany Hall to augment his law practice, and he was elected to the state assembly in 1904, where he focused on legislating cheaper fares on rapid transit and other reform efforts, such as child labor laws and workmen's compensation, which soon became signature issues for urban liberals. He won a seat in the state senate in 1908. By 1910, at the age of thirty-three, he could afford a second home on the shore of Long Island due to the great success of his law practice (Huthmacher 1968, p. 22).

After rising to the leadership of the state senate through working on reform measures related to social welfare and labor law, which drew him closer to all of the New York City reform groups, in 1918 Wagner was elected to the state Supreme Court. After leaving the court for a successful race for a U.S. Senate seat in 1926, he characteristically devoted his first speech to the problem of unemployment and over the next few years introduced a series of bills to deal with the issue through government employment offices, public works programs, and unemployment insurance. He thus took on "the familiar role as spokesman for advanced social thinkers and reformers that he had filled at Albany," meaning that he was very close to the AALL, the League of Women Voters, the National Consumers' League, and the Russell Sage Foundation (Huthmacher 1968, p. 63). At the same time, he listened to experts from the new think tanks: "No member of Congress makes more frequent use of the research facilities of The Brookings Institution," according to one observer at the time (Huthmacher 1968, p. 110). His biographer notes that he was so dependent upon these outside experts for his policy proposals (he had only one paid staff member) that some people wondered what he brought to the process. In fact, he brought the sensibilities of an urban liberal with a vast legislative experience, an incredible degree of patience, and the ability to persist in the face of criticism from business leaders. As crisply stated by a Columbia University law professor, one of the people who worked with Wagner on labor issues in 1933–1934, he had the following qualities: "First, his ingrained, humanitarian, progressive philosophy; second, his uncanny capacity to recruit good men to do the detail work for him; third, his masterful ability to maneuver bills through the legislative mill; and fourth, and most important of all, his willingness and determination to stick to his basic convictions" (Huthmacher 1968, p. 115).

Frances Perkins, who became the first woman to be appointed to the Cabinet, served for all thirteen years of Roosevelt's presidency as the secretary of labor. Her father was a successful business owner in Worcester, Massachusetts, and both he and her mother came from early and respected New England families. She went to a private academy and Mount Holyoke College, where she helped organize a campus branch of the National Consumers' League and met Frances Kelley, later calling her a major influence on her life (see Downey 2009 for biographical information on Perkins). After graduation in 1902, she taught at an elite prep school for girls outside of Chicago, volunteered at the Hull House on weekends, and worked on a project for the Women's Trade Union League. She left her teaching position for work with a social service organization in Philadelphia and then moved to New York, where she lived in a settlement house founded by Mary Kingsbury Simkhovitch and earned an M.A. degree at Columbia University. She then went to work for the New York office of the National Consumers'

League, where she became an expert on factory health and safety issues. She also lobbied for NCL legislation in the state capitol, where she came to know reformist politicians in both parties, including Wagner and Roosevelt.

Like Kelley, who had become friends with Marx's collaborator, Frederick Engels, while she studied in Europe, and even translated his book on housing problems into English, Perkins considered herself a socialist at the time. When she was asked in 1912 to join Theodore Roosevelt's Progressive Party, she wrote her future husband, himself a reform economist from a wealthy background, that "They were shocked and pained when I said I guessed I'd stick by the proletariat and that I believed more in class struggle than I did in politics" (Cohen 2009, p. 173). In 1918, however, she switched to the Democratic Party so she could become the first woman to serve on the New York State Labor Commission after a New York City machine Democrat and reformer, Al Smith, won the governorship. When Franklin D. Roosevelt was elected governor of New York in 1928, she became the first woman to be a state industrial commissioner, which put her in charge of eighteen hundred employees, the largest state labor department in the nation. Speaking to a luncheon crowd of a thousand guests honoring her appointment, she said she stood for the idea that "social justice is possible in a great industrial community" (Cohen 2009, p. 181). After Roosevelt won the presidency and asked her to join his cabinet as secretary of labor, she did so only on the condition that he would promise to enact her list of labor reforms:

> At her meeting with Roosevelt, she said she would only accept if he promised to back her agenda. At the top of her list were aid to state and local governments for unemployment relief and a large-scale public works program. She also wanted a federal minimum wage and maximum hours laws, a ban on child labor, and unemployment and old-age insurance (Cohen 2009, p. 192).

Notably, the list did not include legislation to help unions. Given her difficulties trying to work with unions on protective labor legislation in New York, she always made clear that "I'd much rather get a law than organize a union" (Cohen 2009, p. 168). For their part, union leaders expressed disappointment that the head of the Teamsters Union was not appointed secretary of labor. Reflecting the tensions between organized labor and liberals, John L. Lewis, the forceful and eloquent leader of the United Mine Workers, who had voted Republican in 1932, called Perkins "a mere social worker" (Cohen 2009, p. 193). However, she quickly won over most labor leaders by making a visit to the president of the AFL's office and then holding a one-day conference on labor issues at the Department of Labor.

Harry Hopkins, who became a very close advisor to Roosevelt as the head of New Deal relief and civil works programs, came from a background very different from that of either Wagner or Perkins, but he shared their focus on using government to help low-income people. He was born and raised in Iowa, where his father was a small-town retail businessman, and his upbringing included church attendance as often as six days a week and singing hymns around the family's organ with his four siblings. His mother, who frequently volunteered at the Methodist Home Missionary Society of Iowa, emphasized the importance of good works in finding salvation. He studied at Grinnell College, a small liberal arts school in his home state that was founded by an abolitionist minister. Upon graduation he moved to New York City to become a counselor for Christodora House, a settlement house on the lower east side, which brought him into a world of Italian and Jewish immigrants that was, of course, entirely new to him. But he thrived because of his restless energy, openness, and ability to relate to people of all class, racial, and religious backgrounds. He soon began working nights at the Association for Improving the Condition of the Poor, a New York charity, and then became head of its employment bureau, which led him to an appointment at age twenty-five as the executive secretary of the city's Board of Child Welfare when a reform mayor came into office in 1915 (Cohen 2009, p. 259). After the new mayor lost the election two years later, Hopkins went to work for the Red Cross in New Orleans and Atlanta before returning to New York to direct the New York Tuberculosis Association. When Roosevelt and Perkins created the Temporary Emergency Relief Administration for New York in August 1931, with a $20 million budget, they put Hopkins in charge. This position soon brought him into contact with the nationwide network of welfare organizations through meetings with leaders of other public and private relief agencies. He joined the New Deal as the head of the Federal Emergency Relief Administration in late May 1933, then directed the Civil Works Administration and its more famous successor, the Works Progress Administration.

As the Roosevelt Administration took office, the liberals who were part of his coalition were in considerable agreement on their goals, but there were several different camps in terms of what they should do to reach those goals (see, for example, Hawley 1966). Moreover, with the exception of Wagner and perhaps a few other elected urban liberals, they did not have strong ties to organized labor due to long-standing disagreements over minimum wage and protective labor legislation. Nor did they have much respect for AFL leaders. They saw them as narrow, weak, unimaginative, and self-seeking, not at all public regarding, and often corrupt. They also knew that the union movement had been opposed in principle to the use of the federal government to improve social conditions until its apparent change of heart at its 1932 convention. For several reasons, then, the liberal-labor coalition only began to emerge as the New Deal unfolded. Liberals and union leaders first cooperated in early 1933 in forcing legislators to include some rights for organized labor in the National Industrial Recovery Act, which was otherwise fashioned by business interests, as demonstrated in Chapter 3. This cooperation increased in the 1934 elections, grew stronger in working for the National Labor Relations Act of 1935, and played a significant role in sealing the presidential election for Roosevelt in 1936, including large-scale financial donations from organized labor (Brinkley 1995; Webber 2000).

THE COMMUNIST PARTY

The Communist Party was not a major power actor during the New Deal, but it did figure in many of the events we discuss. Its role is also relevant in assessing the theoretical claims of both Marxists and protest-disruption theorists. It had more power resources than was realized at the time; in the end, however, its political influence was minimal at the national level and sometimes counterproductive for the causes it espoused. It strongly opposed all three pieces of legislation that are central to this book, objecting in the strongest possible terms in testimony before Congress to both the National Labor Relations Act and the Social Security Act. Moreover, members of the liberal-labor coalition repudiated the Communists because they knew from the party's newspaper and public statements that many of its policy stances were shaped by the needs and desires of the Soviet Union, especially on foreign policy. For several reasons, then, the party usually has been dismissed as irrelevant in recent decades because it was small and isolated.

However, on the basis of research by Harvey Klehr (1984) and sociologists Judith Stepan-Norris and Maurice Zeitlin (2003), as well as secret papers in Soviet and American archives that were released in the 1990s (Haynes, Klehr, and Anderson 1998; Klehr, Haynes, and Firsov 1995), we believe that the Communist Party (hereafter usually called the CP, as it always was by its members) did have some impact despite its fierce disdain for liberals and the AFL during the first several years of the New Deal. It did so first of all through the disruption it was able to generate in several major cities immediately after the stock market crash, thereby heightening class tensions, causing some non-Communist workers to take action, and putting pressure on local governments for welfare payments. A few years later it had a significant role in organizing industrial workers into unions. It was able to have this impact, we believe, for three intertwined reasons: an energizing ideology, a powerful organizational form, and far more financial support than is generally realized, all of which are important ingredients for a social movement organization.

Marxism, as a theory of how history inevitably unfolds as well as a strong assertion about the certainty of socialism in the imminent future, provided an ideology that proved useful in recruiting new members and shoring up morale because it allegedly had "predicted" the Depression. The theory thereby lent credence to Marxism's main moral vision, the inevitable replacement of the competitive and profit-driven capitalist system by a cooperative socialist system. American Communists could take heart from their belief that the Depression demonstrated the accuracy of the Marxist analysis of capitalism and its inevitable demise, as propounded in books and speeches coming from Stalin and other Communist leaders in Moscow. Their ideological convictions were further reinforced by the fact that the Soviet economy was not greatly affected by the Depression.

Second, the CP had the advantage of a highly centralized structure that allowed the top leaders to have a rapid and cohesive impact. Building on a base of "units" or "sections" in factories and neighborhoods, the party was governed in theory by a central committee that varied in size from two to three dozen members and that met only periodically. For the most part, party policy was set by the Politburo, an elite subcommittee of five to seven people. A general secretary directed the paid staff, consulted with the Communist leaders in Moscow, served as the party's spokesperson, and managed day-to-day affairs. Members of the central committee, along with many paid organizers, also served as leaders within "front" organizations created to agitate on specific issues or causes that could engage the interest and energies of non-Communists. To the degree that these "mass organizations," as they were called, were successful in attracting members, they extended the potential impact of the CP leaders. In addition, CP organizers and members joined non-Communist organizations as individuals and then attempted to exert influence in them by acting as a cohesive "fraction" with a unified common viewpoint.

Although many new members quickly decided that the party had an overly hierarchical structure and was too subservient to the Soviet Union, leading to a massive turnover in membership each year, those who remained in the party accepted this top-down organizational structure, partly because they believed that the Soviet Union was poised to lead a worldwide Communist revolution but also because the structure of the party was couched in a concept developed by Lenin that merged an aspect of participatory democracy with strong centralized leadership. Called "democratic centralism," it claimed that decisions about new political directions would begin with open and frank discussions within the various units of the party. These discussions supposedly made it possible for everyone to air their opinions and take sides. However, the participants had to agree beforehand that they would stifle any doubts and follow the new policies once the majority decided on the direction to take, which meant that at the end of the process the members would be as focused and unified as if they were part of a totally top-down hierarchical system to begin with. In practice, however, the lower-level units usually had to take their cues from the Politburo and General Secretary, turning the discussions among members into a sham that at best reinforced group solidarity. Thus, just as Marxism provided an all-encompassing theoretical framework and social identity for people seeking to bring about large-scale egalitarian social change, so too Leninism provided a powerful organizational innovation for maximizing the impact of the relative handful of committed activists.

Third, the American Communist Party had a large funding base that made it possible to take full advantage of the internal morale and hierarchical bureaucratic structure provided by Marxist theory and the Leninist form of organization. A significant portion of this funding, which may have added up to as much as $3 to $5 million in the first seven or eight years of the New Deal (that's $45 to $80 million in 2010 dollars), came from the Soviet Union in a variety of ways that ranged from smuggled diamonds to cash payments to a share of the profits from a Soviet trading company and a Soviet travel agency in New York City (Haynes, Klehr, and Anderson 1998, Chapter 2). Even more money came from a handful of wealthy Americans who sympathized with the Soviet Union as a model for the future and supported its projects (Klehr 1984, pp. 374–378). Although members were told that their dues were crucial to the functioning of the organization, only a small portion of CP money came from fundraising events and membership dues. Instead, the obligatory process of paying dues in effect served as a way to increase the commitment of members to the organization through their financial sacrifices for it.

Even though historical research demonstrates that most people who joined the party quickly left it, the net result of this combination of factors was "hordes of functionaries," including three thousand to four thousand paid organizers, who could be mobilized to put their bodies on the line in demonstrations and strikes on very short notice, sometimes traveling a hundred miles by automobile or train to participate in an action (Klehr 1984, pp. 374, 378). Party members serving as leaders within the mass organizations also had the potential to mobilize non-Communist individuals on a range of specific issues.

Despite this potential to exercise power, the history of the American Communist Party from its founding in September 1919 to a purge of its leadership by Stalin in 1929 was one of decline, failure, and fights with rival leftist groups that left it despised and isolated (Klehr 1984, p. 4; Weinstein 1967). The party also alienated the leaders of the labor unions that it tried to take over or displace, especially in the United Mine Workers and Amalgamated Clothing Workers, first by creating left-wing caucuses within these unions, later by trying to organize rival unions (Klehr 1984, pp. 39–44).

But even with this unbroken record of failure throughout the 1920s, and even though its arch-enemy, the Socialist Party, was far larger at the outset of the Depression, the Communist Party's motivating ideology, tight organizational form, and significant financial backing made it possible for the few thousand remaining Communists to capitalize on the stock market crash and the ensuing depression. It did so by taking the lead in street-level agitation and disruption while at the same time formulating a policy proposal for very generous social insurance payments that were about equal to average local wages in each city. The proposal added up to an early version of a guaranteed annual wage (Manza 1995, p. 351). The party also had several veteran leaders who provided it with a continuity of top-level leadership at very low wages throughout the New Deal period. Several of them had spent one or more years in Moscow or traveled to other parts of the world for the Soviets.

Crowds at Communist-led demonstrations of up to fifty thousand in New York and Detroit in late 1929 and early 1930 led the party to organize International Unemployment Day in March, 1930, when a march to city hall in New York by twenty-five thousand people led to rioting and arrests. Buoyed by the disruption it had created, the party then started Unemployment Councils to agitate in a wide range of cities (Kerbo and Shaffer 1992; Valocchi 1990, 1993). However, neither Moscow nor the American CP leaders were satisfied with these actions because they did not strengthen the Unemployed Councils or the party, although they did play at least some role in causing local governments to provide relief funds for the unemployed. Soon thereafter, the party turned to rent strikes and hunger marches (Klehr 1984). Well aware that Stalin controlled the Communist Party and provided much of its money, Roosevelt insisted that Stalin cut down on the disruptions as part of the deal that led to American recognition of the Soviet government in 1933, but in fact Stalin did not attempt to rein in the party until two years later, when he decided that a "popular front" against fascism was necessary to save the Soviet Union from Nazi Germany (Morgan 2003, pp. 136–138).

It quickly became difficult to organize unemployed workers and rent strikes in the face of the new sense of hope generated by the relief programs legislated by New Dealers, so the party revived its efforts to develop its own industrial and agricultural unions. This effort to supplant the established AFL unions failed completely even though those unions were very weak. It also, of course, not for the first time, totally alienated leaders within the AFL. Although both the Unemployed Councils and union-organizing efforts proved to be futile, they did serve as a training ground for a cadre of seasoned and hardened organizers who later became active in the organization of major industrial unions in steel, automobile production, and other heavy industries after 1935. At that point the leaders of the nascent Congress of Industrial Organizations (CIO), which we discuss in Chapter 5, reached a secret understanding with the top leaders of the CP that they would hire several dozen of the party's top organizers as part of their attempt to create new industrial unions (Haynes, Klehr, and Anderson 1998, p. 54). In part because of the willingness of local Communist trade unionists to ignore national party directives when these did not make sense to them, by 1939 members of the Communist Party were the leaders in eighteen of the thirty-four CIO affiliates, which accounted for 25 percent of the total CIO membership (Stepan-Norris and Zeitlin 2003, p. 19, Table 1.1). A 1938 report discovered decades later in files in Moscow estimated that "about 7,500 party members hold official positions in the trade unions ranging from shop steward to national union presidencies" (Morgan 2003, p. 175). In particular, they were the main leaders in the sixth-largest CIO union in 1940, the United Electrical, Radio and Machine Workers Union, with an estimated 72,900 members, although that membership total was far below the estimated 528,300 in the United Mine Workers, the 299,000 in the United Steel Workers, and the 246,000 in the United Automobile Workers (Troy 1965, Table A-2).

Aside from the United Electrical, Radio and Machine Workers, the Communist-led unions all had fewer than forty thousand members before the war began, half of them had fewer than ten thousand members, and only a small number of their members were also members of the Communist Party or sympathetic to socialism or communism (Bernstein 1969, p. 783). However, it is the party's moral and scientific certitude, tight organizational structure, control over significant financial resources, and ability to motivate disruptive actions by workers that matter the most in terms of the analysis of power that is the focus of this book.

With the context provided by this chapter as a backdrop, it is now possible to explain how the power groups did battle on agricultural, labor, and social security issues.

CHAPTER TWO

The Agricultural Adjustment Act

World War I was a time of rising prosperity for American farmers because they could sell their increasing productivity overseas, but problems soon developed for them after the war as Europeans began to grow their own food again and American farm productivity continued to increase faster than the market demanded. Faced with sunk costs and no way to reduce them, individual farmers reacted by putting more land into use and intensifying production in order to sell more crops to make up for the lower market prices. This process of course created a vicious downward cycle. Farm income fell from $17 billion in 1919 to $5 billion in 1932 at a time when farming employed 30 percent of the American workforce and indirectly involved another 20 percent.

The policy adopted by the New Deal to solve these problems—voluntary reductions in crop acreage by plantation owners and farmers in exchange for government payments—had its origins in the corporate moderates' policy-planning network. The rudiments of this "domestic allotment" policy, as it was soon called, were first brought to the attention of relevant experts, business leaders, and policymakers in 1928 by Beardsley Ruml, the president of the Laura Spelman Rockefeller Memorial Fund, and were based on a program that seemed to be working in Germany. However, Ruml did not immediately push the idea into the public realm because he knew it needed refinement and political legitimacy. He also was cautious because a plan championed by conservative Democratic businessmen and eagerly supported by many farm leaders already existed.

THE PARITY PRICE PLAN

The plan that Ruml wanted to displace came from the combined efforts of two men employed by Bernard Baruch, a super-wealthy Wall Street speculator, who was the fifty-ninth-highest individual taxpayer in 1924 and worth an estimated $37.5 million (which is $490.3 million in 2010 dollars) (Lundberg

1937, p. 28). Baruch was born and raised in South Carolina, and his family moved to New York City when he was eleven, where his father practiced medicine as a surgeon and his mother's family was in the shipping business. He graduated from City College of New York, quickly made a fortune on Wall Street, and affiliated with the Democratic Party, giving large donations to its candidates in the years before World War I. He rose to great public prominence during the war after President Woodrow Wilson appointed him to oversee the War Industries Board that coordinated the industrial mobilization. He thereby came to know most of the businessmen and many of the policy experts who would figure in the next twenty-five years of American politics. His success in handling the job, along with his generous campaign contributions, also gave him great stature with politicians, and he enjoyed close relations with several leading Southern Democrats in the Senate.

Baruch's first employee, George Peek, had worked his way up to vice president for sales of Deere and Company, a farm machinery manufacturer, before joining Baruch in Washington as "commissioner of finished products" (Ohl 1985, p. 42). The second was General Hugh Johnson, a graduate of West Point in 1903 and the University of California, Berkeley law school in 1916, after which he became an aide to Baruch in Washington. Following the war Peek decided to take his chances as president of a farm implement company, Moline Plow. He asked Johnson to join him as assistant general manager and general counsel, but the company soon went bankrupt. Peek and Johnson then went to work for Baruch investigating business opportunities, writing position papers, and helping him lobby for legislative policies he favored. Peek served as a link to the Farm Bureau and Johnson lobbied for Baruch's idea that the army should have a preparedness plan (Ohl 1985, Chapter 5).

Baruch, Peek, and Johnson blamed agriculture's problems—and the failure of Moline Plow—on the workings of the tariff, which supposedly forced farmers to pay higher prices for industrial goods but did not protect the price of farm products. Their solution was to figure a ratio based on average crop prices and average general prices for the ten years before World War I, and then to adjust the tariff on the basis of yearly changes in that ratio. They claimed that farmers would then receive a fair-exchange price, which came to be called the "parity price." Just as important, any price-depressing surpluses would be bought by the government at the parity price and then sold for a loss in foreign countries. The losses on the world market would be paid for by a tax on the crops farmers sold, called an "equalization fee" (David Hamilton 1991).

Peek and Johnson first wrote down their ideas in August 1920. Their plan was then circulated to a small group of politicians by officials of the Farm Bureau. A year later Peek and Johnson expanded their ideas into a pamphlet titled *Equality for Agriculture*. By 1924 the plan was supported by most farm groups and, not surprisingly, by farm equipment manufacturers and processors who favored increasing farm production. The bill changed somewhat over the next few years in the face of criticism and rejection by Congress in 1924, but the heart of it remained the government purchase of surplus crops that would then be sold at a loss in foreign countries. Most industrialists and bankers opposed the plan, especially those who wanted to expand international trade markets. They believed it would increase the problem of agricultural overproduction and invite retaliation against American manufactured goods by angry nations whose farmers would suffer from the dumping of American surpluses overseas. The opposition to the bill, which was led by Secretary of the Treasury Andrew Mellon, a banker-industrialist of great wealth, also included most economists, often speaking in the name of the average consumer, and the editors of many farm journals (see Ferrell 1998, pp. 30, 92–93, for a good summary account). Congress nonetheless passed the bill that embodied the plan in 1927 and 1928, but Republican President Calvin Coolidge vetoed it both times (David Hamilton 1991, pp. 20–21).

THE DOMESTIC ALLOTMENT PLAN

Ruml first approached agricultural experts to do a feasibility study of his domestic allotment plan in 1928 after the parity price program had been rejected once again. He did so knowing that a plan to create reductions in the number of acres planted would have great appeal to many corporate moderates precisely because, unlike the parity price plan, it would reduce surpluses. By that point Ruml already had strong connections with agricultural experts because he had been supporting their efforts since 1923. In that year he had first made contact with agricultural economist Henry Taylor, the head of the Bureau of Agricultural Economics, a small research and forecasting agency within the Department of Agriculture, to see if there were any projects in the field of agricultural economics that the Memorial might support. Taylor replied that there was a small project in Montana that was trying to deal with the problems of tenant farming in dry climates through the use of new scientific methods, so Ruml hired him as a consultant to develop the project further (Reagan 1999, p. 160; Rowley 1970, p. 31).

The project Taylor became involved in, called Fairway Farms, was run by agricultural economist M. L. Wilson, who had taken courses in the social sciences at the University of Chicago and the University of Wisconsin, where he had worked with John R. Commons, before settling down in Montana as a part-time farmer and a professor in agricultural sciences at the University of Montana. Wilson, as we shall soon see, played a central role in developing the domestic allotment plan and helped convince future president Roosevelt of its feasibility. Chester Davis, another agricultural economist who would later support the development and administration of the domestic allotment plan, helped Wilson with the project. Ruml was soon serving as its treasurer and provided small grants from the Memorial for two years, at which point Rockefeller himself personally provided a line of credit for $1 million (Reagan 1999, p. 161). The money was used to buy abandoned farms and lease them to tenants, who would work the land with modern machinery and have the opportunity to buy their own land from the project if they were successful. It was hoped that the project would be a demonstration of how tenants could be helped to "climb the 'agricultural ladder' to land ownership" (Rowley 1970, p. 31). The project was not successful, but it did give visibility and legitimacy to Wilson, who was thereafter seen as "a leading authority on the experimental method of research in agricultural economics" (Kirkendall 1966, p. 13). Thus, even though the project failed, it reveals how the careers of experts often become tied to wealthy business leaders as well as administrators in the policy-planning network.

In 1925 Ruml and his colleagues on the board of the Social Science Research Council (SSRC) appointed Taylor to be the chair of the council's newly formed Committee on Social and Economic Research in Agriculture. When Taylor unexpectedly lost his position at the Bureau of Agricultural Economics later in the year due to a newspaper report that he allegedly lobbied for an agricultural bill advocated by farm organizations, friends at the Institute for Research in Land Economics at Northwestern University hired him with special funds provided by Rockefeller philanthropies. Taylor later wrote in his memoirs, which remain unpublished, that the Rockefeller group "saved my career" (Reagan 1999, p. 287, ftn. 66). It should come as no surprise, then, that Taylor was the agricultural economist Ruml turned to for advice when he decided it was time to see if a plan to reduce agricultural acreage might be feasible. Taylor responded that he had recalled Ruml talking about the plan a year or two earlier, and that he thought it had possibilities, but due to lack of time he suggested that Ruml contact John D. Black, an agricultural economist at Harvard University (Reagan 1999, p. 162). Black was no stranger to Ruml because he, too, was a member of the Committee on Social and Economic Research in Agriculture from its inception.

The first contact with Black came in June 1928, through a letter from Ruml's assistant, Edmund Day, later to be the director of the Social Sciences Division for the Rockefeller Foundation, asking him if he would be interested in a grant to study a domestic allotment plan being used in Germany (Day 1928; Klass 1969, pp. 54–55). At about the same time, Taylor wrote to Black urging him to consider doing the research for Ruml. His statement gives a good indication of the rudimentary nature of the idea as a baseline for how much it changed as research and discussions unfolded:

> There is another item I want to take up with you. For about two years Dr. Ruml has been interested in a method of surpluses control which approaches the problem from the standpoint of certificating production for the domestic market on the basis of what individual farmers have been producing in past years, certificating to each one his pro rata share of the domestic needs, then requiring that all additional quantities produced by these farmers or any other farmers shall be for export and shall not be sold on the domestic market. An appropriation of $5,000 [that's $64,000 in 2010 dollars] has been made for carrying on the research to figure out just what this would mean if attempts were made to put it into effect (Taylor 1928).

Black accepted the assignment, quickly assembled a team of researchers, and produced a book, *Agricultural Reform in the United States* (1929a), that became the basis for a major behind-the-scenes lobbying campaign for the program. As Black's papers at the Wisconsin State Historical Society Archives make clear, he stayed in close touch with Ruml by mail while he worked on the project. In late November, just four months after accepting the assignment, Black sent Ruml an outline that he hoped to fill out as a preliminary report in early January 1929. In that letter he also asked Ruml for a little more detail on his own ideas so he could make clear how they related to the ideas of a government agricultural economist, William J. Stillman, who had published a book, *Balancing the Farm Output* (1927), that contained similar ideas:

> I wish you would send me a brief statement of the essential features of your plan as you have thought it out so that we may have the record straight. In one important aspect it is like the plan which Dr. Spillman has described in his book called *Balancing the Farm Output* (Black 1928).

Ruml replied two days later saying that he was "astonished at the ground which you are going to cover and I am delighted that it is going to come out so promptly." He also attached "an outline of the plan we have discussed," as per Black's request (Ruml 1928a). At this point Ruml also conveyed his pleasure with the way this work was proceeding to one of Rockefeller's personal employees, Arthur Woods, president of the Memorial Fund at the time. It is memos such as this one that provide evidence that executive and managerial levels were being kept in touch with what the hired experts were doing:

> You will be interested, I think, in the progress which is being made in the agricultural economics matter, which the Executive Committee [the inner circle that met with Rockefeller] gave me some assistance on. I think you will agree that I am getting on rather well (Ruml 1928b).

Meanwhile, Black received help from several of his colleagues in agricultural economics, including Taylor, but most especially from Davis of the Fairview Farms project, who by this time was working for the Illinois Agricultural Association—the Farm Bureau affiliate in that state. Davis sent Black eight letters with detailed suggestions, not only on the substance of the issue, but on the politics as well. Davis liked the plan very much, but at one point worried that Black had "hung the fodder pretty high for the members of Congress, farm groups, press, etc., to reach"; he therefore counseled simplifying the language (Davis 1929).

As promised, Black sent a draft of the plan to Ruml in late January, as well as two follow-up letters, but did not hear back from Ruml until March 6 because of illness. At that point Ruml expressed his general approval of the chapters, but asked that "any personal reference to me be eliminated, if this is practicable." In the end, neither Ruml nor the support from the Memorial was mentioned in Black's book (Reagan 1999, p. 162). Ruml also expressed caution about Black's eagerness to advocate for the plan in Washington. His comments help to explain why the corporate moderates and their closely associated experts are often lost from view:

> I think it is very important that we continue to maintain a strictly "academic" attitude with respect to the whole situation. It would be very unfortunate for the opinion to be current that we have a "plan" for which we are agitating. It seems to me that we have fulfilled any public responsibility which we may have had in bringing this plan, together with such data as we have been able to assemble, before the people who are responsible for the working out of a national program, and of course the contribution which you will have made in your book is likely in the long run to be far more important than the development of any particular plan which we can envisage at the present time (Ruml 1929).

Ruml then sent the plan to mainstream agricultural economists for their comments, which were not positive, to Black's disappointment. He expressed his concern about Ruml's caution to Taylor:

> Dr. Ruml's plan would have been forced harder than it has if that part of it had been left to me. Dr. Ruml said that he had some excellent connections and that he would handle that end of it. What he did was to send the description of the plan to Julius Barnes and Dr. E. G. Nourse. Barnes of course found reasons to object to it, most of them of a conventional nature. Dr. Nourse praised the workmanship on the plan and indicated that he thought it would be a considerable improvement on any of the other plans, but does not think that any plans of this nature should be adopted (Black 1929b).

At this point Black also asked for and received counsel from employees at the Bureau of Agricultural Economics. As a result, he received feedback from Stillman (the author of the similar plan mentioned in the early letter from Black to Ruml), who seemed to approve of the new plan but thought that his recent studies made it seem likely "that wheat and cotton are the only two commodities to which it is necessary to apply this plan in order to put agriculture on its feet." More generally:

> I have read the enclosed chapter of Dr. Black's book with a great deal of inter-est. He presents here a plan for farm relief which is a development of the idea proposed in my little book entitled *Balancing the Farm Output* and it appears to me has made many important improvements in the plan as originally proposed (Stillman 1929).

The rush of events in Washington in 1929, along with Hoover's cool-ness toward the necessary amount of government involvement, squelched Black's hopes for immediate action on the proposal, and he went on to do work on international agricultural and population issues. Nevertheless, Ruml used Black's book to introduce the domestic allotment plan to Wilson, the economist who had worked for him on the Fairway Farms project (Klass 1969, p. 90, ftn. 2). By then a member of the SSRC's Committee on Social and Economic Research in Agriculture, Wilson spent a good part of the next three years championing the program with farm groups, other agricultural economists, and corporate leaders. Several businessmen who liked the plan aided his efforts by spreading the word about it (Rowley 1970, Chapter 7). The first of them was a grain dealer in Duluth, who purchased five thousand reprints of the key chapter in Black's book to distribute around the country. The second was Gerard Swope, president of General Electric, who figures prominently in all three of the new policies discussed in this book. In ad-dition to his work in the corporate community, he owned a thousand-acre wheat ranch in Montana that had been managed for the previous fifteen years by the president of the state's Farm Bureau (Rowley 1970, p. 120). Swope eagerly spread the domestic allotment idea among industrialists be-cause it fit with some of his ideas about organizing the corporate commu-nity, ideas that in part came to fruition in the National Industrial Recovery Act discussed in the next chapter. Wilson also had the help of Henry I. Har-riman, the Boston utility company executive active in both the Boston and national chambers of commerce, who had been briefed earlier on the plan by Ruml (David Hamilton 1991, p. 186). Wilson also received feedback from Black as the plan evolved.

Wilson in turn was very enthusiastic about the plans that Swope and Harriman were developing for industry. Harriman arranged for him to join a Chamber committee on agriculture, where he was able to convince other business leaders that the domestic allotment plan made sense in terms of their larger interests. Harriman also offered important suggestions on how to finance the program through a processing tax. This committee is a textbook example of what we mean by "policy-discussion groups" within the policy-planning network.

Wilson made an important modification in the plan in early 1932 so that farmers could vote on whether or not they wanted to participate, and allowed them to set up local committees to administer the plan if they approved of it. This addition was extremely important because it was more democratic and offered a way to induce individual farmers to take sensible collective action. According to historian David Hamilton (1991, pp. 190–193), the reformulated plan provided a new answer in the long search for a means of achieving cooperative action in agriculture that reconciled individual and collective action on the part of farmers while sustaining some degree of self-governance. However, Wilson's emphasis on self-governance does not mean that he was concerned with small or marginal farmers. Instead, he shared the mainstream agricultural economists' general view that small farmers would have to leave farming for some other line of work. Nor did the plight of the rural poor concern him (David Hamilton 1991, pp. 183–185).

At this point Wilson also enlisted the help of a young government agricultural economist, Mordecai Ezekiel, who had received his Ph.D. in economics from The Brookings Graduate School in 1926. After working in the Department of Agriculture for a few years in the type of applied work that Brookings hoped to encourage, Ezekiel made a careful study of European farm policy during a year abroad in 1931–1932 on a Guggenheim Fellowship. His new synthesis of the subsidy plan fused Ruml, Black, and Wilson's contributions with Harriman's tax idea to provide a direct payment to those farmers who agreed to accept acreage reduction. The work by Wilson and Ezekiel is evidence for the way in which experts provide new ideas, as historical institutionalists would emphasize, but we also think their efforts have to be viewed within the larger framework of the support provided to them by the SSRC and the U.S. Chamber of Commerce. The fact that Ezekiel was trained at The Brookings Institution also fits with our emphasis on the role of the policy-planning network.

Wilson and Harriman hoped that the plan would be attractive to both Republicans and Democrats, and it did receive sympathetic attention from several important Republicans in Washington. But President Herbert Hoover thought the program went too far in terms of government involvement in the economy. It thus mattered more that the plan attracted interest from key Democrats and their advisors. In the spring of 1932 Ruml, by then serving as dean of the social sciences at the University of Chicago, explained the plan to Rexford Tugwell, a liberal economics professor at Columbia University, who had the primary responsibility for formulating future president Roosevelt's agricultural policy as one of the three members of his Brain Trust (Kirkendall 1966, p. 44; Rosen 1977, Chapter 7). Tugwell's conversation with Ruml, reinforced by a similar conversation with Ezekiel, inspired him to go to Chicago for a crucial meeting with Wilson and other agricultural experts. As Schlesinger (1958, p. 403) tells the story:

> Tugwell, regarding his own thinking on the subject as stale, rather desperately decided to attend a meeting of farm economists held in Chicago shortly before the convention. From Beardsley Ruml in Washington he had heard hints of new developments in the domestic allotment plan; at Chicago he could talk with M. L. Wilson of Montana, who had become the plan's apostle. When he arrived in Chicago, he found not only Wilson, but Henry Wallace of Iowa. For several days they talked late into the night in the dormitory rooms at the University of Chicago where they were billeted. Tugwell was finally persuaded that he had found what he was seeking—a workable means of restricting agricultural production on which the farm leaders might agree.

Wilson and Tugwell then introduced the plan to Roosevelt, who was impressed by it. They were soon joined by Harriman, and the three of them spent several days with Roosevelt at Hyde Park discussing agricultural plans (Rosen 1977, pp. 317, 335–337). Wilson was assigned the task of writing the first draft of a speech on agriculture for Roosevelt to deliver at a key campaign stop in Topeka. Wallace, who had served on the SSRC's agricultural committee in the past, and became a supporter of the domestic allotment plan at a 1931 conference of farm experts, was asked to join Wilson in providing a memo that could serve as the basis for a speech. Roosevelt used this memo, as edited by Raymond Moley, a professor of public administration at Columbia University and the leader of the Brain Trust, as the basis for his speech. At the same time, Wilson drew closer to Roosevelt's campaign, describing himself as a "Roosevelt Republican" (David Hamilton 1991, pp. 21–212; Rowley 1970, Chapter 8). Wallace, who had been a longtime Progressive Republican, also decided that Roosevelt was the real thing and began campaigning for him throughout the Corn Belt. Shortly after Roosevelt's Topeka speech, an angry President Hoover called Harriman to the White House and spent two hours telling him that the plan was unconstitutional and a threat to liberty (Rosen 1977, p. 340).

SHAPING THE FINAL ACT

The domestic allotment plan was a genuinely new approach to the long-standing problem of achieving cooperative action in agriculture that also made sense to most corporate moderates. But the supporters of the parity price plan nonetheless opposed it because they did not like the idea of curtailing production. Peek, as the main proponent of the parity price plan, fought for his program by claiming that the domestic allotment program was the product of a group of wild-eyed academics. In other words, rather than attacking the corporate moderates and moderate Republican farm experts supporting the program, he wisely chose to criticize allegedly unworldly experts and professors, a form of scapegoating that preserved a façade of harmony between the real combatants and overshadowed the fact that the domestic allotment and parity price plans were actually two rival business-sponsored plans for dealing with agricultural surpluses, one more nationalistic in orientation, the other more sensitive to creating an international economy.

Due to their commitment to the parity price plan, leaders of the Farm Bureau and other farm groups did not support the domestic allotment scheme until late 1932. However, the Farm Bureau nonetheless had the opportunity to shape the final version because Roosevelt was not prepared to enact any program opposed by the major farm groups (Campbell 1962, pp. 51–53). Instead, he accepted an idea suggested to him by Wallace and Tugwell to create an omnibus bill that included both plans as well as one or two other possible policy tools, which meant that the farm groups would be able to modify any provisions of the domestic allotment plan that did not suit them. Not surprisingly, then, one of the two drafters of the final legislation was a lawyer hired by the Farm Bureau (Saloutos 1982, p. 45).

Moreover, as part of its price for accepting the general outlines of the plan, the Farm Bureau and other farm leaders insisted that "the benefit payments should be determined by the fair exchange ratio" that had been part of the first versions of the parity price bills (David Hamilton 1991, p. 221). Tugwell, Wilson, and Ezekiel resisted this change because they feared the use of the parity formula would undercut production controls and any move toward responsible planning in agriculture, but to no avail. As subsequent events showed, the act was shaped in practice to reflect the interest group approach of the farm leaders, not the planning approach of the agricultural economists (David Hamilton 1991). Thus the Farm Bureau and its allies not only had veto power over this legislation, but shaping power as well.

However, it is important to emphasize that not all commercial farmers had opposed acreage controls in the past. In fact, the commercial farmers who mattered the most in terms of the Democratic Party, the Southern plantation owners, had understood the usefulness of acreage restrictions since early in the century (Saloutos 1960, pp. 160, 277–278). But they had not pushed the idea because they did not suffer as much from overproduction and low prices in the 1920s as did farmers in other parts of the country. Even when cotton prices collapsed at the outset of the Depression, cotton growers held back from production control schemes in part because they differentially benefited from loans made by the federal government's Federal Farm Board (Saloutos 1960, p. 274).

Strong evidence that plantation capitalists understood the usefulness of limiting surpluses comes from the enactment of state laws in South Carolina, Louisiana, Mississippi, and Texas between 1930 and 1932 that allowed for acreage controls if other farm states passed similar laws. It therefore came as no surprise to Southern Democrats in Congress when plantation owners and their allies made it clear to Roosevelt in late 1932 that some form of production control was essential at the federal level (Saloutos 1960, p. 281). When it is added that cotton accounted for fully one-third of all agricultural production in the United States at that point, it seems certain to us that Northern corporate moderates and Southern planters were the key power actors in creating the context in which Roosevelt was receptive to a last-minute push for introducing the Agricultural Adjustment Act into the special session of Congress. With payments to take acreage out of production (in other words, subsidies) as part of the plan in order to induce cooperation more readily, and with considerable control of the program at the local level through elected committees, it seems unlikely to us that very many farmers anywhere in the country would have been opposed to the program now that the Depression was hurting them so badly.

Nevertheless, there were many conflicts and a month-long delay in the Senate after the bill passed the House by a wide margin a week after it was introduced, including support from 96 percent of the Southern Democrats. These delays reflected a number of problems, starting with an attempt by agricultural processors to get out from under the processing tax that Harriman had suggested in order to raise money to pay the subsidies to cooperating farmers (they failed in this effort). The bill was also delayed by an amendment that expressed the demands made by more radical farmers for a guaranteed price that met their costs for producing their crops (see, for example, David Hamilton 1991, pp. 229–235). As the argument dragged on, farmers in some states began to take militant direct action in late March and April. One such farm group in the Midwest, the Farmers' Holiday Association—formed in May 1932 in Iowa by activist members of the liberal Farmers' Union to convince farmers to withhold crops from the market—called for a farm strike on May 3 if legislation including its amendments did not pass (Schlesinger 1958, pp. 42–44; Shover 1965, Chapter 6). Nonetheless, agreement to leave out the amendment ensuring cost of production was reached shortly thereafter in Congress. Thus any emphasis on the role of militant action by farmers in relation to the domestic allotment program can be easily overdone because this legislation, eagerly sought by plantation owners and commercial farmers, was as certain to be approved as any law could be.

On the other hand, it was the series of disruptive protests by the Farmers' Holiday Association, and a near lynching of a judge in Iowa in late April (because he refused to suspend foreclosure proceedings "until the state courts passed on recently enacted state legislation"), that helped add two additional titles to the bill before it passed (Schlesinger 1958, pp. 42–43). The Emergency Farm Mortgage Act authorized the newly created Farm Credit Administration to refinance farm mortgages at low interest rates. This legislation was on Roosevelt's agenda when the latest round of protests and disruption began, but they very likely speeded up the process. The second additional title gave the president the authority to use one or more of six mechanisms (such as printing more paper money and reducing the gold content of the dollar) that would put more money in circulation, ease credit, and create a mild inflation useful to farmers suffering heavy debt payments (Freidel 1973, pp. 336–337). The Farm Credit Administration loaned over $100 million in the next seven months, four times more than federal programs had loaned to farmers in the previous year. It drove down interest rates as well, leading Roosevelt's vice president, John Garner, a small-town Texas banker, to grumble to the secretary of the treasury that in the past he had "averaged 16 percent on our money, and now we can't get better than 5" (Schlesinger 1958, p. 45).

As straightforward as the domestic allotment plan might seem in terms of implementation, the corporate and farm leaders did not leave the details of carrying it out to independent experts or long-time government employees, as historical institutionalists might expect. Instead, they defied historical institutionalism and the idea of government independence by insisting that people from corporate and agricultural networks should manage the programs. They did so in part because they still had disagreements among themselves as to which policy options within the omnibus legislation should be emphasized, but also because they feared and distrusted the liberals within the New Deal coalition, such as Tugwell, by then an assistant secretary of agriculture, whom they pejoratively called "the New Dealers." Saloutos (1982, Chapter 5) provides the evidence for this point by listing the many business leaders and farmer-connected people who managed the Agricultural Adjustment Administration (AAA) from top to bottom.

The first leader of the AAA was Peek, the Baruch employee and former plow company executive, who was offered the job by Roosevelt in the hope that he would come to accept the program and to ensure that Baruch and his loyalists would not become vocal critics. Peek then hired the Farm Bureau lawyer who had helped to draft the bill as his personal lawyer because he did not trust the liberal "city" lawyers who were appointed to the legal staff of the AAA at the urging of Tugwell (Conrad 1965, p. 39; Kirkendall 1966, p. 66).

When Peek could not be convinced to give greater emphasis to the domestic allotment provisions of the legislation, his friend Davis, the participant in Ruml's Fairway Farms project who also had helped Black with the original allotment plan, replaced him within a few months. Just below the top, the chief of finance was the former manager of a cotton plantation in Mississippi. The chief of processing and marketing was an executive from Sears, Roebuck. The chief of the cotton section was a Southern journalist close to plantation owners, and M. L. Wilson was chief of the wheat section. An executive from Cudahy Packing Company was in charge of the processing businesses that were under the jurisdiction of the corn-hog section. In all, six of nine leaders came from business circles. These appointments are typical of the kinds of high-level appointments that have been made to key government positions throughout American history, including during the New Deal (Burch 1980; Mintz 1975).

However, there were a few liberals and government employees in positions of power. For example, the chief of the corn-hog section was a liberal professor of agricultural economics at Iowa State College, and the leader of the tobacco section was a government employee (Saloutos 1982, pp. 57–58). Most relevant in understanding why the corporate and agricultural chieftains wanted people they knew and trusted in positions of power, the liberal lawyers in the legal department of the AAA later caused unexpected trouble for the plantation capitalists.

SUMMARY

The origins of the Agricultural Adjustment Act demonstrate several points that support our class-dominance theory over any of its rivals. First, we see in great detail that Northern corporate moderates were responsible for developing the main ideas in the legislation through their employees in the policy-planning network and then in lobbying for those ideas. The path from Ruml, as president of the Memorial Fund, to the Agricultural Committee of the Social Science Research Council to the Chamber of Commerce to the Democratic presidential candidate is quite clear, with major assists along the way from Black, Wilson, Swope, Harriman, and Tugwell. (But recall that Ruml also communicated directly with Wilson, Harriman, and Tugwell concerning the plan as well as with Black.) Second, we see that the government experts, Stillman and Ezekiel, were only brought into the process when it was well along, although it is also clear that they had similar ideas or added new wrinkles.

Third, it is certain that the plantation capitalists were major supporters of this legislation because they desperately needed it by 1932. Fourth, we see that the leading farm groups, led by the Farm Bureau, were able to shape the plan so that it was even more to their advantage and acceptable to the Southern Democrats who represented the plantation capitalists and controlled the key committees in Congress. Fifth, it is obvious that the corporate and agricultural leaders were not prepared to leave anything to chance or to the institutional imperatives emphasized by institutional theorists, or even to the structural economic dominance and ideological hegemony enjoyed by capitalists according to Marxist theorists. Instead, they wanted to manage the program themselves. Sixth, and finally, we see that social disruption by dissident middle-income farmers was not a factor in creating this program, but rather a last-minute push that speeded up the addition of other provisions to the legislative package.

It is now time to see if other pieces of New Deal legislation fit a similar pattern.

CHAPTER THREE

The National Labor Relations Act

With the passage of the Agricultural Adjustment Act, Roosevelt was inclined to end the special session of Congress because he thought that the Emergency Banking Act, the Agricultural Adjustment Act, and the Federal Emergency Relief Act dealt with the most pressing problems facing the nation even though industrial production had dropped by half between 1929 and 1932 and the stock market had lost 90 percent of its value. He had been alerted through memos from members of his Brain Trust (especially from lawyer A. A. Berle Jr., who specialized in antitrust and corporate law at Columbia University) that corporate leaders had been working on plans for industrial reorganization that would free them from the constraints of the antitrust laws, thereby making more cooperation possible. He also had received memos and personal White House visits from representatives of the National Association of Manufacturers (NAM) and the U.S. Chamber of Commerce urging such plans upon him. However, Roosevelt was not convinced that any of these plans had jelled sufficiently or were politically feasible (Himmelberg [1976] 1993, Chapter 10).

But the political equation began to change on April 6, 1933, when the Senate unexpectedly approved a liberal bill concerning wages and hours that would cut the workweek to thirty hours for the same daily wage, a significant pay raise despite a likely decrease in productive output. Sponsored by one of the few Southern liberals in the Senate, Hugo Black, later to be appointed to the Supreme Court by Roosevelt, the bill was based on the argument, heartily supported by organized labor, that the measure would spread work and increase purchasing power at the same time. Neither Roosevelt nor any business group liked the idea, for a variety of reasons. Leaders of the National Association of Manufacturers, along with Henry Harriman, Gerard Swope, and Walter Teagle, testified against it. Frances Perkins found the legislation unacceptable because it did not include a minimum wage provision.

Faced with so much disagreement, but deciding that the time might be right, Roosevelt then insisted on an industrial reorganization plan that was acceptable to both organized business and organized labor. The search for an alternative began on April 11 when Roosevelt told Raymond Moley, who became the key contact between Roosevelt and the corporate community on this issue, to ask Senator Wagner to bring together a drafting group. The resulting legislation, the National Industrial Recovery Act, which passed in June 1933, was supposed to do for trade and industry what the Agricultural Adjustment Administration would do for farmers. On the basis of a two-year suspension of the antitrust laws, the new National Recovery Administration authorized by the act would bring together business owners in each sector of the economy, usually through their trade associations, to create codes of fair competition that would set minimum prices, minimum wages, maximum hours, and levels of productive output. The business owners were supposed to be joined in this effort by representatives of workers and consumers, although in practice labor was only represented by even one person in fewer than 10 percent of the cases, usually in various garment trades (McQuaid 1979; Hawley 1966, pp. 56–57). In theory these separate and self-policed code authorities would eliminate cutthroat competition, reemploy workers, and increase purchasing power, thereby restarting the economy.

The National Recovery Administration (NRA) began with parades and speeches that generated high hopes for a new era of cooperation among business, labor, and government, but the program was ineffective and generally ignored after its first year (see, for example, Colin Gordon 1994, Chapter 5). Many people—including most business leaders, labor leaders, liberals, and consumer advocates—rejoiced for their own separate reasons when the National Industrial Recovery Act was declared unconstitutional by the Supreme Court in May 1935, just twenty-three months after it was launched. However, it did acclimate business and organized labor to the idea of minimum wages, maximum hours, and the abolition of child labor, all of which were included in the Fair Labor Standards Act of 1938. Moreover, the industries that most eagerly sought government regulation to deal with their problems were able to obtain it very quickly after the act was declared unconstitutional. For example, the Bituminous Coal Conservation Act of 1935 and the Bituminous Coal Act of 1937 authorized the National Bituminous Coal Commission to set minimum coal prices and provide a safeguard for labor standards. The Connally Hot Oil Act of 1935 saved the oil industry from itself by prohibiting the shipment of oil in excess of quotas set by individual states (where the industry dominated quota setting). The Miller-Tydings Fair Trade Act of 1937 gave small retailers protection from chain stores by allowing them to set minimum resale prices of retail goods.

In addition to failing on what organized business saw as the National Industrial Recovery Act's most important objectives, it had the unexpected consequence of inspiring several unions, and especially the coal mining and garment workers' unions, to mount massive organizing drives that led to hundreds of strikes. As sociologist Rhonda F. Levine explains (1988, p. 82): "Ironically, contrary to its design, the National Industrial Recovery Act and the NRA's implementation of the act actually worked to disorganize the capitalist class and to organize the working class." This turmoil in turn led to the creation of the hastily formed National Labor Board, proposed by corporate leaders, and then two years later to the passage of a bill supporting the right of workers to form unions and bargain collectively. The National Labor Relations Act of 1935, which was adamantly opposed by virtually all corporate leaders, whether moderates or ultraconservatives, is a classic example of how a new law, in this case the National Industrial Recovery Act, can lead to unintended consequences, that is, outcomes that no group anticipated or desired, but it is also a demonstration of the importance of government in shaping—and even supporting—class conflict.

Most generally, then, as the rest of the chapter shows, the failures of the National Industrial Recovery Act show that any attempts to create cooperation between employers and workers on the basis of common interests in such matters as eliminating wage cuts as a form of destructive competition are very difficult to sustain because there are plenty of people on both sides of the class divide who want to take advantage of the opportunity to make gains on other issues, which often concern power and control. In our view the few industries where such bargains have been achieved are exceptions based on highly unusual circumstances, such as the small size of the business enterprises, making them easier for unions to defeat, or the common ethnicity and culture that are shared by both capitalists and workers in some business sectors, such as the garment industry in New York.

ORIGINS OF THE NATIONAL INDUSTRIAL RECOVERY ACT

Although the National Industrial Recovery Act was a hasty response to Black's thirty-hour bill, corporate leaders had been discussing its basic ideas for over a decade. According to every historian who has studied the matter, the fingerprints of various corporate leaders and policy experts can be found on every part of it (see, for example, Hawley 1966; Himmelberg [1976] 1993; Schlesinger 1958; Vittoz 1987). The basic ideas were developed in the aftermath of the seeming success of the business-government partnership during the limited industrial mobilization for World War I under the auspices of Baruch and the War Industries Board. The concept was widely discussed by businessmen through their trade associations over the next twelve years. Roosevelt, as president of the American Construction Council from 1922 to 1928, was one of those "encouraging industrial self-government as an alternative to government regulation," so the idea was not foreign to the new president (Schlesinger 1957, pp. 374–375).

Not only was Roosevelt familiar with the basic plan and the corporate support for it, he knew he was trying to bring about recovery within the constraints that were likely to be set by the Supreme Court if the executive branch tried to regulate the economy. Roosevelt and his advisors feared that the court, as it had ten years earlier, would find legislation regulating wages to be unconstitutional on the grounds that it was an infringement on the right of individuals to freely negotiate contracts. The only way to obtain the minimum wage and maximum hour laws he and Secretary of Labor Frances Perkins wanted was through agreements hammered out by businessmen and labor leaders in each industry. Unfortunately, the White House had to find ways to induce those agreements by giving business something it wanted even more, the ability to set minimum prices and restrict output without fear of antitrust prosecution (Schlesinger 1958, p. 101).

Two versions of a general plan of cooperation that the corporate community and the Supreme Court were likely to accept had gained a fair amount of visibility by 1931. The same two corporate leaders who championed the domestic allotment plan, Swope and Harriman, were the prime movers behind them. Swope's plan called for industrial self-government with a minimum of government oversight, but with provisions for company-sponsored unemployment, health, and old-age insurance for workers. Labor would have a say in administering company-level benefit plans, but there was no provision for collective bargaining (see, for example, Bernstein 1969, pp. 20–21). Harriman's plan, which was developed by the Committee on Continuity of Business and Employment in the U.S. Chamber of Commerce, differed only in that labor had even less participation and government even less of a role. Hoover opposed both plans completely, likening them to fascism, which widened the schism between Hoover and the corporate moderates (Nelson 1969, p. 144).

When Wagner began drafting legislation at Roosevelt's behest, he based it on a plan developed by the president of The Brookings Institution, Harold Moulton, with the help of a Brookings economist, Meyer Jacobstein, who had a Ph.D. from Columbia University and earlier had served in Congress from a district encompassing Rochester, New York. Once again demonstrating Wagner's close ties to the corporate policy-planning network, he recruited the following people in addition to Moulton and Jacobstein to help him fashion the National Industrial Recovery Act:

- Virgil D. Jordan, president, National Industrial Conference Board
- James H. Rand Jr., president, Remington Rand, and a leader in the National Association of Manufacturers
- Malcolm C. Rorty, an electrical engineer and statistician for AT&T who helped found the National Bureau for Economic Research
- Fred I. Kent, a highly admired retired banker from Bankers Trust Company in New York City
- David L. Podell, a lawyer who specialized in work for trade associations
- Senator Robert La Follette Jr., a Progressive Republican from Wisconsin
- Congressman Clyde Kelly of Pennsylvania, a friend of the coal industry and the co-sponsor of an unsuccessful coal stabilization bill that included regulatory ideas

In addition, there was one labor-oriented member of the Wagner group, W. Jett Lauck, an economist who was an advisor to both John L. Lewis of the United Mine Workers and Congressman Kelly. Significantly, Lauck had served as the secretary for the National War Labor Board during World War I, so he was familiar with the tradition of accepting government involvement in collective bargaining in times of social upheaval.

The most interesting question in terms of the concerns of this book is how the substance of the act came to include the idea that labor should have the right to bargain collectively through representatives of its own choosing even though labor had only minor direct representation in the Wagner group. The clause that eventually gave support to this right began as a one-sentence declaration that came to be known simply as "section 7(a)": "that employees shall have the right to organize and bargain collectively through representatives of their own choosing." However, it embodied principles that were first articulated by the National Civic Federation at the start of the twentieth century and that organized labor had insisted upon in exchange for its participation in the National War Labor Board sixteen years earlier (Conner 1983, Chapter 11).

There are slightly conflicting claims on the origins of section 7(a). The specific language seems to have been suggested by Lauck, drawing on his experience with the National War Labor Board and the coal industry, and then agreed to by Moulton of Brookings when he and Lauck were delegated by the Wagner group to write a draft (Vittoz 1987, p. 87). There is also some evidence that at least a handful of business executives and economists from the policy-planning network supported the idea because they believed unions could play a positive role in stabilizing such highly competitive and wage-cutting industries as coal mining and garment making (for example,

Colin Gordon 1994, Chapter 3; Vittoz 1987, Chapters 2 and 3). However, as subsequent resistance to union involvement in the code authorities demonstrates, most of the corporate leaders who at first seemed willing to accept some degree of union involvement as part of a cross-class alliance became highly opposed to unions. It is also clear that the most important labor leaders of the 1930s, Sidney Hillman of the Amalgamated Clothing Workers, John L. Lewis of the United Mine Workers, and William Green, president of the American Federation of Labor, spoke directly with several of the people involved in drafting the bill.

Ultimately, the act included section 7(a) because labor leaders and liberals demanded it (see, for example, Bernstein 1950, Chapters 2 and 3; Schlesinger 1958, p. 99). The two most important liberals, Wagner and Perkins, were unequivocal in their insistence that it be included. Wagner, as the most respected and visible spokesman for urban liberals in Congress, told Roosevelt that there would be no law without the clause. Perkins, who had supported unions since her days as a socialist, even though she found them narrow and shortsighted, made an appointment for her and Green to see Roosevelt, who decided the conflict by agreeing that the clause would remain in the legislation (Cohen 2009, p. 240). The liberal-labor coalition had the power to put their clause in the bill for two reasons; first, the disruptive potential of organized labor through strikes, boycotts, and property destruction, and second, the inclusion of liberals as one part of the New Deal coalition.

The Wagner draft went to Assistant Secretary of Commerce John Dickinson, a corporate lawyer from Philadelphia for the sugar manufacturers' trade association and a professor of law at Columbia University. Dickinson was working on a similar plan with a group of industrialists, mostly from the National Association of Manufacturers and the U.S. Chamber of Commerce, which is an early example of Roosevelt's famous penchant for asking several different groups to work on the same problem. The Wagner and Dickinson groups quickly reached agreement on a common draft satisfactory to the businessmen involved. In fact, these business leaders were highly enthusiastic about the outcome (Himmelberg [1976] 1993, pp. 204–205). However, they became apprehensive when they learned that still another group of Roosevelt advisors was working on its own proposal; they feared it might give too much regulatory power to government and strengthen the pro-union clauses (Himmelberg [1976] 1993, pp. 204–205; Vittoz 1987, p. 91).

General Hugh Johnson, the former military officer who had worked with Baruch and Peek on the unsuccessful parity price recovery plan for agriculture, was in charge of crafting this worrisome draft. He had become a speechwriter for Roosevelt when Baruch offered Johnson's services to him as a peacemaking gesture after he won the presidential nomination in 1932 despite attempts by Baruch and other conservative Democrats to thwart him. Baruch also had become Roosevelt's largest campaign contributor ($711,000 in 2010 dollars), suggesting to some historians that Johnson served as a Baruch outpost in the Roosevelt camp, a quid pro quo for the campaign donation (Ohl 1985, pp. 83–85; Rosen 1977, pp. 311–312). It is also likely that Roosevelt wanted to neutralize Baruch because he believed Baruch had great influence through his personal loans and campaign contributions to many Democratic members of Congress, especially Roosevelt's three main Southern senatorial allies: Byrnes of South Carolina, Robinson of Arkansas, the majority leader, and Harrison of Mississippi, chair of the Finance Committee (Robertson 1994, pp. 101–103, 127–131). Whatever the reasons for Johnson's presence, he won over Roosevelt's wary academic advisors, including the Brain Trusters, with his hard work, good humor, and ability to turn a phrase (Ohl 1985, p. 85).

At this point Roosevelt decided that members of the various drafting groups should join together to find a compromise. Johnson, Wagner, Perkins, Dickinson, and Donald Richberg (a lawyer for the railroad unions who had been in the Johnson drafting group) constituted the final working group, along with one person new to the process, Lewis Douglas, Roosevelt's extremely conservative director of the budget and the scion of a copper mining fortune in Arizona. The corporate leaders who had worked with Dickinson then went to Roosevelt and insisted that they, too, wanted to comment on the draft before it went to Congress. Historian Robert Himmelberg ([1976] 1993, p. 206) reports that the business advisory committee emerging from this request was generally satisfied with the final draft.

Although the final draft of the National Industrial Recovery Act was very similar to the Wagner group's proposal, the Johnson version did prevail in three ways that caused major difficulties. First, the congressional guidelines and loan guarantees for industries called for in the Wagner-Dickinson version were replaced by Johnson's broad delegation of powers to the president, a decision that would be one basis for the Supreme Court finding the act unconstitutional two years later. Second, the Johnson version included every industry engaged in interstate commerce, right down to dog food, ice cream cones, and wigs. This decision led Moulton and other mainstream economists to oppose the legislation because they thought the extension of the act beyond a handful of major industries would make it unmanageable and would lead to too much government control over the economy (Critchlow 1985, pp. 120–121). (Moulton proved to be correct; within a year Roosevelt directed the NRA not to try to organize codes for small industries.) Third, the president could limit business licenses to one year at a time in industries where there were widespread code violations; the granting of this power, which Roosevelt later used to threaten the steel and coal industries into compromises, was seized upon by ultraconservatives to invoke the specter of a dictatorial state.

There also was concern on the part of Southern Democrats about the possible inclusion of agriculture as an "industry" because they did not want to provide any encouragement toward unionization on the part of what was at the time a completely subjugated workforce. In response, Wagner insisted that agriculture was excluded from the purview of the legislation, although there is no record of this fact in the written act (Farhang and Katznelson 2005, p. 12). There was also implicit agreement that any issues having to do with agriculture and its labor force came under the jurisdiction of the Agricultural Adjustment Administration (AAA), which was known to be safely in the hands of conservative Democrats. Thus this potentially divisive issue did not cause any further problems during the legislative process.

In terms of the central issues in this book, the most important successful amendments concerned the AFL's insistence before the House Ways and Means Committee that language from the pro-labor Norris-LaGuardia Act of 1932 be added to the simple declaration of the right to collective bargaining in section 7(a). The additional clause stated that employees "shall be free from the interference, restraint, or coercion of employers of labor or their agents. . . ." (Bernstein 1969, p. 31). Moreover, in a second clause stating that "no employee and no one seeking employment shall be required as a condition of employment to join any organization or to refrain from joining a labor organization of his own choosing," Green demanded that the word "organization" be replaced by "company union," which raised the corporate moderates' hackles immediately (Bernstein 1969, p. 31). These changes were included in the bill passed by the House despite the NAM's desire to eliminate section 7(a) entirely. However, at this moment the NAM did not have the support of its more moderate ally, the Chamber of Commerce, which remained neutral because it had made a private agreement with the AFL that it would accept the collective bargaining provision in exchange for labor's support for the price-setting provisions (Bernstein 1950, p. 35). Here we see again one of the small but important differences between the moderate conservatives and the ultraconservatives in the corporate community.

The ultraconservatives represented by the NAM carried their fight against section 7(a), and especially the amendments to it, to the floor of the Senate. This time they had the support of the Chamber of Commerce, which felt that the AFL amendments went too far. But their united effort to soften section 7(a) was soundly defeated, 46 to 31, by the overwhelming Democratic majority. This vote clearly showed the potential power of the liberal-labor coalition within Congress when the Southern Democrats, who were willing to accept the legislation because they had been assured that section 7(a) did not include agricultural workers, did not oppose it.

Once the legislation passed, the moderate conservatives and ultraconservatives reacted very differently to the success of the liberal-labor coalition
in carving out a small space for union initiatives within the framework of
the NRA. The corporate moderates believed they could live with collective
bargaining if they had to, an attitude reinforced by the way in which the
Railway Labor Act of 1926 had led to a moderate railroad unionism focused
on a few skilled jobs. They also had confidence that employee representation plans, as honed by the efforts of Industrial Relations Counselors, Inc.
(IRC), could keep out independent unions. Most of all, corporate moderates
believed they had won the day against unionism. Thus Himmelberg ([1976]
1993, p. 107) concludes that "few" corporate reformers felt modification
of the new language in section 7(a) was an "absolute condition" for their
support of the whole bill.

On the other hand, the National Association of Manufacturers and
other ultraconservatives opposed section 7(a) to the bitter end. Moreover,
NAM's general counsel believed Wagner had betrayed business on the issue
when he agreed to the AFL amendments in the course of his own testimony
before the House committee. Thus began an increasingly acrimonious relationship between NAM and Wagner. But for the time being, the ultraconservatives, recognizing that there were no penalties for violating section 7(a),
decided to stonewall the pro-union provisions by claiming that the law did
not outlaw company unions or designate trade unions as the sole bargaining
agents within a plant. Everything now depended on who administered the
NRA and how the vague guidelines were interpreted.

THE NRA AND CORPORATE INVOLVEMENT

On the basis of the direct and overwhelming corporate involvement in the
creation of the National Industrial Recovery Act, and the fact that the inclusion of section 7(a) had some semblance of a business rationale and no enforcement mechanism, most social scientists and historians seem to accept
Himmelberg's ([1976] 1993, Chapter 10) conclusion to his highly detailed
analysis of the origins of this legislation: it marked "the triumph of business
revisionists," the group of business leaders we call corporate moderates.
The only slight dissent comes from political scientist Donald Brand (1988),
who believes that pro-government ideas from the Progressive Era also were
behind the act. He therefore makes much of the fact that "in the later stages
of the legislative drafting, interest groups even found their official representatives excluded from decision making" (Brand 1988, p. 86). Since the
final drafting group included Johnson, Dickinson, and Douglas, who were
part of the corporate community, Brand has a very narrow definition of
the business world if he restricts its leadership to heads of interest groups.

Moreover, the fact still remains, as Himmelberg ([1976] 1993, pp. 206–207) emphasizes, that major business leaders from the National Association of Manufacturers and Chamber of Commerce asked for and received access to the final draft.

Any qualms about the administration of the act seemed to disappear when Johnson was appointed as the NRA director—against the advice of Baruch, who thought he was too unstable and undisciplined for such a position. To the great satisfaction of ultraconservatives, Johnson immediately made an interpretation of the collective bargaining section that discouraged unionization. He also accepted many other suggestions made to him by businessmen, including various mechanisms for setting industry-wide prices. Further, he ended any lingering concerns on the part of Southern Democrats by ruling that the AAA would deal with any issues concerning agricultural labor, a ruling that was backed up with a series of executive orders by Roosevelt (Farhang and Katznelson 2005, p. 12). Although Johnson staffed the Consumer Advisory Board mandated by the legislation with economists, sociologists, and representatives of the National Consumers' League, many of them liberals, he generally ignored their advice. Nor did he pay any attention to suggestions from the social scientists in the Research and Planning Division, underscoring once again how little expertise mattered if it did not fit with a corporate outlook.

To provide him and the many business leaders in the NRA with advice, Johnson set up an industrial advisory board. He drew its members from a unique governmental advisory agency formed in the early spring of 1933 by Roosevelt's Southern-born secretary of commerce, Daniel Roper, a former lobbyist for corporations with extensive contacts throughout the corporate world. The new advisory committee, originally called the Business Advisory and Planning Council of the Department of Commerce, soon shortened its name to the Business Advisory Council (hereafter usually BAC).

Although the BAC was a government advisory group, the corporate community itself selected its members. Through consultation with the leading policy groups and trade associations, the corporate leaders who set it up made a deliberate attempt to enlist "statesmen of business" (McQuaid 1976, 1982). At the outset it had forty-one members, representing a cross-section of business and financial executives. Several members of the Special Conference Committee were in this group, as well as officers of other large banks, retail firms, policy groups, and trade associations. According to our research in biographical reference sources, eighteen of the sixty largest banks, railroads, utilities, and manufacturing corporations of the day were linked to the BAC through the multiple corporate directorships held by some BAC members. There were also numerous regional and local businessmen from across the country.

Swope was named chairman of the council, and Teagle was selected as chairman of the council's Industrial Relations Committee, which demonstrates their central role in the corporate community once again. One of Teagle's first decisions was to appoint all the members of the Special Conference Committee to the Industrial Relations Committee, thereby making that private group into a governmental body. Rockefeller's personal employee, Edward Cowdrick, the aforementioned secretary of the Special Conference Committee, was made secretary of the new BAC committee. Reflecting the seamless overlap of the corporate community and government in the early New Deal, Cowdrick wrote as follows to an AT&T executive. The memo deserves to be quoted because it reveals one of the ways the corporate leaders explained their involvement in government advisory groups, as well as a decision to avoid any mention of the Special Conference Committee even though the government advisory meetings were part of Special Conference Committee meetings. The members are told they would be there as individuals, not as representatives of their companies or as members of the Special Conference Committee:

> Each member is invited as an individual, not as a representative of his company, and the name of the Special Conference Committee will not be used. The work of the new committee will supplement and broaden—not supplant—that of the Special Conference Committee. Probably special meetings will not be needed since the necessary guidelines for the Industrial Relations Committee's work can be given at our regular sessions (U.S. Senate 1939, p. 16800).

Not surprisingly, perhaps, the first task of the new Industrial Relations Committee was to prepare a report on employee representation and collective bargaining, which favored employee representation plans and criticized unions (Scheinberg 1986, p. 163). However, it did not really take a report from the new BAC to prod the corporate community into defensive action by quickly installing employee representation plans (Jacoby 1997, pp. 157–159). As if to signal that it meant to continue the central role it had always taken in resisting unions, U.S. Steel hired the longtime director of Industrial Relations Counselors, Inc., Arthur H. Young, as its vice president in charge of industrial relations. Young, who had worked for both International Harvester and Colorado Fuel and Iron before joining IRC, received a personal letter of congratulations from John D. Rockefeller that thanked him for his years of service and told him that "I shall follow with interest your course in this new position" (Rockefeller 1934). Young soon announced a new employee representation plan and assured everyone that the plan would generate "sound and harmonious relationships between men and management," which he likened to the "sound and harmonious relationship between a man and his wife" (Bernstein 1969, p. 455). Within a year, at least ninety-three steel companies had employee representation plans that covered over 90 percent of the workers in the industry.

At the BAC's first general meeting in Washington on June 26, 1933, ten days after the NRA itself was created, Johnson asked Teagle to chair the NRA's Industrial Advisory Board, which drew the majority of its members from the BAC as well (McQuaid 1979, p. 685–686). Teagle brought Clarence J. Hicks, his recently retired industrial relations vice president at Standard Oil of New Jersey, to join him in Washington as his personal assistant. (At this point Hicks was paid about $97,500 a year as a personal consultant to Rockefeller, in addition to his $162,500 a year pension from Standard Oil of New Jersey—both those figures are in terms of 2010 dollars). Teagle, along with Swope, Harriman, and other business executives, then spent the summer of 1933 overseeing the development of the NRA. In short, the overlap between the corporate community and the NRA was very extensive, especially when it is added that other top businesspeople came to Washington to serve the NRA as "presidential industrial advisers" on temporary loan from their corporations. Once again, that is, the capitalist class was subsidizing, staffing, and building a new state agency.

THE NATIONAL LABOR BOARD

But the many efforts to prevent worker unrest and labor organizing did not work out as expected. The inclusion of section 7(a) in the enabling legislation for the National Recovery Administration turned out not to be benign after all. Instead, it inspired a huge organizing drive. "Those provisions," conclude protest-disruption theorists Frances Fox Piven and Richard Cloward (1977, p. 110), "were to have an unprecedented impact on the unorganized working people of the country, not so much for what they gave, as for what they promised." The idea of collective bargaining seemed to have arrived due to its legitimation and support by the state. Organizers for the United Mine Workers told workers "the president wants you to join a union," leaving it somewhat unclear as to whether they were referring to the president of the United States or the president of the union that employed them.

Labor's organizing efforts met with success in some industries, especially those in which the companies were small or the workers were organized into one industry-wide union that included many different types of craft workers as well as unskilled workers. This success was greatest for the United Mine Workers, who were able to thwart attempts by mine operators to bring in replacement labor. Similarly, the Amalgamated Clothing Workers grew rapidly by organizing the men who worked for the many small clothing companies in New York and other Eastern cities; the International Ladies Garment Workers did the same for women. (For an excellent analysis of the relatively unique situation in the coal and clothing industries, see Swenson (2002, pp. 146–160).)

In fact, the unexpected labor upheaval six weeks after passage of the NRA was so great that major business figures felt it necessary to contemplate a compromise with organized labor, which was represented in the NRA by the six-member Labor Advisory Board that included Lewis, Hillman, and Green as the key figures. The BAC members on the Industrial Advisory Board hosted a private meeting with the Labor Advisory Board on August 3, 1933, in the first attempt to deal with the increasing militancy. BAC minutes reveal that Teagle opened the meeting by suggesting a "truce" (this war-derived metaphor suggests that Teagle believed that there was a class struggle going on) until the NRA could establish the numerous codes that would set prices, hours, and wages in a wide variety of industries. He emphasized that he had no complaint with labor's efforts. "It was only natural," he said, "for labor to try to use this opportunity to organize and for employers to resist" (McQuaid 1979, p. 688). But some degree of harmony was needed, he continued, so that the recovery process could begin. Teagle therefore proposed that the two boards create an agency to arbitrate the problems that were being caused by differing interpretations of section 7(a).

The labor leaders were skeptical about Teagle's proposed truce because he also was asking that organizing drives and strikes be halted. Hillman countered that he might agree to forego strikes if the right to continue organizing was stated clearly by the Industrial Advisory Board, but Teagle did not like this suggestion. Swope, searching for compromise, then suggested that a small subcommittee of four people, including himself, meet for a short time to see if it could work out a common declaration on labor policy.

The subcommittee came back to the full meeting a few minutes later with a proposal for "a bipartisan arbitration board composed equally of IAB and LAB members and headed by an impartial 'public' chairman" (McQuaid 1979, p. 680). The similarity of the proposed board to the earlier War Labor Board was not lost on any of the participants; several of them had been involved in management-labor cooperation during World War I. The problem of union organizing was left unmentioned, but to reassure the labor leaders, Swope suggested Senator Wagner as the public member and chairman. While there was general acceptance of Wagner, Hillman remained doubtful about the overall plan. He repeated his opinion that the "right to organize on the part of labor" should be announced as an overall board policy, whereupon Green, who was far more cautious than Hillman or Lewis, responded that Hillman's view was as "extreme" as Teagle's proposal to halt all organizing drives for the duration. Green, like Swope, wanted to maintain a "cooperative spirit" by leaving the issue of organizing rights for the future (McQuaid 1979, pp. 689–690).

After further discussion, the two groups reached general agreement on the subcommittee proposal, and they formally approved it the following day. President Roosevelt accepted the agreement immediately and the next day announced the formation of the National Labor Board to arbitrate strikes and seek voluntary consent to section 7(a). Corporate moderates had forged a compromise with labor leaders in the way that their general approach to most problems and the earlier efforts of the National Civic Federation on labor issues would lead us to expect. In the process they developed a new government structure (another example of state building) and thereby gave renewed legitimacy to collective bargaining and government mediation of labor disputes.

For the most part, the board consisted of men who had been present for the meeting during which it was proposed. The labor representatives on the new board were Lewis, Green, and Leo Wolman, an advisor to Hillman and a professor of economics at Columbia University. The three business members were Teagle, Swope, and Louis Kirstein, a vice-president of William Filene & Sons, the Boston department store. Like Teagle and Swope, Kirstein was a member of the NRA's Industrial Advisory Board and had been present at the August 3 meeting with the labor leaders. The Filene family for whom he worked, one of whose members was on the BAC, had been proponents of liberal business policies for several decades. They also had a role in the formation of the U.S. Chamber of Commerce in 1912 (Eakins 1966, p. 226).

There is no direct information as to why Swope suggested Senator Wagner as the public member. Wagner's biographer reports that Wagner was on a long summer vacation in Europe when the decision was made, and that he had to cut his trip short to come home to his new duties (Huthmacher 1968, p. 152–153). But as we noted earlier, both moderate conservatives and labor leaders respected Wagner, and he was close to experts at The Brookings Institution and the American Association for Labor Legislation.

From the tenor of the August 3 meeting of corporate and labor leaders and the composition of the new labor board, it appeared that moderate conservatives within the corporate community were prepared to adopt a more cooperative stance toward organized labor. It seemed that they might be willing to accept the collective-bargaining solution that had been urged by the National Civic Federation and the commission on industrial relations in the Progressive Era, implemented for the duration of World War I, reluctantly accepted by railroad executives in 1926, supported by the Norris-LaGuardia Act, and legislated by Congress as a suggested part of the NRA. The presence of Swope and Teagle seemed to signal that two of the most respected and powerful corporate leaders in the country were now in favor of a more cooperative approach to labor strife.

The new board registered considerable success in its first few weeks by establishing regular procedures and settling several strikes. On August 11, just six days after the board was created, it announced a five-step procedure that was successful in ending a strike at forty-five hosiery mills in Reading, Pennsylvania. Drafted by Swope, and soon to be known as the "Reading Formula," the procedure was as follows, with the provision for secret elections conducted by the National Labor Board as the most crucial aspect:

1. The strike would end immediately.
2. The employers would reinstate strikers without discrimination.
3. The National Labor Board would supervise a secret election by workers to determine whether or not they wished to have a union as their representative.
4. The employer would agree to bargain collectively if the workers voted for a union.
5. All differences not resolved by negotiation would be submitted to an arbitration board or the National Labor Board itself for decision (Gross 1974, pp. 20–21; Loth 1958, pp. 228–229).

Most of the successes under the Reading Formula were with small businesses in minor and fragmented industries that were neither big enough nor organized enough to resist worker pressure and a government board, especially coal mining, clothing, and building construction, which accounted for half of all union members in 1934; the capitalists in those industries also had reason to hope that bargains with unions might help put an end to destructive competition through cuts in wages and prices (Swenson 2002, p. 144). Despite its auspicious start, however, the National Labor Board's authority and prestige were diminished in late 1933 by the lack of a legal underpinning and enforcement powers to overcome opposition by the large industrial employers organized into the Special Conference Committee, the NAM, and strong trade associations, all of which refused to accept the board's decisions. In October, for example, several companies declined to appear at its hearings, and on November 1 the NAM launched a vigorous public attack on the legitimacy of the board itself. The NAM claimed that the procedures of the board were unfair and objected in particular to Swope's idea of representation elections, 75 percent of which were won by trade unions from August through December of 1933. The NAM even objected to the business members of the board, claiming "the representatives of the manufacturers are usually chosen from among those who are known from their expression of views to have a strong leaning towards labor" (Gross 1974, p. 44). In two major cases in December 1933, Weirton Steel and Budd Manufacturing openly defied the National Labor Board and brought the agency to its knees (Bernstein 1969, p. 177).

Workers in large-scale industries were therefore defeated in the first surge of unionizing efforts, but it was not simply because the companies they were up against were large, well organized, and treated gingerly by Roosevelt and his advisors. They also were handicapped by the fact that union organizers were under the jurisdiction of numerous craft unions that, in keeping with the principles that had led to the original success of the AFL, had little interest in organizing the growing number of industrial workers.

By December 1933, Wagner had decided that the basic principles established by section 7(a) and the Reading Formula, along with various board rulings concerning procedures for implementing them, had to be written into law outside the structure of the NRA (Bernstein 1950, p. 62). To that end he held a meeting in early January with labor leaders and a lawyer from the Department of Labor to decide what topics would be covered. Since this meeting began a process that led to an eventual defeat for the corporate moderates, we are going to use our new archival findings to document in considerable detail just how this unusual turn of events came about over the space of the next sixteen months.

THE GROWING OPPOSITION TO COLLECTIVE BARGAINING

Although no employer representatives were present at that first meeting to plan for new labor legislation, it did not take long for Hicks to write Wagner on January 16 saying that he liked section 7(a) as written because in many cases workers did need unions. However, he did not like the possibility that section 7(a) would be modified at labor's request so that employee representation plans would be forbidden because they were allegedly company dominated:

> I have noticed, however, that the A.F. of L. is recommending a change in this Section which would forbid employers to cultivate friendly relations with their own employees. Such a change would in my opinion, work a great injustice to both employers and employees (Hicks 1934a).

Hicks went on to explain that it would not be fair to allow union leaders to "have a free hand to secure members on a voluntary basis" while at the same time saying that "such men as Mr. Teagle, Mr. Swope, and Mr. Kirstein should be forbidden to encourage and cultivate cooperative relations with their own employees. . . ." Wagner replied with a cordial thank-you letter two weeks later, but a prohibition against employee representation plans sponsored by a company nonetheless appeared in the first draft of the legislation in early February. At that point the corporate representatives on the National Labor Board began planning a dinner with Wagner for February 13 during which they hoped to convince him to adopt their plan for organizing the board for its current work, with Hicks playing an administrative role. We know of this meeting because Kirstein (1934) made an effort to convince Swope to change his schedule and join them. But no changes were made on the basis of the dinner meeting.

As these maneuverings signal, the strong opposition from steel, autos, and the NAM soon led to differences of opinion within the board itself, which had been enlarged from seven to eleven members so there would always be three business people able to come to Washington at relatively short notice to deal with new cases that needed immediate attention. One of those new members was BAC member Pierre S. du Pont, chairman of DuPont Corporation and a member of the then closely knit du Pont family of Wilmington, Delaware, the third-richest family of the era (Lundberg 1937, pp. 26–27). The family's main corporate base was in the DuPont Corporation, which had grown very large during World War I through munitions orders from the government. It was the tenth-largest American corporation in 1933, when it earned $26 million despite the Depression; by 1936, its profits were over $90 million (Zilg 1974, p. 345). In addition, the family owned about 25 percent of the stock in General Motors, the third-largest corporation in 1933, and about 20 percent of the stock in United States Rubber. It also owned the National Bank of Detroit and the Wilmington Trust Company and had at least partial ownership in Continental American Life Insurance, North American Aviation, and Remington Arms Company.

Although highly conservative and anti-government, the du Ponts had become Democrats in the 1920s to push for repeal of Prohibition, which they favored for reasons that are still disputed—to make federal income taxes less necessary through the collection of taxes on alcoholic beverages, to keep the role of the federal government in American life to a minimum, or both (Okrent 2010; Webber 2000, Chapter 2, for a discussion of these issues). They also were drawn to the Democrats because one of their top employees, John J. Raskob, who served as vice president for finance for both General Motors and the DuPont Corporation, backed fellow Catholic Al Smith for president in 1928 and then took over as the head of the Democratic National Committee.

Raskob and the du Ponts were anti-Roosevelt at the Democratic National Convention in 1932, but they were pleased with the repeal of Prohibition, which did lead to a significant increase in federal tax revenues, and other early New Deal measures. Then tensions gradually developed over labor policies in 1934 and both tax and labor policies in 1935, with a special du Pont animus toward the pro-union clauses in the National Labor Relations Act. In 1934 the du Ponts and their allies led a successful effort by ultraconservatives to install new leadership and take over the NAM at a point when its financial situation was at a low ebb due to the loss of small-business members hit hard by the Depression (Burch 1973). They then increased its advertising and public relations budget from $36,500 in 1933 to $467,759 by 1936 (Lichtman 2008, pp. 62–63).

In May 1934, Pierre du Pont stopped making regular donations to the Democratic National Committee to help pay off its campaign debts, and then joined with Raskob in August of that year to form the American Liberty League, an ultraconservative political action group funded by a handful of multimillionaire ultraconservatives. The league immediately began media attacks on the New Deal that were based on traditional conservative principles. In 1935, it published and disseminated more than 135 pamphlets to members, newspapers, and universities. It also supported numerous radio broadcasts and recruited college students and conservative professors in an effort to publicize its cause. In addition, it supported legal challenges to the constitutionality of most New Deal legislation through a lawyer's committee headed by the general counsel of U.S. Steel (Lichtman 2008, pp. 70–71). Needless to say perhaps, it hoped to defeat Roosevelt in the 1936 elections by publicizing criticisms of him, starting with those by highly visible Democratic leaders from the past who had become disenchanted with the New Deal (Webber 2000; Wolfskill 1962).

These details on Pierre du Pont, the du Pont family, and the American Liberty League are important because he became a key figure in the split that was about to emerge in the National Labor Board. He made his first public dissent on March 1, 1934, when the majority on the board ruled that the union or employee representation plan chosen by a majority of the employees voting in a representation election had to be recognized as the sole bargaining agent for all the employees in the plant, factory, or office. This decision, if enforced, would have cut the ground from under one of the major tactics of anti-union employers, who insisted, on the basis of a doctrine called "proportional representation," that they had the right and duty to bargain with their company unions and individual employees as well as trade unions. Although the industrialists' claim was based on lofty arguments about the rights of numerical minorities and individuals, it was believed by most observers at the time to be a divide-and-conquer strategy that would allow them to avoid serious negotiations with unions. Corporate lawyer Lloyd K. Garrison, who chaired the reconstituted labor board for several months in the summer and fall of 1934, subsequently said that "I have never yet seen a case in which these arguments were advanced by a *bona fide* minority group generally concerned with negotiating a collective agreement applying to all" (Bernstein 1950, p. 103n, emphasis in the original).

For many years thereafter Pierre du Pont was portrayed as the villain in contrast to Teagle and Swope. For example, the former general counsel employed by the National Labor Board, Columbia Law School professor Milton Handler, remembered du Pont as a person who tended to vote automatically for the business side in a dispute. This was in contrast to Teagle and Swope, whom he recalled as "very, very fair-minded men and they called the shots as they saw them" (Gross 1974, p. 44). Another member of the board's staff said,

> My experience with Pierre du Pont [was] that when he spent a little time in Washington subject to discussions with us, he would be well educated to the purpose of the act and interested in carrying out its functions . . . and then he'd go back to Wilmington for two weeks . . . (listening . . . to the people in his own organization who must have told him what a horrible thing the whole 7(a) idea was) . . . and by the time he came back again, we'd have to go through the whole process all over again" (Gross 1974, pp. 44–45).

However, our new findings in the General Electric Archives suggest that du Pont was not the only major business leader on the National Labor Board who opposed the March 1 decision establishing majority rule. Surprisingly, Swope also opposed it. As he wrote in a letter to du Pont on February 26, he was on the panel that heard the Denver Tramways case in December and "the officers of the Amalgamated had at no time asked for Tramways to deal exclusively with them as representing all employees, and the contract recites that they were dealing on behalf of the members of the union who were employees of the Tramways" (Swope 1934b). Swope therefore was "heartily in agreement" with du Pont's view that the decision should say that "the Amalgamated shall represent the 353 employees who voted for them, and the representatives for whom 325 employees voted shall represent them, and the Tramways is to deal individually with the 36 employees who cast no ballot, until such time as part or all of them choose some method of collective bargaining" (Swope 1934b). He added that he had told Wagner that this was his conclusion.

March 1 was also the day that Wagner introduced his labor disputes bill into the Senate. Swope did not like it any better than the ultraconservatives did, revealing that the differences between the liberal-labor coalition and the corporate moderates were beginning to emerge more clearly. A clear-cut class division was developing. Swope immediately wrote to one of his vice presidents at the company's plant in Schenectady on March 2 asking him what he thought:

> I suppose you saw in the paper this morning about the bill of Senator Wagner for the strengthening of the National Labor Board and also combat the company union. Senator Wagner's statement to me was that it would not affect our so-called company unions, but the way I read this bill, I am not so sure of this. What do you think? (Swope 1934a).

The vice president quickly wrote back on March 5 saying he read the bill in the same way: "The provisions are far reaching and my feeling is like yours that they do touch the General Electric Company's various Employees Representation Plans as they operate today" (Peck 1934). On March 12 Swope sent a rush telegram to Wagner in Washington outlining his objections to the bill and suggesting ways to change it. He first of all wanted to make sure that employee representation plans could survive by adding language that would specify that employers could be paid for the time they spent meeting with managers and that a manager would have the right to discuss "matters relating to his business" (Swope 1934c). He also thought that the act in general was unfair because it "imposes no obligations whatever on employees." Further, he did not think the board should be permitted to make decisions "without legal evidence and to proceed in disregard of ordinary rules of evidence." In short, the corporate moderate Swope had as many reservations about the direction Wagner was heading as the ultraconservative du Pont.

While the du Ponts and the NAM made plans to block any labor legislation that would strengthen section 7(a), Teagle, Kirstein, Swope, and Hicks lobbied Wagner for modifications in the draft legislation that would make it more palatable to them in case it did pass. They did so through a memorandum of suggested changes, many of them similar to Swope's comments via telegram. Teagle and Kirstein handed the memorandum to Wagner when the three of them had dinner in Washington on March 14 (Teagle 1934b). As Teagle summarized the results of the meeting in a letter to Swope the next day, "Generally speaking, the Senator expressed himself as feeling that most of the points we had made were sound and that the draft of the Bill should be modified accordingly" (Teagle 1934a).

One of the suggestions eventually accepted by Wagner concerned a change in the title for his "Labor Disputes Bill." Teagle felt that the word *disputes* contained what today would be called a self-fulfilling prophecy. As the memorandum dryly noted, "some of the provisions of the law, unintentionally of course, seem to have been framed expressly to invite such industrial disagreement." Teagle's memorandum then went on to suggest that henceforth the term *labor relations* be used: "I am sure that you, as the sponsor of this measure, had quite the opposite field in mind and I, therefore, take the liberty of suggesting that the title be made "Labor Relations Act" (Teagle 1934b). (When a new board was constituted by a presidential executive order three months later, it was called the National Labor Relations Board, and the law that Roosevelt eventually signed in July 1935 was called the National Labor Relations Act.)

The memorandum made several other suggestions that were standard parts of the employers' argument by then. For example, coercion by labor organizers as well as coercion by employers should be banned and efforts should be made to solve problems through cooperative means. But the sticking point in the memorandum at the dinner discussion concerned a section of the draft legislation that banned employee representation plans that had been founded and financed by companies. Teagle and Kirstein argued that the issue was domination, not origins, but Wagner held firm, at least for the time being:

> The principal point, on which the Senator seemed to be still in doubt, was as to our suggestion that on Page 5 "Section 5 (3)" [which in effect outlawed all employee representation plans] should be struck out. We had quite a debate about this, and I am sorry to say that I am doubtful whether the arguments we advanced were in themselves sufficient to convince the Senator as to the desirability of the elimination of this paragraph" (Teagle 1934a).

As the tensions increased over labor issues, Raymond Fosdick wrote an extremely revealing letter to Rockefeller on March 22 warning him that he and IRC had to keep a very low profile because there were likely to be strong clashes with labor. Fosdick began by stressing the importance of IRC, but then said he had "to introduce a caveat which is not in any sense inconsistent with the enthusiasm which I have just expressed"(Fosdick 1934). He then noted, "One of my responsibilities in the twenty-one years I have been associated with you has been to point out possible dangers ahead in connection with your multifarious interests." By this he meant that Rockefeller and IRC might be drawn into the conflict between corporations and unions, which he deftly reframed and softened as "a head-on collision between the labor union and the company union." Due to these conflicts, he was "not entirely convinced that the detached attitude which we have thus far held can be maintained."

Fosdick then brought Hicks's opinion into the picture by saying that "Mr. Hicks with entire frankness has pointed out to me that the very nature of the work of Industrial Relations Counselors implies a sympathy toward the company union which as an organization we do not have toward the labor union." He then delivered the clear warning: "If this is true—and I fear it may be—it is possible that the charge might be made that you were financing an organization to fight union labor, and you might thereby be maneuvered into an uncomfortable public position." He then qualified this warning by reminding Rockefeller that "I am not saying you *would* be dragged in" (the emphasis is in the original). Indeed, he thought it likely that "Industrial Relations Counselors might—and indeed probably can—steer clear of this fighting issue in the future as we have in the past." Fosdick then closed by saying "I feel I have a duty, however, just to mention the possibility of unpleasantness—and with this mention I again subscribe to my belief in the value of the organization" (Fosdick 1934).

It seems likely, then, that employees of Industrial Relations Counselors were told to be circumspect about union issues. However, Hicks and Teagle continued their individual efforts to influence the legislation. On March 26, four days after Fosdick's letter to Rockefeller, Hicks wrote another long letter to Wagner on the issue of employee representation plans, agreeing that employers initiated "practically all" of them but denying that the employers "have in any sense dominated employees." He pointed to the higher wages paid by Standard Oil of New Jersey as evidence for this point, along with the company's willingness to accept outside arbitration when workers and management disagreed. Then he reminded Wagner that Teagle, Swope, and Kirstein felt strongly about this matter:

> Mr. Teagle tells me that he and Mr. Swope and Mr. Kirstein are agreed in feeling that these provisions would be disastrous to the plans now in operation in the companies which they represent. I know that you believe in the sincerity of these men and I hope that you will see to it that these particular provisions, which they and many others deplore, are stricken from the bill (Hicks 1934b).

A DEFEAT FOR THE CORPORATE MODERATES

As a result of the preceding lobbying, the provisions banning all employee representation plans were removed from the draft legislation in late March. This series of events suggests that Teagle and Swope still had some leverage with Wagner, especially when it is added that amendments to the Railway Labor Act in 1934 banned company unions, but Teagle and Swope obviously did not have the clout to bring about all the changes they wanted. In any case their partial success proved to be unnecessary. At the moment when Wagner was making the requested changes, Roosevelt intervened in a conflict between the National Labor Board and the automobile industry over unionization that put an end to their concerns for the time being. As part of his decision to move jurisdiction over automobile companies to a separate labor board, he rejected the principle of majority rule. It seemed to be a clear concession to the du Ponts and General Motors, and it was a great disappointment to liberals and union leaders. Roosevelt's decision meant that company unions could flourish alongside trade unions, thereby undercutting serious negotiations by employers with independent unionists (Gross 1974, pp. 61–62). If there had been any hope of restraining anti-union employers, this decision by Roosevelt killed it, at least for the time being.

However, there may have been more to Roosevelt's decision than pressure from the du Ponts and the automobile industry. First, he needed the automobile industry to lead the way to recovery; the industry had accounted for one-fourth of the increase in national payroll between January and February 1934 and was in general, along with large steel and rubber corporations, leading the economic rebound (see, for example, Levine 1988, pp. 104–106). Second, he was well aware that the AFL union could not win a strike against the powerful and well-organized automobile executives, who were widely known for their willingness to use strong-arm methods. It may even be that some union leaders conveyed their desire to avoid a showdown to the president (Fine 1969, pp. 220–222).

Whatever Roosevelt's reasons for his decision, the moderate conservatives Teagle and Kirstein were privately pleased with it. They believed the National Labor Board now would fall by the wayside. They were in effect abandoning a government agency they had played a major role in creating. As Teagle wrote to Kirstein in a private note in April 1934:

> Just between you and me and the lamp-post it strikes me that the President's decision in the automobile controversy has put the Labor Board out of the running. I am sure that neither you nor I will shed any tears if such is the case (McQuaid 1982, p. 46).

Any hope for Wagner's revised legislation also collapsed at this point. The new draft was handed to another Democratic senator, David I. Walsh of Massachusetts, whose Committee on Education and Labor proceeded to suggest legislation that was even more sympathetic to employer concerns. However, the committee's revised legislation act did not include any mention of excluding agricultural and domestic labor, a glaring omission in the eyes of the wary Southern Democrats. That problem was remedied by five of the Democrats on the committee, including the senator from Alabama, Hugo Black, who had introduced the legislation that caused Roosevelt to set the wheels in motion for the creation of the National Recovery Administration (Farhang and Katznelson 2005, p. 13). Helping workers in the North in 1933 through the introduction of legislation to create a thirty-hour week was one thing, apparently, for a Southern liberal; supporting the unionization of agricultural labor in the South was another.

Once the exclusion of agricultural and domestic labor was in the bill, there was no further mention of the issue by either supporters or opponents of the bill. Industrial workers were the focus of the floor debate and the amendments that were offered. Despite the many amendments that were added, the NAM, Chamber of Commerce, Special Conference Committee, and industrial trade associations worked to make sure that even this tepid legislation did not pass. Large numbers of employees involved in employee representation plans in several different companies were brought to Washington to testify to their satisfaction with the plans and their distaste for unions, which Cowdrick thought to be the most influential statements heard by the Senate (U.S. Senate 1939, p. 16807). Corporate executives who supported employee representation plans were especially vigorous in their criticism. Arthur H. Young, identified as the former director of Industrial Relations Counselors as well as the vice president for industrial relations at U.S. Steel, criticized the bill as "in its entirety both vicious and undesirable because of its fundamental philosophy as to the certain and complete clash of interest as between employer and employee" (Stark 1934, p. 1).

We believe the refusal by the moderate conservatives to accept majority rule in March 1934, when they still had control of the overall legislative and administrative situation, encapsulates the complex change in class forces that had occurred over the previous four to six years. At the surface level, the corporate moderates had an obvious concern to protect the employee representation plans they had established in their various companies. At a deeper level, they were committed to proportional representation because it allowed them to deal with craft workers separately from industrial workers, thus helping to maintain the segmentation of the working class. Proportional representation had been the basis for the agreement between big business and organized labor during World War I, and it had allowed the craft-oriented AFL to look after its workers while leaving industrial workers at the tender mercies of their anti-union employers. In suggesting a similar board in 1933, the business leaders were assuming that AFL leaders once again would accept the same sort of cross-class bargain (McQuaid 1979, 1982).

However, the leaders of at least some AFL unions were no longer willing to accept this alliance because of changes in their own circumstances. First, Lewis and Hillman wanted to organize industrial unions, so they refused to go along with proportional representation. In particular, Lewis was determined to organize the steel workers because the steel companies would not allow him to organize the coal miners in the many mines owned by steel companies. These "captive mines" left the United Mine Workers completely vulnerable to the employers who almost destroyed the union in the 1920s, so Lewis was determined that such a near-catastrophe would not happen again (Dubofsky and Van Tine 1977). Hillman also had strategic reasons to support industrial unions. He needed to organize textile workers to protect his clothing workers union (Fraser 1991).

If it were only a matter of Lewis and Hillman in coal and garments, perhaps the corporate moderates might have conceded the point on majority rule, although the du Ponts and other ultraconservatives would have objected mightily. However, there was an even more serious issue: the growing unity and militancy among both craft and industrial workers, especially in steel, rubber, autos, and other heavy industries. The moderate conservatives did not want to see most workers organized into industrial unions, especially unions supported by national laws. The idea of collective bargaining was acceptable if it was voluntary and involved craft workers, but not if it was mandatory and contained the potential for uniting all workers. There is also evidence that some business leaders, usually in highly competitive sectors with many small companies, could see the benefits of unions in helping to limit competition among businesses by means of making wage reductions. However, even the historian who presses this point the furthest concludes that in the final analysis almost all business owners rejected unions as a threat to the right to manage their enterprises exactly as they pleased (Colin Gordon 1994, p. 238). At the most general level, then, as one historical institutionalist concludes in a rare but strong nod to the importance of class conflict, a large part of the problem boiled down to the fact that virtually no corporate leaders, whether moderate conservatives or ultraconservatives, wanted the government to have the power to help create a fully organized working class (Skocpol 1980, p. 181).

The rejection of majority rule by the corporate moderates meant that labor policy would be decided by the president and Congress, not corporate executives, in the context of labor unrest on the one side and a corporate willingness to use physical attacks to resist unionization on the other, as exposed in great detail by Senate hearings in late 1936 and early 1937 (Auerbach 1966). Roosevelt, as a member of the labor board for naval shipyards in World War I and a participant in discussions at the National Civic Federation in the 1920s, was most closely identified with those corporate leaders who favored a conciliatory approach toward workers and an acceptance of limited trade unionism. But as his decision to give the automobile industry its own labor board clearly showed, he was willing to make temporizing decisions that reflected the complex balance of issues and political alliances at any given moment. Francis Biddle (1962, p. 220), a corporate lawyer who served as chair of the temporary National Labor Relations Board in 1934–1935, reflecting many years later on Roosevelt's approach to labor conflict, admiringly concluded that he had "a strong sense of the incidence of power. . . . "

Although they surely understood the shifting power equation, Roosevelt, most corporate leaders, and top AFL leaders probably did not fully grasp the growing militancy of industrial workers or the increasing acceptance of trade unionism by Congressional liberals, which of course fed on each other. The corporate policy-planning network had helped to legitimate an idea—collective bargaining—and create a mechanism—the National Labor Board—that were fast taking on lives of their own, just as historical institutionalists would argue, although it is more accurate to say that these ideas had gained new supporters in the changing circumstances of the New Deal. The moderate conservatives had lost control of the concept of collective bargaining to liberals and industrial unionists. Senator Wagner, Lewis, Hillman, and the lawyers for the National Labor Board, most of them corporate lawyers or law school professors, would come to center stage to fight for an improved version of the labor board that corporate moderates had created and then abandoned.

PROGRESS TOWARD THE NATIONAL LABOR RELATIONS ACT

Roosevelt's decision to establish an automobile labor board, in conjunction with the watering down and forthcoming defeat of the 1934 version of Wagner's bill, was deeply disheartening to militant unionists and gave activists inspired by Marxism their opening. The result was a series of violent strikes that broke out in April and May in San Francisco (where Communists joined with syndicalists and independent radicals to lead the way), Toledo (where small Marxist groups sparked the confrontation), and Minneapolis (where Marxist-Leninists who followed Leon Trotsky had the lead role). At the same time, the Senate, under enormous lobbying pressure from the corporate community, rejected Wagner's attempt to codify the practices and case law developed by the National Labor Board (see Levine 1988 and Brecher 1997, for detailed accounts of these strikes that give a full accounting of leftist leadership and police violence).

For all the tensions and calls for repressive forces by the ultraconservatives, Roosevelt was able to deal with all three of these serious upheavals when they reached the boiling point that summer by sending special mediators to bring the two sides to the bargaining table, where temporary arrangements acceptable to them were hammered out after several deaths, scores of injuries, and hundreds of arrests (Bernstein 1969, Chapter 6). Despite all this violence and the militancy of the striking workers, Roosevelt might have put aside labor legislation entirely except for a problem that could not be easily handled, the threat of an industry-wide steel strike in mid-June, which might slow economic recovery as well as lead to more violence. The strike was first proposed by a small group of leftist labor leaders who had taken over several moribund locals of the Amalgamated Association of Iron, Steel, and Tin Workers. It was then agreed to by the union as a whole in mid-April as a last resort if the steel companies would not bargain with it. As the steel companies prepared for physical conflict by stocking munitions, putting up barbed-wire fences, and hiring extra employees, the top AFL leadership was able to head off the strike, which the union almost surely would have lost, by convincing Roosevelt to set up an impartial committee to mediate the dispute (Bernstein 1950, pp. 76–77). Once again, leftist activists, including Communists, had forced an issue that top labor leaders and Roosevelt did not want to face.

The near collision in steel was enough to convince Roosevelt that he needed a new labor board to handle unexpected disputes while at the same time buying him time to see if the National Recovery Administration would be able to bring back economic prosperity. The result was a public resolution, written by Roosevelt on the basis of suggestions from lawyers in the Department of Labor, which Congress immediately adopted in late June. It gave the president the power to appoint a temporary National Labor Relations Board that would have what corporate leaders felt confident were very limited powers. Young of U.S. Steel, who had made the spirited attack on Wagner's proposed legislation two months before, wrote a private memo expressing his pleasure with the outcome, suggesting that victory could be declared:

> I view the passage of the joint resolution with equanimity. It means that temporary measures that cannot last more than a year will be substituted for the permanent legislation proposed. . . . I do not believe there will ever be given as good a chance for the passage of the Wagner Act as exists now, and the trade is a mighty good compromise. I have read carefully the joint resolution, and my personal opinion is that it is not going to bother us very much (Bernstein 1950, p. 81, ellipses in the original).

However, Young may have misunderstood Roosevelt's perspective on labor issues. As Roosevelt wrote to one of his most trusted advisors, Harvard Law School Professor Felix Frankfurter, in August 1934, his long-term goal was to salvage the National Industrial Recovery Act's provisions for "(1) minimum wage, (2) maximum hours, (3) collective bargaining and (4) child labor," which would require legislation that could pass muster with a Supreme Court dominated by eight former corporate lawyers (four ultraconservatives, two moderate conservatives who provided the swing votes, and two liberals); Frankfurter then passed this information along to Justice Louis Brandeis, one of the two liberals, in a handwritten note (Kenneth Davis 1986, p. 517).

Moreover, the new board proved to be more formidable than Young expected, in part because its new chair, Garrison, the corporate lawyer quoted earlier in the chapter, who was at the time the dean of the University of Wisconsin Law School, took the board in a more legalistic direction. In the process he prepared it to become a mini-Supreme Court for labor law. With the aid of two equally competent board members and a staff of excellent young lawyers, some of whom were former law school professors, some fresh out of law school, he began to create the "common law" on labor issues that would provide the basis for a stronger version of the National Labor Relations Act in early 1935. When Garrison resigned after several months to return to the University of Wisconsin, he was replaced by Biddle, even more experienced and liberal, whose firm boasted the Pennsylvania Railroad as its most prominent client among several blue-chip corporations (Biddle 1962; Bernstein 1969, pp. 318–319).

It was at this point that Industrial Relations Counselors began printing its brief, recurring bulletin *Memorandum to Clients*, which updated a wide range of industrial relations executives, primarily in the Special Conference Committee and the many companies related to Rockefeller interests, but also a few others as well, such as Sun Oil and Union Carbide, on unfolding events in Washington relating to labor relations, unemployment insurance, and old-age pensions. These memorandums, which appeared on an as-necessary basis, provide us with a new window into the perspectives of corporate moderates during these years (Kaufman 2003, was the first to make use of these memorandums and kindly provided us with copies of them). Generally speaking, the memorandums are very circumspect in discussing labor issues, perhaps in keeping with the admonitions that Fosdick and Hicks had expressed to Rockefeller in Fosdick's letter in March, but they prove that IRC employees kept a close eye on the personnel, inner workings, and decisions of the new labor board. (As we show in the next chapter, the memorandums are much more revealing of insider information on the Social Security Act, which IRC openly supported and on which it could provide considerable detail because its employees were involved in writing it.)

The first memorandum, dated July 10, provided a two-page overview of the powers of the new labor board and the backgrounds of its three appointees. It noted that the president's executive order "gave it more authority than was contemplated" in the resolution passed by Congress, then went on to characterize the three board members for its clients. An accurate account of Garrison's impressive career is provided, followed by the reassuring information that "Apparently he has a pleasant personality and has favorably impressed the business men with whom he has been in contact." It is further stated, "He is said to have 'advanced ideas on economics,' but not to be radical on labor questions." Similar positive comments are provided on the other two board members, who were judged to be open to established employee representation plans (Industrial Relations Counselors, Inc. 1934a, pp. 3–4).

Meanwhile, the leaders of most craft unions continued to reject the idea of organizing workers into industrial unions despite continuing failure for craft forms of organizing and the presence of an activist ferment that might be capitalized upon. In particular, the head of the machinists union was totally opposed to industrial unions even though virtually no machinists in the automobile industry belonged to a union. If machinists in heavy industry were somehow organized into a temporary industrial union, he insisted, they would have to be reassigned to his craft union at some point (Bernstein 1969, pp. 353–354). The same balkanization obtained in the rubber industry. Sixteen internationals claimed jurisdiction over one or another subset of rubber workers, thereby disregarding the fact that most of the men in the plants thought of themselves simply as rubber workers and wanted to belong to industrial unions. Lewis and Hillman remained in near isolation at the top of the AFL when it came to sympathy for this approach. But labor organizing went nowhere from 1934, following a devastating defeat for textile workers in the autumn of that year, until after the passage of the National Labor Relations Act in the summer of 1935, which at first glance suggests that the corporate community and the New Dealers were not as afraid of labor militancy as some Marxist and protest-disruption accounts have claimed.

Disruption or no disruption, Wagner was determined to continue his work toward legislation that would give workers the right to unions and collective bargaining. His revised version of the National Labor Relations Act, introduced in February 1935, benefited greatly from the experience of the temporary board appointed by Roosevelt in the summer of 1934. The new version also may have had more legitimacy with political leaders through Biddle's numerous speeches to business groups and middle-class voluntary associations across the country about the proposed legislation's sensible approach and its basis in long experience and many legal precedents (Biddle 1962). With Biddle and other board members overseeing their efforts, the board's legal staff, led by former Harvard Law School professor Calvert Magruder, produced the key provisions in the act (Gross 1974). Wagner's lone staff member, Leon Keyserling, a twenty-four-year-old Columbia law school graduate, then put these ideas into traditional legislative language (Casebeer 1987).

The new version established the National Labor Relations Board as a "Supreme Court" that would focus on the enforcement of rights, not on mediation. It would have the right to enforce its decisions concerning the appropriate bargaining unit for each case, the use of unfair labor practices by employers, and the appropriate remedies for workers who had been fired for union activities. The proposed legislation based the board's procedures in the precedents set by earlier quasi-judicial government regulatory agencies, such as the Federal Trade Commission, that had been approved by federal courts (Bernstein 1969, pp. 323–324). However, there was one aspect of the 1934 version that remained unchanged. Agricultural and domestic labor was excluded with the same language that the Committee on Education and Labor introduced in 1934. And once again, there were no questions raised about this exclusion in the floor debates (Farhang and Katznelson 2005, p. 13).

Significantly, Teagle and Swope made very little effort to influence the legislation this time around, probably because they knew that they could not have any general impact. In February 1935, Teagle sent Wagner a copy of a new booklet that Standard Oil of New Jersey had created to sing the praises of its employee representation plan and employee benefits. Wagner replied that the booklet was "quite helpful," adding "the need for social legislation would be much less pressing than it is" if "conditions everywhere were such as described in your booklet" (Wagner 1935b). On a more important note, Swope made a successful effort to amend a section of the bill pertaining to employee representation plans by sending Wagner a letter containing language suggested by Teagle. Creating an employee representation plan would not be prohibited, but dominating or interfering in one would be illegal. In addition, language was once again added to make it possible to pay workers for the time they spent in meetings with management as officers of an employee representation plan (Swope 1935).

The IRC *Memorandum to Clients* No. 8, dated March 1, reported on the new version of the legislation in a descriptive and neutral tone. It included a comparison of the 1934 and 1935 drafts provided by an unnamed "client company." It also contained a list of questions and answers, mostly pertaining to the status of employee representation plans, which once again was provided by a client company. The first question asked whether an employee representation plan can still "continue to function if the bill were passed," and the answer was "yes" as long as "it is not dominated by the management and involves no practices ruled illegal by the bill" (Industrial Relations Counselors, Inc. 1935c, attachment, p. 1). The illegal practices were then listed, including financial support beyond paying workers their wages while meeting with management. The memorandum's assured tone in claiming that employee representation plans remained legal fits with the language that Wagner added to the bill at Teagle and Swope's request.

The IRC *Memorandum to Clients* for March 27, No. 9, reported that "spokesmen for employee representation plans in a number of steel plants testified before the committee March 26, asserting that many thousands of employees were satisfied with employee representation plans as a method of collective bargaining." But it also said on the basis of "advice received from Washington this morning" that the new bill was likely to pass. Again documenting IRC's concern for the preservation of employee representation plans, the memorandum added that "it is hoped that certain amendments which have already been considered by the Senate Committee on Education and Labor will be adopted; these amendments are designed principally to ensure recognition of employee representation" (Industrial Relations Counselors, Inc. 1935d, p. 8).

Although the hoped-for amendments were adopted, Cowdrick and the Special Conference Committee nonetheless coordinated an all-out battle against the act, a fact revealed in documents subpoenaed by a Senate investigating committee (Auerbach 1966; U.S. Senate 1939, pp. 16806–16809). Contrary to those researchers who claim that some corporate leaders were willing to accept the new labor legislation (for example, Ferguson 1995), we do not think that any business sector or visible corporate leaders supported it. Most of the favorable testimony came from Garrison, Biddle, and others who had worked for earlier incarnations of the labor board. The act also had the support of a number of labor relations experts who had in effect parted company with the IRC-oriented industrial relations network on this issue, including several who had worked with Commons, as discovered in work by sociologist Jeff Manza (1995, Chapter 3).

In late April, Cowdrick reported to members of the Special Conference Committee that Roosevelt might have struck a deal with Hillman and Lewis to support the act in exchange for labor support for the renewal of the National Industrial Recovery Act:

> There is much speculation over the question of whether or not Roosevelt has made a deal with Wagner and the American Federation of Labor, as a result of which the Administration will support the Wagner bill and receive labor's aid for some of its own projects in exchange. People who suspect a deal of this kind had been made point out that Wagner switched his vote on the prevailing wage amendment on the public works bill, and that a few days later Green and Lewis agreed to the appointment of Donald R. Richberg as head of NRA. For this concession the labor leaders ostensibly received no other consideration except the appointment of an additional representative on the NRA Board. Some people suspect, however, that there was an understanding about the Wagner bill (U.S. Senate 1939, p. 17017).

Cowdrick added that he was not certain the deal had taken place: "One point against this story is the fact that the Wagner bill was not included in the list of 'must' legislation which Roosevelt gave to Senator Robinson just before the President left for his Florida vacation this week" (U.S. Senate 1939, p. 17017). But an economist close to Hillman, George Soule, was confident that a bargain was in the making. He reported to liberals and leftists in *The Nation* on April 3 that informal talks between Hillman and Roosevelt were going on about industrial unions to work with the government (Soule 1935).

For all the speculation about Roosevelt's backroom dealings, there is no certain evidence as to what he had promised and not promised to key labor leaders. The most likely inference is that he was playing for time to see what the Supreme Court would rule on the constitutionality of the NRA. On May 14, he refused Wagner's request to make the act "must" legislation, but the Senate nonetheless passed the bill two days later by a strong 63-12 vote, just as Cowdrick had feared. The Senate's approval, which included virtually all of the Southern Democrats, made the final outcome a foregone conclusion because the Democrats also had an overwhelming majority in the House. On May 20 the lawyers at the National Labor Relations Board wrote to Wagner that they thought it was imperative that the bill go to the White House "this week" because of "the imminence of a decision in the Schechter case which will in all probability be adverse to the government" (Levy 1935). In other words, the lawyers at the National Labor Relations Board expected the National Industrial Recovery Act to be declared unconstitutional, which would eliminate the foundation for labor relations in section 7(a). With further urging from Wagner, Roosevelt finally made a public statement in favor of the act on May 24, three days before the Supreme Court issued its unanimous negative verdict, to Roosevelt's apparent surprise.

The certain passage of the National Labor Relations Act once Roosevelt expressed his support was the final straw for most corporate leaders, who had become increasingly uncomfortable with the direction the New Deal was taking. They had expressed their dissatisfaction in early May by replacing Harriman as the president of the Chamber of Commerce with an ultraconservative, who made fiery speeches about the perfidy of the New Dealers. From that point forward most corporate leaders were in all-out revolt against New Deal policies, with the important exception of the Social Security Act, discussed in the next chapter. Young of IRC and U.S. Steel was so incensed by the act that he told the assembled audience at a banquet on May 24, where he received a gold medal from the American Management Association for "his outstanding and creative work in the field of industrial relations," that he would "prefer to go to jail or receive a conviction as a felon and yet be true to the principles of peaceful cooperation in industry" than to accept any provision of the National Labor Relations Act. He claimed the act was being "imposed on us by demagogues," a claim that was strongly contested at the same banquet by a labor relations expert from Harvard (*New York Times* 1935).

Shortly before the House was due to vote, the opponents of the act were momentarily heartened by the unanimous Supreme Court decision on May 27 declaring the National Industrial Recovery Act unconstitutional because it was both an impermissible delegation of congressional power to the president and an overreach on the power that Congress had to regulate commerce unless there was a direct impact on interstate commerce. Concerned by the substance of the court's ruling in relation to interstate commerce, Wagner asked that the House delay its vote so he could change the preamble to the act in light of the court's argument. It now omitted any appeal to the general welfare clause of the Constitution. It focused instead on the fact that the failure of employers to recognize and bargain with unions was a major cause of strikes, which did stop production of goods intended for interstate commerce, and therefore had a very direct effect on the flow of goods beyond single states (Bernstein 1950, pp. 120–122; Cortner 1964, pp. 82–83). The revised bill passed the House by a voice vote and then was supported once again in the Senate.

Two days before Roosevelt signed the new legislation on July 5, IRC's *Memorandum* No. 13 provided a summary of the bill, along with a criticism of it for efforts to upend employee representation plans:

> Many provisions of this act are clearly intended to prevent not only coercion but also any active interest on the part of the employer in the matter of collective bargaining so far as it concerns employees. It may fairly be stated that the act encourages the organization of outside unions and discourages employee representation plans" (Industrial Relations Counselors, Inc. 1935g, p. 1).

The memorandum further claimed that union organizers were using the act to argue that employee representation plans had been "outlawed," but the memorandum then reminded readers that "[t]he bill states otherwise, and employers and employees should bear in mind that employee representation plans are specifically named in the act as a recognized form of 'labor organization for dealing with employers concerning grievances, labor disputes, wages, rates of pay, hours of employment, or conditions of work,' and employers and employees should be prepared to maintain before the Labor Board and in the courts their right to continue friendly relations" (Industrial Relations Counselors, Inc. 1935g, pp. 1–2).

The memorandum then urged employers to "study carefully the list of five specified unfair labor practices and under advice of counsel instruct all connected with management to refrain from any statements or actions which could be construed as coming within that list" (Industrial Relations Counselors, Inc. 1935g, p. 2). It next presented six steps that needed to be taken to ensure that an employee representation plan could not be banned because it was deemed to be employer-controlled. They included employee-controlled elections, separate meetings of employee representatives in addition to their meetings with management, statements by employee representatives to fellow employees assuring them that the organizations were independent of management, and the withdrawal of any company subsidies to the organizations.

Clearly, IRC was not prepared to give up on its employee representation plans. In fact, the memorandum argued, "genuine employee representation plans should be strengthened rather than weakened by this legislation" (Industrial Relations Counselors, Inc. 1935g, p. 2). But in spite of all the hope and effort on the part of Industrial Relations Counselors and the members of the Special Conference Committee, the union movement overwhelmed most employee representation plans in 1937, as we discuss in Chapter 5, quickly winning the support of most of the 2 million members enrolled in these plans. As late as 1962, however, when the Industrial Relations Section at Princeton last supported a study, there were still 1,400 "single-company" unions, as employee representation plans were called at that point, most of them descendants of earlier employee representation plans, representing 400,000 workers. (By comparison, there were about 14.8 million members in independent unions at that time.) Interestingly, single-company unions were "the dominant form of labor organization in the chemical industry and close to being so in the telephone and petroleum industries," which means that the employee representation plans at the DuPont Corporation, AT&T, and various Standard Oil companies were able to hold on with the help of higher salaries and better employee benefits than in most industries (Shostak [1962] 1973, p. 1). (For a detailed account of company unions after the New Deal through the lens of a major manufacturing company heavily involved in the leadership of the NAM, see historian Sanford Jacoby's *Modern Manors* (1997, Chapter 5).

Meeting shortly after Roosevelt signed the act, members of the Special Conference Committee reaffirmed their decision taken two months earlier to challenge its constitutionality, asserting, "It is generally agreed among industrialists and their legal advisers that the Wagner Act is unconstitutional as applied to manufacturing industry" (U.S. Senate 1939, p. 16809). They also stressed that the behavior of corporations should look good in the eyes of the general public. Executives should make themselves more accessible to newspaper reporters. "Industrial relations" and "public relations" were declared to be interdependent (U.S. Senate 1939, p. 16850).

SUMMARY

The major question that must be answered by any theory attempting to understand the American power structure is how such an act so vehemently opposed by organized business groups could pass so easily despite their very large lobbying effort. For historical institutionalists, the passage of the act shows that corporate leaders had lost whatever power they once had in Washington (see, for example, Finegold and Skocpol 1995; Skocpol 1980). For many Marxists and protest-disruption theorists, the increased unity and militancy of the working class forced a worried corporate community and a timid New Deal to accede to labor demands (for example, Goldfield 1989).

An emphasis on a general loss of power by the corporate community is contradicted by the way in which the same Senate and House that passed the National Labor Relations Act treated other liberal legislation, namely, public utility regulation, changes in the Federal Reserve System, and proposed increases in taxes on high incomes and large inheritances ("the wealth tax"). First, business was successful in removing the most stringent forms of utilities regulation (see, for example, Parrish 1970). One historian concludes that the House was rebuking Roosevelt in this vote because a majority of its members were "annoyed at what they considered Roosevelt's undue hostility to free enterprise" (Patterson [1967] 1981, p. 56). Second, the proposed reforms in the Federal Reserve Act were changed so that New York bankers retained some of their traditional power through the Open Market Committee, and the act ended up acceptable to the American Bankers Association (Schlesinger 1960, pp. 300–301). Finally, the wealth tax had very little immediate impact once it was moderated in Congress, although it did raise the effective tax rate on the top 1 percent of income-earning households from 11.3 percent in 1935 to 16.4 percent in 1936, and in the process prepared the way for greater reliance on highly progressive income taxes rather than sales taxes during World War II (Brownlee 2000, p. 51, Table 2.4; Schlesinger 1960, pp. 333–334; Thorndike 2009). It therefore seems that the National Labor Relations Act was a unique piece of legislation even for a liberal Congress, which means it is not possible to explain its passage with generalities such as "loss of business power."

Nor does it seem likely that the labor militancy of the spring and summer of 1933 and 1934 can provide an explanation because the 1934 version of the National Labor Relations Act was defeated in the midst of that militancy (see Goldfield 1989, for a contrary view that we discuss in the final chapter). Moreover, there was relatively little militancy in the following year, when the new—and stronger—version did pass. Finally, the labor movement was clearly divided over the issue of organizing industrial unions, making it unlikely that the unity and zeal necessary to defeat major corporations could be mustered without the backing of the federal government.

We therefore think it is more likely that liberals and labor leaders were able to pass this legislation for very different reasons than what historical institutionalists, Marxists, or protest-disruption theorists claim. First and foremost, the liberal-labor coalition was able to convince most moderate and conservative Democrats in Congress to vote for the act willingly by excluding agricultural and domestic labor from its purview. This purposeful exclusion meant that the great bulk of the Southern workforce would not be covered, making it easier for Southern Democrats to support the legislation (compare with Farhang and Katznelson 2005). The exclusion of farm labor also made it possible for the Progressive Republicans of the Midwest to vote for the act without any hesitation. Translated into class terms, the exclusion of agricultural and domestic workers meant that the Southern segment of the ownership class did not have any direct stake in opposing the act, so Southern Democrats in Congress were free to support their Northern counterparts instead of voting with Northern Republicans, as they usually did on labor legislation. Moreover, we think the Southern Democrats, with little fear of industrial unions at a time before the Congress of Industrial Organizations was created, may have seen some advantages for the South in the act in terms of attracting businesses in the North that did not want to deal with unions. This is in fact what had already happened in the textile industry, and the process was repeated in many other industries after the passage of the National Labor Relations Act, a gradual industrial revolution that brought many companies into Southern states in search of low-wage, non-unionized workers. Contrary to historical institutionalists, then, and one of our major disagreements with them, the corporate leaders did not lose power in general despite the calamity of the Depression. Instead, they lost on this issue because their key allies, the plantation capitalists, did not stick with them.

Wagner understood the necessity of this exclusion. As far back as the debate over the National Industrial Recovery Act, he had insisted that the act did not cover agricultural labor, and he had seen the 1934 version of his anti-lynching bill die without even making it out of committee. That is, he fully realized that Southern Democrats still controlled the Democratic Party and Congress despite the large majority of Democrats from the North and West. He knew that they would not be reluctant to use the filibuster in the Senate if all else failed, as they did against the 1935 version of the anti-lynching bill. When the leader of the Socialist Party, Norman Thomas, wrote to Wagner to complain about the exclusion of farm labor, Wagner replied as follows on April 2, 1935, a month before the bill was voted on in the Senate:

> I am very regretful of this, because I should like to see agricultural workers given the protection of my bill, and would welcome any activity that might include them. They have been excluded only because I thought it would be better to pass the bill for the benefit of industrial workers than not to pass it at all, and that inclusion of agricultural workers would lessen the likelihood of passage so much as not to be desirable (Wagner 1935a).

The importance of satisfying Southern Democrats is also seen in an interview many years later with Keyserling, the Wagner employee who drafted the National Labor Relations Act on the basis of the concepts and arguments given to him by labor board lawyers. As he told the interviewer, Secretary of Agriculture Henry Wallace did not want to include farm labor because "[h]e was entirely beholden to the chairmen of the agricultural committees in the Senate and House, who were all big Southern landowners like Senator Smith and Congressman Bankhead" (Casebeer 1987, p. 334).

The National Labor Relations Act passed handily because in addition it was acceptable to the centrists and liberals who controlled the executive branch on this issue, meaning Roosevelt, Perkins, and the corporate lawyers and law professors who worked for the National Labor Relations Board. These were people who believed through long experience that unions were a safe and sensible method for dealing with workers. And from the point of view of moderate and liberal corporate lawyers, the act had a very respectable regulatory pedigree that had worked well for the corporate community in the past, including the Interstate Commerce Commission, the Federal Trade Commission, the Securities and Exchange Commission, and the Railroad Labor Board. From a historical perspective, the New Deal's collective bargaining legislation "gathered up the historical threads and wove them into law" (Bernstein 1950, p. 18).

Third, the legislation passed because of the newly developed electoral cohesion between the native-born craft workers and predominantly immigrant and African American industrial workers in the Northern working class, who began to vote together for Democrats in the late 1920s, helping to overcome the divisions that had existed since at least the 1880s (see, for example, Mink 1986; Voss 1993). Many of them also worked together in an effort to create industrial unions in heavy industry, and almost all of them supported union leaders and liberal elected officials in their efforts on behalf of the National Labor Relations Act. The AFL leaders had some reservations about the act because they knew it would put them at the mercy of labor board decisions on voting procedures and on the determination of the size of bargaining units, but they backed the act even though none of their suggested amendments to the proposed legislation was incorporated (Tomlins 1985, pp. 139–140).

Finally, the Wagner Act passed because Roosevelt had entered into a political alliance on this issue with leaders of the industrial segment of the working class, which had gained his attention through the disruptions its activists and leaders had been able to generate, a point that puts us in partial agreement with Marxists and protest-disruption theorists. That is, the key labor leaders on this issue were Hillman and Lewis, precisely the people who would create the new movement for industrial unions after the passage of the act. Roosevelt was faced with a choice between trade unions regulated by the government and the continuing use of force to repress militant labor activists. As far and away the most important leader of the new liberal-labor coalition, as well as the most cautious and enigmatic, he chose unions over periodic violence and property destruction of the kind that had first broken out in 1877, but only after the liberal-labor coalition proved that it could produce a voting majority in Congress that included the Southern Democrats.

In summary, then, the National Labor Relations Act passed for a confluence of reasons, starting with the fact that the Great Depression led to both social upheaval and a united working class, which in turn led corporate moderates to suggest a new government institution, a labor board, that soon took on a life of its own—in the sense that liberals, a handful of corporate lawyers serving in government, and labor leaders refashioned it to their own liking. The union leaders who spoke for the working class found allies in the liberal Democrats they had helped to elect to Congress and in the pragmatic patrician liberal they helped elect to the presidency. It was possible for the liberals and Roosevelt to work with labor on this issue because the plantation capitalists and large-scale farmers outside the South had been satisfied by the removal of their workforce from the purview of the legislation. Although the election of moderate-to-liberal Northern Democrats to Congress and the militancy of a united working class were necessary conditions, Southern Democrats had the final say on this critical piece of legislation.

This analysis is supported by the decline in the importance of the National Labor Relations Act after 1938. For reasons we explain in Chapter 6, the Southerners turned against the act in 1937 when the new CIO unexpectedly tried to organize racially integrated industrial unions in the South, raising the possibility that they would make use of a tactic, the sit-down strike, that was proving to be very effect in the North. This sudden and very resolute change of heart on the part of Southern Democrats meant that the entire ownership class became united against the National Labor Relations Act. At the same time, the American Federation of Labor and the Congress of Industrial Organizations entered into an intraclass war, which meant that the working class was divided at a time when the ownership class was united. When the Republicans gained enough seats in the House and Senate in 1938 to forge an effective conservative voting coalition with the Southern Democrats, which could stop any legislation that employers North and South did not want, the handwriting was on the wall for the development of a strong union movement in the United States.

CHAPTER FOUR

The Social Security Act

As the Agricultural Adjustment Act and the National Industrial Recovery Act were being turned into administrative structures, the two main policy issues that came to be embodied in the Social Security Act—old-age insurance and unemployment insurance—were moving along at a slower and more measured pace. Moreover, old-age insurance and unemployment insurance were being discussed on somewhat separate tracks within the corporate community and the policy-planning network that only came together in the spring of 1934. More generally, the Social Security Act had a much longer and very different history from that of either the Agricultural Adjustment Act or the National Labor Relations Act.

ORIGINS OF THE SOCIAL SECURITY ACT

Although we focus in this chapter on old-age insurance and unemployment insurance because of their later impact and their importance in the theoretical disputes that concern us, the Social Security Act included several other policies as well. There was a title, for example, called "old-age assistance," which provided means-tested benefits for the elderly. The proponents of old-age insurance always saw this means-tested benefit as a potential threat to their own program because ultraconservatives insisted that it was all that was necessary. From the moderate conservative and liberal point of view, an ultraconservative victory on this issue, which reappeared several times during the ensuing decades, would have stigmatized funds for the elderly as "welfare" and led to a reluctance to raise benefits to keep pace with inflation (Altman 2005). There was also a title advocated by liberal women activists that provided benefits for unmarried mothers, but it was reshaped and soon stigmatized as welfare for undeserving women (Poole 2006, Chapter 5).

In the case of old-age pensions, there had been government pensions as far back as the nineteenth century for some types of government employees. Thanks to the government budget surplus generated by the high tariffs imposed by Republicans during the Civil War to protect Northern manufacturers, veterans of the Civil War—and later their widows and children—received government pensions that lasted into the early twentieth century (Skocpol 1992). As for unemployment insurance, it first gained attention in the first decade of the twentieth century and received extended discussion in the 1920s, in part based on the experience of European countries with various forms of social insurance.

Although veterans' pensions, mothers' pensions, and the European experience had a general influence in legitimating the idea of social insurance, it is important to make clear at the outset that the specific principles embodied in the old-age and unemployment provisions of the Social Security Act came from corporate experience with private insurance plans, and that the experts in the policy-planning network built on this corporate experience in designing their proposals.

When it came to private old-age pensions, corporate leaders always saw them as having two main purposes, which varied in their importance from era to era depending on circumstances. Starting with a program put into place in 1875 by American Express, whose employees handled freight from railroad cars as well as securities and currency, old-age pensions were seen as a way to replace superannuated workers with more productive younger workers. However, after the strikes and property destruction by railroad workers in 1877, the promise of old-age pensions for loyal employees came to be regarded by a few companies as a potential way to quell labor unrest, although death benefits, accident insurance, and unemployment compensation were seen as more important in this regard (Graebner 1980; Sass 1997). By 1900 the Pennsylvania Railroad, the third-largest railroad in the country at the time, had a full-fledged pension plan for all employees at age seventy.

Workmen's Compensation

The first push for government social insurance for private-sector workers, primarily on a state-by-state basis and always based on what were considered to be sound business principles that would appeal to the moderate conservatives in the National Civic Federation, came from the American Association for Labor Legislation (AALL), discussed in Chapter 1. As we noted in that chapter, the more liberal members of the organization advocated insurance for accidents, health, unemployment, and old age, but almost all companies resisted government unemployment and old-age insurance, and physicians and insurance companies opposed health insurance (Moss 1996). However, the AALL did enjoy success on one insurance issue, workmen's compensation, because industrial accidents were a major personal tragedy for tens of thousands of workers and a costly and disruptive problem for American industry. The result was worker discontent and numerous individual liability lawsuits in which juries found against the companies and awarded expensive settlements to injured workers. As corporations lost more and more lawsuits, they became open to new alternatives.

In an effort to provide accident insurance for workers in a way that would be acceptable to employers, the AALL developed a plan that was structured to induce companies to reduce their rate of accidents in exchange for lower insurance payments. Just a year after the AALL began its campaign in 1906, which consisted of sending its model legislation to business executives, labor leaders, academic experts, and government officials, the members of the National Civic Federation decided to support the AALL initiative as a way to reduce uncertainty and expenses; some corporate chieftains also argued that workmen's compensation might help reduce agitation for unions as well because the high accident rate was such a contentious issue (Weinstein 1968, Chapter 2).

By 1910 most members of the National Association of Manufacturers (NAM) also favored workmen's compensation as a legal right, but they did not want to pay taxes for a plan administered by state governments. They therefore urged private insurance companies to develop commercial plans, which led to a trip to England by insurance experts and NAM representatives to study European precedents (Klein 2003; Sass 1997). The result was a rival proposal for legally enforceable mandates that would stipulate that companies had to provide their employees with private accident compensation insurance. This approach also came to be preferred by many members of the National Civic Federation, reflecting once again their inclination toward as little government involvement in their affairs as possible.

The original reaction by Samuel Gompers and other AFL leaders to the AALL's model legislation had been to oppose any form of social insurance that involved the government because of their strong belief that the domination of government by business would lead to unsatisfactory programs. Instead, labor leaders preferred to continue to take their chances in individual court cases. By 1908, however, they had been persuaded by their corporate counterparts in the NCF to support insurance on this specific issue. But then they reacted negatively to the NAM push for the involvement of private insurance companies, as did many reformers and all members of the rising and highly visible Socialist Party of the pre–World War I era. The result was two rival camps that were pushing for two different approaches to government-mandated accident insurance programs. The AALL, NCF, and NAM were on one side and organized labor, liberal reformers, and the Socialist Party were on the other. When the AALL, NCF, and NAM campaign for legislation began in 1910 and 1911, the battles primarily centered around the disagreement over government versus commercial insurance, although there were also arguments concerning compensation rates, breadth of coverage, and other particularistic but vital issues. In the end, corporate executives usually held firm for private insurance and conceded higher payout rates in exchange, generally above 50 percent of a week's pay, a compromise that organized labor and their liberal and Socialist Party allies reluctantly accepted. By 1920, only six states, all in the South, lacked workmen's compensation laws (Fishback and Kantor 2000; Weinstein 1968).

Over and beyond the immediate impacts of this legislation for the tens of thousands of workers injured each year, the battle over accident insurance had two long-lasting effects that influenced debates about social insurance during the New Deal. First, success on workmen's compensation reinforced John R. Commons and his AALL colleagues in their belief that the use of sound business principles and the right incentives might convince corporations to drop their opposition to unemployment compensation. As a result, the AALL developed a company-specific unemployment insurance plan that was structured to encourage companies to minimize layoffs for their workers through better anticipation of market fluctuations and more careful planning of production schedules. Under this plan, lower layoff rates would lead to lower payments into the unemployment insurance fund. And once again, legislation would be passed by individual states.

Later experience revealed there was no chance that individual companies could have any effect on a systemic problem such as unemployment. For that reason the AALL emphasis on company layoff rates, individual company accounts, and state-level legislation became major points of conflict when other experts within the policy-planning network came to believe that a federal system with uniform tax rates was necessary. But what we want to underscore here is that the long policy battle on unemployment insurance we are about to discuss was between rival business-oriented plans, which is fundamentally an argument about how much government involvement could be forced on the well-organized ultraconservatives in the corporate community and the Southern Democrats. Put another way, these battles do not have the implications about the decline of business power during the New Deal that historical institutionalists attach to them.

Second, the outcome of the legislative conflicts over workmen's compensation insurance convinced insurance companies that they might be able to underwrite other forms of group social insurance, starting with group life insurance programs and maybe old-age pensions as well. Two of the three largest insurance companies, Equitable Life and Metropolitan Life, which had many directors in common with major banks and corporations, began making the analyses necessary to offer such packages to corporations as a way to head off government insurance programs. Both of them also came to believe they could do a better job than individual corporations with private pensions if contributions were made by both the companies and their employees (Klein 2003; Sass 1997). (Plans that mandated contributions by both the company and its employees are called "contributory" plans.)

The gradual move toward actuarial soundness for old-age pensions received a boost in 1918 from the president of the Carnegie Foundation for the Advancement of Teaching. He put the foundation's program for pensions for university professors on a better footing by founding the Teachers Insurance and Annuity Association, a life insurance company, which then fashioned the first fully insured pension system (Sass 1997, p. 65). At this point the experience of the insurance companies and the Carnegie Foundation for the Advancement of Teaching also began to have an influence on pension programs for government officials, as seen in the pension program designed for federal civil service employees in 1920 by the Institute of Government Relations, which was mentioned in Chapter 1 as one of the forerunners of The Brookings Institution (Graebner 1980, pp. 77, 87; Saunders 1966, p. 25). In other words, by 1920 large corporations and an organization in the policy-planning network, the Carnegie Foundation for the Advancement of Teaching, were shaping government insurance programs on the basis of their own principles and experience. Any influence from past government pension plans had been swept aside by this point.

During the 1920s the group insurance plans provided coverage for only a small percentage of the elderly who had pensions in the United States. Most people bought old-age insurance from actuarially unsound plans sponsored by fraternal organizations, ethnic lodges, or trade unions, but by the end of the 1920s almost all of those plans had failed. As a consequence of these failures, there was a gradual movement toward support for government pensions by organizations such as the Fraternal Order of Eagles and some local and state union federations, using plans drawn up for them by the AALL. They were joined in these efforts by a new left-oriented reform group in 1925, the American Association for Old Age Security, which advocated comprehensive social insurance at the state level paid for by general taxes, thereby directly challenging the AALL approach (Loetta 1975). In the late 1920s and early 1930s, as many as twenty-five states passed legislation allowing for old-age pensions, usually without any state funding and at the option of individual counties. As a result, few people received a pension, and the benefits were meager if they did so. These efforts are sometimes credited with preparing public opinion for what came later, but we think that is a very generous assessment, a manifestation of the general desire in the United States—and mainstream academia—to assume that public opinion matters unless proven otherwise (Domhoff 2010, Chapter 5, for an explanation of why public opinion often can be ignored in formulating new government policies).

As for plans for unemployment insurance, which continued to be based on the AALL's emphasis on encouraging employers to prevent unemployment with an incentive-based insurance plan, they went nowhere in the 1920s (Nelson 1969, Chapter 6). Most unions ignored plans for government unemployment insurance and tended to favor the company-oriented incentive plans offered by the AALL and corporate moderates. One of the few exceptions involved the pragmatic leftists in the clothing industry, who combined the ethnic solidarity of the immigrant workers—primarily Italian and Jewish Americans—with a socialist ideology to push for programs to which companies and workers both contributed (Nelson 1969, Chapter 6).

Individual Corporation and Insurance Company Plans

Despite these grassroots and leftist efforts, the major developments of the 1920s, the ones that had an impact on the Social Security Act, were being made by the individual corporations that had pension plans of their own and by the insurance companies that made their group programs more sound and less expensive by having both employers and employees contribute. This is the point that was missed by the historical institutionalists who examined the literature on social security in the 1980s, as shown by the later work of historians and economic historians (Klein 2003; Sass 1997). By 1923, Metropolitan Life was confident that it had a group pension plan that was better than anything any one corporation could offer on an equally sound basis. One of its main spokespersons therefore eagerly presented the new plan to the corporate executives that his company invited to a special conference. However, even though he presented evidence that most corporate plans were unsound, the biggest corporations of the era were not prepared to abandon their own plans, which they still believed to be helpful in controlling their workforces and limiting strikes. (For example, some corporate plans had clauses saying the pension could be lost if the individual participated in a strike.) The corporate leaders present also liked the fact that they had complete control over the plans and did not legally have to pay benefits if they decided not to do so.

When an executive from Otis Elevator frankly told the Metropolitan Life speaker that the circumstances of each corporation varied too greatly to go along with what the insurance companies had to offer, the insurance representative argued back. His reply led to a sharp rebuke by none other than Clarence Hicks of Standard Oil, who put an end to the discussion with these words:

> It is impossible and impracticable. For twenty years the [Standard Oil] company has been experimenting on plans. I do not know why it becomes suitable at this time to stop experimenting. If we had done this a week ago, we would not have had the benefit of what we did today (Sass 1997, p. 72)

When Hicks concluded his remarks, the executive from Otis Elevator made a motion to end the meeting and offered Metropolitan Life a "hearty thanks," which led to immediate adjournment (Sass 1997, p. 72).

But in fact the individual company plans did not help with control of the workforce, and they were not actuarially sound. Shortly after the Metropolitan Life conference, for example, a meat packing company went bankrupt, sold its assets, and left its four hundred retirees with fourteen months of benefits (Sass 1997, p. 57). So it was not long before the Metropolitan Life plan became more attractive to smaller companies, especially when it packaged group old-age pensions with life, health, or disability insurance.

IRC Research

It was at this juncture that the recently incorporated Industrial Relations Counselors, Inc., decided to pay more serious attention to company-level old-age pension and unemployment compensation plans to see if they needed to be reorganized. This new emphasis was signaled by the employment of two very-well-trained independent experts on these issues, Murray Latimer and Bryce Stewart, who ended up at the center of the legislative drafting for the Social Security Act in 1934. Latimer, a twenty-five-year-old instructor in finance at the Harvard Business School at the time he was hired in 1926, was born and educated in Clinton, Mississippi, where his father had an automobile dealership, and received an M.B.A. degree at Harvard in 1923 before joining the faculty. During his years at IRC he helped to establish new pension plans at Standard Oil of New Jersey as well as three other Rockefeller oil companies and an independent steel company, American Rolling Mill. His 1932 book for IRC, *Industrial Pension Systems in the United States and Canada*, was well known and respected at the time, and is still frequently cited in historical accounts (Klein 2003; Orloff 1993; Sass 1997). Latimer also did a study of union plans for the American Federation of Labor in 1928–1929, shortly before the stock market crash, concluding that "the experiments are far from having reached a sound basis and that unless drastic financial reorganization is made they are almost certain to end in failure in the relatively near future" (Klein 2003, pp. 56–57).

Stewart, forty-four years old when he joined the IRC staff in 1927, was a Canadian with many years of experience working with employment and labor issues. A graduate of Queens University in Kingston, Ontario, he earned a Ph.D. degree at Columbia University and worked as a researcher, chief statistician, and editor for the Canadian Department of Labor, and then as an organizer and director of the Employment Service of Canada (Kelly 1987). Most interesting of all in terms of our emphasis on the relative openness of moderate conservatives in the corporate community on unemployment and pension issues, Stewart came back to the United States in 1922 to develop and administer an employment exchange for the Amalgamated Clothing Workers in Chicago, which was later supplemented by an unemployment insurance fund. Created at the insistence of Sidney Hillman, the union leader who figured so prominently in Chapter 3, the employment exchange and the insurance fund were jointly financed by labor and management but controlled by the union. Stewart (1925) wrote an article for the *International Labor Review* about this "American experiment." After joining the IRC staff, he became its director of research in 1930 and held that position until his retirement in 1952, except for a return to Canada as deputy minister of labor during World War II. Like Latimer, he was well known in the early 1930s for his publications on social insurance (Stewart 1928, 1930).

Latimer and Stewart were often joined in their efforts by economist J. Douglas Brown, the director of the Rockefeller-financed Industrial Relations Section of the Department of Economics at Princeton. The son of an industrial executive in Somerville, New Jersey, Brown received his B.A. and Ph.D. degrees at Princeton and taught for a year in the industrial relations program at the Wharton School at the University of Pennsylvania before returning to Princeton as a professor. Brown also worked closely with Hicks and later helped him write his autobiography, which is highly critical of the National Labor Relations Act while praising the Social Security Act (Hicks 1941, pp. 163–167). He also met with and sent reports to John D. Rockefeller III, who oversaw IRC for his father in the late 1920s and early 1930s before turning his full attention to philanthropic endeavors. One of Brown's tasks was to talk with corporate executives around the country and make periodic reports to Hicks and Rockefeller III. Brown also hosted an annual industrial relations conference at Princeton in conjunction with Hicks, Edward Cowdrick, and the IRC staff.

Cowdrick's pamphlet, written for the American Management Association in 1928, best exemplifies the pre-Depression thinking about company pensions within the Rockefeller circle and other corporate moderate organizations in the policy-planning network. According to this detailed analysis, which contains discussions of the moral, economic, and technical issues involved in industrial pensions, a pension is part of a good personnel program. Especially in the case of corporations that have been around for many years, a pension is "a means, at once humane and approved by public opinion, of purging its active payroll of men who, by reason of age or disability, have become liabilities rather than assets" (Cowdrick 1928, p. 10). Pensions also provide the "opportunity to promote their younger subordinates" (p. 11). Cowdrick concluded with the prediction that industrial pensions will be "increasingly valuable to employers" (p. 21).

IRC undertook its first consulting for a government agency in 1928 when Frances Perkins, recently appointed by Governor Franklin D. Roosevelt as

New York's industrial commissioner, established the Advisory Committee on Employment Problems "to effect some improvement in the State Employment Service" (Perkins 1930). Very striking in terms of our emphasis on the policy-planning network, the legislation enabling the demonstration project called for private funding. After Perkins wrote Beardsley Ruml, the director of the Spelman Fund, that "[a]lready one of the large foundations has indicated its willingness to subscribe funds for the support of this project," she asked him "if the Spelman Fund of New York would grant an annual appropriation of $25,000 for a period of three to five years," which was one-third of the estimated annual expenses (Perkins 1930).

It was in this context that Arthur H. Young became the chair of Perkins's advisory committee. As mentioned in earlier chapters, Young was the director of IRC before he became the outspoken anti-union vice president for industrial relations at U.S. Steel. His report to Perkins recommended that demonstration projects be developed to test the effectiveness of public employment centers. The recommendation led to a demonstration project in Rochester in 1931 that was based on a grant of $75,000 over a three-year period by one of the Rockefeller philanthropies. Stewart was put in charge of the project as chair of the Committee on Demonstration, through which he came to know Perkins. The Rochester project also brought Stewart into contact with a transplanted Southerner, Marion Folsom, the assistant treasurer of Eastman Kodak, who had taken a leadership role since the early 1920s in experimenting with forms of unemployment insurance, with the approval and support of the company president (Jacoby 1993; 1997, pp. 206–220). During the same year Stewart also worked for a three-person federal government study group on unemployment that included Senator Wagner as one of its members (Huthmacher 1968, p. 83). Clearly, then, IRC and the Spelman Fund had developed close connections with the liberals who would shape the New Deal on social insurance issues well before the 1932 presidential elections.

Although corporate moderates had a strong interest in old-age pensions and unemployment compensation plans, there was no desire on the part of either corporate executives or IRC employees to move toward government social insurance, a point demonstrated in a report by the National Industrial Conference Board in 1931. On the basis of work by IRC employees and a survey of a large number of industrial executives, *Elements of Industrial Pension Plans* concluded that pension plans were becoming more important in the minds of industrialists and urged that the plans be made actuarially sound, in part through having employees contribute to them. No longer was there any mention of the usefulness of these plans in controlling employees. Now the emphasis was on staving off government plans by demonstrating that industry can "take care of its worn-out workers through pension plans resting on voluntary initiative and cooperation" (National Industrial Conference Board 1931, p. vi). Even more frankly:

> In proportion as such plans are established and become successful there is thus effected a reduction in the number of dependent aged that must be taken care of by society or the state. The extension throughout the field of industry of pension plans adequate in their provisions, equitably administered, and soundly financed will do much toward removing any real need or excuse for resort to the dubious expedient of state pensions (National Industrial Conference Board 1931, p. vi).

At the same time that the insurance companies and IRC were shoring up company pension plans, IRC employees also became involved in the growing problem of unemployment. Although most members of the Rockefeller group had accepted the cautious and optimistic approach to dealing with the Depression that Hoover insisted upon—indeed, as noted in Chapter 1, Teagle served as chair of Hoover's Share-the-Work Program—they nonetheless began to take new initiatives. Very quickly, the Rockefeller Foundation came to the fore as the center of Rockefeller efforts to help combat the growing Depression. The Rockefeller Foundation's first step in this new direction was the creation of the Economic Stabilization Program in early 1930, a framework used to fund a variety of initiatives over the next three years. The second step was to tell the Social Science Research Council (SSRC) there would be no further grants for general academic research; only socially useful applied research would be supported from that point onward. We find this decision to be another telling commentary on the limited power of experts when they do not have immediate relevance in a time of economic crisis.

Shortly thereafter, in February, the SSRC created a committee to consider unemployment. Arthur Woods, the Rockefeller employee who was also a friend of Hoover's, chaired it; his vice chair was Joseph Willits from the Wharton School and the SSRC (Fisher 1993, p. 122). Stewart of IRC was a member, as were two other men who figured later in the creation of the Social Security Act: William Leiserson, a Wisconsin-trained economist, well-known labor mediator, and a professor at Antioch College; and Morris Leeds, the corporate moderate and AALL director mentioned in Chapter 1 as the president of Leeds & Northrup.

Hoover's Emergency Committee

By October 1930, Hoover was becoming less certain that prosperity was just around the corner, so he appointed the President's Emergency Committee on Employment, drawing heavily on the policy-planning network. In spite of his concerns, Hoover was at the same time fearful that such a committee might contribute to an atmosphere of pessimism and a call for greater involvement by the federal government in creating employment. He therefore stressed the temporary nature of the committee and limited its options to voluntary efforts at the state and local levels. He chose his friend Woods as the chair, who then dovetailed the work of the emergency committee with that of the SSRC committee he also chaired (Fisher 1993, p. 122). Joining Woods on the thirty-three-person presidential committee were ten business leaders and eight experts from the policy-planning network, including Ruml, Willits, Stewart, and Brown from the network of Rockefeller-supported experts. In addition, the Rockefeller Foundation gave the committee $50,000 in 1930 and $75,000 in 1931 to help with its work. Ruml's Spelman Fund provided an additional $25,000 in 1931.

The committee's experts drafted a proposed message to Congress for Hoover that presaged what the New Deal would eventually do, calling for "a public works program, including slum clearance, low-cost housing, and rural electrification" (Schlesinger 1957, p. 170). They recommended speeding up a large program of highway construction. They also advocated a national employment service, but there was no mention of unemployment insurance. These suggestions were resisted by Hoover, however. When Woods asked Hoover to start an emergency program in the near-starvation conditions of Appalachia, he was sent to the Red Cross, which refused to help because the problem was not due to a natural disaster such as a flood or drought. At that point the Rockefeller philanthropies provided money to charitable and community groups for the Appalachian relief effort (Bernstein 1960, p. 301).

Woods later removed most hints of the considerable tensions between Hoover and the committee from the historical account of the committee's efforts, leading to a long delay in the appearance of the book. As one of Woods's aides later wrote to a key Rockefeller lawyer, "Colonel Woods was somewhat doubtful as to the wisdom of publishing the report in exactly the form as first prepared by Mr. Hayes, since it went into considerable detail as to certain differences of view which arose between the Committee and President Hoover" (Eden 1936). Willits was assigned the task of making the manuscript revisions. We think these conflicts highlight the difference between anti-government ideological purists such as Hoover and the more pragmatic approach of the moderate conservatives within the corporate community. The libertarian strain that exists in the rightist community is not always useful to corporate leaders.

Despite the obvious failure of the emergency employment committee, it had longer-term research consequences, although they were not at first apparent. It did so through its supplemental Advisory Committee on Unemployment Statistics chaired by Willits, with Stewart as its technical advisor. The committee sent out questionnaires to businesses and government agencies all over the country; its main finding was the inadequacy of unemployment figures and the impossibility of determining the number of people needing direct relief (Hayes 1936, p. 29). This finding supported later SSRC efforts to develop better data-gathering capabilities under governmental auspices.

The work by Hoover's emergency committee also led to research collaboration between IRC and the Economic Stabilization Research Institute at the University of Minnesota on a pilot program on the usefulness of employment centers. The Rockefeller Foundation's Economic Stabilization Program awarded a two-year grant for $150,000 to carry out the research, which was supplemented by smaller grants from the Carnegie Corporation and the Spelman Fund. One of the outcomes of this collaboration was a book presenting a plan for unemployment insurance, written by Stewart in conjunction with three University of Minnesota employees. The first of these three co-authors, economist Alvin Hansen, who later had a staff role in the formulation of the Social Security Act, was soon to be appointed a professor at Harvard, where he became persuaded of the correctness of Keynesian theory in 1937. The second, Merrill Murray, trained in economics at Wisconsin and previously employed by the Wisconsin Industrial Commission, was in charge of the actual field study and took part in an unsuccessful campaign to pass an unemployment insurance bill in the state. Four years later he joined with Stewart in writing a draft of the unemployment insurance provisions of the Social Security Act. The third co-author, Russell Stevenson, the dean of the School of Business Administration at the University of Minnesota, had no further role in the events we recount in this chapter.

Although this multi-authored book is only of historical interest now, its preface has a noteworthy comment that highlights the way in which research carried out in the policy-planning network helps to bring about a new consensus. Hansen, Murray, and Stevenson reported that they had come to doubt the usefulness of the AALL plan to create incentives that presumably would induce businessmen to reduce unemployment. Now they favored a national-level rather than a state-level plan, crediting Stewart for their change of view: "Many of the modifications in the original plan are the result of the research and thought brought to bear upon the subject by Bryce M. Stewart of the Industrial Relations Counselors, Inc., and his staff" (Hansen, Murray, Stevenson, and Stewart 1934, p. v).

THE INFLUENCE OF THE POLICY-PLANNING NETWORK

Throughout 1931 the Rockefeller Foundation's Economic Stabilization Program made a series of grants to IRC, drawing what had been a business-oriented consulting group further into the policy arena. The first, for $30,000, provided at Woods's request, paid for a study of unemployment insurance plans in Great Britain. The second, for $16,000, supported a study of the administration of employment offices, supplemented a year later with $7,500 to support IRC's role in the demonstration projects on employment offices in Rochester and Minneapolis. Another $16,000 made possible a study of employment offices in Europe. Finally, IRC received $10,000 to help it set up the New York State Employment Service, which brought it into collaboration with Perkins once again. In short, IRC was on its way to developing unique expertise on the administration of employment offices and on unemployment insurance.

Even with this increased support from the Rockefeller Foundation, the great bulk of IRC's funding continued to come directly from Rockefeller himself, who was still kept informed of its activities by John D. Rockefeller III, Hicks, and Raymond Fosdick. A letter from Fosdick to Rockefeller in early 1933 expresses the high regard Rockefeller's most trusted advisor on domestic policy had for work by IRC:

> As to the value of the work of this organization I cannot speak too highly. In reviewing the current year's work, I would mention the completion of our series of reports on Unemployment Insurance, which are everywhere acclaimed as authoritative and timely, and the publication of the report on Industrial Pension Systems (Fosdick 1933).

Fosdick also notes that the quality and visibility of the work of IRC "has led to engagement of our staff by the Wisconsin Industrial Commission and the Minnesota Employment Stabilization Research Institute to assist in shaping and administering legislation." But he does not neglect what IRC was doing to stabilize company pension funds by switching them to contributory plans:

> There is much concern over the problem of funding of pensions plans just now, and in the last two years we have directly aided the New York Transit Co., National Transit Co., Buckeye, Northern, Indiana, Cumberland, Eureka, Southern and South West Pennsylvania Pipe Line Companies, Standard Oil Company of Ohio, Solar Refining Co., Ohio Oil Co. and other clients in revising and refunding their plans on a sound basis, in nearly all cases securing adoption of a plan providing for assumption of part of the cost by the employees, and other desirable and conservative provisions that have aggregated several millions of dollars in savings to those companies as well as affording greater security to the employees. This work has required intimate consideration of the financial status of the companies and on several occasions has permitted us to make suggestions of general management and economic value which I believe Mr. Debevoise [Rockefeller's lawyer for business matters and a close friend] or Mr. Cutler [a personal Rockefeller employee who was a director of Metropolitan Life] could attest (Fosdick 1933).

Fosdick's mention of concern about pensions reflected a new reality that now faced corporations: by 1932 the ongoing Depression was starting to take its toll on even the best of the company plans. More workers were reaching retirement age and retirees were living longer at a time when corporate profits had been flat or declining for three straight years. In addition, low interest rates meant that the investments by corporate pension funds were not generating the cash flow that was needed to pay current monthly obligations. As economic historian Steven Sass (1997, p. 88) concludes, "The Great Depression of the 1930s sent a massive shock wave through the nation's fragile private pension system." This was especially the case for the railroads, which had an older workforce than that of many industries, on top of unsound pension plans. Even the switch to contributory plans over the previous three years had not been enough to save the railroad pension plans. But it was not just corporate plans that were in trouble: the handful of small pension plans controlled by the AFL and other unions also began to suffer, as Latimer had predicted they would even before the Depression began.

As the Depression deepened and Roosevelt took office in March 1933, the Rockefeller Foundation created the Special Trustee Committee to administer emergency funds of up to one million dollars in an expeditious manner (to keep things in perspective, that's $16.5 million in 2010 dollars). The committee consisted of Rockefeller, Fosdick, and Walter Stewart, an investment banker (no relation to Bryce Stewart) who served as a trustee of the Rockefeller Foundation. In addition, Woods and other advisors were sometimes present for the committee's deliberations. The largest of ten projects for that year was $100,000 for work by the SSRC's Committee on Governmental Statistics and Information Services, which followed up on concerns expressed by Willits, Stewart, and others about the dismal state of government statistics. This project, the largest undertaken by the SSRC to that date, led to the creation of a new Central Statistics Board for the federal government, the first small exercise in state building on social insurance at the national level by the policy-planning network (Fisher 1993, pp. 128–129). Then, too, the foundation gave $5,000 to the SSRC's Committee on Unemployment for a study of unemployment reserves by Bryce Stewart.

Members of IRC contributed their first direct official service to the New Deal in 1933 when Stewart became chair of a committee to advise Perkins on selecting the members for her Advisory Committee to the Department of Labor. He also served as a member of the Advisory Council of the United States Employment Service and chaired its Committee on Research (Stewart 1933). At the same time, Latimer provided the Department of Commerce with estimates on the amount of pension income that was being paid out in the country and then became a member of the Advisory Committee of the Department of Labor, where he spent part of his summer months assisting "in the revision of the employment and payroll indexes and in making studies which would lead ultimately to the revision of the price indexes" (Latimer 1933).

As this mundane statistical work was grinding along, a grassroots effort by the railroad workers in craft unions, which had been building since 1929, began to pick up momentum. It did so in good part because the railroad owners announced they would be making 10 percent cuts in both salaries and pensions. In a context in which at least 84 percent of railroad workers had been covered by pension plans since the early 1920s, and with young workers backing the older workers so they could move into the senior jobs, the rank-and-file organized on their own because of the lack of interest in government pensions on the part of their union leaders (Latimer and Hawkins 1938; Klein 2003; Sass 1997). In 1931 and 1932, the railroad workers' independent actions—organized as the Railway Employees National Pension Association, which was outside the confines of their union leadership—generated enough support among workers in the face of the impending pension crisis in the railroad industry to convince Senator Henry D. Hatfield, a one-term Republican Senator from West Virginia, to introduce legislation in 1932 that ended up having a major impact on corporate thinking about government pensions.

A physician who was a staunch supporter of unions and a former governor of his home state, Hatfield had a special sympathy for railroad workers because he had worked for eighteen years as a surgeon for the Norfolk and Western Railroad. Significantly, the legislation he introduced, written for the most part by the Railway Employees National Pension Association, called for contributions by workers and employers as well as an option for early retirement and generous benefits. This legislation grabbed the attention of the railroad union leaders. "As pension agitation mounted," concludes sociologist Jill Quadagno (1988, p. 73), "labor leaders began to recognize that their indifference to the pension issue was alienating them from the rank and file, and in the same year they succeeded in inducing Senator Robert Wagner to introduce an alternative proposal." The liberal Hatfield version and more cautious Wagner version were eventually reconciled, and Congress passed the Wagner-Hatfield bill in 1933 despite strong opposition from railroad executives, (Huthmacher 1968, p. 177; see also Graebner 1980, pp. 171–176).

Although the federal coordinator of transportation advised Roosevelt to sign the legislation because "it is in line with sound social policy," he added that he would have preferred to wait in order to improve it (Latham 1959, p. 160). One of the problems he worried about was the actuarial soundness of the plan. This concern caused him to bring Stewart, Latimer, and Brown to Washington in late 1933 as members of the Employment Advisory Council, which would design the new social insurance system for railroad workers. As Brown tells the story:

> The group of us that went down [to Washington] on that centered very much on Industrial Relations Counselors, in New York. . . . So Latimer and I began working on the old-age protection of railroad workers. We put Hawkins [a student of Brown's] to work on the dismissal compensation. Bryce Stewart worked on the unemployment insurance" (Brown 1965, p. 6).

Latimer, Stewart, and Brown lacked the information needed for the actuarial studies on which to base a sound program, and they did not have an army of clerks at their disposal to develop the information. They therefore applied for a $300,000 grant from the recently established Civilian Works Administration and then hired laid-off railroad clerks who had dealt with the relevant employment records for their respective companies—1,500 people ended up collecting records on 400,000 employees and 110,000 pensioners. The threesome also hired a staff of 500 in New York to analyze the data (Brown 1965, pp. 8–9; Latimer and Hawkins 1938, p. 111). The result was a new set of records within the space of a few months, which proves how rapidly government capacity can be created when there is the desire to create it.

Latimer, Stewart, and Brown then crafted a plan that was satisfactory to all concerned even though the benefit levels were lower than those originally proposed, due to the fact that the study discovered the original actuarial assumptions were unsound (Latimer and Hawkins 1938, pp. 123–127). Employers were pleased because they were relieved of the cost of private pensions and their tax rates were lower. Railroad workers accepted the plan because the pensions were satisfactory—in fact, much higher than those later established for the Social Security Act—and there were disability and survivor benefits as well (Latimer and Hawkins 1938, p. 274). In the end the Railroad Retirement Act was a victory for all those who were willing to allow the government to play a role in providing social insurance. Because of this work Latimer was appointed chairman of the three-person Railroad Retirement Board in the summer of 1934.

Strikingly, the railroad workers' success did not lead to similar efforts by other workers, which Quadagno (1988, p. 74) attributes to the division of American workers along craft lines. This lack of involvement by other unions supports our contention that pressures from organized labor in general had very little to do with the development of the Social Security Act over the next two years. However, the lessons from this successful effort were not lost on Latimer, Stewart, and Brown. They began to understand the possibilities for using the group insurance policies developed by the private insurance companies, with whom they were always in close contact, as a model for government insurance plans. They realized they could package old-age pensions and unemployment compensation in a way that would be compatible with the major concerns of corporate leaders. They also realized that such plans would be far less expensive for corporations than having their own programs, some of which were on increasingly shaky grounds in any case. From this point forward they worked to convince corporate executives, fellow experts, liberal reformers, and social workers of the soundness of their ideas. Their efforts are a textbook example of how experts function in the United States, which contradicts the historical institutionalists' emphasis on independent experts as well as anything could, while at the same time showing there is originality and complexity built into their role.

The large amount of time being spent in government service by IRC employees led to another series of grants from the Rockefeller Foundation to IRC beginning in January 1934. The first grant request, titled "Grant from Rockefeller Foundation to Cover Expense of Cooperation with Government Agencies," captures much of the argument we have been making for the growing importance of IRC in the policymaking process. The grant request, written by Young, also relates to the issue closest to the hearts of historical institutional theorists, state-building. It begins by noting "increasing inroads have been made on our time by such agencies as the New York State Advisory Council on Employment Problems, the Labor Statistics Committee of the American Statistical Association and the Social Science Research Council" (Young 1933, p. 1).

The proposal then outlines the many governmental and SSRC tasks undertaken by Stewart and Latimer, including work on the railroad retirement program, and in addition reports that another employee had been serving full time as the assistant director of the United States Employment Service for the previous six months. Young then listed his own government involvements "as a member of the Federal Advisory Council of the United States Employment Service, as a member of the Executive Committee, and chairman of the Committee on Veterans' Placement Service and, since June as a special representative of the United States Department of Labor, actively assisting the Director of the United States Employment Service in the organization and administration of the National Reemployment Service" (Young 1933, p. 2).

All of this service, the grant proposal continues, was voluntary, and it had been costing IRC money in both salary expenses and lost opportunities to do paid consulting work for businesses. The proposal concludes with a request for "an emergency appropriation of twenty-five thousand dollars," which was granted by the foundation shortly thereafter (Young 1933, p. 3). Similar supplemental grants were approved for $10,000 in June 1935 and $6,000 in February 1936. Even when Latimer began to be paid by the government, he stayed on the IRC payroll and turned over his government salary to the organization, which is one reason why the Rockefeller Foundation grants for 1935 and 1936 could be smaller (Latimer 1934).

We think this series of grants has theoretical implications that are even more profound than the formulation of the domestic allotment plan or the creation of the first National Labor Board in 1933 by corporate moderates. In effect, the Rockefeller Foundation became part of the government by paying the salaries of men who were de facto state employees. The foundation thereby provided the capacity to build new processes and agencies into the government through the expertise of a private consulting firm, Industrial Relations Counselors, Inc. Contrary to the conclusions of historical institutionalists, the American federal government did not build its own capacity, and those who administered it were not independent of the corporate community and its closely affiliated policy-planning network.

By November 1933, the experts in the policy-planning network who had been working on social insurance for nearly four years felt confident enough with what they had accomplished to bring it to the attention of experts just outside their circles. They did so through a small conference in Washington under the auspices of the SSRC. Meredith Givens, an economist trained by Commons at the University of Wisconsin, who had been a member of the research staff at the National Bureau of Economic Research since 1928, made the arrangements. Givens also became the executive secretary to the SSRC's Advisory Committee on Industry and Trade in 1929 and was the main force behind the successful effort to create the aforementioned Central Statistics Board within the government. In addition, he served as a staff member for the SSRC's Committee on Unemployment Insurance, often working with Stewart. His example, like those of Alvin Hansen and Merrill Murray in the case of the IRC and University of Minnesota collaboration, suggests that the line between the John R. Commons and Industrial Relations Counselors camps was not a hard and fast one.

Twenty-two people attended this conference, representing a wide range of social service organizations as well as government agencies related to social insurance and social provisioning. Fourteen of the twenty-two had served on an SSRC committee or were connected to the policy-planning network in some other way. Several were affiliated with the local-level policy-planning network created in good part by Rockefeller philanthropies and housed by the Public Administration Clearing House at the University of Chicago (Roberts 1994). The most prominent representative of the social service organizations was Edith Abbott, one of the most famous women reformers of the Progressive Era and since 1921 the dean of the School of Social Service Administration at the University of Chicago. The social welfare representatives also included the director of the Public Administration

Clearing House and leaders from the Institute of Public Administration and the American Association of Social Workers.

Perhaps the most important government official present was Harry Hopkins, the head of the Federal Emergency Relief Administration, whose career we overviewed in Chapter 1 (see Cohen 2009, Chapters 8 and 9, for more details on Hopkins). Arthur Altmeyer, Perkins's main assistant on social insurance issues, was second only to Hopkins. Yet another former Commons student, Altmeyer had been the executive secretary of the Wisconsin Industrial Commission for many years before joining the New Deal. Also present were John Dickinson, the assistant secretary of commerce, who had helped draft the National Industrial Recovery Act just a few months before; Isador Lubin, a former Brookings Institution employee who had been appointed by Perkins as the commissioner of labor statistics; and Mary Anderson, the director of the Women's Bureau in the Department of Labor, which had jurisdiction over the "mother's pensions" that would become known as "welfare payments" when they were enfolded into the new Social Security Act. (Anderson, who grew up in the working class, became involved in social reform through the outreach efforts of Jane Addams and Hull House [Anderson and Winslow 1951, p. 32].) There were also several experts present who worked closely with government agencies, starting with Wilson, the person who did so much to improve the domestic allotment plan after serving on the SSRC agricultural committee; Brown, the director of the Industrial Relations Section at Princeton, who had worked on the railroad retirement plan; and Frank Bane, head of the American Public Welfare Association, who had played a key role in the November 1932 conference in Chicago that established the principles for the new federal relief program, and by then was serving as an advisor to Hopkins.

The starting point for the discussions at the SSRC conference was a document prepared by Stewart listing the nature of the studies needed to understand several problems that had to be resolved to design a comprehensive social insurance program. It set the stage by noting that his earlier work, which focused strictly on issues of unemployment and relief, had soon led him to the realization that these issues were linked to many other questions. For example, they related to the inability to return to the workforce due to old age or physical or mental disabilities. Others involved the relation of government unemployment insurance to programs for vocational training and to government employment centers that had been established recently to aid job seekers. He added that it also would be necessary to explore the need for minimum wages to guard against any tendency by employers to reduce wage rates to help pay their unemployment insurance taxes.

In the case of old-age pensions, the draft plan embodied three basic principles that the corporate moderates insisted upon given several years of experience with private pension plans, especially in conjunction with the efforts of the major life insurance companies (Klein 2003). First, the level of benefits must be tied to salary level, thus preserving and reinforcing the values established in the labor market. Second, unlike the case in many countries, there would be no government contributions from general tax revenues, if at all possible. Instead, there would be a separate tax for old-age pensions, which would help to limit the size of benefits. Third, there had to be both employer and employee contributions to the system, which would limit the tax payments by the corporations.

Although the attendees were unanimous in encouraging the SSRC to move forward in refining its proposal, the liberals and reformers of that era, many of them social workers, did not give their approval without expressing their disagreements with what they called "the insurance crowd," which meant experts such as Latimer and Stewart. This difference flared up most prominently over the issue of funding old-age pensions, when Abbott stated her preference for "one welfare statute" that would be paid for out of general tax revenues and "available to all without stigmatizing qualifications" (see Linda Gordon 1994, p. 261 for Abbott's general views; see Witte 1963, pp. 15–16, for the fact of disagreement). Moreover, liberals and social workers did not like the idea of employee contributions to unemployment compensation because they agreed with labor leaders that unemployment was a failure of the economic system that should be paid for by its primary beneficiaries, the owners, perhaps with the help of general tax contributions. These differences of opinion suggest that Stewart and other insurance-oriented experts in the policy-planning network were not liberals in the eyes of the liberals of that era.

The same group of people then met for a second SSRC conference in early April 1934 to consider a second version of Stewart's proposal, this one co-authored with Givens. However, they did so under very different circumstances because Senator Wagner had introduced a new state-oriented unemployment insurance bill on February 5. He did so on behalf of the AALL reformers, who were being provided with ideas, advice, and encouragement from behind the scenes by Supreme Court Justice Louis Brandeis. Brandeis conveyed his policy ideas through a number of different people, the most important of whom was his daughter, Elizabeth Brandeis, who became a professor of economics at the University of Wisconsin in the late 1920s after studying with Commons. He also conferred with her husband, Paul Raushenbush, also an economist at Wisconsin, who was in charge of administering the state's unemployment insurance law passed in 1932, which included the AALL's incentive policy. Both Elizabeth Brandeis and Paul Raushenbush were leaders in the AALL and championed its basic principles.

Louis Brandeis also had an extensive network of legal and political contacts, especially among lawyers who had clerked for him or former Justice

Oliver Wendell Holmes (see, for example, Carter 1934, pp. 315–316). His most important confidant was Felix Frankfurter, a professor at Harvard Law School and an informal advisor to Roosevelt since working with him during World War I; Frankfurter was renowned for sending his students both to corporate law firms and to work for the New Deal (Irons 1982). One of those students, Thomas Corcoran, worked very closely with Roosevelt and served as a direct communication link between Brandeis and Roosevelt. In short, the AALL was not simply a group of academic experts by the time of the New Deal, but a part of the prestigious Brandeis-Frankfurter network rooted in the stature and resources of the Supreme Court, Harvard Law School, the University of Wisconsin, and the state government in Wisconsin, along with the financial help of a handful of well-to-do donors and corporate moderates.

In addition to the incentive provisions, the legislation introduced by Wagner included a new feature suggested by Brandeis that would apply strong pressure on states to create unemployment insurance plans. Called the "tax offset plan," it imposed a federal tax on employers to pay for federal unemployment insurance, but it would not be collected if they paid an equivalent tax to their state government. This was of course an incentive for state-oriented employers and elected officials to urge passage of an unemployment insurance plan in their states (Nelson 1969, p. 199).

Reformers to the left of the AALL, such as those involved in the American Association for Old Age Security, which had just changed its name to the American Association for Social Security, vowed to defeat the AALL-Wagner bill because it was so cautious. They also feared it would undercut their efforts toward more liberal programs in several states, which they thought had a good chance of legislative success. At the same time, most business groups were equally opposed to the AALL-Wagner bill for their own reasons. Nonetheless, Perkins urged Roosevelt to push for this legislation and held a conference on February 14–15 to drum up support for it. However, Roosevelt soon made clear in the midst of all the strong disagreement that he wanted a contributory unemployment compensation plan as part of a larger social insurance plan that included old-age pensions (Nelson 1969).

Within this context, Roosevelt invited Swope to the White House on March 8 (Swope was in Washington for a meeting of the BAC) for a long discussion of social insurance that may have had considerable impact on him. During their discussion Swope argued that it was feasible to have government social insurance for everyone that would begin at birth with a government life insurance policy that would require small payments from the parents; at age twenty both the individual and the employer would contribute (Loth 1958, p. 234). He also outlined plans for unemployment and old-age insurance that had been shown to be workable through the experience of private corporate plans, stressing the need for employee contributions. Although Swope thought that one-third from employees and two-thirds from employers would be sufficient, Roosevelt thought that the split should be fifty-fifty.

According to Swope in extensive interviews with his biographer, Roosevelt expressed enthusiasm for these ideas and asked for a detailed memo outlining a plan, which Swope sent him two weeks later (Loth 1958, p. 235). These plans later were seen as too ambitious by Roosevelt's other advisors, but at the very least the visit from Swope may have led Roosevelt to anticipate support for a comprehensive social insurance program from the corporate moderates on the BAC in the way that is stressed by Swenson's (2002, Chapters 9–10) expectations theory of why the Roosevelt Administration moved ahead with social insurance legislation despite the possible opposition of ultraconservatives in the corporate community. According to this view, political leaders often put forth plans that they have reason to believe will be accepted by groups that are initially hesitant or skeptical.

With the legislative disagreements in Congress swirling around it, in early April the SSRC-sponsored group gave its general approval to the evolving plan that had emerged from the combined IRC, Rockefeller Foundation, and SSRC efforts over the past several years. Stewart and Givens then revised their report to take into account concerns expressed at the meeting and to emphasize their support for a unified plan of the kind Roosevelt also was talking about. As they explained in a report to the SSRC: "In a draft report, revised following the April conference, the unified character of the task of planned protection was developed, and the several phases of relief and social insurance were considered in terms of (a) the problems of planning, administration, and coordination, (b) the present state of knowledge in each field, and (c) further work specifically required for the proper integration of each major segment into a unified program" (Stewart and Givens 1934b, p. 1).

Stewart and Givens sent Perkins and Hopkins copies of their conference report in an effort to reinforce the idea that general, not piecemeal, legislation was necessary. From their point of view, their efforts were successful in influencing the creation of the Cabinet-level Committee on Economic Security, as explained in the same SSRC report of November 16 that we just quoted. We find the following paragraph to be strong evidence that the experts within the policy-planning network were working closely with Perkins and Hopkins to shape the government's agenda:

> At the request of officials of the Department of Labor and the Federal Emergency Relief Administration, these materials were made informally available in the formulation of plans for a government inquiry. A draft plan for such an inquiry, developed upon the basis of the exploratory study, was placed in the hands of a Cabinet committee, and these plans have eventuated in the

establishment by Executive Order, June 29, 1934, of the Committee on Economic Security. Thus the original project became merged in a major planning venture at the Administration (Stewart and Givens 1934b, p. 1).

Once the Roosevelt initiative was announced, Stewart and Givens anticipated (on the basis of the liberal social workers' dissents at the two SSRC conferences and the strength of conservatives in Congress) that there might be aspects of the final legislation that would not be acceptable to corporate moderates. They therefore revised their earlier proposal for immediate research funds from the SSRC to make it a call for a large SSRC study that would begin after the shape of the final legislation became clear. They argued it was very unlikely that any new legislation would be thoroughly satisfactory, which meant that future SSRC studies would be important in influencing inevitable revisions in the program (Stewart and Givens 1934a, p. 1). Thus members of the policy-planning network were already preparing for likely amendments—and for shaping the administration of the Social Security Act—well before the plan was finalized and sent to Congress in early 1935 (compare with Fisher 1993).

As this brief history demonstrates beyond any doubts that might linger for historical institutionalists, experts from the policy-planning network were actively involved in developing plans for social insurance right up until the moment the governmental process began. They also had plans to draft amendments to the legislation if they thought changes would be necessary. Our next step is to determine whether or not they were involved in the drafting processes inside the government and, if so, whether they had any impact.

DRAFTING THE SOCIAL SECURITY ACT

Roosevelt announced the plan for a comprehensive study of a program for economic security on June 8, 1934. It would be conducted by a cabinet-level committee, the Committee on Economic Security (CES), chaired by Perkins and including Hopkins, who always was in attendance at its meetings, along with the secretary of agriculture, who sometimes sent Tugwell to represent him; the secretary of the treasury, who often sent one of his economic advisors; and the attorney general, who always sent an assistant who was instructed to vote with Perkins. The CES was assisted by what was called the "Technical Board," a group of twenty government-employed experts drawn from several different agencies (several of the "government" experts had been employees of foundations, think tanks, and universities until shortly before the process began). It also had the input of the Advisory Council on Economic Security, which was made up of twenty-three private citizens, including many prominent corporate moderates, labor leaders, and social welfare advocates. The business representatives included Swope of General

Electric, Teagle of Standard Oil, Leeds of Leeds & Northrup, Lewisohn of Miami Copper, and Folsom, by then the treasurer at Eastman Kodak, who had worked on unemployment insurance with Perkins and Stewart in upstate New York. (Although the president of Eastman Kodak supported Folsom in his efforts on behalf of the Social Security Act, he was an officer of the NAM and an opponent of the New Deal, which suggests the complexities of sorting out moderate conservatives and ultraconservatives in the corporate community (Jacoby 1997, p. 319, ftn. 64).) There were also five labor leaders, including the head of the AFL, but they attended few meetings and generally had very little impact except for one critical issue relating to unemployment insurance. There were also several public members who came from advocacy organizations that stretched back to the Progressive Era and the social service organizations housed at the Public Administration Clearing House (Chambers 1952, pp. 255–256; Witte 1963, pp. 49–53). In addition, the National Grange (a farm organization) and the Fraternal Order of Eagles, which had advocated for old-age pensions since the 1920s with an AALL model bill, were represented. The members of the advisory council were supposed to have a minimal role and serve in part as window dressing, but they nonetheless inserted themselves into the process with considerable vigor.

To do the necessary detail work, there was a research staff made up of experts brought in from IRC, the SSRC, other think tanks, and universities. It was the staff's job to draft the proposals to be discussed by the appropriate committees of the Technical Board and the Advisory Council on Economic Security before they were passed up the hierarchy to the CES (and Roosevelt from behind the scenes through his interactions with Perkins and Hopkins). Finally, there was an executive director to lead the staff and serve as secretary to the CES.

Significantly, the most visible reformers on this issue, who had worked for social insurance at the grassroots level for well over a decade and written several influential books, such as Abraham Epstein, the leader of the American Association for Social Security, and Isaac Rubinow, who had both a Ph.D. in economics and an M.D. degree, and made his living as an actuary, were not included in the formal process. Like the liberals and the social workers, they advocated protection for everyone without qualification and wanted to finance the program out of general taxes. But they were far less willing to compromise than were the social workers, who were part of the New Deal coalition through their many connections to Eleanor Roosevelt, Perkins, Anderson of the Women's Bureau, and several other government appointees.

Rubinow, Epstein, and their colleagues and followers made it clear that they would disagree with several of the basic premises of the corporate moderate-IRC approach, which would only slow down the drafting process.

In addition, it was feared that their involvement would serve as a red flag and rallying point for ultraconservative opponents in the corporate community and Congress. Their agitation, writing, and lobbying may have helped to create a more favorable climate for doing something about old-age pensions, and it was their phrase—"social security"—that came to designate what had been called "economic security," "social insurance," or "industrial pensions" up until that time (Klein 2003, pp. 78–80). Although they were briefly consulted when the process was well under way, they had no direct involvement in formulating the act, which led to many tensions among the supporters of Social Security.

On the basis of a strong recommendation from Altmeyer, Perkins offered the important position of staff director to Edwin Witte, who had studied with Commons at the University of Wisconsin and then was appointed the executive secretary of the Wisconsin Industrial Commission in 1917. In 1922 he became the chief of the Legislative Reference Library, a service for state legislators who needed help in writing their bills, and in 1933 he became a professor of economics at the University of Wisconsin, shortly before he was hired to direct the social security drafting process. He did collaborative work with Commons and wrote reports on labor law for him, but he respectfully disagreed with Commons and the AALL that incentives to encourage employers to reduce unemployment would have any impact (Nelson 1969). Once again, not all AALL members were of exactly the same mind.

Unknown to anyone at the time, Witte maintained a diary of the unfolding events to help him keep things straight in a complex situation. The diary became the basis for a memorandum he wrote in 1936 at the request of the SSRC's Public Administration Committee, which used it as part of its efforts to help shape the administration of the Social Security Act (Witte 1963, p. xi). Later the SSRC asked Witte if it could have his permission to publish his memorandum as a book, which appeared in 1963 and became the basis for just about every analysis of the origins of the Social Security Act since that time. It remains a valuable book, but it is too brief to tell the whole story in detail, which is one reason why accounts by historical institutionalists sometimes go astray.

With this background material on Witte and his book in mind, we can open our inquiry into the impact of the policy-planning network on the act itself with the fact that the structure and process for the program and much of its research agenda were developed by Altmeyer, Givens, and Stewart and were based on the report written after the second SSRC conference, as explained by Witte's biographer, Theron Schlabach (1969, p. 99). This conclusion, based on interviews and a statement in the CES files written by the three men for Roosevelt, is consistent with Stewart and Givens's (1934b) statement in their SSRC report that their proposals were made informally available to government officials. In addition, Witte (1963, pp. 15–16) notes that he made "some little use" of the research suggestions in this report "in outlining the fields to be covered by various members of the staff." Moreover, Stewart was put in charge of unemployment studies and Givens in charge of the study of employment opportunities (Witte 1963, pp. 13–14, 31). All in all, this is impressive preliminary evidence that the policy-planning network was an integral part of the governmental process.

To our unexpected good fortune, it is at this point that the IRC experts also began to provide inside information on the drafting process to industrial relations executives through the periodic IRC memorandums prepared for the organization's clients and the members of the Special Conference Committee. These memorandums give us a new window into the thinking of the corporate moderates on government social insurance that has never been utilized in detail. The first of them, for July 10, provided a thorough overview of how the drafting process would be carried out, concluding that "[i]t is patent that the Administration is determined to develop a program of social welfare to be presented at the next session of Congress, and that broad departures in the field of industrial relations may be anticipated" (Industrial Relations Counselors, Inc. 1934a, p. 2). Two paragraphs later it reminded its readers "to prepare for the advent of various forms of social insurance."

Three pages later it began an analysis of the various alternatives for unemployment insurance by noting that "[t]he United States Chamber of Commerce has suggested to the code authorities [in other words, the NRA] that they should consider the development of industrial plans of unemployment insurance, and the Industrial Relations Committee of the Business Advisory Council [readers should recall that this committee was made up of members of the Special Conference Committee] has also been giving the subject much attention" (Industrial Relations Counselors, Inc. 1934a, page 5). The analysis that is presented outlines the advantages of a plan such as Stewart would be proposing to the Committee on Economic Security. It is noteworthy that the Annual Report for the Special Conference Committee for 1934 also stated that "there probably will be need for funds built up and administered under the direction of public authorities" (Colin Gordon 1994, p. 256).

Old-Age Insurance

The corporate moderates and IRC experts had extensive day-to-day involvement in the development of the plan for old-age insurance. Describing his search for a staff to study old-age pensions and draft a proposal, Witte (1963, p. 29) reported that "[i]t was agreed by everyone consulted that the best person in the field was Murray Latimer, who was unavailable because he was chairman of the Railroad Retirement Board." However, Latimer was able to serve as chair of the Technical Board's Committee on Old Age

Security, an important policy role in itself, and in any case he worked closely with the research staff in drafting the legislation. Latimer also was given the opportunity to recommend a leader for the staff. He suggested Brown, one of his collaborators on the railroad retirement study, whom he also knew through IRC and annual conferences at Princeton on social insurance (Witte 1963, p. 3). When Brown decided that he could only give part of each week to the work at hand, Professor Barbara Nachtrieb Armstrong, a professor in the law school at the University of California, Berkeley, was placed in charge of the old-age study (Armstrong 1965, p. 36). Latimer and Brown worked very closely with her, along with Otto Richter, an actuary on loan from AT&T.

Armstrong is an intriguing and interesting figure who also figures in theoretical arguments with the historical institutionalists because she is one of their few examples of an independent expert who was important in the process (Hacker and Pierson 2002, pp. 102–104, 395ftn. 71). Armstrong earned her law degree in 1915 at the University of California, Berkeley, and went to work for California's Commission on Social Insurance, producing a report on sickness as a cause of poverty in California that earned her a Ph.D. at Berkeley in 1921. She then taught both law and economics at UC Berkeley for the next several years before becoming the first woman to be appointed a professor of law in the United States. During the 1920s she immersed herself in the study of European social insurance systems and produced one of the most respected books in the field at the time, *Insuring the Essentials* (Armstrong 1932), with the help of an SSRC grant. She is indeed an example of the kind of independent expert that historical institutionalists emphasize out of all proportion to their frequency and impact.

Armstrong (1965, p. 38) reports in an oral history that she knew no one in Washington when she was asked to join the research staff and never learned who suggested her inclusion. She says she had received positive letters about her book from Roosevelt intimates Swope and Frankfurter and speculates that Swope may have been responsible for her selection (Armstrong 1965, p. 30). However, since she also knew many of the experts in the field and was highly respected for her book, it may be that one of the other experts recommended her.

Originally hired to work on the unemployment compensation program, she was switched to old-age insurance when she arrived because Latimer and Brown did not have the time to take on the task. Like them, she favored a nationwide contributory system administered by the federal government. Armstrong therefore clashed with Witte because she had little use for his ideas about social insurance, derived in good part from the AALL-Wisconsin tradition, calling them "absurd" (Altmeyer 1968, pp. 5–6; Armstrong 1965, p. 42). Nor did she have much respect for Perkins, who never bothered to meet with her, which Armstrong attributed to Perkins's preference for the AALL-Wisconsin approach (Armstrong 1965, p. 31). In turn, Perkins was highly critical of Armstrong; she characterized Armstrong as an "arrogant academic" (Downey 2009, p. 234).

On the other hand, Armstrong had the highest regard and affection for Brown and Stewart, whom she describes as kind and gentle people. She told the interviewer for the oral history project that she felt sorry for Stewart because he was not as tough as she was. "He suffered awfully at their hands," she continued, meaning Perkins, Altmeyer, and Witte (Armstrong 1965, p. 36). After playing a central role in the drafting process, she returned to California, never returning to Washington to testify before Congress, in part because of time pressures, in part because she feared she might be too acerbic as a witness before congressional committees (Graebner 1980, p. 187).

The plan prepared by Armstrong and her colleagues, which contained all the provisions IRC had come to advocate, sailed through the Technical Board's Committee on Old Age Pensions, but its two main features, its national scope and the inclusion of employee contributions, were worrisome to Perkins and the other members of the CES for a combination of political and legal reasons. However, the original plan prevailed on both issues when the CES finally voted. Thus the process produced a clear policy victory for the approach first developed by the insurance companies and the experts at Industrial Relations Counselors, Inc. But it did contain one funding issue that emerged later and caused last-minute problems. To keep taxes on both employers and employees as low as possible, there would be a need for a government contribution from general tax revenues beginning in 1965 and lasting for another fifteen years unless payroll taxes were increased (Witte 1963, pp. 147–149). When Roosevelt grasped the details of this funding plan several months later, just before the proposal was about to be sent to Congress, he insisted that payroll taxes should be set at a higher rate to maintain his rhetorical fiction that the funding came from "contributions," not taxes. The result would be a very large reserve fund; this result led to amendments in the plan after it passed, which are discussed in Chapter 5.

Of more immediate concern, the plan may have faced a different kind of challenge. There may have been some inclination on the part of Roosevelt, Perkins, and Witte to exclude old-age insurance from the final package sent to Congress because they feared that opposition to it might interfere with the passage of the program that mattered the most to them, unemployment insurance. Perkins and Witte always denied there was any such move afoot, but Armstrong, Latimer, and Brown were convinced otherwise. They quickly spoke off the record to reporters to that effect after they were jolted to attention by an ambiguous comment by Roosevelt in a speech to a national conference on economic security in Washington in November 1934.

"I do not know," Roosevelt intoned, "whether this is the time for any federal legislation on old age security" (Davies 1999, p. 60). The immediate uproar in the newspapers led to assurances by all concerned that old-age pensions would be included in the legislative proposal (Armstrong 1965, pp. 88–89; Brown 1965, p. 13; Schlabach 1969, p. iii, based on his interview with Latimer).

Shortly after the public phase of this dust-up ended, the corporate moderates came into the picture in a supporting role through their membership on the Advisory Council on Economic Security. According to Armstrong (1965, pp. 82–83) and Brown (1972, p. 21), they were crucial in convincing Roosevelt and Perkins to retain the old-age provisions in the legislation. As Brown recalled it:

> The likelihood of gaining the support of the Cabinet Committee for our proposals was still in doubt. At this critical time, December 1934, help came from an unexpected source, the industrial executives on the committee's Advisory Council. Fortunately included in the Council were Walter C. Teagle of the Standard Oil Company of New Jersey, Gerard Swope of General Electric, and Marion Folsom of Eastman Kodak, and others well acquainted with industrial pension plans. Their practical understanding of the need for contributory old-age annuities on a broad, national basis carried great weight with those in authority. They enthusiastically approved our program. Just as the newspaper writers had carried us through the November crisis, the support of progressive industrial executives in December ensured that a national system of contributory old-age insurance would be recommended to the President and Congress (Brown 1972, p. 21).

Brown later summarized what he called the "American philosophy of social insurance" in a retrospective book. Echoing Cowdrick in his 1928 pamphlet for the American Management Association, Brown's (1972, pp. 90–91) emphasis was on "the need for a perpetual corporation to assure a flow of effective and well-motivated personnel for the year-by-year operation of the company." More specifically, "retirement programs with adequate pensions became necessary to prevent an excessive aging of staff or the loss of morale which the discard of the old without compensation would involve;" thus, old-age insurance was simply "a charge on current production to be passed on to the consumer" (Brown 1972, pp. 90). This is exactly the conclusion most corporate moderates and some ultraconservatives had reached by the late 1920s. However, as we mentioned earlier in this chapter, it did take the "massive shock wave" of the Great Depression (Sass 1997, p. 88); the grassroots efforts of the Railway Employees National Pension Association; and careful actuarial work by Latimer, Stewart, Brown, and other experts to convince the corporate moderates that they would have to realize their purposes through a narrowly circumscribed government program.

Unemployment Compensation

When we turn to unemployment compensation, the other major title of the Social Security Act of theoretical interest, the story begins as even more of a triumph for the corporate moderates and experts in the policy-planning network than were old-age pensions. Not only was Stewart put in charge of the staff study, he installed one of his co-authors from the Minnesota study, Murray, as his principal assistant, and then insisted on using employees of IRC to make the study. As Witte explained, Stewart would only take the position if he could also stay with IRC in New York and use his own staff as well:

> It developed that he did not feel that he could leave his position and would consider only an arrangement under which his work for the committee could largely be done in New York, and under which he could use his own staff to assist him. Such an arrangement was objected to by some members of the technical board, but was finally made. Almost the entire research staff of the Industrial Relations Counselors, Inc., was placed on the payroll of the Committee on Economic Security, so that the arrangement in effect amounted to employing the Industrial Relations Counselors, Inc., to make this study (Witte 1963, p. 29).

Witte then explains a little further in a footnote:

> Dr. Stewart himself was never on the payroll of the Committee on Economic Security, pursuant to his express request. Instead, his staff was put on the payroll, with the understanding that both he and the staff would work simultaneously for the committee and the Industrial Relations Counselors, Inc. (Witte 1963, p. 29, ftn. 24).

This seems to us to be a strong set of demands for a government free of corporate dominance to accept. To retain the services of the expert it needed, the CES had to hire staff members from a private firm that everyone in Washington knew to be closely affiliated with Rockefeller and Standard Oil of New Jersey, and it had to allow them to stay in New York as well. On top of that, Stewart and his staff were also consulting directly with Teagle, who was chair of the Business Advisory Council's newly formed Committee on Unemployment Insurance in addition to being on the Advisory Council on Economic Security. It therefore seems very likely to us that Teagle, Stewart, and IRC were the main links between the corporate moderates and the executive branch of the federal government on the issue of unemployment compensation. If the full network of personal and financial ties could be drawn, we believe they would be at the center. The substance of the IRC memorandums that we cite in the remainder of the chapter also supports this inference.

It would thus appear the story should have a similar ending to the one on old-age insurance, but it doesn't. Stewart did recommend that unemployment compensation should be a national system, not a state-by-state one, to ensure adequate and uniform standards of taxation and benefits, and that employees—and general government tax revenues in the distant future—should contribute to the fund as well as employers. But these recommendations generated enormous conflict, causing the CES to change its recommendation several times. In the end, Stewart and the corporate moderates lost because the CES finally decided on the federal-state system favored by the AALL and Southern Democrats. The CES also eliminated contributions by employees and the government. Nor were there any minimum standards that states had to meet, to the chagrin of both Stewart and members of the AALL. In terms of the theoretical issues addressed in this book, the interesting problem is why the corporate moderates' lost on these issues, which we explore as the story unfolds and then discuss more fully at the end of the chapter.

Stewart's report first went to the Technical Board's Committee on Unemployment Insurance, which was chaired by Murray, the economist who had worked with him on the Minnesota project and was his principal assistant in writing the report for CES. The executive secretary of the Business Advisory Council, Edward Jensen, also served on this committee, along with another one of Stewart's former co-authors, Hansen, by then in the Harvard economics department. In addition, the committee also included Leiserson, the economist who had been a member of the SSRC's Committee on Unemployment; economist Jacob Viner from the University of Chicago, an advisor to the Department of Treasury, who had often substituted for the secretary of treasury at CES meetings; and Thomas Eliot, a lawyer from a long-standing upper-class family who worked for Perkins at the Department of Labor. The committee was unanimous in its general support for Stewart's proposal, but differed on a few details (Witte 1963, pp. 112–113).

The committee's recommendations then went to the executive committee of the Technical Board, where Altmeyer presided. The executive committee made a very general statement of endorsement, but expressed concern about the idea of any "public contribution," meaning funds from general taxes, and about the constitutionality of a national-level system. Because of this hesitation, Perkins and other members of the CES asked for more definite recommendations before they reached any conclusions. A month of discussions then followed that included experts who had not been consulted before on this specific issue, such as Armstrong and Brown, who weighed in on Stewart's side. As disagreement and acrimony increased, the germ of a compromise was finally proposed. It would allow the federal government to collect taxes from employers and employees but then return the money to the individual states "subject to the state's compliance with standards to be prescribed by the federal government" (Witte 1963, pp. 115–116). This became known as the "subsidy" plan even though there were no subsidies involved, but it was sometimes called the "federal" plan as well. Stewart, Armstrong, and Brown saw it as an acceptable fallback position because it gave some assurance of federal standards; that is, it helped ensure that firms in low-wage states would not be able to undercut large national firms by paying less into the fund for unemployment insurance.

IRC *Memorandum to Clients* No. 4, for October 31, provided readers with an overview of most of these issues, but first it urged its clients to keep the memorandum confidential:

> We have refrained from comment until we could have the advantage of the discussion in meetings held during the past week. Because this organization has worked with various committees and interests, much of our information is confidential. Therefore, to avoid any possible embarrassment, we request that the following discussion be limited to confidential circulation among the executives of our client companies" (Industrial Relations Counselors, Inc. 1934b, p. 1).

In addition to discussing the conflicts over unemployment insurance along the lines we already have outlined, the memorandum notes that there was talk of delay for old-age insurance because "the administration is trying to improve business psychology," that is, postpone any program that business thought to be an impediment to recovery. But the memorandum is certain that unemployment insurance would be enacted in the next Congress: "At this stage the outstanding feature of the development is that some kind of legislation on unemployment insurance seems fairly certain to be enacted in the next Congress" (Industrial Relations Counselors, Inc. 1934b, p. 2).

The first-round success enjoyed by Stewart's plan did not last long because the unemployment insurance committee of the Technical Board reversed its earlier decision when it met again in early November. Now it unanimously supported the cooperative federal-state system favored by Roosevelt, Perkins, Witte, and the AALL. This plan differed from the federal approach in that states would collect the money and set their own tax levels and benefit payments. The Technical Board apparently was influenced by questions of constitutionality and political viability (Schlabach 1969, p. 118).

When the proposal went to the CES for a second look, the members met with Altmeyer, Hansen, Stewart, and Viner to hear a debate on the issues before making a decision. The CES members then concluded that a fully national system was out of the question, but the issue of the federal plan favored by Stewart versus the cooperative federal-state one favored by many AALL members was left somewhat open. Nonetheless, Perkins immediately told Roosevelt the sentiment was primarily in favor of the federal-state system. Roosevelt liked that recommendation and supported it in a speech on November 14, the same speech mentioned earlier in which he gave the impression that the old-age insurance plan might not be included in the legislative package (Witte 1963, pp. 118–119). Put another way, it now seems clear that Roosevelt was using this speech to try to shape the legislation before it was sent to Congress. As we have shown, he failed to postpone the old-age provisions. Now we shall see if he had his way on unemployment insurance.

After all, it would seem to be the end of the matter because the president had spoken. But Stewart and his colleagues would not accept the decision. The next day Stewart discussed the issue with a group of experts that he personally invited to an informal discussion. They voted fourteen to three in favor of a national plan over a state-federal one (Witte 1963, p. 121). Stewart also contacted the business members on the Advisory Council on Economic Security; three of the five (Teagle, Swope, and Leeds) were also members of the Business Advisory Council's unemployment insurance committee, for which Stewart and IRC were serving as consultants. Stewart and Armstrong also lobbied the chair of the Advisory Council on Economic Security, Frank Graham, the president of the University of North Carolina, at a dinner party arranged by a mutual friend (Burns 1966, p. 44).

There then followed a battle within the Advisory Council on Economic Security, much to the consternation of Roosevelt, Perkins, and Witte. The full council heard directly from Stewart, Armstrong, and Murray. Then it created a committee on unemployment insurance to draft its own proposal with the help of Stewart and Murray. But the committee's efforts failed because the same divisions appeared with the Advisory Council (Witte 1963, pp. 56–57). Finally, on December 9, the Advisory Council on Economic Security voted nine to seven in favor of the nationally oriented federal plan over the AALL's federal-state plan. Three liberals and the president of the AFL joined with the five business executives in supporting the federal plan. Voting in opposition to a federal plan were the representative from the Fraternal Order of Eagles, the president of the Wisconsin Federation of Labor, and five people from charity and social work backgrounds who were not supporters of the insurance crowd. That is, one of the corporate moderates' major problems had surfaced once again: they were not able to gain the full support of the social workers and liberals they first tried to persuade at the SSRC conference in November, 1933.

However, the corporate moderates were not deeply concerned, as Folsom explained in a long letter to Frank W. Lovejoy, the president of Eastman Kodak, after discussing the outcome of the vote:

> The Committee was almost evenly divided as to the Wagner-Lewis type [AALL type in our terms] and the subsidy [federal] type of bill. The employers all favored the subsidy type because under that plan it would be possible to set up

inter-state industry funds, in which Mr. Teagle, Mr. Lewisohn, and Mr. Swope are very much interested. The subsidy plan received a majority vote but it seems that the Cabinet Committee and the Technical Board favor the Wagner-Lewis bill. We have it protected, I think, so that under either plan the plant reserve system can be set up with the decision left to the states (Folsom 1934).

Folsom's mention of the importance of the "plant reserve system" as a fallback position if the "inter-state industry funds" were not included is an important reminder that market considerations were a major issue for the corporate moderates. They could gain a cost advantage if they maintained their workforce at a steady size and therefore have lower unemployment insurance payments than smaller companies that were more likely to take on or drop workers with small swings in demand. That is, the need to maintain a company reserve might give them a competitive advantage in the pricing of their products (Swenson 2002, pp. 226–231 for a detailed discussion of this issue).

Meanwhile, the CES already had agreed to reconsider the issue even before it received the report from the Advisory Council on Economic Security, partly because it had received a new report sent to Roosevelt by the BAC's Committee on Unemployment Insurance urging the federal plan; as might be suspected by this point, the BAC report was written by Stewart (Schlabach 1969, p. 140). The CES then decided on a federal system after all, but soon changed back again after floating the federal option with key members of Congress. As Perkins later explained:

> After long discussion we agreed to recommend a federal system. We went back and informed colleagues in our own Departments. Within the day, I had telephone calls from members of the Committee saying that perhaps we had better meet again. There was grave doubt, our latest interviews with members of Congress had shown, that Congress would pass a law for a purely federal system. State jealousies and suspicions were involved. So we met again, and after three or four hours of debate we switched back to a federal-state system(Perkins 1946, pp. 291–292).

In the end, we believe that the corporate moderates and IRC lost to members of Congress on the federal-level versus state-level issue, not to Roosevelt, the AALL, or those who wanted to protect the unemployment program that had been launched in Wisconsin. That is, the decision was a political one, not a constitutional one. But what were the state jealousies and suspicions to which Perkins alluded? Historical institutionalists argue that supporters of the AALL and Wisconsin's state program were the key opponents, but it seems to us, given the objections that soon surfaced in Congress, that the most important opponents of Stewart's plan were the Southern Democrats. As Latimer wrote in a frank personal letter to a professor at the University of Virginia early in 1935 that anticipated the outcome of the congressional debate:

> Almost without exception, congressmen and Senators from the South indicated extreme skepticism of the wisdom of any legislation of a social character which would concentrate further power in Washington. Behind this feeling was obviously a fear that unsympathetic administrations in Washington would require southern states to pay Negroes a benefit which would be regarded locally as excessive (Latimer 1935).

The opponents are more clear and visible when it comes to the rejection of Stewart's proposal to have both employers and employees contribute. Contributions by workers were opposed by both organized labor and reform-oriented social workers because they believed that unemployment was the fault of the corporations, which therefore should take full responsibility for compensating workers when they lost their jobs. In their eyes this fact made unemployment compensation different from old-age pensions, where employee contributions were considered to be fair. Unfortunately for the reformers, this line of reasoning reduced unemployment benefits, made them easier to stigmatize, and put payment levels and the number of months of coverage at the mercy of Congress in later decades. In a word, it seems to us that the liberal-labor victory was a shortsighted one.

The failure to include employee contributions to the unemployment insurance fund is also very telling in light of Roosevelt's statement at the outset of the process that he favored a contributory plan for both old-age pensions and unemployment compensation. Nevertheless, he quietly accepted the narrow demands by the liberal-labor coalition on this issue. We think future commentators on the New Deal should keep this point in mind when they praise Roosevelt for claiming that he insisted on contributions by workers "to give the contributors a legal, moral, and political right to collect their pensions and unemployment benefits" and thus ensure that "no damn politician can ever scrap my social security program" (Schlesinger 1958, pp. 308–309). But workers did not contribute to unemployment benefits, the program that seemed to be most important to him at the time. We think he decided not to challenge the liberal-labor coalition on an issue about which it felt very strongly. We also think this is a classic example of how elected officials provide politically appealing rationales for policy outcomes that are based in power battles that the rationales obscure.

THE LEGISLATIVE GAUNTLET

The CES's overall legislation for a range of social insurance programs was introduced into Congress in mid-January, 1935, with the apparent support of a wide cross-section of the corporate community, including a committee of the National Association of Manufacturers (Brents 1984; Jenkins and Brents 1989). Then, too, a committee of the Chamber of Commerce endorsed the bill in March 1935, while it was still being dissected by Congressional committees, and went one step further by favoring the nationally oriented federal plan for unemployment insurance that Teagle and Stewart advocated (Nelson 1969, p. 214). The plans embodied in the draft legislation also had support from reformers and labor leaders. Nevertheless, the proposal had to survive a seven-month legislative gauntlet that included highly critical testimony by NAM leaders and the leaders of NAM affiliates in leading industrial states, a complete redrafting in the House, near defeats in key Congressional committees, and changes in the preamble due to a Supreme Court decision (Altman 2005, for an insightful account of the legislative battles). It also faced a last-minute amendment to allow companies with their own pension plans to opt out of the government plan, which was so controversial that it almost led to a deadlock between the House and Senate. In the end, however, all of the policy provisions survived even though Southern Democrats insisted upon further restrictions on federal regulation of both the old-age and unemployment insurance provisions.

IRC's *Memorandum to Clients* No. 5 provided a detailed eight-page overview of the bill on January 25, eight days after the bill was introduced. It then criticized the unemployment insurance plan because it would lead to forty-eight sets of state records, causing many costly problems in transferring files in what was coming to be a nationwide labor market. It also was disappointed by the small measure of control that the federal government would have over state plans. It predicted opposition to the unemployment provisions for several reasons, all of which reflected Stewart's ongoing preferences: a national plan, a tax on employees as well as employers, and uniform federal standards that must be adhered to by all states.

The memorandum was more favorable toward the old-age insurance provisions, noting that the contributions to the program were low "as compared with the pension plans of progressive companies . . . " (Industrial Relations Counselors, Inc. 1935a, p. 10). However, it did worry that the government might not be able to "assure the contractual character of this obligation so long as Congress has the power later to change the terms of the law." It also expressed concern that the bill gave "no recognition to industrial pension plans that have been adopted in several industries, and a number of which have become well established and have accumulated considerable reserves" (Industrial Relations Counselors, Inc. 1935a, p. 10). Within a few days, however, they saw this lack of recognition for established industrial pension plans as a very real opportunity for the companies that had them.

Testimony Before Congress

As Roosevelt and Perkins had feared, most of the discussion in Congress focused on old-age social insurance. This part of the legislation was explained and defended at length and in detail by Witte, Brown, and Latimer. Latimer and others believe that Witte was by far the most creditable witness for the great majority of congressmen (Schlabach 1969, p. 144). However, Brown and Latimer's testimony is of greater theoretical interest to us because it stressed labor market concerns, which supports the argument that the program was created with industrial relations in mind, not social welfare (compare with Graebner 1980, pp. 187–189). For example, Latimer's only concern was that higher benefits might be needed to induce the large number of retirements that he thought necessary to help improve the unemployment problem. (Armstrong's oral history suggests the same kind of emphasis, which is worth mentioning because she speaks from an independent perspective. She told her interviewer that the objective "was not only to protect the older worker, but it was also to get him out of the labor market" (Armstrong 1965, p. 255).)

Responding to the concerns of companies that already had their own pension plans, IRC's *Memorandum to Clients* No. 6, for February 1, explained for the first time that the government plan would be less costly for these companies. It also proposed that the current company plans could be seen as supplementary to the government program, making it possible to provide more attractive pensions for higher-income workers: "The combined cost to companies of the revised company plan and the national plan would presumably be less than the cost of their present plans, since the contribution rates levied by the Security Bill are set below actual cost on the assumption that the additional amounts needed later will be drawn from general tax funds" (Industrial Relations Counselors, Inc. 1935b, p. 1). This memo is very important to our argument because it proves that Industrial Relations Counselors realized there would be cost savings and the opportunities to provide better retirement benefits for executives much sooner than previous accounts state (see, for example, Hacker 2002; Klein 2003).

Memorandum No. 6 then explains why the employees themselves might prefer Social Security to company plans that claimed they would pay higher benefits. These reasons also are an admission of the weaknesses inherent in company pension plans discussed by Sass (1997). It first notes that there is an "absence of real guarantees" in company plans, which is a damning admission if there ever was one. Second, it notes that there had been "widespread cuts in the amounts paid to pensioners and reductions in the rate of pension which have occurred during the past four years," which is an admission that many company plans were not actuarially sound over the long run (Industrial Relations Counselors, Inc. 1935b, p. 2).

Memorandum to Clients No. 6 is also important because it provides the first mention of "contracting out," which would "permit a company to operate a separate plan outside the federal scheme if it is in no way less favorable than that of the government and has its current credits fully financed." The memorandum concedes that such a provision would have "a decided appeal from the industrial relations viewpoint of the individual company," implying that privately controlled pension plans might help the company in retaining and restraining employees. But it then adds "we understand that *the experts who drafted the bill* believe such a provision would weaken the effectiveness of the measure for the great number of wage earners who are not under company plans" (Industrial Relations Counselors, Inc. 1935b, p. 2, emphasis added). In other words, the IRC experts, as exemplified by Latimer and Stewart, had decided that contracting out was not a good idea for the corporate community. The memorandum then added that a separate plan would be burdensome besides: "Certainly the inclusion of the proposed provision would be accompanied by requirements for financial guarantees from the companies of a character that might prove burdensome and difficult to meet and to that extent would lessen its acceptability" (Industrial Relations Counselors, Inc. 1935b, p. 2).

We see such comments as part of the process of disseminating a new perspective within the corporate community, starting with the Rockefeller-related oil companies and the large companies with membership in the Special Conference Committee. We also see them as the first of several pieces of evidence that the historical institutionalists who have written in the greatest detail about the origins of the Social Security Act are wrong when they conclude that the majority of the corporate moderates were in favor of contracting out because of their alleged continuing opposition to federal old-age insurance (Hacker 2002; Orloff 1993, p. 293).

The depth of the IRC experts' concern over contracting out is revealed in a letter that Brown sent to Witte shortly thereafter, on February 13, reporting on what he had learned through his discussions of contracting out with corporate executives at the annual meetings of the American Management Association. Once again serving as the eyes and ears of the Rockefeller circle, Brown reported that most of them understood that this provision was not to their advantage. He also had learned that the Philadelphia insurance agent who was lobbying for the idea, Walter Forster, had very little support among insurance agents or the large insurance companies, with the exception of Prudential and Metropolitan:

> The Prudential Company has been rather inept in the matter and I think that you will find that the dozen or more companies other than the Prudential and the Metropolitan are not particularly in sympathy with the tactics of those two companies. I heard in Pittsburgh, however, that the Metropolitan, at least

on the surface, is saying the bill will be a boon to the insurance companies in expanding the demand for supplementary group annuity contracts. Both the Prudential and the Metropolitan are somewhat frightened by the threat of investigation of industrial insurance, and may not be as anxious to push the amendment on account of a backfire in this respect (Brown 1935a).

Brown had further encouraging conversations that he reported on in a letter to Witte on February 23. The list of companies he provides that lacked interest in contracting out is long and impressive. It is also noteworthy that Young of IRC and U.S. Steel was in agreement on this issue:

> I am continuing to receive word from industrial relations executives of their lack of interest in the contracting out amendment. Confidentially, the last word I had was from Art Young, Vice-President of the United States Steel Corporation. I have been in touch also with the American Telephone and Telegraph Company, Socony-Vacuum, DuPont, United States Rubber, Union Carbide and Carbon, Western Electric, and a number of other companies. The men in question are the chief personnel officers, and since I have known most of them for six or eight years, I have confidence in what they tell me (Brown 1935b).

While committees in the House and Senate were deciding whether to permit the report from the Committee for Economic Security to be voted upon by the full House and Senate memberships, Stewart and the SSRC hosted a conference in Atlantic City on March 22–23 based on the funding request from spring 1934, when they had anticipated that amendments to the final legislation would be necessary. This conference unanimously recommended funding for studies of the new social security administrative board. Two SSRC committees, the Public Administration Committee and the Committee on Social Security, would carry out the studies. The Rockefeller Foundation immediately gave approval to this request, which led to donations of $611,000 between 1935 and 1940 (Fisher 1993, p. 139). The members of the Committee on Social Security and the impact of their efforts are discussed in the next chapter.

Shortly after the SSRC conference, IRC's next *Memorandum to Clients* included two attached statements from insurance companies stating their belief that the legislation would "result in renewed appreciation and greater stimulation of life insurance activities both individual and group rather than the reverse" (Industrial Relations Counselors, Inc. 1935d, p. 8). This is further evidence that IRC and at least some insurance companies understood the potential of the Social Security Act well before the date claimed by other researchers.

At the same time IRC and the insurance companies were realizing that contracting out was not a good idea, the administration's general legislative proposal was being totally rewritten in the House Ways and Means

Committee for reasons that had nothing to do with IRC and the insurance companies. Minimum benefits and merit hiring of state-level administrators were eliminated at the insistence of Southern Democrats on the committee, which is of course further good evidence for our emphasis on their power during the New Deal (Witte 1963, pp. 125, 143–145).

IRC's *Memorandum to Clients* No. 10, dated April 10, provided a thorough summary and evaluation of the revised legislation that the Ways and Means Committee introduced into the House on April 4, starting with the fact that the title had been changed from the Economic Security Act to the Social Security Act. It noted that the unemployment section of the new bill "makes no provision" for any of the major concerns expressed in *Memorandum to Clients* No. 5, leaving that portion of the legislation very unsatisfactory:

> Coverage is reduced and federal supervision of state personnel is struck out. In short, the principles of board coverage and competitive equality insisted on at the outset have been violated while a door has been opened to permit political appointments and high administrative costs (Industrial Relations Counselors, Inc. 1935e, p. 2).

There were also changes in the plans for old-age insurance that did not meet IRC's expectations. For example, benefits would now be higher for low-wage workers than they were in current company plans and lower than they would be for high-wage workers. Death benefits would now be higher than planned after short periods of employment and lower than after lengthy periods of employment.

When the revised legislation reached the House floor on April 12, it first had to survive two brief challenges—one by the Communist Party, the other by a pressure group for the elderly, who advocated a grassroots plan, the Townsend Plan. Both received attention in the media at the time and subsequent attention by historians and social scientists, but in fact neither alternative had any chance of passage or any influence on the proceedings. They are worth a brief comment here because they document that any opposition to the New Deal from the left was very weak, and the Townsend Plan is discussed more fully in the final chapter as part of our critique of alternative theories. The Communist bill, with its sweeping call for a guaranteed annual income adjusted for region of the country, received only forty votes, and the Townsend Plan, which originally called for payments of $200 per month to every person over age sixty, with the proviso that all of it be spent within the month, only fifty-six. Moreover, over half of the votes in both instances came from conservatives who opposed any form of government social insurance (Witte 1963, p. 99). If the votes on the Communist and Townsend bills are any indication, there were not more than fifteen to twenty representatives in the House who stood to the left of the New Deal. Contrary to claims by historical institutionalists, the corporate community had nothing to fear by way of a worse alternative if the Social Security Act did not pass (Hacker and Pierson 2002, 2004).

Restoration in the Senate

The Senate Finance Committee, which Witte feared as the biggest threat to the legislation because it contained many Southern conservatives, finished its hearings in February, but then postponed further action on the proposal until April. It did not approve a report until May 17, after coming within a vote or two of stripping the bill of old-age insurance. During the final weeks of deliberation, a new element was added to the picture when corporate anger over the imminent passage of the National Labor Relations Act spilled over to a harsh attack on the Social Security Act in early May by the newly elected ultraconservative president of the Chamber of Commerce at the group's annual meeting in Washington. It came as a surprise because the previous Chamber leadership had been quietly accepting of the Social Security Act.

In response to this criticism, the Business Advisory Council decided that it had to restate its support for Social Security by going to the White House the next day despite its opposition to the National Labor Relations Act. "Business Leaders Uphold President," said the *New York Times* in its front-page headline on page 1 on May 3. Among the twenty people appearing at the White House were the presidents or chairmen of Remington Rand, Kennecott Copper, United States Rubber, Cannon Towels, Proctor and Gamble, and Chase National Bank (Domhoff 1970, pp. 214–215 for the full list and their corporate affiliations).

However, in spite of Witte's fears, the Senate Finance Committee's bill ended up much improved over the version passed by the House. According to IRC's *Memorandum to Clients* No. 12, for May 27, 1935 (Industrial Relations Counselors, Inc. 1935f, p. 1), it "restored to the bill several features that appeared in it originally but were omitted in the House draft." This may have been in good part because the Southern-dominated committee was extremely impressed by the testimony of their fellow Southerner, Folsom of Eastman Kodak, which led to changes in the details of the bill's unemployment provisions that were more in keeping with the corporate moderates' top preferences (Jacoby 1993; 1997, pp. 211–212; Swenson 2002, p. 228–229).

The bill also had a new preamble due to a Supreme Court decision in early May declaring the Railroad Retirement Act unconstitutional. Because the reduction of unemployment and the efficiency and morale of the workforce were not judged to be within the purview of the constitution, the emphasis in the revised preamble was on the country's general welfare. This change, which obscured the major role of industrial relations experts such as Latimer and Stewart in writing the act, was made because the constitution allows the government to support the general welfare through its taxing power:

> Now, to achieve the original purpose, the administration turned to the taxing power and the general welfare clause of the Constitution. In the process, the ideology of social security was given formal sanction. After May 1935, proponents of retirement legislation talked less about efficiency, economy and unemployment relief than about social security and the needs of older workers, which were now a central policy goal rather than ancillary to some larger purpose (Graebner 1980, pp. 162–163).

We think it is worth highlighting that this change is the mirror image of the change that was made in the preamble to the National Labor Relations Act just a few weeks later, which eliminated any appeal to general welfare and focused on the direct effects of strikes on interstate commerce. Put another way, both the National Labor Relations Act and the Social Security Act were concerned with labor relations, but neither act could state that fact directly due to the composition of the Supreme Court and the nature of its past decisions. It was therefore necessary to refer instead to impacts on the flow of commerce in the case of the National Labor Relations Act and to the general welfare in the case of the Social Security Act.

Just as the bill was about to pass the Senate, it faced one final obstacle: an amendment to allow the contracting out that was so vigorously opposed by Industrial Relations Counselors and most of the corporate moderates interviewed by Brown a few months earlier. The amendment was formally offered by a conservative Democrat from Missouri, Bennett Champ Clark, so it came to be called the Clark Amendment. From the point of view of the corporate ultraconservatives and senators who opposed the whole social insurance program, the amendment was a perfect way to undercut the Social Security Act without voting against it. Despite protests from Roosevelt and Perkins, along with actuarial arguments against the amendment by Witte and other experts, it passed by the wide margin of fifty-one to thirty-five on June 19, followed by passage of the act in general by a seventy-seven to six vote the same day (Witte 1963, p. 106). The large vote for the Clark Amendment is revealing—and supportive of our general analysis—because it underscores the power of Southern Democrats and others sympathetic to corporate ultraconservatives in a seemingly liberal Senate that just a month before had passed the National Labor Relations Act by a large margin.

Roosevelt then made it clear that he would not sign legislation that included the Clark Amendment because it would create major actuarial and administrative problems, especially when companies—or their pension plans—went bankrupt, or when employees left companies with private pension funds before they retired. The standoff led to a two-month delay while the conference committee argued about the issue and searched for a compromise. Congress finally agreed that the bill would be passed without the Clark Amendment, but with the provision that the Clark Amendment would be reconsidered in the next session of Congress after experts had a chance to see if contracting out could be made compatible with the overall system. Roosevelt signed the legislation on August 14.

IRC sent out a brief summary of the act's provisions on August 16. The memorandum first repeated its disapproval of the Clark Amendment, concluding, "it seems clear that from the practical operating viewpoint such companies would have nothing to gain from the amendment" (Industrial Relations Counselors, Inc. 1935h, p. 1). It then noted that members of the IRC staff were meeting with "the representatives of leading insurance companies and other interests concerned primarily with the sections on pensions." Finally, the memorandum announced that the organization already was working on supplemental plans:

> Industrial Relations Counselors is now engaged in the formulation of several types of private plans which will supplement the pension benefits provided under the federal scheme and more adequately cover employees in the *higher salary brackets*. Our recommendations on future procedure may vary as between companies installing a plan for the first time and companies that have operated a formal plan for some years" (Industrial Relations Counselors, Inc. 1935h, p. 1, emphasis added).

This brief memorandum was followed on August 23 by a longer and more reflective one, No. 15, which nicely reveals the moderate conservative viewpoint and presages the moderates' agenda for defeating the Clark Amendment. By and large, IRC experts were satisfied with the overall legislative outcome, calling it a program that "will increase mass purchasing power and act as a shock absorber for our economic system" (Industrial Relations Counselors, Inc. 1935i, p. 2). The memorandum also said that the old-age pension provisions "were much better drawn than the unemployment compensation phase," a conclusion that comes as no surprise because IRC experts—and their ally, Barbara Armstrong—wrote them (Industrial Relations Counselors, Inc. 1935i, p. 3). Indeed, we see this satisfaction with federal old-age insurance as further support for our claim that IRC experts were involved in creating it.

In addition, the memorandum also contained some surprisingly moderate and even progressive comments that explained the empirical basis of their policy analyses. For example, the report said that IRC's cross-national studies of social insurance systems convinced its authors "that a very considerable proportion of the costs must be borne by the public treasury," which put them in greater accord with the social workers than originally seemed to be the case (Industrial Relations Counselors, Inc. 1935i, p. 3).

The summary also contained several criticisms of the Clark Amendment that past memorandums had refrained from mentioning because IRC's leaders wanted "to avoid any comment which might have been misconstrued as being political argument . . . " (Industrial Relations Counselors, Inc. 1935i, p. 6). First, contracting out would be more costly for corporations by as much as 33 to 100 percent. Second, the need to make back payments to the government for "each employee leaving a company before retirement age would subject a company fund to an unpredictable cash withdrawal, which would tend to force investments into a form suitable for commercial banks rather than proper insurance investments" (Industrial Relations Counselors, Inc. 1935i, p. 7). Third, private plans would have "burdensome administrative and reporting problems" so that the government could oversee them properly. Finally, the existence of private plans "would tend to weaken the actuarial basis of the government old-age benefit plan" due to the fact that companies with the lowest costs were most likely to set up their own plans, leaving the government "to deal with the poorest risks" (Industrial Relations Counselors, Inc. 1935i, pp. 6–7).

This list of objections to the Clark Amendment was the opening salvo in the effort to make sure that it was not adopted. In the end, no substitute for the Clark Amendment was ever offered, but the behind-the-scenes effort to deal with it will be discussed in the next chapter because it provides further evidence for the power of the corporate moderates in and around the Rockefeller, IRC, and SSRC network.

SUMMARY

The process leading to the drafting and passage of the Social Security Act was long and drawn out, but the final outcome fits well with the class-domination theory that underlies this book. It also provides excellent evidence for state building by the capitalist class. The corporate moderates proposed a sophisticated and comprehensive program based on years of experience with their own company plans and with group plans developed by life insurance companies, as adapted and fine-tuned for them by experts in the policy-planning network. Many ultraconservatives originally went along reluctantly with the proposal on its merits and then turned against it on general ideological, anti–New Deal grounds. But the ultraconservatives could not stop the program or bring about any changes in it.

Restive workers made their presence felt through the grassroots activity of the Railway Employees National Pension Association, which forced the corporate community to consider government involvement in worker pensions. Then, too, the AFL's decision in 1932 to end its opposition to government insurance removed an obstacle to trade union support for a government program. On a more negative note, the AFL demonstrated its power on the Social Security Act by helping to foist its crabbed non-systemic view of the economy into the provisions for unemployment insurance by shortsightedly rejecting contributions by workers. As for liberals and social workers, they wanted something better and more generous than the corporate moderates' plan when it came to old-age pensions and unemployment compensation, but they ended up as lobbyists for the plan that emerged from the policy-planning network. They also played a self-defeating role in refusing to allow employee contributions to unemployment insurance. Finally, the agitation and plans from the Communists and Townsendites, while drawing headlines at the time and many academic what-if and if-only analyses decades later, had little or no impact on the formulation or passage of the act (compare with Manza 1995, p. 345, for a similar conclusion).

As for the Southern Democrats, they were once again the Disposers. They were the reason why agricultural and domestic workers were not covered by old-age insurance until 1950, even though an early study by the Committee on Economic Security's research staff said that such coverage was feasible (Alston and Ferrie 1999). We also think the legislative battles in Congress and the concerns expressed by Latimer and Witte at the time strongly suggest that the Southern Democrats were the main reason why unemployment insurance was placed under the control of the states. Southern Democrats also eliminated the civil service requirements for the staff that administered the programs and any minimal federal standards for payment levels, which both the IRC experts and the AALL reformers favored. This allowed the representatives of the plantation capitalists to put their local cronies in charge of agencies and keep benefit payments low enough to maintain both full control of their workforce and the strict racial segregation that was one of their primary motivations on every policy issue they considered (see Quadagno 1988, for detailed information on the powerful impact of the Southern Democrats on this legislation).

CHAPTER FIVE

Aftermath and Implementation

The three previous chapters demonstrated the power of the ownership class in creating and shaping the three most important pieces of New Deal legislation. But as historical institutionalists and public administration practitioners rightly point out, we also can learn about power through the way in which policies are implemented. In the words of political sociologist Bill Winders (2005, p. 387), "focusing on trajectories rather than merely policy formation more clearly demonstrates the influence of class coalitions over state policy." That is, passing legislation is one thing, but keeping the winning coalition together and keeping opponents from undoing or distorting its aims is another. This chapter explains how the implementation of the Agricultural Adjustment Act, the National Labor Relations Act, and the Social Security Act provides further evidence for corporate dominance in the United States in the face of class conflict, especially in the complex case of the National Labor Relations Act.

THE AAA AND CLASS CONFLICT

As we recounted at the end of Chapter 2, Northern business executives and the representatives of Southern planters staffed the Agricultural Adjustment Administration (AAA) and allowed farmers complete discretion in dealing with their workers and tenant farmers. Farmer committees packed with members of the Farm Bureau and county agents controlled the program at the local level (Kirkendall 1966, p. 154; McConnell 1953, pp. 75–76). For example, the degree of Farm Bureau involvement in the AAA in 1936 can be seen in the large number of its members on state-level committees. In states where there was a Farm Bureau, which means most major farm states, 117 of the 169 state committee members were members of the Farm Bureau. Further, in some states "90 percent or more of the county and township committeemen were Farm Bureau members" (McConnell 1953, p. 78).

The importance of the Farm Bureau in shaping the Agricultural Adjustment Administration is also seen in the changes it instigated in the program in 1935 and 1938 (Campbell 1962, pp. 106–114; McConnell 1953, pp. 77–78). The 1935 legislation led to administrative changes that provided "a clear organizational gain for the Farm Bureau on three scores," writes McConnell (1953, p. 78):

> First, administrative organization was now general and not broken along commodity lines. Second, it paralleled the local Farm Bureau structure. Third, it was more amenable to direction through the county agents. In the South the county agent automatically became the secretary of the local association.

When it came time for hearings in 1938 on legislative changes to the AAA, the Farm Bureau leadership stated to a Congressional committee that the farm organizations were asked by the Department of Agriculture to draft the bill (McConnell 1953, p. 78). To help it with the task, the Farm Bureau once again employed the lawyer who assisted in the drafting of the original act (Saloutos 1982, p. 45). Farm Bureau leaders then lobbied vigorously for the bill (Albertson 1961, p. 113; Saloutos 1982, pp. 78–79). McConnell (1953, p. 79) concludes on the basis of the legislative hearings and Farm Bureau reports that "[w]ith the passage of the 1938 act, the Farm Bureau had accomplished its basic legislative program." Now the domestic allotment program was a permanent one that was at the service of the plantation capitalists and other commercial farmers to the tune of many hundreds of millions of dollars each year in the 1930s and several billion dollars a year thereafter.

In spite of this administrative control by corporate and farm interests, the AAA became a source of class conflict because plantation owners saw their AAA payments as an incentive to fire farm hands and terminate leases with tenants and sharecroppers. Not every tenant farmer was cut loose, of course, but historian Pete Daniel (1985) likens New Deal agricultural policy in the South to a modern-day enclosure movement. This enclosure movement triggered disruption in the South and an African American exodus to the North that only grew more intensive later as planters used their domestic allotment payments to mechanize agriculture and as African American workers and soldiers were needed during World War II. Although as many as 15 to 20 percent of Southern tenants and sharecroppers were evicted between 1933 and 1935, the plantation owners nonetheless wanted them available as low-wage labor when needed (Grubb 1971, pp. 25–26). They therefore resisted any liberal-inspired programs to give unemployed farm workers better welfare payments or to settle them on their own land. Despite what most outside observers and government officials saw as a surplus of labor, the landowners were afraid that they were going to run short of inexpensive employees at peak seasons (Mertz 1978, pp. 45–50).

But it was not only evictions that were causing problems for the tenants and sharecroppers. Even those who were allowed to stay on the land were receiving smaller incomes from subsidy payments than they had received for growing crops. Through a variety of contractual devices and southern customs, the landlords found ways to keep a very large share of the subsidy payments for themselves. For example, on one typical plantation "the landlord's gross income increased under the AAA from $51,554 in 1932 to $102,202 in 1934, while the average gross income of his tenants fell from $379 to $355" (Grubb 1971, p. 20).

Still, the power of Southern landowners was not so great that they could keep the rural poor in total destitution. There were two countervailing influences: the disruptive potential of the people who were being displaced or underpaid, which was aided and augmented by leftist organizers, and the leverage that liberals gained within the federal government because they were part of the Roosevelt coalition. The exploited tenants and evicted farm hands were a source of tension and disruption in many ways. They wrote letters of protest about their situation to officials in Washington, generating conflict within the White House, Congress, and the Department of Agriculture. Their poverty was highly visible to journalists, writers, and photographers, who publicized their plight and thereby caused embarrassment for officials in Washington. Most of all, their turmoil and despair held out the potential for radical action of the kind that leftists, and especially Communists, were trying to organize (Conrad 1965; Grubb 1971).

Liberals within the Roosevelt coalition, both Southerners and Northerners, responded to the exclusion and exploitation of tenants and sharecroppers by demanding relief and reform for all Southerners, black or white, who had lost their livelihood. In effect, they assumed the leadership of the farm workers' battle with plantation owners. Their presence within the Democratic Party, along with their ability to stir up public opinion through their access to the media, gave them a toehold in some federal agencies, including the Department of Agriculture, and a few pipelines to the White House itself. In reaction, there was an attempt by the White House to create agencies and programs aimed at relieving some of the devastating poverty in the South without alienating the wealthy whites that controlled the regional Democratic Party. Put another way, the Democratic Party and plantation owners faced the classic dilemma about relief payments analyzed by Piven and Cloward ([1971] 1993): such spending is necessary to forestall disruption, but it must be accompanied by rituals of degradation and eliminated as soon as possible so that work norms and the willingness to work for low wages are not undermined. The harsh way in which this dilemma was handled in the South during the New Deal has been demonstrated in great detail by several historians (Conrad 1965; Grubb 1971; Mertz 1978), who go unmentioned by the historical institutionalists who write about the AAA without any consideration of class conflict.

The protest movements did not go very far in the South because they were met by racial epithets, violence, and incarceration (see, for example, Grubb 1971, pp. 70–71). Nor did the meager emergency relief payments disrupt the labor market. Despite protests by liberals, local relief administrators cut off payments when more workers were needed for planting or harvesting (Mertz 1978, p. 49; Schulman 1994, pp. 31–32). Nonetheless, the Southern landlords were extremely disturbed by the farm workers' protests, and by the involvement of "outside agitators" (that is, liberals and leftists). The Department of Agriculture therefore had to deal with strong pressures from the landlords and liberals outside government who were the most visible combatants in a class struggle that pitted the better-off farmers and plantation owners against the massive number of displaced farm hands and their liberal allies, with small family farmers somewhere in between.

The scope of what began as a one-sided class struggle in Southern agriculture was widened by clashes in California, where there was a long history of large agribusinesses and migratory wage labor (see, for example, Majka and Majka 1982; McWilliams 1939; Weiner 1978). Strikes and organizing efforts were frequent in the first summer after the passage of the Agricultural Adjustment Act, often led by Communists and sometimes taking place in labor camps set up by the federal government (Dyson 1982; Klehr 1984, Chapter 8).

Moreover, conflict between the farmer-business alliance and the liberal-farm labor coalition was not limited to the South and California. There was also an increasing use of wageworkers in the Southwest, Midwest, and even to some extent in the Northeast because farms had expanded in size throughout the 1920s and 1930s. In 1935, when 3 percent of the farms were hiring 40 percent of the roughly 2.5 to 3 million farm laborers, the largest 184,000 farms employed 1.1 million workers for some part of the year (Majka and Majka 1982, p. 104; McWilliams 1942, p. 353). For example, the 70,000 growers of sugar beets in Colorado and the Midwest used 158,000 workers, 110,000 of whom were migrant contract workers. These migrant workers were increasingly Mexican and African American in their origins due to the legislation in 1924 shutting off large streams of immigrants from Europe. The ethnic and color differences between the predominantly white farm owners and the darker-skinned farm hands made the class differences even more obvious.

The strikes by farm workers outside of California, usually to protest wage cuts but sometimes when led by Communists to demand union recognition, were usually not large, frequent, or dramatic, and they only rarely succeeded in restoring wages, but there were many work stoppages in several different states between 1933 and 1935 after virtually no strikes in the preceding three years. They occurred in such varied crops and places as beet fields in Michigan, hops fields in Oregon, onion fields in Ohio, cranberry bogs in New Jersey, citrus groves in Florida, and tobacco fields in Connecticut and Massachusetts. As for unions, they rarely lasted for more than one summer (see, for example, Jamieson 1945, p. 39).

Nevertheless, this labor turbulence was very important politically because it helped to generate greater class consciousness and solidarity among farm interests in all parts of the country, not just the South and California. Since their harvests were at risk if there were strikes or work stoppages, especially with highly perishable crops, the farmers often reacted even more harshly than industrialists to challenges from their workers. The fact that some of the strikes in the Midwest and Northeast were led by organizers from the Communist Party, although not as frequently as in California, made it all the easier for the farm owners to become highly agitated about them and to be successful in enlisting local and state governments against the strikers (Jamieson 1945, pp. 39–42; Klehr 1984, Chapter 8).

Within the context of these highly visible and often violent strikes, along with Communist leadership in some of them, the small group of pro-labor lawyers in the legal department of the AAA, most of them liberals (but two of them, it was learned later, secret members of the Communist Party), in February 1935 triggered a years-long battle with the Farm Bureau and other organized farm groups by ruling that plantation owners who received subsidy payments from the AAA could not remove their tenants (Kirkendall 1966, pp. 99–103; Schlesinger 1958, pp. 78–79). The ruling caused an immediate firestorm of protest in the South and within the AAA itself. Davis, the director of the AAA, who was far closer to the Southerners and the Farm Bureau than he was to the liberals, told Secretary of Agriculture Henry A. Wallace that the liberal and Communist lawyers had to go or else he would resign.

The liberals had calculated that Wallace would back them, but they were wrong because he feared a confrontation with the Southern Democrats and Roosevelt feared that they would block his entire legislative program. Moreover, Southern congressmen warned Roosevelt himself that no more agricultural legislation would be passed if he supported Wallace (see, for example, Lowitt 1979; Saloutos 1982, pp. 117–122). The ruling was rescinded and the liberal and Communist lawyers were fired. The Southern rich won because "almost every major committee in the House and Senate was chaired by a southerner who represented the planter interest" (Kenneth Davis 1986, p. 478). Schlesinger (1958, p. 376) puts it even more bluntly and hints at the police violence that plantation capitalists were ready to employ: "The landlords dominated not only the local administration of the AAA, but the sheriffs at the county court house and the Congressmen in

Washington; it was this situation that drove the legal staff to the reinterpretation of the contract which led to the agricultural purge of 1935."

As Grubb (1971, p. 59) concludes from his study of farm workers during the 1930s, the outcome of this conflict was a clear indication that liberals would be kept in check within the department. Indeed, this incident presaged what happened in every major battle thereafter that might limit the ability of plantation and commercial farmers to control their labor force. Every liberal initiative was pared down to the point where it was acceptable to them, or else it was rejected. Thus, whatever room liberals or independent-minded government officials had to maneuver actually existed at the sufferance of the Farm Bureau and the Southern landlords inside and outside Congress.

Once liberals were ousted from the AAA, their battle with plantation owners and other large-scale farmers over the mistreatment of farm workers and tenant farmers was waged from within other agencies in the Department of Agriculture. The first scrimmages occurred within the Farm Security Administration (FSA), a small agency created in September 1937, as the heir to the temporary programs of relief, loans, and resettlement for rural areas once provided by the Federal Emergency Relief Administration (1933–1935) and the Resettlement Administration (1935–1937). Although the FSA was widely perceived as a liberal agency because it employed many of the remaining liberals within the Department of Agriculture, the Farm Bureau and southern legislators set strict limits on what it could do (see, for example, Alston and Ferrie 1999; Baldwin 1968). Liberals wanted it to focus on cooperative farms, the resettlement of poor farmers from bad soil to good, the upgrading of tenants to farm ownership, and the unionization of farm workers, but the primary emphasis of the agency was limited to rehabilitation loans for small family farmers and an underfunded program to help tenant farmers become owners.

Even within this narrow framework the liberals and farm labor suffered further setbacks. One of the issues liberals inside and outside the government wanted to address through the FSA was the inadequacy of tenancy laws, which made it very difficult for tenants to save money and buy their own land. But the President's Committee on Farm Tenancy, appointed in 1936 to suggest programs to be incorporated into the FSA, "side-stepped the problem of obsolete and inadequate tenancy laws" (Benedict 1953, p. 360). The agricultural economists serving as technical advisors to this presidential committee wrote a draft report containing suggestions on a variety of issues that annoyed several members of the committee, and especially the president of the Farm Bureau. These members "regarded the draft as too critical of tenancy, landlords, the South, and race relations and, in spite of objections from some of the social scientists, forced the technicians to alter the draft" (Kirkendall 1966, p. 127). This outcome provides still another example of experts being cast aside when their advice is not to the liking of the power holders.

Farm and plantation owners restricted the FSA even further by mandating that committees made up of the most prosperous local farmers had to approve any home ownership loans (Grubb 1971, pp. 154–155). They also eliminated a provision that would have allowed the government to buy land it could then divide into smaller farms and sell to tenants (Mertz 1978, p. 150). When all is said and done, and very significantly in a theoretical sense, the basic provisions of the law creating the FSA in 1937 ended up as "almost exactly the tenancy 'cure' that southern planters and established, upper-middle-class dominated farm organizations had been advocating" (Grubb 1971, p. 155). Moreover, the FSA actually functioned in part to help landlords shed their traditional responsibility to provide cash, seed, and equipment advances for their tenants. Now the FSA was fulfilling that obligation for the plantation owners with emergency rehabilitation loans and other forms of relief payments (Mertz 1978, p. 198).

In addition, the FSA programs were meager in size compared to AAA programs or what was needed. To give some idea of the magnitudes involved, Kirkendall (1966, pp. 129, 131) reports the FSA was authorized to expend $85 million in grants and loans between 1937 and 1940, but that the AAA made $133 million in benefit payments to Texas farmers alone in 1936. Looked at from another angle, $500 million of the $644 million in annual appropriations for agriculture in 1938 went for AAA subsidy programs, compared to $26 million for the bureau that supported and inspected the livestock industry, $24 million for the Soil Conservation Service, $18 million for the Forest Service, $13 million for the Extension Service, and only $10 million for the FSA for helping tenant farmers (U.S. Bureau of the Budget, 1938, p. 145).

However, in spite of its limited charter and small budget, the FSA was nonetheless threatening to local power structures in agriculture. As the most detailed analysis of the FSA puts it, the agency was a challenge to the "economic status quo" at the local level even though it was "economically irrelevant" at the national level (Baldwin 1968, p. 263). This challenge to the local status quo occurred in every part of the country. Most of all, the FSA was viewed as a threat by established farmers because it could provide organizing assistance to workers. Its camps for workers could be used as organizing sites, for example. The most important struggle between farm owners and the FSA occurred in the South, where the FSA tried to undermine the traditional Southern power structure by helping poor farmers, tenants, and agricultural laborers, six million of whom were African Americans. The seriousness of the conflict can be seen in an exchange between the FSA and Senator Byrnes of South Carolina when Byrnes learned in 1937 that African

Americans were being appointed to FSA committees in Southern states. He immediately wrote a letter to the head of the FSA warning that "the Negro will be the one to suffer" if the practice continued; he further warned that the FSA should "not disturb the friendly relations now existing between the races" (Baldwin 1968, p. 307). When the FSA refused to back down, Byrnes went to Wallace, who quickly removed the African Americans from the committees even though he had originally supported the plan.

Byrnes's vehement reaction to the FSA's attempt to empower African Americans in the South is of special relevance because, as we noted in Chapter 1, he was one of Roosevelt's most important Southern allies. He was instrumental in keeping Southern delegates behind Roosevelt at the Democratic convention in 1932, and he played an even bigger part in gathering Southern support for Roosevelt's program during his first term. By 1937, however, he was in the process of quietly organizing the Southern revolt against Roosevelt that stopped most New Deal legislation in its tracks and provided the basis for the conservative voting coalition when Republicans gained many seats in Congress in the 1938 elections. Moreover, as explained in the next section, Byrnes's clash with the FSA came at a time when he was very upset by the CIO's organizing attempts in the South, especially because they were interracial in nature.

The FSA suffered serious setbacks in the early 1940s. Roosevelt needed the cooperation of the conservative voting coalition and its corporate allies to have success in the industrial mobilizations for war production, and their price for cooperation was the dismantling of liberal initiatives such as the FSA (Albertson 1961, p. 286; Waddell 2001). The agency's employees were refused long-sought civil service status in 1941 due to Farm Bureau pressure on Congress, which kept the pay of FSA employees 10 to 15 percent below that of other government workers, greatly demoralizing the agency and hastening the departure of many of its best employees (Baldwin 1968, pp. 315–316; McConnell 1953, pp. 101–102). The agency was disbanded in 1946.

While the attacks against the FSA were unfolding, liberals also tried to revive their earlier hopes for agricultural planning by convincing Wallace in late 1938 to try to reshape departmental programs, including the AAA subsidy program, by transforming the minuscule Bureau of Agricultural Economics (BAE) into a departmental planning agency. The reorganization plan called for the bureau to make studies of the budgets and plans it received from all agencies within the department. It also was charged with developing local committees to formulate land-use policies, which was seen as a direct challenge by the Farm Bureau and leaders within the AAA.

Although it may not seem apparent at first glance, land-use planning raised issues of class conflict in the 1930s because it could be used to benefit landowners or help tenant farmers and farm workers. From the successful farmers' point of view, land-use planning was a way to make commercial farming more profitable by increasing the size of their farms and eliminating marginal farmers, which could be accomplished by ending government land grants for new homesteads, purchasing marginal farm lands and turning them into pastures and parks, and encouraging industries to move to rural areas in order to employ displaced agricultural workers (David Hamilton 1991, p. 184; Rowley 1970, p. 39; Saloutos 1982, pp. 31–32). Liberals, however, had other policies in mind when they talked of land use. They thought a proper land-use policy should help turn tenants into owners and that some land could be used more productively if it were farmed cooperatively. They also wanted to resettle poor and tenant farmers on good land rather than force them out of farming, and to bring low-income farmers into the political process.

As might be anticipated by this point in the story, the liberals' land-use concepts were shelved. All farmers, not just wealthy ones, resisted the idea of resettlement, and it was difficult for the government to buy productive land for possible resettlement in any case. Plans for cooperative farming were abandoned because of resistance from both poor and prosperous farmers. All that was left of the liberal notion of land-use planning was the democratic participation of all farmers in the planning process through membership on BAE committees, but members of the Farm Bureau who did not want any changes in their composition dominated those committees. They saw any reconstitution of the committees as a threat that had to be eliminated because the committees would report directly to the BAE and could be used for training programs and discussion groups (Kirkendall 1966, p. 180).

By early 1940, the BAE's attempts to increase grassroots involvement in the planning committees had alienated the AAA and other agencies in the department that were aligned with the Farm Bureau, and its criticisms of the AAA in its annual reports were the final straw (Kirkendall 1966, Chapter 10). It then suffered major budget cuts in arguments before the House Appropriations Committee in 1941 and 1942, which led to the assignment of the planning committees to the AAA. It was officially demoted in 1945 after being attacked in Congress for allowing its experts to write reports that provoked powerful agribusiness interests in Mississippi and California. The report on life in a Mississippi county suggested that race relations there might be less than idyllic (Kirkendall 1966, p. 235). The report on two small towns in central California claimed that the quality of life in the town surrounded by small farms was better than in the one surrounded by large agribusinesses. When growers protested, the BAE withheld the report from publication, once again showing that experts—in this case, sociologists and anthropologists—did not have the independence while in government service that historical institutionalists attribute to them (Kirkendall 1964).

THE AFTERMATH OF THE NATIONAL LABOR
RELATIONS ACT

Although the corporate community suffered a major defeat when the National Labor Relations Act passed, its leaders and trade associations nonetheless continued to resist unionization through a multipronged attack. With Industrial Relations Counselors, Inc., frequently reminding its clients that employee representation plans were legal if the employer did not control them, industrial relations executives restructured their plans with the hope they would find favor with their employees. Top corporate chieftains made preparations to challenge the constitutionality of the act in the Supreme Court, with the long list of corporate lawyers employed by the American Liberty League taking the lead by means of a lengthy brief they already had prepared (Shamir 1995, pp. 85–92, for the most complete list of corporate lawyers and Wall Street law firms that filed cases against the National Labor Relations Act or supported the American Liberty League). Further, they obtained injunctions to prohibit the National Labor Relations Board from carrying out the duties assigned to it by the legislation until the Supreme Court ruled on the constitutionality of the act. Finally, many corporations prepared for violent confrontations with labor organizers by stockpiling guns and dynamite, hiring labor spies and infiltrating union groups, organizing squads of men to attack pro-union activists, and in a few cases making contact with right-wing vigilante groups. These efforts were uncovered in Senate hearings in early 1937 that embarrassed the corporate community and put many corporations on the defensive (Auerbach 1966; Huberman 1937). Among the corporations preparing to use violence against their employees were General Motors and Goodyear Tire and Rubber, both members of the Special Conference Committee (Scheinberg 1986, Chapter 7).

Labor leaders were of course elated by the passage of the National Labor Relations Act, and many workers at the plant level were inspired to make new demands, with the number of strikes increasing significantly in 1936. Although spontaneous sit-downs by workers in the rubber industry in the face of wage cuts in early 1936 led to an increase in the membership of the United Rubber Workers, top-level AFL leaders made no immediate attempt to take advantage of the new labor act with massive organizing drives. Three important issues delayed organizing efforts until early 1937, giving the corporate community ample time to put all its defenses in place.

First, there was the ongoing disagreement over the form the new unions would take, craft or industrial, which heated up within four months after the National Labor Relations Act passed. It was not resolved until November 1936, when several union leaders, including one from a craft union, decided to start the Committee for Industrial Organization to build industrial unions. Three years later it became the Congress of Industrial Organizations. For the leaders of traditional craft unions, ranging from carpenters to railroad engineers to photoengravers, the battle involved both long-standing principle and the desire to continue to dominate the AFL. Harking back to the early days of the AFL in the 1880s, they insisted that only craft unions were strong enough in the long run to resist employer pressures. But John L. Lewis and Sidney Hillman, the main force behind the CIO effort, argued that large corporations could only be organized if workers with varying levels and types of skills were part of one industrial union, pointing to the failure of most union drives in heavy industry in 1933 and 1934 and the success of their own unionization efforts. They also claimed, as we also noted in Chapter 3, that workers in industries such as steel, rubber, and automobiles wanted to be in one industrial union (Bernstein 1969, Chapters 8 and 9).

Even if there had been agreement within the AFL, which would have made it possible to issue charters for both craft and industrial unions, there was another difficulty: the need for experienced organizers, who were woefully few within the AFL. Lewis decided to solve this problem in good part by reaching out to his perennial enemies in the Communist and Socialist parties, which had opposed him on many occasions in the 1920s, leading him on one occasion to have the Communist members beaten up and expelled. These overtures to his former opponents, which were formally denied at the time, began with an interview Lewis gave to the Communist Party's *Daily Worker* in December 1935. They were made possible by the fact that the American Communists had quietly signaled a change in strategy by closing down their rival unions and allowing their organizers to work with the most militant local trade unionists. This change of line was formally announced in February 1936, after Moscow gave its reluctant approval. Months of negotiations then ensued, finally ending with an agreement in mid-1936 that led to the hiring of many dozens of Communist labor organizers, highly experienced due to their past organizing efforts. Because the Communists had to gain approval for this new alliance from Moscow, the detailed reports in the Soviet archives opened in the early 1990s make it possible to see the arrangement in detail from the Communist perspective (Haynes, Klehr, and Anderson 1998, pp. 53–70).

Third, Lewis and Hillman knew that they could not successfully organize large corporations run by ultraconservatives unless Roosevelt won reelection in 1936 and non-Southern Democrats gained enough seats in Congress to fend off a potential pro-employer alliance between Southern Democrats and Northern Republicans. Labor leaders also wanted to elect sympathetic governors and local officials in key industrial states such as Pennsylvania, the home of the steel industry, and Michigan, the center of the automobile industry.

The unions were particularly concerned about a possible Republican victory because of the highly visible but ultimately futile efforts of the American Liberty League. The du Pont family and their close allies, the Pew family, which owned Sun Oil, gave nearly $1 million to the Republicans (that's $15.2 million in 2010 dollars), and one-third of the Republican National Finance Committee was identified with the Liberty League (Wolfskill 1962, pp. 205–206). The du Ponts also gave another $350,000 and the Pews an additional $20,000 to the Liberty League and other extremely right-wing groups, with names such as the Crusaders, the Sentinels of the Republic, and the Southern Committee to Uphold the Constitution (see, for example, Webber 2000, p. 27). This money was used to supplement the Republican campaign in a variety of ways.

To help win Democratic victories against the combined Republican and Liberty League efforts, labor played a major role in a political campaign for the first time in American history as foot soldiers for candidates and as financial contributors to campaigns. Between 1906 and 1935, the AFL had given a meager $95,000 to national political campaigns, but in 1936 organized labor contributed $803,800 to the party and political organizations aligned closely with it, which represented 16 percent of the $5.1 million spent by the Democrats (Overacker 1937, p. 46; Webber 2000, page 116, Table 7.2). A little over three-fourths of that money came from just three unions—the United Mine Workers ($470, 349), the International Ladies Garment Workers Union ($90,409), and the Amalgamated Clothing Workers of America ($62,938). What makes these donations all the more unexpected is that Lewis had voted for President Hoover in 1932 and the leaders of the other two unions, David Dubinksy and Sidney Hillman, had voted the Socialist Party ticket.

Contrary to claims that Roosevelt had major backing in the corporate community from a capital-intensive international segment of the capitalist class, as one political scientist insists (Ferguson 1995), or from proto-Keynesians in mass-consumption industries (such as department stores, chain stores, manufacturers of household electrical equipment), as one historian believes (Fraser 1989, 1991), he did not have significant support in any business sector except the production of alcoholic beverages, which simply "paid its debt of gratitude to the Democratic Party" by providing 5.7 percent of the party's donations of $1,000 or more (Overacker 1937, p. 487). Using campaign contributions as an indicator of political preferences in an election in which virtually no business executives gave to both parties, two different studies found that Roosevelt had support from only 17 to 20 percent of the 35 percent of corporate executives who gave $100 or more to either party. The first study used the directors of the 270 largest corporations of that era (Allen 1991). The second used a large random sample of 960 executives and directors listed in *Poor's Register of Corporations Executives and Directors* (Webber 2000, p. 13). Four factors that are often ignored by social scientists who focus on power structures, but not by those who study voting patterns, were the best predictors of business support for Roosevelt: region (Southerners in most business sectors gave more to Democrats than to Republicans); religion (Catholics and Jews in the capital-intensive and mass-consumption sectors were much more likely to give to Democrats than Protestants were); the size of the business (smaller businesses tended to support Roosevelt); and involvement in the manufacture or sale of alcoholic beverages. On the other hand, and contrary to many past claims, Roosevelt did not lose any of his 1932 business backers except the du Pont family and their key employees and close associates (Webber 2000, for detailed evidence for all these points).

Nor did any of the corporate moderates who supported the Social Security Act provide any financial support for the Roosevelt campaign. Rockefeller, conspicuously absent from the list of American Liberty League donors, was at the same time the largest single donor to the Republican National Committee ($105,000), along with an additional $10,000 to the state party and $5,000 to the Republican senatorial candidate in New York. John D. Rockefeller III, still playing a prominent role in Industrial Relations Counselors, gave $5,000 to the Republican National Committee, $5,000 to the state party, $5,000 to the Republican senatorial candidate in New York, and $5,000 to Republican congressional candidates. Swope and Teagle did not contribute to either party, but Teagle revealed his conservatism with a $2,000 contribution to the Crusaders, a super-patriotic organization that had some trappings of a vigilante group.

Due to the strong corporate support for the Republican challenger, Roosevelt was outspent $8.8 million to $5.1 million, and most major newspapers endorsed his opponent. Nevertheless, he won 62.5 percent of the two-party vote, documenting once again that those with the biggest war chest don't always win and that the influence of the mass media can be overstated. The ultraconservatives' appeal to traditional values, their claims that the Constitution was being shredded, and their insistence that the New Deal was socialism in liberal clothing fell on deaf ears. Organized labor's efforts seemed to make the difference in Ohio, Illinois, Indiana, and Pennsylvania, including "crucial local elections in the steel and coal towns of Pennsylvania and Ohio" (Dubofsky 2000, p. 157). The Democrats increased their already overwhelming margins in both the Senate and House, and also elected New Deal Democrats to the governorships in Pennsylvania and Michigan.

With New Deal Democrats in key positions of power, the newly hired organizers employed by the CIO targeted an automobile assembly plant in Flint, Michigan, in early January 1937 for a sit-down strike that would serve as an ideal starting point and a signal of what was to come. The automobile factory was chosen because it belonged to General Motors and was a critical link in the company's network of factories. Success would bring much of General Motors's production to a halt. Moreover, a victory over the third-largest corporation in the country was likely to bring hope to industrial workers everywhere because its profits had rebounded in 1935 and 1936, leading to $10 million in salaries and bonuses for 350 officers and directors in 1936 while its workers averaged $900 a year, well below the $1,600 that was considered to be the minimum necessary for a family of four (Zilg 1974, p. 330). Led in good part by Communist and Socialist factions in the fledgling United Auto Workers, the sit-downers held the factory for six weeks despite attacks by police, legal threats from local authorities, and demands by the owners that the liberal governor put an end to this illegal takeover of private property (Fine 1969, for a detailed account). However, neither the governor nor Roosevelt would accede to the corporation's demands, forcing its leaders to negotiate with the union and thereby providing a major triumph for the CIO.

While the Flint drama unfolded, the chairman of U.S. Steel decided for several reasons that it was time to make a deal with the unions, starting with the fact that New Deal Democrats controlled Pennsylvania, where the company had many of its mills (Bernstein 1969, pp. 466–473; Colin Gordon 1994, p. 229). Furthermore, the CIO's Steel Workers Organizing Committee was in any case winning over many members of the company's employee representation plan. In effect, union organizers were building an industrial union at U.S. Steel, and elsewhere, through the employee representation plans (Jacoby 1997, pp. 158–159; Zieger 1995, pp. 54–59). As a result, the steel company's chairman began secret meetings with Lewis that led to a signed agreement shortly after the United Auto Workers' victory over General Motors. The agreement saved Lewis from expending resources on what could have been a very long and tough battle, kept the many Communist organizers from rising to important positions in what was basically a top-down union, and provided a visible symbolic victory because U.S. Steel was still the largest industrial company in the United States. Change came easily and more completely at General Electric, where Gerard Swope and Owen Young, a director of Industrial Relations Counselors since the 1920s, were still in charge. When the workers voted to unionize, Young and Swope recognized the union immediately and began bargaining. That the union was the largest of the Communist-dominated unions made the bargaining all the more notable, but the fact that the leaders were Communists made no difference in terms of the company's willingness to deal with the union. As a result of these and other victories, the percentage of the nonagricultural workforce in unions rose from 6.9 percent in 1933 to 19.2 percent in 1939 (see, for example, Cohen 2009, p. 304).

By 1937 Industrial Relations Counselors was keeping its distance from labor conflicts. As Rockefeller wrote to Mackenzie King, the creator of his employee representation plan, in late April 1937, just a few days after the Supreme Court ruled that the National Labor Relations Act was constitutional, such plans "were generally doomed." Rockefeller went on to note that "the Harvester Company, the Goodyear Company, and now the subway company in New York City, have given up their industrial relations plans, which have worked successfully for many years, and are carrying on collective bargaining with the union, while the Steel Company has recognized the unions, which I assume is tantamount to the same thing." Although he did not look forward to unions "in our own companies," he did not think it "either wise or possible to withstand the pressures from outside for union recognition even though the employees themselves may prefer the present plan" (Rockefeller 1937). As it turned out, and as we mentioned in Chapter 3, Standard Oil of New Jersey and several other Standard Oil companies were among the relative handful of companies that were able to maintain their employee representation plans at least into the 1960s.

Moreover, several problems soon arose that slowed the CIO's progress. With the help of the state police in Ohio, Indiana, and Illinois, along with layoffs for thousands of workers due to the economic downturn triggered by Roosevelt's decision to balance the budget, the ultraconservatives in Little Steel were able to defeat unionization efforts in the summer and fall of 1937. A similar drive in the heterogeneous textile industry was stalled later in the year for the same combination of reasons.

At the same time, Southern Democrats were deeply upset by the sit-downs in the North and by attempts by the CIO to organize in the South, starting in early 1937 with the textile industry, which was by then the largest industry in the South due to the rapid movement of Northern mills into the region. The fact that the CIO organizing drives were interracial in both the North and South only added fuel to the fire. Led by James Byrnes of South Carolina, the Southern Democrats began a series of actions within Congress that created problems for the CIO and the National Labor Relations Board, ranging from passage of a "sense of the Senate" resolution that sit-downs were illegal to attacks on the labor board's budget (Gross 1981; Patterson [1967] 1981, pp. 135–137). Capitalizing on the growing animosity in Congress over Roosevelt's unexpected court-packing scheme, introduced as a complete surprise on February 5, 1937, which stirred fears in Southerners of an attack on the Jim Crow system, the effort to hamstring the National Labor Relations Board helped to revive the conservative voting coalition that had dominated Congress since the Compromise of 1877 (Patterson [1967] 1981). (In 1939, the Supreme Court ruled that sit-down strikes were illegal, thereby depriving union organizers of a potent tactic that makes it impossible to bring in replacement workers.)

To make matters worse for pro-union forces, the AFL became extremely bitter toward the National Labor Relations Board because of its belief that the board's decisions favored the CIO. As the AFL had feared might happen before passage of the act, the board was using its power to create large bargaining units that included workers in a wide range of occupations. AFL leaders felt from early 1937 on that the NLRB was aiding the CIO, but the decision that "could not be forgiven" occurred in June 1938, when the board ruled that the entire West Coast would be the bargaining unit for longshoremen and warehousemen, thereby eliminating the AFL in the four ports where it had small locals (Gross 1981, p. 56). Then the board voided an AFL contract because it was allegedly a sweetheart deal between the company and the AFL that was meant to keep out the CIO. AFL officials also were upset by the ruling in the Mobile Dry Dock Company case in Alabama that allowed for plant-wide elections in which the five hundred "white, highly skilled mechanics" would be outnumbered by the one thousand African American laborers (Gross 1981, pp. 59, 85).

The AFL retaliated by claiming that Communists dominated both the labor board and the CIO. It charged that a Communist Party member, with allegedly great power as the board's executive secretary, had manipulated information in the West Coast longshoremen's case in favor of a seemingly pro-Communist CIO union. It also charged that one member of the board, a former industrial relations manager at the liberal William Filene & Sons department store, had become pro-Communist. It is highly likely that these AFL charges are true, but the important point is that the craft segment of the working class had gotten into a public political battle with the industrial segment. In our view, the Communists in the CIO and at the National Labor Relations Board were primarily a useful rallying cry and an ideal scapegoat.

The result of Southern and AFL disenchantment with the National Labor Relations Board was a new alignment of class forces. The Southerners were once again in an alliance with a united Northern business community that had planned for amendments to the National Labor Relations Act from the day of its passage. The working class, on the other hand, was now split. Moreover, the most conservative segments of the ownership and working classes entered into an alliance after decades of unrelenting hostility. Beginning in July 1938, leaders of the NAM began meeting in private with AFL lawyers to decide upon those amendments to the National Labor Relations Act that would best serve their common interest in thwarting the CIO (Gross 1981, pp 67ff.).

At this point the Roosevelt Recession of 1937–1938 entered into the equation once again because it contributed to the large gains for the Republicans in both the Senate and the House in the 1938 elections, thereby changing the balance of power in Congress. The result was a nearly unbeatable conservative voting coalition that could weaken the National Labor Relations Board and slow any further union gains. (Roosevelt joined with the Communist Party in blaming the new recession he had started on a "capital strike" by his corporate enemies, a laughable concept because eager regional and smaller capitalists would have taken advantage of the new opportunities that large corporations were in effect giving them if there had been any such opportunities.)

Buoyed by the 1938 election results, the political leadership that was needed to stop the drive for industrial unions was provided by a Southern Democrat in the House, Howard Smith, who also was chairman of a local bank in his hometown of Alexandria, Virginia. The new Southern Democrat, NAM, and AFL coalition greatly weakened the NLRB in late 1939 and early 1940 through damaging revelations in House committee hearings, undermining the board's credibility and causing Roosevelt to make changes in its personnel (Gross 1981, p. 2). Moreover, it was the bill fashioned by this coalition that was the basis for the Taft-Hartley Act, a fact the AFL later tried to deny or ignore. As Gross (1981, p. 3) summarizes his discoveries:

> The Hartley Bill was written in Smith's office using Smith's 1940 bill as a model, and the Taft-Hartley Act of 1947 contained most of the more severe provisions of the Hartley Bill. The AFL-business-conservative southern Democrat alliance during the first half of the twelve years between the Wagner and Taft-Hartley Acts has had a lasting effect on labor history and on labor law.

Despite its complaints about the labor board, the AFL nonetheless was growing in the late 1930s in regulated industries, such as railroads and trucking, where both owners and workers could benefit from the higher prices made possible by government oversight (Nelson 2001). Construction unions also grew in the late 1930s when the economy revived, partly due to the gradual rise in defense spending. In addition, the AFL made gains in service industries. By 1941 the AFL had almost twice as many members as the CIO (5.2 million versus 2.7 million), a fact that was masked at the time by the CIO's inflated membership claims (Bernstein 1969, p. 774). Furthermore, its 106 affiliates were in a far wider range of business sectors than the 41 CIO unions, which were concentrated in mining and manufacturing, with its mining, automobile, steel, electrical, clothing, and textile unions accounting for 71 percent of its membership.

On the basis of the setbacks the CIO suffered in Little Steel and textiles in the latter half of 1937, and in Congress from 1938 to 1940, and despite the gains made by the AFL, we think the union movement was stalled at best and most likely on the defensive by 1940–1941. However, the weaknesses of the union movement at that point were obscured by the country's need for class harmony after 1941 to carry out the huge industrial and military mobilizations that were necessary to win World War II against two formidable enemies. Recognizing that the war could be lost, Roosevelt was firm in insisting upon a suspension of class warfare within the United States until the wars with Germany and Japan were over. He therefore created a temporary National War Labor Board consisting of four employers, four union leaders, and four government representatives, which decreed that new employees had to join existing unions in exchange for a no-strike pledge from organized labor. The result was large gains in membership by unions because corporations could not employ their usual instruments of intimidation and repression (see, for example, Winders 2005). In a context in which everyone was employed, including previously excluded women and African Americans, union leaders and many members of the rank-and-file began to think they had a more solid power base than they actually did.

The growth in membership during the war caused the union leaders to develop the same illusions about their strength that their predecessors harbored during World War I. At the same time, the AFL muted its antagonism toward the CIO in the postwar years because it had gained strength and members at the expense of the CIO. Moreover, the AFL and CIO started to work together in the months after the end of the war as workers lost ground due to inflation once price controls were lifted. But their strike actions failed in the face of united opposition by the reinvigorated corporate leaders and instead created a backlash that gave Congress the opportunity in early 1946 to legislate many of the restrictions that the Southern Democrats and the NAM had decided upon several years earlier. Only a veto by Truman kept these restrictions from becoming law at that early juncture. Then, in the election a few months later, only 75 of 318 candidates endorsed by organized labor's political action arm were elected, and the Republicans gained control of Congress for the first time in eighteen years, with 246 seats in the House and 51 in the Senate; it was a clear sign that a majority of the electorate, which consisted of only 38 percent of those eligible to vote in that election, was not sympathetic to organized labor, including some liberals who thought the labor leaders had acted in an irresponsible fashion (see, for example, Griffith 1988, p. 145). The result was the passage of the Taft-Hartley Act in 1947 despite Truman's veto, which crippled unions in numerous ways (Gable 1953).

For one thing, the Taft-Hartley amendments included new language that downgraded the importance of collective bargaining in the name of free speech for both employers and workers. In practice, this meant employers could refuse to bargain and more readily propagandize workers through pamphlets, flyers, and speeches at meetings workers had to attend. Veiled threats to move the plants elsewhere were often made, and companies did increase their efforts to move factories to the South whenever possible. In addition, the board's chief staff lawyer gained some independence from the board itself, and union leaders had to sign affidavits swearing they were not members of the Communist Party. There were other changes as well, such as bans on secondary boycotts and unauthorized ("wildcat") strikes by the rank-and-file on the shop floor, all of which hindered union organizing (see, for example, Gross 1995, Chapter 1). In addition, the softening of provisions against unfair management practices aided in the defense and extension of company unions (Jacoby 1997, pp. 183–191, 200–203).

In 1948 the AFL and CIO worked together even more closely to help restore strong Democratic majorities to both houses of Congress. They also worked very hard for the re-election of Truman, but their efforts were complicated by a third-party challenge by former Secretary of Agriculture and Vice President Henry A. Wallace on the Progressive Party ticket. Although Wallace ran for his own reasons, union leaders were sure, on the basis of information from their own informants, that the Communist Party and the CIO unions it controlled were the backbone of the new party. Communists denied these claims at the time, and there were some non-Communist leftists in the Progressive Party, but in fact the AFL and CIO leaders were absolutely correct, as historical archives fully demonstrate.

The decision to back Wallace was made by the left wing of the Communist Party in late 1947 as the best way to fulfill Moscow's October directive that everything should be done to stop the Marshall Plan (Stepan-Norris and Zeitlin 2003, pp. 292–295). Sympathetic histories of the Progressive Party, often by its former members, tried to argue that the Communists did not dominate it (for example, MacDougall 1965). However, the full records available in recent years prove otherwise. Even several key left-liberals close to Wallace, who were said to be the best evidence that Wallace was not surrounded by Communists, turned out to be secret Communists (Devine 2003). In any event, the head of the CIO believed he had solid information on this issue from informants, including Communist union leaders who refused to accept the CP directive, so he began the process of eliminating Communists from the union movement. This decision was the beginning of the end for the Communist Party in terms of any influence within the CIO, leading to the demise of the "combative, class-conscious industrial union movement" it had built within the larger context of the CIO (Stepan-Norris and Zeitlin 2003, p. 296).

Despite the initial threat posed to the liberal-labor coalition within the Democratic Party by the Progressive Party challenge, the Democrats nonetheless returned Truman to the White House and reclaimed majorities in both houses of Congress, in part due to the efforts of organized labor. Labor

leaders therefore had every hope that they could reverse some of the changes
brought about by the Taft-Hartley Act. In particular, labor wanted to remove a clause that legalized state-level anti-union "right to work laws,"
which allowed newly employed workers to refuse to pay union dues if they
so desired. Eleven states already had passed such laws, all of them in the
South and Great Plains, and seven more in the same regions were to do so
in the 1950s (Dempsey 1961, pp. 25–27). However, the union movement
was stopped cold in its effort to make any changes in Taft-Hartley. Once
again, the power of the Southern segment of the ownership class was the
determining factor. As historian Robert Zieger (1986, p. 119) points out, a
united working class could do nothing against the Southern Democrats, who
of course had the support of most Republicans as well:

> But despite labor's electoral and financial contributions and the Democrats'
> successes in 1948, the Eighty-first Congress failed to move energetically on
> Taft-Hartley. Although President Truman dutifully supported revision of Taft-
> Hartley, even under Democratic control Congress remained in conservative
> hands. Southern Democrats, almost uniformly hostile to the labor movement,
> dominated key congressional committees. While the tally sheets of labor lob-
> byists suggested that most Democratic senators and congressmen from north-
> ern, eastern, and blue-collar districts loyally supported labor's goals, they also
> revealed that labor simply could not muster the strength to gain significant
> revision of the law.

From that point forward, the union movement lost its momentum.
Although its members enjoyed another twenty-five to thirty years of good
wages and improved benefits in several mass-production industries, including
steel and autos, the percentage of the non-agricultural labor force in unions
peaked at 35.5 percent in 1945, stagnated at an average of about 33 percent
for the next thirteen years, and then began a gradual decline in the late 1950s
from which the union movement never recovered (Goldfield 1987). By the
1970s unions had begun to fail rapidly for two separate reasons: (1) another
all-out effort on the part of corporations to weaken the National Labor
Relations Board, beginning in the late 1960s (Gross 1995) and (2) the defection of many blue-collar and white-collar Democrats, North and South,
to the Republican Party in reaction to the demands being made by African
Americans for better jobs, school integration, and housing integration (see,
for example, Carmines and Stimson 1989; Carter 2000; Edsall and Edsall
1992; Sugrue 2008). Both of these changes in turn made the movement of
industrial jobs to the South and third-world countries much easier because
of decisions by President Richard Nixon's conservative appointees to the
National Labor Relations Board (Gross 1995). With both labor unions and
the Civil Rights Movement on the defensive, the corporate moderates were
able to take a right turn on key policy issues in the mid-1970s in the face of

both inflation and rising unemployment (see, for example, Domhoff 2007; Piven and Cloward 1982, for analyses of the right turn).

REVISING THE SOCIAL SECURITY ACT

When we last looked at the Social Security Act, it had been signed by Roosevelt in August 1935 to the general satisfaction of the corporate moderates, with the proviso that several changes had to be made to make it fully to their liking. The way in which those changes were worked out is highly revealing in terms of the role of the policy-planning network in implementing social policies that are favored by the corporate moderates. In this instance, two SSRC committees, the Public Administration Committee and the Committee on Social Security, both mentioned briefly in Chapter 4, were the key links with government, but it is also noteworthy that the Rockefeller Foundation was standing behind them with both advice and money (Fisher 1993).

As the SSRC committees positioned themselves to play a major role in shaping the Social Security Board and any legislative amendments that might be needed, the Rockefeller Foundation and the SSRC committees gradually edged Industrial Relations Counselors, and Stewart in particular, to the sidelines because they were too closely identified with employers. However, this decision did cause hard feelings, which we know due to two letters in the Rockefeller Archive Center. The first was sent by Stacy May, the coordinator for public administration programs for the Rockefeller Foundation, to Joseph P. Harris, the research director for the SSRC's Public Administration Committee. May told Harris that "it is entirely sound for you to attempt to straighten out on the feeling of strain between your committee and the Industrial Relations Counselors" (May 1936). May then stated the basis for the tension, namely, a decision to give the SSRC the visible role because it would have more legitimacy as a disinterested source: "It seems to me clear that your group is much more apt to be accepted than the Industrial Relations Counselors as an objective body the advice of which might be of service to the Social Security Board" (May 1936).

Nonetheless, IRC would continue to be valuable, the letter continues, because it had compiled very useful information and might be helpful in reassuring reluctant companies that it made sense to support the Social Security Administration:

> On the other hand, the Industrial Relations Counselors has done an impressive amount of work in the field and, as I have reviewed their publications recently, it seems to me that they have collected a considerable amount of material even on the detailed administrative aspects of the problem such as forms, etc. Furthermore, the field is so huge that I am all in favor of having everyone who is equipped to make any contribution to it proceed to do so. Everyone, I suppose,

accepts the fact that administrative procedure will not get very far unless it is able to win the support of industrial groups, and it is likewise agreed that those industrial groups have a considerable experience which may be drawn upon for guidance in the operation of their own pension schemes, etc., because of the fact that many of the largest firms have operated abroad and have had actual experience in working under social insurance schemes of a number of types. If, then, the Industrial Relations Counselors are interested in continuing their past work and have the resources to do so it would seem to me that they might be encouraged to make it their special task to see that the industrial side of the case is heard and that the industrial experience is available (May 1936).

According to a memo on March 26 to top foundation officials from one of their employees, John Van Sickle, who was associate director of the foundation's Division of Social Sciences and its major contact with the SSRC's two committees working to shape the Social Security Board, Stewart probably came to terms with the new arrangement:

> I lunched today with Bryce Stewart. The main purpose of the meeting was to discover to what extent he felt aggrieved by the Foundation's recent action in appropriating funds for the investigations of the Public Administration Committee notably in the field of unemployment insurance administration and employment office procedures. He appeared to have accepted our action as evidence that it would not be feasible for him to push ahead with his own project (Van Sickle 1936).

Van Sickle's two-page memo, which is also of general interest to us because it once again spotlights how the Rockefeller Foundation combined money and information to play a pivotal role in the implementation of the Social Security Act, then went on to summarize the work that IRC was doing and discuss how that work might fit into the SSRC committees' larger plan. A possible grant request to the foundation from Stewart is mentioned, along with the fact that IRC would remain valuable in advising employers about meeting the requirements of the Social Security Act. In short, IRC and Stewart would now have a more peripheral role than they did in the drafting of the act.

Although the Public Administration Committee made many contributions to the development of the Social Security Board between 1935 and 1937, the Committee on Social Security took primary responsibility for Social Security in 1937 so that the Public Administration Committee could concentrate on other governmental issues. In 1937–1938 industrial relations expert Joseph Willits of the Wharton School, whose work with the Rockefeller industrial relations experts and the SSRC reached back to the early 1920s, took over as chair of the Committee on Social Security. In addition, J. Douglas Brown joined the committee and thereby provided another close link to the Rockefeller industrial relations circle and to the staff that wrote the Social Security Act as well; he became chair of the committee the next year. The committee also included an AT&T executive, Chester I. Barnard, the president of New Jersey Bell Telephone, who made somewhat of a scholarly name for himself with his lectures on enlightened management that became a Harvard University Press book titled *The Functions of the Executive* (Barnard 1938). The other member from the corporate community was Albert Linton, the president of a major insurance company in Philadelphia, Provident Mutual Life Insurance. In addition to Brown, there were three other university professors with expertise on unemployment or old-age benefits, along with the director of the Russell Sage Foundation, the head of the railway and steamship clerks union, and representatives of the American Public Welfare Association and the American Association of Social Workers.

There is evidence that the officers of the Rockefeller Foundation were "exerting direct control over appointments to the committee" (Fisher 1993, p. 148). For example, they vetoed the idea of including Leo Wolman, the professor of economics at Columbia who served as an advisor to Hillman, which led to the appointment of the union leader for railway and steamship clerks. Then, too, the SSRC accepted a Rockefeller Foundation suggestion that a representative of the American Public Welfare Association be added to the committee.

The Clark Amendment Once Again

The first key issue facing the SSRC committees concerned the defeat of any attempt to revive the Clark Amendment. The task was assigned to the Committee on Social Security, which hired a highly respected actuarial expert, Rainard B. Robbins, who had first worked on old-age pensions for the Carnegie Foundation for the Advancement of Teaching fifteen years earlier. Robbins began by writing to the industrial relations officers at a wide range of companies, along with the relevant executives at six major insurance companies, to find out if they were favorable to the amendment. The way in which he operated can be seen in an exchange of letters he had with Marion Folsom of Eastman Kodak, who had served on the Committee on Economic Security's Advisory Council on Social Security.

Robbins's letter to Folsom on December 16, 1935, began by calling attention to the well-known people who served on the committee: "The Committee indicated by this letterhead has asked me to find for them, if possible, the views of a number of leading employers with reference to a provision for "contracting-out" in the old age annuity sections of the Social Security law" (Robbins 1935). He then asked if Eastman Kodak had "reached a decision as to how it will modify its retirement plan, if at all," and invited Folsom to lunch if he happened to be coming to New York City in the next few weeks.

Folsom replied two days later saying he would be happy to discuss the issue, but first he noted that "I was quite interested in seeing the personnel of your committee; it is a high-grade committee and I am sure that this investigation will be very helpful" (Folsom 1935). He then went on to say he had originally supported the Clark Amendment, but that he had changed his mind because of the headaches of transferring funds to the government when an employee leaves before retirement and of dealing with government oversight. (Readers will recall that these two issues were among the concerns mentioned in IRC's *Memorandum to Clients* No. 15.) After noting that Eastman Kodak already had supplemental plans to attract higher-wage workers to its factories in France, Belgium, and the Netherlands, where government pensions were low, Folsom said that the company would turn its current American pension plan into a supplemental plan.

According to the report written by Robbins (1936), there were many executives with views similar to those expressed by Folsom. Of the seventeen who were acquainted with the details of the amendment, thirteen were opposed to it, two were working to improve it, and two were undecided. When Robbins asked executives if they were aware of the various restrictions and standards built into the amendment, most of them replied, "I had not thought of that" (Robbins 1936, p. 9). Given this line of questioning, we infer that the questions asked by Robbins were also meant to educate executives about the amendment and to discourage them from supporting it.

In the case of insurance companies, Robbins found that five of the six had "no enthusiasm for the Clark Amendment" (Robbins 1936, p. 22). However, they did favor "the general idea of an employer being permitted to conduct his retirement plan independently of the government plan if a way can be found" (Robbins 1936, p. 9). At the same time, they did not see any practical way to improve upon the unsatisfactory Clark Amendment, so they were advising corporate employers to develop plans that supplemented the government plan (compare with Klein 2003, Chapter 3). Most corporate executives caught on fast, although a few ultraconservatives used the passage of the Social Security Act as an opportunity to shrink their plans (Quadagno 1988, p. 118).

Robbins's findings were made known to both friends and critics of the Clark Amendment. In addition, they were used by Latimer as one basis for a report he submitted to the Social Security Board on March 23, 1936. Latimer also drew upon his own personal discussions with executives and a letter to him from Brown, which reported that he had talked to "scores" of executives on a visit to several western states, but found "never even a wishful thought for the Clark Amendment." (Brown then added that "I think Forster [the insurance agent who led the lobbying effort for the Clark Amendment] and Graham [an executive for one major insurance company] will have something to explain away" (Brown 1935c). Latimer concluded his memorandum summarizing what he had learned from Brown's letter, the SSRC report, and his own inquiries by asserting, "With the possible exception of Standard Oil Company of New York, I know of no industrialists favoring the Clark Amendment, if such amendment has all or most of the following features" (Latimer 1936, p. 1). The report then lists several basic features, such as being at least as favorable as the Social Security Act.

When it came time for a joint Congressional committee to convene in the spring of 1936 to discuss the Clark Amendment, the meeting was cancelled. According to the recollections of one labor department lawyer assigned to help draft a new version of the Clark Amendment, the meeting was cancelled because Forster and the insurance companies that had sided with him no longer had any interest in it (Eliot 1992, p. 130–131). We therefore conclude yet again that the advantages of accepting and then building upon the government's social security program were understood by corporate moderates and their experts a few years earlier than historical institutionalists realize when they overlook the role of IRC in creating the Social Security Act and of the SSRC in its implementation (see, for example, Hacker and Pierson 2002; Klein 2003).

The 1939 Amendments to the Social Security Act

Once the Clark Amendment was finally out of the way, SSRC committee members could turn their full attention to providing advice on Social Security Board procedures and suggesting changes in the Social Security Act. The SSRC also arranged "for the employment of people when the government was unable to hire [them] because of the inflexibility of federal personnel recruitment or because of the restrictions against the employment of noncitizens" (Fisher 1993, p. 155). Even before the Social Security Board was established, the Committee on Social Security was providing technical assistance and helping with the selection of personnel: "The committee assisted in the selection of personnel, brought together officials and nongovernmental experts, advised on research plans generally, and, on the details of specific studies, called attention to sources of pertinent data or accumulated experience, participated in innumerable technical conferences and discussions, and facilitated interagency coordination" (Fisher 1993, p. 150).

In addition to the massive informational, organizational, and staffing problems that faced such a major undertaking, the SSRC committees and the Social Security Board had to deal with the many criticisms that had been raised about the program by organized business, liberals, social workers, and supporters of the Townsend Plan and similar senior citizen pressure groups. (These pressure groups had gained strength, not lost it, after the passage of the Social Security Act, and often were able to directly influence state legislatures to improve their old-age assistance programs; this meant they were in a position from which they could have an indirect influence on the Social Security Board and Congress to improve benefits (Amenta 2006, Chapter 7, especially p. 173).) Corporate leaders were most exercised by the reserve fund that Roosevelt and his secretary of treasury had insisted upon at the last minute so that general tax revenues would not have to be used to finance the program decades later. They first of all worried that a large reserve fund would lead to pressures to raise benefits or be used to buy public enterprises, a concern that Teagle (1935) expressed to Swope three years earlier. They also feared that the money might be used to help pay for other government social welfare projects, such as public housing.

On the other side of the fence, liberals, social workers, and advocates from old-age groups wanted to raise pension payments and extend them to more occupational groups than were originally covered, including the self-employed, agricultural workers, and domestic workers. Most worrisome of all to the centrist social insurance experts and leaders of the Social Security Board, many social workers and liberals wanted to merge the old-age insurance program with the old-age assistance plan for those who had not earned enough money over the years to qualify for old-age insurance. The centrists rejected this option, also supported by the Townsend Plan and its imitators, as a form of welfare that could be easily stigmatized and cut back by conservatives. Furthermore, the social workers still wanted to pay for this generous old-age benefit for everyone out of general tax funds.

In the face of the corporate community's criticisms of the reserve fund, which were soon voiced by Republicans in the Senate, the Social Security Board's chair, Arthur Altmeyer, Perkins's former assistant in the Department of Labor, reluctantly agreed to a temporary Advisory Council that would examine the issues closely and recommend any needed amendments to Congress. Brown, still serving on the SSRC's Committee on Social Security, became chair of the twenty-five-member Advisory Council, on which one other member of the Committee on Social Security, Linton of Provident Mutual Life, joined him. The committee also included six other business leaders in addition to Linton (Swope and Folsom were among them, along with a high executive from U.S. Steel). Six union representatives were appointed, three from the AFL and three from the CIO. There were six other professors in addition to Brown, including Witte, the former executive director of the Committee on Economic Security, by this time teaching economics at the University of Wisconsin, and Hansen, a former member of the Technical Board, from Harvard. The general secretary of the National Consumers' League was appointed, along with a recent president of the Association of Schools of Social Work.

According to historian Edward Berkowitz's (1987, pp. 62–66) analysis of the Advisory Council's minutes, which were almost verbatim transcripts of the meetings, Witte, Linton, Folsom, and Brown took the lead in the arguments and compromises, with the labor leaders seldom attending meetings and having very little impact. It seems likely, then, that the historian who studied the issue from the perspective of the Rockefeller Foundation's internal documents and exchanges with the SSRC's Committee on Social Security, Donald Fisher (1993, p. 155), is correct when he concludes that research and reports by the Committee on Social Security "laid the basis for the 1939 amendments to the Social Security Act." For example, in a study similar to the earlier analysis of business leaders' attitudes toward the Clark Amendment, the Committee on Social Security surveyed organized labor, insurance companies, and other businesses on their attitudes toward various proposed modifications of the act, which provided Brown and Linton with a good sense of which amendments would be acceptable to all parties.

After months of negotiations, usually with Witte in one corner and Linton and Folsom in the other, Brown was able to fashion a compromise that satisfied just about everyone. To begin with, all parties agreed that the reserve fund should be whittled down to a "reasonable contingency" size by several means. They included raising benefits, providing higher benefits for married couples, extending benefits to widows at age sixty-five and to the dependent children of deceased recipients, and starting to pay out benefits in 1940 rather than waiting until 1942, as originally planned (Berkowitz 1987, p. 72). Furthermore, all concerned could agree to a payment schedule that gave a slight boost to low-income retirees while restraining benefits at the top. Liberals, social workers, labor, and Townsendites favored these changes because of their concern that low-income people might not otherwise have enough money to live on. The changes suited Keynesian economists such as Hansen because they avoided the drag on the economy that a reserve fund might create and put money into the hands of those most likely to spend it.

As part of this bargain, the insurance companies and other corporations gained agreement that payroll taxes would be kept as low as possible. In addition, insurance companies liked the compromise because it created a market for their profitable private plans for employees with higher incomes, especially for the corporate executive plans that were their biggest customer target. Indeed, this desire was so great that Linton even helped finance some of the liberal reformers who lobbied for "adequacy" in old-age pensions (Sass 1997, p. 282, ftn. 17). As for the corporate moderates, they of course appreciated the fact that the reserve fund would decline, although the issue of its continuing existence was purposely left ambiguous.

Congress accepted most of the Advisory Council's recommendations, but not all of them. Reflecting the continuing concerns of the Southern Democrats and ultraconservatives, no new occupational categories were added (Berkowitz 1987; Manza 1995). Nevertheless, the passage of the 1939 amendments brought Social Security close to the form the corporate moderates desired and that would endure for the next forty-four years. They had eliminated any possibility of contracting out, cut the size of the reserve fund, fended off pressure to enhance the old-age assistance program, and left plenty of room for private pensions for corporate executives.

By the late 1940s, the corporate community as a whole was in general agreement that expansionary changes could be made in the system, thanks in good part to proselytizing efforts by Folsom, who chaired the social insurance committees of both the NAM and the U.S. Chamber of Commerce (Manza 1995). A new Advisory Council created in 1947 made recommendations for amendments that Congress adopted in 1950. Full-time farm and domestic workers were now included, as well as the self-employed, and they were immediately eligible for support. However, most agricultural workers in the South were still excluded (Quadagno 1988, p. 148; Winders 2005, p. 400). Benefits were increased by 77 percent, but a large portion of this increase simply undid the erosion in benefit levels due to the inflation of the previous decade (Altman 2005, Chapter 9; Hacker 2002, p. 140; Manza 1995, pp. 370–372).

Social Security as amended in 1950 remained about the same for three decades, with the extremely important exception of the indexing of Social Security for inflation in the early 1970s. However, funding problems emerged in the late 1970s that led to a new compromise in the early 1980s that created a reserve fund that has been used by Republican administrations to help pay for the massive tax cuts they provided to the wealthy few. This means that general revenue taxes or Social Security taxes, or some combination of the two, will have to be raised to pay off the U.S. Treasury bills that Social Security holds in a legally protected trust fund (Baker 2001; Greider 2009). However, these issues are beyond the time frame of this book (see Altman 2005; Baker and Weisbrot 1999; Light 1985; Rogne and others 2009, for information and perspective on recent decades).

SUMMARY

The findings and analysis on the implementation of the Agricultural Adjustment Act, the National Labor Relations Act, and the Social Security Act support and extend our conclusions based on our study of the origins of these policies: the owners and managers of large income-producing properties dominated the federal government during the New Deal on the policy issues of greatest moment for them.

The AAA program was expanded and its structure refined because it was appreciated by the agribusiness interests of that era. Although liberals did not oppose the enabling legislation, they did try to shape specific policies carried out by the Agricultural Adjustment Administration because of the unfair way these affected farm labor, especially African Americans in the South. At the same time, leftists of various types tried to organize farm workers into unions so they could improve their wages and working conditions. The result was defeat for the liberals and leftists: class conflict was quelled. The farm bloc's ability to amend the act to its liking and fend off challenges from liberals and farm labor in the years after it passed is further support for a class-domination theory.

The Social Security program grew and prospered because corporate moderates, including the top executives of most insurance companies, supported it, especially after some annoying aspects of the original act were removed in 1939. The act also prospered because the plantation capitalists felt insulated from any potential impact on their racial and class domination in the South by the changes in the legislation that they insisted upon before it passed. Moreover, the act did not generate any class conflict and may have reduced it by holding out hope for younger workers that they would eventually have the jobs vacated by retirees. It also meant that middle-aged working adults could worry less about having to support their elderly parents.

In the case of the National Labor Relations Act, which was heartily opposed by all corporate chieftains in both its 1934 and 1935 versions, the record demonstrates that it suffered from constant challenges and was finally altered when mistakes by Roosevelt—his court-packing scheme and his decision to balance the budget—provided an opening for the conservative voting coalition to reclaim its power on labor issues due to the large increase in Republicans in Congress after the 1938 elections. The decision by the AFL to join forces with the NAM and the Southern Democrats to stymie the CIO and the Communists then sealed the board's fate. This ability to thwart the act and contain the upsurge of unionization is evidence that a united ownership class is difficult to defeat in the political arena in the United States, especially when the working class is divided by the re-emergence of divisions based on skill levels, ethnicity, or race. This sequence of events thereby directly contradicts the historical institutionalists' claim that "legislative reversals" are rare because of the "stickiness" of political institutions and the numerous "institutional veto points" at which changes can be blocked (Hacker and Pierson 2002, p. 285). The more important factor is the alignment of class segments for or against the effects of the new legislation. When class coalitions shift, legislation may change despite any institutional inertia, stickiness, or veto points (Winders 2005).

More generally, the corporate community wielded its great power quite dramatically in the face of worker demands in the years between 1877 and 1948 by the way in which it was able to narrow the conflict between capital and labor to the limited matter of collective bargaining over wages, hours, and working conditions, and to undercut collective bargaining with welfare capitalism, human relations initiatives, judicial rulings, outright repression, and the post-1938 limitations on the National Labor Relations Board (McCammon 1990, 1993, 1994). As we noted in Chapter 1, collective bargaining is the one area in which the two sides potentially have some economic interests in common if bargaining can be confined to wages, hours, benefits, and working conditions, but this focus on cooperation and common interests is rarely realized without government actions. Collective bargaining is also the area in which their power resources are even vaguely comparable due to the ability of workers to strike, block shipments of raw materials and finished products, and destroy machinery. Still, labor's strike power is conditioned on the neutrality of government. If government officials decide to use the law or force on striking workers, as it always did before 1937, and sometimes after that date as well, then the workers are far less powerful. Labor history therefore suggests that domination of the relevant institutions of the government is a crucial issue in sustaining corporate power in the United States, as our version of class-domination theory expects.

Then, too, the failure of the liberal-labor coalition to amend the Taft-Hartley Act after the 1948 elections once again points to the plantation capitalists as the tipping point in the power system in that era (compare with Winders 2005). Their complete domination of workers in their region through segregation, intimidation, and violence translated into great political power in the Democratic Party and in Congress, giving them a virtual veto power over any legislation that threatened them. This situation did not change until the massive disruption by the Civil Rights Movement in the 1960s once again forced a breakdown in the North-South employers' alliance, only this time it was conservative Northern Republicans who deserted the Southern Democrats. The Republican refusal to continue to participate in the Southern Democrats' lengthy filibuster resulted in the passage of the Civil Rights Act of 1964 and the more ready acceptance of the Voting Rights Act of 1965, thereby opening the way for major changes in power relations in the South.

With these conclusions as a starting point, it is now possible to take a closer look at historical institutionalism, Marxism, and protest-disruption theory in order to examine the defects in their claims about the origins and implementation of the three main policy initiatives that emerged from the New Deal.

CHAPTER SIX

The Shortcomings of Alternative
Theories of the New Deal

Historical institutionalism, Marxism, and protest-disruption theory each emphasize different aspects of the New Deal and have different weaknesses. Historical institutionalists have written on all three of the acts discussed in this book. Their primary concern is the Social Security Act, and they focus on the role of government officials and independent experts, although they also point to pressures from social movements. Marxists, on the other hand, have placed most of their attention on just one case, the National Labor Relations Act; they emphasize the role of class struggle in its passage and at the same time claim that the act was a co-optation strategy used by liberals, labor leaders, and corporate moderates to forestall even greater militancy from the industrial working class. As for the protest-disruption theorists, who discuss both the National Labor Relations Act and the Social Security Act, they of course focus on the role of social disruption in bringing about their passage.

INSTITUTIONALIST THEORY AND THE NEW DEAL

Reacting to the structural Marxists of the 1970s, who insisted that the deep inner dynamics of capitalism necessarily make government in a capitalist society a "capitalist state," even if capitalists do not try to shape it or are not directly part of it (see, for example, Poulantzas 1969, 1973), the original starting point for the historical institutionalists was the idea that government is at least "potentially autonomous" (Skocpol 1979, 1980). This is because of its monopoly on the legitimate use of force in the territory it controls, its important role in dealing with invaders and rival governments, and its essential role in regulating a wide range of activities within its domain. Historical institutionalists built on this theme, and the key insight was later summarized by the claim that "the logics of state-building and the international state system are not reducible to an economic or class logic" (Orloff 1993, p. 85). The theory further emphasizes the importance of state "capacity" in understanding government independence—the more capacity that the leaders of the government could develop, the more likely they were to realize the state's potential for autonomy.

More recent historical institutionalists have made additions to the theory. For example, Jacob Hacker and Paul Pierson (2002) claim that there is greater business power in some eras than others, such as the decades before the New Deal, when the small and decentralized nature of the American government made it possible to play one state government off against the other, giving corporations "structural" economic power. In this context they go on to assert that business lost power after 1929 because the massive economic crisis shifted policymaking issues to the federal level, at which corporations had little or no structural power. While business did not lose power entirely during the New Deal, it had to rely far more on lobbying and other forms of direct influence, and it had to do so under difficult circumstances: "Moreover, they did so in a political environment characterized by relative organizational weakness on their part, divisions among business sectors, widespread public mobilization, and well organized populist challenges, such as the Townsend Movement for old-age pensions" (Hacker and Pierson 2004, p. 187).

Hacker and Pierson (2002) also bring forth an argument that decreases the importance of any seeming successes that the corporate moderates may have enjoyed during the New Deal by reducing those successes to "induced" or "strategic" preferences because they supposedly were not their first preferences. That is, achieving an induced preference, one that is on a list of options they did not create, "should not necessarily be construed as a sign of great influence" (Hacker and Pierson 2002, p. 283). By this argument, the large role of the National Civic Federation (NCF) in the creation of the Federal Trade Commission is not much of a victory after all, even though the NCF met in a satisfactory way a number of challenges that faced the corporate community. Nor is the creation of the Social Security Act, in spite of the serious actuarial problems that confronted some corporations' private pension plans.

In the following discussion we bring together evidence and arguments that raise doubts about all of the historical institutionalists' main claims when it comes to the New Deal. However, before we begin, we want to reiterate our agreement with the view that governments are potentially autonomous and cannot be reduced to an economic logic, or be seen simply as extensions of the economic system. We also agree that history and institutional structures matter in understanding differences between nations. It is not a foregone conclusion that the capitalists always rule in a society with a capitalist economic system. At the same time, we would also note that the possibility of variation in power structures from country to country was the precise reason for the empirical study of power structures by Floyd Hunter

(1953, 1959), Mills (1956), and those who shared their general approach (see Domhoff 2007 for a history of this research tradition and its empirical findings for the United States). Mills's (1962) critique of Marxism therefore contains many of the same claims and admonitions that historical institutionalists later presented.

Institutionalists and the Agricultural Adjustment Administration

Most of the problems with historical institutionalism when it comes to understanding power in the United States during the New Deal can be seen in their analysis of the Agricultural Adjustment Administration (AAA). In their view, the AAA succeeded first and foremost because it had administrative capacity as part of the Department of Agriculture (Finegold and Skocpol 1995). Although we agree that the training of many kinds of experts within the land grant colleges provided the government with the capacity for planning in agriculture, the Department of Agriculture's most important capacity at the grassroots level, the Extension Service, was in good part launched by the Rockefeller's General Education Board and the Rosenwald Fund, with encouragement from local chambers of commerce. This increased government capacity provided the basis for the creation of the Farm Bureau, an organization that went on to severely limit any government autonomy when it came to agricultural policy.

Contrary to what historical institutionalists might expect, the alliance between commercial farmers and county agents meant that "a segment of the public bureaucracy has been captured and made to serve as the bureaucracy of a private association" (McConnell 1953, p. 176). This "structure of power" bridged and blurred the private-public distinction that is the essential starting point of any analysis that stresses government independence (McConnell 1953, pp. 7 and 72, and Chapter 16). Similar findings in the late 1980s for agriculture and three other policy domains—energy, health, and labor—have been reported on the basis of an interview study of members of policy networks that demonstrated there is no distinct boundary between interest groups and government (Heinz, Laumann, Nelson, and Salisbury 1993). This conclusion is best demonstrated by the fact that 80 percent of the officials above the middle levels in the Department of Agriculture had worked for an agricultural interest group in the past (Heinz and others 1993, p. 221). The authors therefore pointedly conclude that any claims of governmental autonomy are not tenable for the United States (Heinz and others 1993, p. 396). In the language of class-oriented theorists, "class interests become embedded in the state by shaping the direction of state expansion (e.g., new bureaucracies)" (Winders 2005, p. 391).

According to historical institutionalists, the domestic allotment program was primarily the product of agricultural economists within the Department of Agriculture, who were working from a "public interest" perspective (Finegold and Skocpol 1995, p. 61). They also assert that there were experienced experts within agencies of the department who could serve as administrators and staff in the new agency. This in turn provided the AAA with autonomy at its outset, although the authors agree with other theorists that the agency eventually came to be controlled by the Farm Bureau (Finegold and Skocpol 1995, pp. 188, 194). Historical institutionalists also emphasize that organized farmers originally opposed the domestic allotment program. This claim is important to them because it purportedly documents that (1) private interests did not develop the concepts for the program and (2) the government forced plantation capitalists and other commercial farmers to accept a program that was not of their own making.

As we demonstrated in Chapter 2, this analysis is empirically wrong. The original idea for the domestic allotment program came from Beardsley Ruml of the Laura Spelman Rockefeller Memorial Fund and a committee of the Social Science Research Council. The fact that an agricultural economist employed by the government's small Bureau of Agricultural Economics suggested something similar about the same time (actually, after Ruml had talked about his proposal) is beside the point because his efforts did not lead to a proposal that made it to the policy agenda. Instead, the agricultural economist from Harvard who agreed to work on the program at Ruml's request later incorporated the government employee's ideas into the new plan.

Nor can the agricultural economist who did the most to promote and modify the plan, M. L. Wilson, be seen as independent of the policy-planning network. He had been the recipient of research support from Rockefeller for the Fairway Farms experiment, a member of the SSRC's Committee on Agricultural Economics, and a member of a U.S. Chamber of Commerce's committee on agricultural policy. The only government expert who was part of the mix, Mordecai Ezekiel, an innovative agricultural economist, received his Ph.D. at The Brookings Institution, which links him more to the policy-planning network than to the university community that provides most independent experts.

In keeping with their focus on governmental independence, historical institutionalists stress that the major conflicts over agricultural policy after the domestic allotment legislation passed were between the AAA and other agencies in the Department of Agriculture. We agree that there is ample evidence for ongoing intradepartmental battles and even attempts by some agencies to free themselves from the influence of commercial farmers in order to aid tenant farmers, farm workers, and the rural unemployed. However, as we demonstrated in Chapter 5, and in keeping with what a class-based theory would expect, the intradepartmental rivalries reflected the class conflict between large commercial agricultural interests and the liberal, left, and farm labor coalition that developed after the legislation passed. The AAA was dominated by leaders of the farm organizations and officials within that agency who disliked the Farm Security Administration and the Bureau of Agricultural Economics, largely because some members of those two agencies were challengers to the major supporters of the AAA. Parenthetically, it can be noted that two other liberal-leaning agencies within the department, the Rural Electrification Agency and TVA, spared themselves any conflict by striking a deal with the Farm Bureau (McConnell 1953, pp. 123–124).

The Supreme Court ruling that struck down the Agricultural Adjustment Act also stands as a challenge to the historical institutionalists' emphasis on an independent government because former corporation lawyers wrote it on the basis of their laissez-faire doctrine, which is patently not a statist ideology. We thus have the irony that one of the three branches of American government, a branch consisting of nine lawyers appointed for life, did not believe the executive branch should be allowed to interfere in a key sector of the private economy, and a majority of them certainly did not believe in the New Deal (compare with Mann 2011, Chapter 8). As political scientist Harvey Feigenbaum (1985, pp. 172ff.) argued in a telling critique of theories emphasizing government autonomy, there has to be a unitary state—one not divided within itself—before it makes sense to talk about an independent government.

Specific arguments aside, are there general power indicators that could be used to decide if it was the government or the property owners that had "the upper hand" on issues related to the AAA, to put the concept of dominance in more conventional terms? The standard approach in political sociology is to look at the evidence that derives from three traditional indicators of power—the distribution of values people seek, such as wealth and income in Western countries; over-representation on key decision-making units inside and outside of government; and case studies demonstrating which side prevails in the unfolding of specific legislative and bureaucratic conflicts when preferences are reasonably clear at the outset.

However, these indicators do not easily lend themselves to an argument with historical institutionalists because their assumption that the government has independence and capacity allows them to interpret the evidence in an unconventional way. For example, if we pointed to the tremendous subsidy benefits obtained by well-off farmers and plantation owners as evidence of their dominant power over government, historical institutionalists could reply that private benefits such as wealth and income are minor issues for government officials. For historical institutionalists, subsidies can be seen as the government's way of paying off business and plantation owners for their cooperation. They also could say, as Hacker and Pierson (2002, pp. 283–285) do in rejecting outcomes as power indicators, that the outcome of any policy battle might be an unintended one.

Similarly, if we noted that farm leaders and their allies held key positions in the AAA and that members of the Farm Bureau were disproportionately represented on local AAA and land use committees, thereby invoking the over-representation indicator of power, historical institutionalists might reply that such positions are merely ways for government officials to co-opt leaders of the agribusiness segment of the capitalist class. They also could argue, invoking classical role theory, that at least some of the people in government that class-dominance theorists see as evidence for their claims, such as plantation owners sitting in Congress, or corporate executives serving for one or two years as head of a division of the AAA, act in terms of the interests of the government when they are in office.

In other words, the only admissible evidence becomes who succeeds on policy issues when there are distinctly different agendas between rival groups. In this regard the historical institutionalists are very similar to another theoretical school once prominent in the social sciences, namely, the pluralists (Dahl 1957, 1958). The main difference is that pluralists emphasized coalitions of interest groups that shift from issue to issue, which gives the system more fluidity and openness than historical institutionalists perceive due to their focus on the "structure of the state and other major political institutions including electoral systems and political party systems" (Amenta 2005, 104).

Even here, though, there may be difficulties in deciding if there are winners and losers because historical institutionalists could argue that government officials make the choices they do because their goals happen to be very similar to those of owners on a given issue. In the case of the AAA's decision to support plantation capitalists in limiting their payments to sharecroppers, for example, historical institutionalists could argue that neither the top government officials or the employers cared much about poor farmers or unemployed farm workers, so the defeats suffered by liberals and low-income farm workers are not necessarily evidence that owners dominated agricultural policy. That is, state officials did what plantation capitalists asked in this instance without giving the request a second thought.

Despite these likely objections by historical institutionalists, which might be more persuasive if there was other, more general, evidence of overall government independence in the United States, it seems clear to us that the weight of the evidence on all three types of power indicators supports a class-dominance theory for the AAA. The distribution of AAA subsidies was far more skewed toward the biggest and wealthiest farmers than would make sense if this largesse were simply a matter of the government giving out enough money to minimize dissent in rural areas. Furthermore, wealthy commercial farmers used the money they received from AAA subsidies to increase their ability to dominate government through strong lobbying organizations and campaign donations to political candidates. Moreover, contrary to Hacker and Pierson's (2002, 2004) general objection to using outcomes as a power indicator, long-term skews in distributions on general systemic benefit indicators such as the wealth distribution, the income distribution, and government subsidies are less likely to be the result of unintended consequences than short-term outcomes on very narrow issues might be.

Turning to the large over-representation of agribusiness and its representatives in positions of government responsibility, we think they reveal that the American government is highly permeable due to the simple fact that there is an electoral system that provides most of its essential leaders. This point also holds for appointed officials because they have close relations with elected officials through campaign finance and other mechanisms. It would have been a rare elected official from the South or California in the 1930s that would have challenged agribusiness leaders by approving a government appointment they did not like. And as seen in the case of Roosevelt and Wallace's replacement of the liberal and Communist lawyers in the Department of Agriculture who wanted to stop plantation owners from ousting tenant farmers, the few liberals appointed against the wishes of employers were removed when there was a confrontation.

As for the question of wins and losses on specific policy issues, it is clear that the agenda of the corporate moderates, Southern plantation owners, and non-Southern commercial farmers prevailed by a wide margin over that of liberals, farm labor, or any officials within the Department of Agriculture who offered opposing positions. Whether the issue was the origins of the domestic allotment plan, the alignment of forces that passed the AAA legislation in 1933, the conflict in 1935 over payments to tenant farmers, the legislative changes in the Agricultural Adjustment Act in 1935 and 1937, the restrictions placed on the Farm Security Administration, or the demise of the Bureau of Agricultural Economics' short-lived land-use planning committees, the dominant class prevailed.

From our class-dominance perspective, the disagreements over agricultural policy after the Agricultural Adjustment Act passed were clearly delineated class conflicts because businessmen and successful commercial agricultural interests were on one side and tenant farmers and farm workers were on the other. Liberals and leftists sided with the tenants and farm workers, and provided much of the leadership, but the fundamental conflict is one of class because agricultural employers were pitted against farm workers over class issues such as wages, profits, unionization, and land ownership. In the final analysis, then, the AAA succeeded because its main constituency, large-scale farmers, was united behind it, whereas its main opponents were unable to have much influence within it after the liberal and Communist lawyers were forced to resign in 1935 for challenging labor relations in the South. The AAA ended up an agency that subdued class conflict and gave money to several million planters and farmers in exchange for acreage limitations.

Institutionalists and the National Labor Relations Act

Historical institutionalists see the National Labor Relations Act first and foremost as strong evidence that organized business had lost power and the government had gained it. Within that context, they first described the act as the product of government bureaucrats who teamed up with liberal legislators to create a National Labor Relations Board and thereby expand their domain. For example, "NLRB administrators achieved their entire raison d'être through the spread of unions: they had a natural institutional bias (as well as legal mandate) in favor of protecting all legitimate unions and union drives" (Skocpol 1980, p. 192). In a later analysis, there is greater emphasis on the role of elected officials rather than appointed state officials (Finegold and Skocpol 1995). Either way, their analysis ignores both the role of the National Civic Federation in helping to formulate and legitimate the practice of collective bargaining and the direct participation of corporate moderates in establishing and serving on the National Labor Board in 1933–1934. It also overlooks the work of industrial relations experts from the Standard Oil of New Jersey, General Electric, and IRC network in establishing procedures to carry out voluntary collective bargaining.

When historical institutionalists make claims about the state-building goals of the government officials, elected and appointed, who are said to be engaged in these efforts, they do not look at their social backgrounds or their subsequent careers, apparently assuming that those factors are irrelevant to the point they are making. However, the backgrounds and subsequent careers of the eight men, aside from Wagner, who were most responsible for shaping the National Labor Relations Act make it unlikely that they were motivated by the state-building and government career goals attributed to them by historical institutionalists. A brief look at their lives suggests that their primary goal was to find ways to ameliorate class conflict over the right of workers to unionize and engage in collective bargaining, thereby making the smooth and productive functioning of the economic system more likely.

The two men who served as chair of the National Labor Relations Board in 1934–1935, Lloyd Garrison and Francis Biddle, who had major roles in shaping the new labor law, were both prominent corporate lawyers from upper-class social backgrounds. Garrison was a member of a family that had been part of the upper class since the eighteenth century. A graduate of

Harvard Law School, at the time an acknowledged bastion of corporate law and predominantly upper-class students, he practiced on Wall Street from 1922 to 1932 and then became dean of the law school at the University of Wisconsin. He returned to the University of Wisconsin Law School for several years after his service to the labor board, was briefly considered by Roosevelt for the vacant Supreme Court seat that eventually went to Hugo Black in August 1937, and later joined a Wall Street law firm, where he practiced for thirty years until his death. Biddle, usually said in New Deal histories to be from an "old" Philadelphia family of considerable wealth, had some overlap with Roosevelt in his years at their high-status private school, Groton. He graduated from Harvard Law School in 1911 and practiced corporate law in Philadelphia for many years before Garrison talked him into taking over as chair of the labor board. Biddle returned to corporate law shortly after the National Labor Relations Act passed, then came back to Washington as solicitor general in 1940 and as attorney general from 1941 to 1945.

The general counsel of the National Labor Board in 1933–1934, Milton Handler, graduated from Harvard Law School in 1926, then became a professor of law at Columbia University, still considered a university for the social elite in that era, specializing in antitrust law. He knew very little about labor law when he joined the board, but helped formulate some of the basic principles followed by it and subsequent boards. He returned to Columbia after a year, but from 1937 to 1948 he also worked as president of a $10 million real estate firm that owned a city block of apartments west of Central Park. He later became a partner in a corporate law firm, but remained a Columbia professor all his life.

The general counsel for the reconstituted labor board of 1934 and early 1935, Calvert Magruder, who oversaw the drafting of the version of the National Labor Relations Act that passed in 1935, came from an upper-middle-class background, graduated from Harvard Law School in 1916, served as a law clerk for Justice Brandeis in 1917, worked as an attorney for the United States Shipping Board in 1919–1920, and became a professor of law at Harvard in 1920. He married into a famous upper-class Boston family, the Saltonstalls, in 1925 and was vice dean of the Harvard Law School when he took a one-year leave to join the labor board. In 1939, after writing a law review article in which he scorched business leaders for their shortsightedness in relation to the National Labor Relations Act, he was appointed to the federal Court of Appeals, where he served for the next twenty years.

One of the general counsel's employees who worked on both the 1934 and 1935 versions of Wagner's labor legislation, William G. Rice, came from a prominent Democratic family. His father was secretary to Grover Cleveland when he was governor of New York, and was made chair of the

National Civil Service Commission when Cleveland became president. Rice was a graduate of Andover and Harvard (B.A., 1914, LL.B., 1920). After serving as a law clerk for Brandeis in 1921–1922, he became a professor of law at the University of Wisconsin. After leaving the labor board in 1935, he became U.S. labor commissioner to the International Labor Organization in Geneva, and in 1937 he returned to Wisconsin as a law professor and special counsel to the Wisconsin Labor Relations Board.

Philip Levy, a graduate of Columbia University Law School in 1933, came to Washington in the summer of 1933 when Handler, who had been one of his teachers, became the National Labor Board's general counsel. Levy was with the labor board in its various incarnations and collaborated very closely with Magruder in ironing out the details of the final bill, then became a legislative aide to Wagner in 1937 (Gross 1974). He entered private practice in 1947, specializing in labor law, arbitration, and foreign claims settlement. Thomas Emerson, another employee of Magruder's who helped with the final version of the Wagner Act, is described by one source as having "venerable New England Puritan forebears" (Irons 1982, p. 235). He graduated first in his class at Yale in 1931, then a school with an overwhelming representation of students from the social elite, and spent two years as a civil liberties lawyer before joining the labor board. In the late 1930s he became a professor of law at Yale and stayed there ever after, writing well-regarded books on freedom and civil liberties.

Leon Keyserling, the son of the largest cotton planter in South Carolina, and an employee in Wagner's office, was responsible for the drafting of the National Labor Relations Act. He earned his B.A. degree from Columbia in 1928 at age twenty and his LL.B. from Harvard at age twenty-three, and then did graduate work at Columbia in economics with Rexford Tugwell, who brought Keyserling with him to Washington when he joined Roosevelt's Brain Trust. Keyserling's home-state acquaintance with Senator "Cotton Ed" Smith of South Carolina, chair of the Senate Agricultural Committee, landed him an immediate job with the liberal lawyers at the Department of Agriculture, but he joined Wagner a few months later as Wagner's only staff member at the time. From 1937 to 1946 he was a lawyer for the federal government's housing agency, and from 1947 to 1953 he was a member of the White House's Council of Economic Advisors. Keyserling was very liberal, but he was also a well-connected Southern Democrat, which made him an ideal go-between within the Democratic Party.

Clearly, these men do not fit the portrait of careerist government experts and bureaucrats painted by historical institutionalists. Most of them were in government for only a short time—their careers were in their professions for the most part, either as corporate lawyers or law school professors. Only Levy and Keyserling stayed in government for an appreciable amount of time. Levy never became an employee in the government agency he helped to create and later put his understanding of labor law to work as a lawyer who helped unions. As for Keyserling, as our recounting of his subsequent career in government demonstrated, he had no further involvement with the National Labor Relations Board. As this quick overview shows, it is very difficult to conceive of an independent government managed by careerist administrative elites if the high administrators and experts said to be motivated by state-building are coming and going all the time.

Institutionalists and the Social Security Act

Historical institutionalists have staked most of their claims about the American government during the New Deal on several studies of the origins of social welfare benefits, as epitomized by the Social Security Act (see, for example, Amenta 1998; Orloff 1993; Hacker and Pierson 2002; Skocpol and Ikenberry 1983; Weir, Orloff, and Skocpol 1988). Collectively, they make five main points. First, the act is the product of a long historical experience with government pensions, starting with the pensions for those who fought in the Civil War (Skocpol 1992). Second, they deny that any but a very few corporate leaders supported the act and insist that most opposed it, making it highly unlikely that corporate leaders could have had a role in bringing about this historic legislation. Third, they say there is a lack of evidence that the experts at Industrial Relations Counselors, Inc., (IRC) had strong connections to the corporate community or that any corporate leaders, including those around Rockefeller, looked upon its prescriptions with favor. Fourth, they stress that those experts involved in formulating the act who were not from IRC were almost certainly independent experts. Fifth, some of them claim that any corporate support for the Social Security Act was in good part because of distaste for the Townsend Plan that might have been enacted if Social Security failed; this fact makes any seeming preference for the Social Security Act an induced preference, not a solution that any corporate leaders actually wanted. (In other words, they supposedly preferred to maintain their strictly private social insurance system.) Overall, then, historical institutionalists conclude to one degree or another that the act is the product of institutional learning, government officials, independent experts, liberal political leaders, and pressures from social movements.

We think all of these emphases are misplaced. As we showed in Chapter 4, and as one of us argued in more detail elsewhere (Domhoff 1996, pp. 234–236), it is very doubtful that veterans' pensions, or any other government pension program, had very much impact on the nature of the Social Security Act, except in terms of making the idea of pensions more acceptable to the general public. Pensions for veterans, and later for their widows, were a way of spending the huge government surpluses built up in the late nineteenth century due to the demand by Republican industrialists for high tariffs, as well as a way to provide patronage in a few swing states, thereby serving a double purpose. They were a very minor issue by 1915, when there were only 424,000 surviving veterans among the 4.5 million people who were sixty-five or older, and most of the veterans and their widows were dead by 1920, when a twenty-year-old from 1865 would have been seventy-five in an era when life spans were far shorter than now. Instead, the specific origins of the Social Security Act can be found in private pensions created by corporations in order to rid themselves of superannuated workers (Klein 2003; Sass 1997).

The evidence the historical institutionalists adduce to downgrade the role of corporate leaders is not convincing. They have to treat company presidents such as Teagle and Swope as window dressing, or make claims, as Orloff (1993, p. 296) does, that the Business Advisory Council was in turmoil due to disagreements over the act and "nearly broke up and did lose several of its members in the course of the drafting and congressional consideration of the law." This is simply not the case. Rather, the BAC's conflicts were with the White House concerning Roosevelt's support for the National Labor Relations Act, his unexpected call in mid-June 1935 for higher taxes on the extremely wealthy, and his attack on the holding companies through which Wall Street financial interests controlled many public utilities around the country. These points were accurately reported in the *New York Times* and *Business Week* at the time. They are also summarized in historian Robert Collins's (1981, p. 59) work on corporate moderates and in historian Robert Burk's (1990, pp. 183–191) study of the du Pont family interest group between 1925 and 1935. Moreover, there is no evidence of resignations in protest from the BAC in mid-1934. For example, although Pierre du Pont did resign from the Industrial Advisory Board of the NRA to protest the direction in which labor relations seemed to be moving, he was still serving on a BAC committee in May 1935 that unanimously opposed the National Labor Relations Act; he did not leave the BAC until January 1936, well after the Social Security Act passed (Burk 1990, pp. 133–135, 189–190).

Historical institutionalists also claim that the corporate moderates lost on several of their specific preferences in relation to the way in which unemployment insurance was handled. More specifically, they assert that the corporate moderates lost because the experts from the Wisconsin network wanted to preserve the state-level unemployment insurance plan they had succeeded in passing in Wisconsin. Aside from the fact that the rival plans were both business oriented, Swenson (2002, pp. 226ff.) points out in a highly detailed rebuttal that corporate moderates in fact ended up with something very close to what they wanted, in part due to the persuasive testimony by Marion Folsom of Eastman Kodak that we mentioned in Chapter 4.

The historical institutionalists who have written about the New Deal also see the Clark Amendment as evidence that business opposed the Social Security Act and lost (see, for example, Amenta 1998; Hacker and Pierson 2002; Orloff 1993). But they rely on either Witte's (1963) brief discussion of this issue, which actually minimizes its support from corporations, or a list of 145 corporations thought to support it (compiled by the insurance agent who lobbied for the amendment), which the SSRC's Committee on Social Security obtained as part of its effort to defeat the Clark Amendment (Hacker and Pierson 2002, pp. 302, 321 ftn. 80). As against this very thin evidence, we have shown in Chapter 4 that Brown, Latimer, and the SSRC's Committee on Social Security found very little support for the amendment in their discussions with corporate executives from major corporations, even those from companies that already had private pension plans. Here we think the historical institutionalists ignore the fact that the views of corporate moderates can evolve as they gain new information, which is not the same as their capitulating to independent experts, government officials, or pressure from social movements.

Historical institutionalists, in their most important argument, claim that the experts at IRC should be seen as independent experts whose policy recommendations may or may not be consistent with the preferences of corporate moderates. One such argument (Orloff and Parker 1990, p. 306) concludes that "by the early 1930s, IRC was a self-supporting industrial relations consulting firm." They base this assertion on a statement by Rockefeller's labor advisor, Raymond Fosdick (1956, p. 186), writing from memory thirty years later, that "By 1933 Mr. Rockefeller was confident that it [IRC] was now capable of supporting itself on a nonprofit basis and that further financial backing from him was no longer necessary." Whatever Fosdick may have remembered, in fact Rockefeller's gradually declining personal donations were the tail end of a five-year commitment that began in 1927 at $150,000 per year. His support was down to $100,000 in 1932–1933 and to $35,000 in 1935–1936, when he still was providing 23 percent of the organization's operating budget. Moreover, one of his sons, John D. Rockefeller III, wrote him in 1934 asking for permission to use his own money to make up a potential deficit of $16,000 (Rockefeller III 1934). In 1936, this same son informed his father that the organization was now almost on its own, attaching a list of nineteen companies that were paying annual retainer fees, starting with Colorado Fuel and Iron and including five Standard Oil companies:

> It occurred to me that you might be interested to glance at the attached chart showing Industrial Relations Counselors' sources of support during the last four years. You will note that, while the total budget has increased during this period from approximately $128,000 to $167,000, the percentage of your contribution in relation to the total has dropped from seventy-eight percent to twenty-four percent (Rockefeller III 1936).

He then suggested to his father that it would be "terribly nice if you were to write" to the head of IRC "expressing your satisfaction with what they have done," which his father did a week later, adding that "I send my hearty congratulations on the splendid showing and on the uniquely useful work which you are doing" (Rockefeller 1936). In short, the reality is that Rockefeller's support for IRC tapered off gradually in the 1930s as IRC relied more on grants from the Rockefeller foundations, as demonstrated in Chapter 4, along with consulting fees from Rockefeller-connected corporations, members of the Special Conference Committee, and a few independent companies.

But even if historical institutionalists conceded that Rockefeller and large corporations funded IRC and other think tanks, they nonetheless might argue that more evidence is needed to demonstrate that the corporate moderates and the experts working for IRC were in general agreement on policy proposals. As we attempted to document in detail through the use of primary historical sources, Fosdick and Hicks did keep Rockefeller abreast of IRC work, so he would have had every opportunity to register his opposition to any tentative plans he did not accept. In addition, the close collaboration between Teagle and Hicks on the workings of the original National Labor Board, and of Teagle, Swope, and other business leaders with Stewart in trying to shape the unemployment provisions of the Social Security Act, seem to us to be good evidence that the corporate leaders and policy-planning experts in and around IRC were in tune with each other on these two key pieces of New Deal legislation.

Here we would also note the highly detailed evidence we presented in Chapter 2 for close collaboration among Ruml, SSRC experts, and corporate moderates in developing the domestic allotment program as support for our general claim that corporate moderates and experts within the policy-planning network were in general agreement at the time. It would be ideal if examples could be provided of the dismissal or shunning of experts because of disagreement with corporate moderates, such as has been found for clashes within the Committee for Economic Development in the 1970s (Domhoff 1998, pp. 152–153), but we know of no such examples for the three legislative issues examined in this book. Nor is there any evidence in the files of IRC that we have examined that any of their clients abandoned them because of their work on the Social Security Act.

In the past, historical institutionalists have responded to the evidence concerning the close relationship between the corporate community and the policy-planning network by focusing on experts from the academic community, such as Barbara Armstrong, a key figure in the formulation of the old-age provisions of the Social Security Act, claiming that they are not given the importance they deserve in our analyses (see, for example, Hacker 2002, pp. 102–103). They then end the argument with a standard academic scare word by saying the class-domination theory makes "conspiratorial claims" in its analysis of the Social Security Act, which implies that the analysis imputes too much power to business leaders working from behind the scenes and is based on the idea of secret instructions and manipulations (Hacker and Pierson 2002, p. 308). It is a claim that in effect ignores the public presence of corporate leaders on the boards of directors of foundations and think tanks; the open and widely known foundation funding of think tanks; the public presence of Teagle, Swope, and other corporate moderates on advisory committees; the involvement of Stewart, Latimer, Givens, Brown, and other IRC and SSRC experts in the actual drafting of the Social Security Act; and the considerable amount of interaction between leading corporate moderates and policy experts in supporting the Social Security Act.

We conclude our specific comments on the historical institutionalists' analysis of the Social Security Act by turning to the claim by several of them that Townsend Plan supporters had an impact on the nature of the Social Security Act and the fact that it passed (see, for example, Hacker and Pierson 2002; Weir, Orloff, and Skocpol 1988). To begin with, the Townsend group was only formalized in early 1934, several months after a sixty-six-year-old physician, Francis Townsend, recently eased out of his city government position, wrote a series of letters to the editor that appeared in a newspaper in Long Beach, California, starting in late September 1933. The letters presented his own version of plans that were being discussed in retirement communities in that city and nearby Los Angeles (Bernstein 1985, pp. 61–66 for a colorful and informative portrait of Townsend). Townsend suggested that in order to revive the economy and at the same time help the elderly, the federal government should give $200 a month to every American citizen over age sixty, with the funds coming from a new 2 percent sales tax, on the condition that they would retire, making room for younger employees, and spend the money immediately. (Later the plan called for a more general transaction tax, roughly akin to the value-added tax that is now used in many European countries.)

On the basis of an enthusiastic local response to his letters, Townsend and one of his former real estate partners incorporated his plan as a nonprofit organization and in the summer of 1934 began to set up local clubs and publish a newsletter. However, their movement did not grow immediately, and there were very few Townsend clubs in late 1934, especially outside of California. Although Witte kept a close eye on the rise of the Townsend Plan, and personally worried that it might eventually prove to be troublesome, the administration's old-age proposal was nearly completed at that point. However, in late November 1934, the organization's barrage of letters against omitting the old-age provisions from the Social Security Act may have had some impact, although the letters began to arrive well after

Roosevelt and Perkins had given public assurances that those provisions would be included (Amenta 2006, p. 76).

Despite the fact that the total membership in the organization behind the Townsend Plan and its ability to lobby were not as impressive even in early 1935 as it appeared to be in some media accounts, Townsend himself was able to draw national media attention during the debate over the Social Security Act. He was even invited to testify before House and Senate committees in February, where his lack of specifics, or even a clear understanding of his own plan, proved to be an embarrassment. When a vote was taken in the House in April on substituting a watered-down version of his original plan for the administration's bill, it lost 206-56, a clear indication that it was no danger to the corporate community. In any case, as we stated in Chapter 4, over half of those fifty-six votes came from conservatives who opposed any form of government social insurance. (Large numbers of House members did not bother to vote on other, more minor, amendments to the administration's plan, so the fact that 173 members did not vote does not mean they were afraid to vote for fear of drawing the wrath of Townsend Plan supporters.) One trio of historical institutionalists (Weir, Orloff, and Skocpol 1988) claims that the Townsend Plan did have an impact in Congress, even though it lost so badly, because it had membership groups in many congressional districts that might challenge legislators who opposed the plan. This claim is contradicted by the fact that at the time the local clubs set up by advocates of the Townsend Plan "had little presence outside the far West and had not yet decided on targeting congressional districts" (Amenta 2006, p. 98).

We therefore believe that any mention by supporters of the Social Security Act of the alleged threat of the Townsend Plan was strictly for rhetorical purposes. For example, when Witte (1963, p. 103) was asked by members of the Senate Finance committee in mid-May, well after the Townsend Plan had been completely rejected in the House, to present the best argument he could for the administration's old-age social insurance proposal, he replied that if the bill did not pass, then something like the Townsend Plan might be forced upon Congress as an alternative. This assertion is taken at face value by Hacker and Pierson (2004, p. 187) when they allege the influence of "well-organized populist challenges, such as the Townsend Movement for old-age pensions." Contrary to their claim, we agree with highly detailed research work by another historical institutionalist, sociologist Edwin Amenta, which appeared after Hacker and Pierson wrote, showing that the Townsend Plan had little or no impact on the passage of Social Security legislation. As Amenta argues:

> [I]t is difficult to identify anything the Townsend Plan did in Washington that buoyed old-age benefits. Almost all the beneficial effects of the Townsend Plan on old-age policy would doubtless have materialized regardless of whether its

leaders had drafted the McGroarty [the sponsor of the Townsend Plan in the House] bill, come to Washington to testify and lobby for it, induced Townsendites to threaten legislators to pass it, to amend it, and to attack the security bill and support no alternatives, as they did" (Amenta 2006, p. 96).

Wrapping up our discussion of the weaknesses of historical institutionalism in regard to New Deal legislation, we think we have shown that all of its key empirical conclusions are wrong. First, the federal government had little or no independence. Its potential autonomy could not manifest itself in the face of long-standing corporate involvement in both political parties and in the face of the dominance of Congress by plantation capitalists through the Southern wing of the Democratic Party. The fact that one branch of government, the Supreme Court, consisted primarily of former corporate lawyers is also highly relevant to this point because the judgments of the Supreme Court are the final backstop in government for the ownership class (Mann 1993, pp. 156–158).

Second, the historical institutionalists' emphasis on government capacity is misguided, first and foremost because the government had very little policy-planning or administrative capability at the time. This point is most directly demonstrated by its reliance on nongovernment experts, who were in good part from the corporate policy-planning network. More generally, the historical institutionalists' use of governmental capacity as an indicator of autonomy is mistaken because governmental capacity—whether reflected through growing budgets, increased staff size, or the creation of new agencies—does not necessarily say anything about how the government is controlled. The government can grow and still be controlled by the ownership class through the policy-planning network, as is amply demonstrated by the fact that corporate leaders and experts from their think tanks carried out a state-building role in regard to both the Agricultural Adjustment Administration and the Social Security Board. The ownership class and the policy-planning network also played a part in the formation of the National Labor Relations Board through their involvement in establishing the original National Labor Board. These findings show it is not accurate to focus on state capacity and simply ignore the traditional indicators of social power— the wealth and income distributions, the over-representation of groups or classes within the governmental agencies under study, and, most important, the detailed historical studies that trace the origins of any new congressional legislation or government agencies in order to determine which group or class had the greatest impact on the legislative process.

This tendency on the part of historical institutionalists to blur the distinction between social power and government capacity leads to our consideration of their third general mistake: an overemphasis on the importance of induced preferences that leads them to downplay the degree of power exerted by the ownership class during the New Deal. We think there is general agreement among theorists that it was the drastic changes in American society created by the unexpected and prolonged collapse of the economic system—everything from falling stock prices, bank failures, and declining production to rising unemployment, increasing social unrest, declining government revenues, and growing electoral support for the Democratic Party—that forced leaders in both the ownership class and the working class to rethink their policy preferences. It was these changing conditions, these "macroeconomic forces exogenous to the institutional system," that determined the new preferences that both classes adopted (Swenson 2004, p. 3).

Thus it is not useful or accurate to claim, as do Hacker and Pierson (2002, 2004), that leaders in the corporate community would have preferred to maintain their private pension plans when the new economic situation had made those plans increasingly untenable, especially given that simply closing down those plans, as they had the legal right to do, might have fed employee discontent and increased class conflict (Sass 1997; Swenson 2002). When the nature of the Social Security Act is examined within the context of the financial problems facing private pensions and the potential for increased class conflict, the act is far greater evidence for corporate power than Hacker and Pierson appreciate, especially when it is recalled that the preferences of liberals and leftists were almost completely brushed aside. Contrary to one of their most important claims, the corporate moderates did not have to choose "from a list of options not of their own choosing" (Hacker and Pierson 2004, p. 187). In fact, they no longer wanted to leave social insurance in private hands because economic and actuarial circumstances had changed dramatically for them by early 1934. They therefore accepted a new plan fashioned for them by hired experts. They also quickly realized as the legislative process unfolded that it made no economic or policy sense even for companies with solid private pension plans to hold on to them, which is why they had no interest—or lost interest, in the case of some of them—in the Clark Amendment. The Social Security Act, the only focus of Hacker and Pierson's attention, is far more than a mere induced preference achieved against rival claimants who in fact did not set out the options. It is a triumph. So, too, is the Agricultural Adjustment Act.

The National Labor Relations Act, however, cannot be seen as a triumph. It is an unintended consequence of a series of mistakes by corporate moderates that were seized upon by liberal and labor leaders in a context of many workers' increasing willingness to demand unionization and vote Democratic. Corporate moderates as well as ultraconservatives made it totally clear in 1934 and 1935 that they thought they could continue to manage disputes with workers in traditional ways despite the changed circumstances, but the liberal-labor coalition was able to create the National

Labor Relations Board nonetheless. It was not until 1947 that the corporate community was able to limit the government labor board in a way that was more satisfactory to its interests. The National Labor Relations Act is the New Deal legislation that best fits the historical institutionalists' framework, but it is nonetheless better understood within a class dominance perspective because it is one battle in an ongoing struggle that continues even today. For the most part, the corporate community and the plantation capitalists have triumphed overwhelmingly in direct class conflict with their employees.

MARXISTS AND THE NEW DEAL

We think Marxists make two major mistakes concerning the New Deal that are in some ways the opposite or mirror image of the mistakes made by historical institutionalists. First, most of them exaggerate the potential for a leftward surge during the Great Depression, mistaking the ability of the Communist Party and other leftist groups to organize disruptive events in the early 1930s and provide organizers for the industrial union movement later in the decade for a desire on the part of large numbers of workers to embrace socialist solutions to the nation's economic problems. They therefore speak of the limited reforms of the New Deal as a lost opportunity for radical change or a co-optation by union leaders, corporate moderates, or both. Second, some Marxists claim that the ownership class was fearful of socialist or revolutionary upheaval, which is why some corporate moderates purportedly helped John L. Lewis and Sidney Hillman rein in the growing labor militancy. As might be expected, most of their claims have focused on union organizing and the National Labor Relations Act.

For sociologist Stanley Aronowitz (1973; 2003, p. 77), a prominent Marxist sociologist since the 1960s, the "industrial rebellions of the first half of the 1930s" were the crucial factor that led to "an extraordinary wave of social reform" as both the capitalist class and leftist groups came to believe that "the long wave of defeats for the workers' movement" may have ended. The surge was led for the most part by younger workers who could keep up with the pace of modern assembly lines and therefore were eminently employable (Aronowitz 1973, p. 236). Section 7(a) was labor's "reward" for cooperating with Roosevelt, but the activism on the left "made it plain to Lewis and Hillman that unless the AFL acted decisively to control the developing mass upsurge among industrial workers, the left could pose a serious threat to conservative and liberal leaders of the unions and upset the emerging Roosevelt coalition" (Aronowitz 1973, pp. 239, 241). The National Labor Relations Act was therefore an attempt to restore order to the workplace; Senator Wagner introduced the legislation "at the behest of Roosevelt and the AFL leadership" in order to forestall "an incipient revolution in

America's key production and transportation industries" (Aronowitz 2003, p. 79). The new labor law imposed restrictions on the ability of labor to use a "wide array of weapons to advance its interests," but the continuation of strikes after its passage is testimony to the fact that workers were "unwilling to surrender their right to engage in direct action" (Aronowitz 2003, p. 80).

While workers struggled, union leaders caved in. The "defection" of Sidney Hillman of the Amalgamated Clothing Workers Union and David Dubinsky of the International Ladies Garment Workers Union from the Socialist Party to Roosevelt began the process whereby "organized labor's most radical battalions" became part of the New Deal coalition; their willingness to support the National Labor Relations Act heralded the "beginning of labor's integration into the prevailing structure of corporate and political power" (Aronowitz 2003, pp. 82–85). But it was not only left-leaning union leaders who undercut the growing power of leftist activists. Although Communist Party leaders presented a blistering critique of the National Labor Relations Act in Congressional testimony, Aronowitz nonetheless claims "there is little evidence that the party mounted criticism of the Labor Relations Act or its winner-take-all [i.e., majority rule] provision" (Aronowitz 2003, p. 85). Instead, the CP made the mistake of joining the Roosevelt coalition at a time when it had a real presence on the shop floor and was making headway in union organizing drives. As a result, the CP "all but scuttled the emerging movement within labor's ranks for the formation of a labor party" (Aronowitz 2003, p. 85).

Similar assertions are found in the work of one of the most visible Marxist historians since the 1980s, Mike Davis. He sees the upsurge of unionization efforts after the passage of the National Industrial Recovery Act as the product of young workers (primarily the children of recent immigrants) who were led by "two species of unofficial vanguards," one made up of "implanted nuclei of revolutionary vanguards," mostly members of the Communist Party, the other of skilled workers who built on "neo-syndicalist craft traditions of a more radical inflection than the AFL mainstream." However, this rank-and-file effort was "harnessed to the rebuilding of the power of established bureaucracies by Hillman and Lewis in the garment and coal-mining industries" (Mike Davis 1986, p. 57). While the origins and impact of the National Labor Relations Act are not discussed, the emergence of the CIO is portrayed as the result of "the intervention of the Lewis-Hillman wing of the AFL bureaucracy, supported by Roosevelt and Secretary of Labor Perkins . . . " (Mike Davis 1986, p. 57). The CIO's purpose was "capturing an already existent mass movement of industrial shop committees and rebel locals—a movement with dangerous embryonic proclivities toward an anti-Gompersian model of 'class struggle unionism'" (Mike Davis 1986, pp. 56–57).

Devising ways to slow the rising tide of labor militancy is also one of the themes in the work of Marxist sociologist Rhonda Levine (1988). Building on the structuralist version of Marxism, which characterizes the state as a relatively autonomous entity that looks out for the general interests of the capitalist class, Levine first argues that the New Deal pursued policies necessary for capital accumulation even though some of those policies might antagonize particular segments of the capitalist class. Confronted by rival segments of the capitalist class that had their own separate views of what policies should be enacted, the state had to "put into motion plans for economic recovery that represented the compromise not only between capital and labor but also within capital itself" (Levine 1988, p. 173).

After the state plan embodied in the National Industrial Recovery Act failed to stimulate the accumulation process, and instead generated labor militancy, the result was a new state plan, the National Labor Relations Act, crafted primarily by Congressional leaders, that offered concessions to industrial labor by providing an institutional mechanism for settling labor disputes through the framework of collective bargaining. Although the National Labor Relations Act was a "pro-union" act, it was not a "pro-working-class" act because collective bargaining "depoliticizes" the class struggle due to the fact that "collective-bargaining arrangements remain within the confines of bourgeois political rule and tend to isolate workers' political struggles from economic struggles" (Levine 1988, p. 135). In addition, the subsequent incorporation of organized labor into the Democratic Party "served to diffuse labor militancy, directing the leaders of the newly emergent industrial-union movement to accept, by the end of the decade, a general consensus in support of the existing political and economic order" (Levine 1988, p. 16).

An emphasis on containing labor militancy is also the main thrust of Marxist political scientist Michael Goldfield's (1989) analysis of the origins of the National Labor Relations Act. While most of his article is devoted to documenting why historical institutionalists are wrong to deny that the strikes and disruption of 1933 and 1934 had any impact on the passage of the act, his views on its origins are very clear: "The virtually unanimous opinion among New Deal Democrats and progressive Republicans (the overwhelming majority in both Houses after the November 1934 elections) was that government regulation was necessary to constrain, limit, and control the increasingly militant labor movement" (Goldfield 1989, p. 1274). However, it was not simply liberals who feared the growing leftist threat within the labor movement. After noting that the 1934 strike wave "may have increased the fear among the rich of revolution," his subsequent focus is on his belief that the strikes were even more threatening to traditional labor leaders: "For AFL leaders, however, these strikes must have had the

appearance of the grim reaper. They signified the existence of an emerging mass-based movement led by radicals outside their control" (Goldfield
1989, p. 1273). In our terms, the act was the product of a liberal-labor
coalition, a conclusion we in part share with Goldfield, but as we will now
explain, we doubt that liberals, labor leaders, or government officials were
fearful that left-wing labor militancy would have any real success.

In actuality, liberals and labor leaders were fearful, as the AFL had been
since its founding, that leftist labor actions and talk of a socialist-communist
revolution would lead to a backlash and the triumph of organized capitalists, who were fully prepared to use violence. To claim otherwise is to overlook the fact that both industrial capitalists and planters were ready for a
violent confrontation with labor of the kind that had brought them success
over the previous sixty years. The ownership class's willingness to employ
physical attacks on workers is seen most obviously in the organized violence
that was unleashed on Communists and other leftists who tried to organize
tenant farmers and farm workers in the South and California. But it is also
documented in numerous instances by many corporations' use of their own
paid gangs of strikebreakers and by their stockpiling of weapons and ex-
plosives, including a few corporations in the Special Conference Committee
(Auerbach 1966; U.S. Senate 1939). Capitalists and government officials
were also supremely confident that they still had control of law enforcement
in the United States.

We think the lack of potential for any left-wing successes can be seen
by imagining what would have happened if the National Labor Relations
Act had not passed. The most likely counterfactual is that leftist organizers
would have taken to the streets and fomented demonstrations and strikes,
as they had in 1919 and 1934. These strikes would have been met with organized violence on the part of corporate leaders because they could claim
the strikers did not have any legitimacy due to the fact that there was no legal framework mandating union recognition or collective bargaining. Then
local police and the National Guard would have stepped in on the side of
the corporations to restore "law and order," as evidenced by the fact that
government at the state and local levels used violence to break up strikes
in late 1937 and 1938, even though the National Labor Relations Act had
passed overwhelmingly in 1935 and survived a constitutional test in the
spring of 1937. The result would have been the destruction of most industrial unions and the shrinkage of the union movement to the few enclaves in
the economy where organized workers had leverage due to their usefulness
in stabilizing highly competitive industries or their capacity to deploy picket-
ing, industrial sabotage, and violence to shut down work sites.

This alternative scenario is based on a very different conception of how
most people approach everyday life than is implied by Marxian theory, in-

cluding during the 1930s. As historian Melvin Dubofsky (2000, Chapter 6) carefully documents in a discussion of the upheavals of the 1930s, there were many ways in which these were "not so turbulent years" even though fifteen strikers were killed in 1933 and forty in 1934 (Piven 2006, p. 88). Very few workers—fewer than 1 percent—actually participated in these strikes, and the major strike wave in 1934 was smaller and less intense in terms of number of strikes, days of work lost, and number of workers involved than the strike wave of 1919 (Dubofsky 2000, p. 138). Lewis's main organizer in Akron reported to him in a confidential note in March 1936 that the successful sit-down just carried out was a "minority strike, starting with only a handful of members and gradually building a membership in that Local Union to a little over 5,000 out of 14,000 workers" (Dubofsky 2000, p. 143). Similarly, the United Automobile Workers local in Flint had been able to sign up only fifteen hundred of twelve thousand workers by late December 1936, after many months of organizing, which is one of the key reasons why the activists resorted to a sit-down to defeat General Motors (Fine 1969, p. 117).

Dubofsky draws upon often-overlooked sociological studies of workers in two very different cities, Muncie and New Haven, to document that the overwhelming majority of workers were first and foremost concerned with living their everyday lives and had little time or sympathy for leftist solutions (Bakke 1940a, 1940b; Lynd and Lynd 1937). Even a study of workers in Akron, which is often cited because the survey results showed that workers there believed human rights were more important than property rights, nonetheless reached the conclusion that workers' general opinions would not have much impact on their behavior:

> Our measurements of opinion and the comments of workers indicate clearly
> that most of them do not want to feel that they have isolated themselves from
> the general run of 'middle class opinion.' The general climate of opinion bears
> in upon them and would make it impossible for them to turn decisively away
> into a workers' world, even if such a thing existed (Jones 1941, 297).

These and other findings lead Dubofsky (2000, p. 143) to reaffirm the importance of "union sparkplugs" in creating unions, citing evidence that the militancy of the remaining workers usually extended no further than a willingness to honor picket lines. He also notes that union contracts with corporations, often seen by Marxist critics as a snare and distraction that limited workers' freedoms in the workplace, were greeted with enthusiasm by workers at the time because of the security they provided. Secure and stable contracts were a major reason why many workers were willing to take the few risks that they did. Dubofsky's reading of the literature on the 1930s, which was first undertaken for a highly regarded biography he co-authored on Lewis (Dubofsky and Van Tine 1977), leads him to a different view of mainstream labor leaders than the one presented by Aronowitz, Davis, and Goldfield. Although he agrees that they of course wanted to retain their positions of authority, they were even more concerned to avoid losing strikes (because "nothing destroyed a trade union as quickly") or to risk a level of militancy that reached the point where it "would produce government repression, an ever-present reality even in Franklin D. Roosevelt's America" (Dubofsky 2000, p. 145). As a result of trying to steer between these two disastrous potential outcomes, "All labor leaders, then, necessarily played a devious and sometimes duplicitous game" (Dubofsky 2000, p. 144).

As readers might expect, we think Dubofsky's analysis of workers' consciousness in the 1930s supports our general understanding of the combination of factors that keep most people focused on their everyday lives. First and foremost, everyday life has many positive features despite the many problems workers face. It is "compelling" due to loved ones, friends, hobbies, and routines that become enjoyable, as well as work that, even for some blue-collar occupations, often provides varying degrees of satisfaction (Flacks 1988, Chapters 1–2). Second, there is also the fact that workers knew they were very likely to lose in a direct confrontation with authorities because most people would have no sympathy for them and the government would use armed force to put them in jail and allow new workers to take their places.

Despite our disagreements with many aspects of the Marxist analysis of the New Deal, we think Marxists are right that a profit-driven economic system based in private ownership of income-producing property, and the resulting class structure, have a large impact in shaping power and political participation in the United States. We also agree that there is corporate dominance of the government on the issues that determine the distribution of wealth and income among the country's inhabitants. However, Marxists encase their insights about classes and class conflict within a Grand Theory that is as much a metaphysic as anything Hegel or Talcott Parsons ever wrote (Mills 1959, Chapter 2). In their case, however, it is a Labor Metaphysic, which means that the theory is rooted in the idea that the increasing alienation and working-class solidarity generated by the growing concentration of capital in a crisis-prone system will inevitably strip away false consciousness and lead to a socialist outcome (Mills 1962, pp. 127–129). It is this certainty about the inevitable rise of a united and revolutionary working class that leads to most of the Marxists' misunderstandings of the New Deal. It causes them to overestimate the depth of the economic crisis, the degree of alienation and anger that most workers experienced, and the likelihood of revolutionary upheaval. At the same time it leads them to underestimate the flexibility of capitalism, to deny the possibility that government could be used to shape a capitalist economy simply by running deficits or expanding the money supply, to ignore the strong positive feelings a majority of people held toward Roosevelt and the Democratic Party, and to overlook the importance of people's commitment to their everyday lives in countering any tendencies to join radical movements.

PROTEST-DISRUPTION THEORY AND THE NEW DEAL

Protest-disruption theory, as we explained in the Introduction, locates power in the interdependencies that lead to institutionalized networks of cooperation. Workers in a capitalist society therefore have potential power through their ability to withdraw their cooperation, a form of protest that leads to disruptions that can take the form of strikes, strategic nonviolence, the destruction of machines and buildings, or the use of physical force against opponents (Piven and Cloward 2003). People have to break the rules that codify and reinforce their domination if there is to be any significant social change.

Protest-disruption theorists support these claims by presenting evidence that protest movements have been the key to understanding whatever gains ordinary people have made in the United States over the past several hundred years, starting with the mob's role in fomenting the American Revolution and workers' use of strikes and sit-downs during the Great Depression (Piven 2006; Piven and Cloward 1977). At the same time, they stress that elections can play a very important part in bringing about egalitarian social change in the United States because disruptive movements increase voter turnout and threaten to destabilize established voting coalitions, as was the case with the efforts of both the Abolitionist Movement and the Civil Rights Movement (Piven 2006).

When focusing on the New Deal, protest-disruption theorists first argued that disruption and fear of disruption were important factors in creating the various relief and government employment programs instituted by the early New Deal. They also described how quickly these programs were cut back or dismantled in the face of fierce conservative criticism of them once any concern with disruption by the unemployed had subsided (Piven and Cloward [1971] 1993). They then provided a similar explanation for the successes the union movement enjoyed, suggesting that labor militancy forced the federal government to adopt the National Labor Relations Act and restrict the use of government violence on strikers in early 1937 (Piven and Cloward 1977, Chapter 3). More recently, Piven (2006, p. 105) has written that several activist groups, including those pushing the Townsend Plan, had a significant role in the creation of the Social Security Act.

While we think there is much to be said for protest-disruption theory in general, we nonetheless believe that it only holds to differing degrees for key policies in the New Deal. We also think that it overemphasizes the degree of spontaneity in these protests and downplays the importance of strong organizations in making them possible. To begin with, we think disruption was indeed the key factor in creating new federal relief and temporary employment programs, but we also believe the evidence supports the point that this disruption was more coherently and efficiently organized because of the efforts of Communists, Socialists, and other leftist activists than the protest-disruption account implies. As sociologists Harold Kerbo and Richard Shaffer (1992, p. 150) conclude on the basis of a detailed coding of newspaper reports on unemployment protests, "In fact, almost all of the protest activity indicated by our *New York Times* data during 1930 involved the Communist-led Unemployed Councils, beginning with demonstrations in February of 1930 involving more than a thousand of the unemployed." Another sociologist, Steve Valocchi (1990, 1993), has reached similar conclusions based on his research on unemployment organizations created by other leftist groups as well as Communists.

The National Labor Relations Act does have some element of spontaneous grassroots discontent behind it, but even here, as Piven and Cloward (1977, p. 110) also say, the upheaval began with the apparent approval of the Roosevelt Administration when it included section 7(a) in the National Recovery Act. Moreover, two established labor leaders, Lewis and Hillman, led the most successful organizing efforts in both 1933 and 1937–1938. As for the many grassroots efforts that failed in factories in 1933 and 1934, Communists and other leftist activists led a significant number of them. In making this statement we are not claiming that the activists were from higher classes, but we are saying that they were highly organized and adequately funded as well in the case of the Communist Party. The role of organized leftist groups in the three most disruptive and carefully studied strikes of 1934—in San Francisco, Toledo, and Minneapolis—is widely agreed upon (see, for example, Levine 1988) and acknowledged by protest-disruption theorists (Piven and Cloward 1977, Chapter 3).

But in general, and in agreement with historical institutionalists on this point, we would stress that the dramatic upheavals in 1933 and 1934 did not lead to the passage of the first version of the National Labor Relations Act, which was in the process of being eviscerated in Congress at the time of the largest and most volatile of these conflicts (Finegold and Skocpol 1995, pp. 134). Instead, Congress passed a public resolution that gave only slightly greater power to a temporary National Labor Relations Board than the earlier National Labor Board had possessed. While it can be argued that fear of future disruption motivated Wagner to introduce an improved version of his legislation in 1935, as Goldfield (1989) does, it is also noteworthy that Wagner—and many other Congressional liberals—had been in favor of legislation supporting unions and collective bargaining at least since their involvement in the formulation and passage of the National Industrial Recovery Act in the spring of 1933 (Finegold and Skocpol 1995, p. 135). Looked at from this angle, the National Labor Relations Act is, as we argued in Chapter 3, the product of a liberal-labor coalition that took advantage of government legitimation of collective bargaining as well as the disruption and the potential for disruption by workers. But we also think it was the burgeoning electoral support for Northern Democrats, which rewarded the party with overwhelming majorities in both the House and the Senate in the 1934 elections, that best registered the discontent that people were experiencing due to the Depression (compare with Finegold and Skocpol 1995, pp. 136–137).

One thing seems certain to us: the labor act did not pass because business leaders feared disruption or were intimidated by it. To the contrary, as we stressed in Chapter 3 and in our discussion of the failings of Marxist analyses of the New Deal, all corporate leaders opposed the act and felt confident they could win any direct confrontations at factory gates and in the streets. When the passage of the act is looked at from the vantage point of past capitalist victories in violent confrontations, the fact that the act passed suggests once again a victory for the liberal-labor coalition, even though it was conditioned on making concessions that induced plantation capitalists to refrain from joining the legislative battle on the side of their Northern counterparts.

When disruption—usually in the form of sit-downs—and the ability to use and fend off physical attacks became important was in the organizing of unions after the National Labor Relations Act was passed. And even though the National Labor Relations Board had little or no role in the events of early 1937 because corporations denied its authority, the assertive actions by labor organizers did happen in the context of the legitimation of collective bargaining by the government. Furthermore, it is crucial to recall that in early 1937 the government refused to use its police powers or to allow the use of corporate-financed violence, either of which could have defeated the strikers in the most pivotal battles against large corporations. Moreover, it needs to be pointed out once again that people at the grassroots level usually did not spontaneously carry out this disruption. Organizers hired by unions largely planned and executed these efforts, many of whom were provided by a very hierarchical organization we have discussed throughout this book, namely, the Communist Party. This was especially true for several of the key organizers who started and directed the sit-down at the General Motors plant in Flint (Fine 1969).

In discussing the possible role of disruption in the case of the Social Security Act, we need to begin by noting that Piven's (2006, p. 105) chronology is faulty when she claims that Roosevelt asked Perkins to chair the

Committee on Economic Security "in the spring of 1935" in the midst of ferment caused by Upton Sinclair's End Poverty In California (EPIC) electoral campaign. She also incorrectly claims that the Townsend Plan, Father Charles Coughlin's National Union for Social Justice, and the Share-Our-Wealth clubs created by Senator Huey Long, a fiery autocratic Democrat from Louisiana, were active at the time. Piven also wrongly claims the legislation was introduced and passed because of Roosevelt's growing concerns over winning the 1936 elections in the face of these insurgencies:

> The sense of crisis among political leaders was intense. As the 1936 election approached and the protests of the aged spread, FDR introduced the Social Security Act, a multitiered and complexly shaped effort to respond to both the aged and their numerous supporters among the electorate, and to limit the emergency relief program ceded earlier in response to the insurgent unemployed (Piven 2006, p. 105).

In fact, as we explained in Chapter 3, plans for comprehensive social security legislation began in the spring of 1934 due to infighting among the Democrats over the nature of unemployment insurance, along with urging by the social insurance experts in and around IRC and the SSRC, who had been studying the issue and carrying out small pilot studies for several years by that point. Nor were the protest and lobbying groups mentioned a moment ago generating any serious pressures while the legislation was working its way through Congress. They had either passed their peak or had yet to reach the point at which they would be likely to have any impact.

To start with, the EPIC electoral campaign, confined exclusively to California at the time, reached its zenith in November 1934, when Sinclair lost his bid for the governorship. He then went back to writing books and most of the EPIC clubs dispersed, with some organizers and members joining other groups, especially those supporting the Townsend Plan. As for the Townsend Plan, it was barely visible while the legislation was being drafted for submission to Congress and had very little impact during the legislative process despite the media attention it received, as we already noted in our critique of the historical institutionalists. Sociologists who think that social pressure can matter have concluded that the Townsend Plan had little or no influence on the passage of the act (Amenta 2006; Manza 1995).

In the case of the radio priest Coughlin and his paper organization, the National Union for Social Justice, he only announced it in the fall of 1934 and did not have any local chapters formed until 1936. His influence in Washington is described as "rapidly ebbing" by April 1935, in a major historical study of his efforts (Brinkley 1982, p. 175). Although he tried to revive his declining hopes with a speaking tour, delivering well-received speeches to very large audiences in Detroit, Cleveland, and New York, he made no efforts to build any local organizations at the time. When reporters at a press conference in New York asked him if he had any local organizers, he replied that "I am the Union of Social Justice" (Brinkley 1982, p. 178). Amenta (2006, p. 127) concludes that Coughlin's "National Union was little more than a mailing list of those who wrote to him in support of his broadcasts" before 1936. We add the obvious point that any local chapters formed in 1936 would have been too late to have any influence on the Social Security Act.

Much the same holds for Long's Share-Our-Wealth Clubs, said to be a potential basis for his possible third-party bid for the presidency in 1936. Brinkley (1982, p. 179) concludes that Long's clubs were "less than they seemed" despite "the impressive facades." They were located primarily in small towns and rural areas in the South, an area that was going to stick with the Democrats come hell or high water, and they often focused on local issues (Brinkley 1982, p. 181). Long was killed in the capitol building in his home state in early September 1935, so it cannot be known if he would have been able to create a viable organizational structure, but it was clearly recognized at the time that he was a highly erratic and self-centered demagogue, running the state of Louisiana as a dictatorship. It therefore seems unlikely to us that he was the national electoral threat he is now portrayed to have been based on a small mail survey in the spring of 1935 by a Roosevelt pollster whose sampling methods are unknown and whose reliability is highly suspect in our eyes (Brinkley 1982, p. 284).

Even more to the point, we do not think that the efforts by the EPIC campaign, the Townsend Plan supporters, Father Coughlin, and Long's Share-Our-Wealth clubs meet the basic prescriptions of protest-disruption theory: they never threatened or carried out any form of social disruption. They were not rule-breakers. EPIC was a temporary insurgent electoral group within the Democratic Party and the Townsend Plan advocates were more of a traditional interest group—a narrow group that seeks to influence specific legislative issues of concern to it—than they were a social movement. The term *social movement* is rightly restricted to collective opposition to established rules and customs by people who have organized to make sustained challenges against elite opponents and authorities (see, for example, Tarrow 1994). Otherwise, the concept has no real meaning beyond the idea of interest groups and pressure groups long familiar and carefully studied in political science. Thus Father Coughlin's radio following was not a social movement by any stretch of the imagination. Nor was Long's Louisiana political machine (which was based in patronage, bribery, and intimidation) any sort of social movement, as shown by the fact that in the first eight months of 1935 it could not even create sustained organizations outside of Louisiana.

In our view, these various groups were simply the 1930s incarnations of a long series of leftist-oriented or demagogic fringe groups that always have flourished in the United States, gaining attention primarily through media coverage and pundit commentary. They are sometimes useful to pragmatic liberals and moderate conservatives in trying to frighten the general public and each other into their own preferred compromise. Further, we think seasoned politicians in the 1930s knew that support for fringe candidates such as Long always suffers a very rapid decline as elections near because most people fully understand that a vote to the left of the Democrats, or the right of the Republicans, is a vote for the candidate they dislike or fear the most. As it turned out, the new third party that Father Coughlin, Townsend, and the main organizer of the Share-Our-Wealth clubs tried to put together in 1936, with a second-term agrarian North Dakota congressman as its presidential candidate, was a complete disaster, gaining fewer than 2 percent of the vote (Brinkley 1982, pp. 255–260).

We think the only organized group that applied any pressure that mattered in terms of the Social Security Act was class-based, namely, the Railway Employees National Pension Association, which formulated and brought about passage of the original version of the Railroad Retirement Act. This success forced the Railroad Commissioner to make the plan viable, which in turn brought Brown, Latimer, and Stewart to Washington for the work that led them to realize that such a plan might be feasible for industrial corporations as well. In other words, we are talking specifically about class conflict to the degree there was group pressure on the corporate community or the government that led to the Social Security Act.

More generally, it was activists with a good organizational base that carried out the major disruptive, rule-breaking protests that occurred with any frequency at any point during the Great Depression. The Communist Party and other small leftist groups were the leaders in the disruptions that began within months of the stock market crash in October 1929, starting with the CP's near riots at city halls in 1930. These events led to police violence and several deaths, and they were followed by the CP's efforts to stop evictions through its Unemployed Councils. Dissatisfied with the results of these actions, the CP leadership turned to militant protests in and around factories, which were complemented by the separate activities of other leftist groups (see, for example, Levine 1988, pp. 53–56, 115–125; Goldfield 1989). Even the union leader most accustomed to using physical force, John L. Lewis, had to turn to the Communist organizers within the union movement when it came time to take disruptive actions against the large industrial corporations in 1936 and 1937 (Dubofsky and Van Tine 1977; Haynes, Klehr, and Anderson 1998). We agree that many workers were ready for unions, better wages, and much else, but as Piven and Cloward say (2003, p. 53), "most of the time, people don't challenge the rules that enforce domination"; they "mainly endure and obey."

Leftist organizations were also the main instigators in the widespread but largely unsuccessful strikes and unionization efforts in agriculture in 1934. Communists were the leaders of the Alabama Sharecroppers Union and the Cannery and Agricultural Workers Industrial Union, and members of the Socialist Party started the Southern Tenant Farmers Association (Dyson 1982). The most successful farm protest organization, the Farmers' Holiday Association, founded in Des Moines in May 1932, also had a strong organizational base because most of its activists were members of the Iowa Farmers' Union, a chapter of the National Farmers' Union, which was created in 1902 to set up marketing cooperatives, support the preservation of family farms, and advocate reformist and liberal policies (McCune 1956, Chapter 4).

The president of the Farmers' Holiday Association, a longtime leader and former president of the Iowa Farmers' Union, immediately called on farmers to withhold their crops from middlemen until there was a legal guarantee that they would at least receive as much money as it cost to grow them (a policy proposal called "cost of production"). Farmers' Holiday Association activists picketed along highways and near storage bins in an attempt to convince other farmers to join them. The protests spread to nearby states and then were suspended in late November to give Roosevelt a chance to meet their demands after he came into office. In the meantime, the activist farmers started a campaign in early 1933 to prevent farm foreclosures by convincing the bidders at auctions to make very low bids and then sell the farms back to their owners; many such "penny auctions" were carried out, some through threats of physical violence. For example, the dramatic abduction and harassment of a judge by masked men in late April 1933, mentioned in Chapter 2, occurred as part of this campaign. It was not at all an example of spontaneous disruption by unorganized individuals.

When the Farmers' Holiday Association regretfully concluded in the summer of 1933 that the new Agricultural Adjustment Administration was dominated by the conservative Farm Bureau and large commercial farmers, it called for a new round of crop withholding until the Roosevelt Administration guaranteed cost of production and did more by way of currency inflation. But the strike failed within a few days, and the organization faded into obscurity. The Farmers' Holiday Association, based for the most part in the long-standing National Farmers Union, was beaten by a stronger organization, the Farm Bureau (see Shover 1965, for the history of the Farmers' Holiday Association).

On the basis of this quick recounting, we think that organization does matter in the creation of effective disruption. Moreover, it is not clear to us, as we noted in our critique of Marxist analyses of the New Deal, that labor leaders such as Hillman and Lewis were acting in an overly cautious and self-serving manner in trying to calibrate the degree of disruption. Given their experience, they worried that a majority of the general public could turn against them, as some polls suggested it already had as early as February 1937 in the face of wildcat strikes and the sit-down strikes: "two-thirds of respondents in a Gallup poll in February 1937 believed that GM was right not to negotiate with the sit-downers and strong majorities sympathized with the employers" (Kennedy 1999, p. 316). Hillman and Lewis also assumed that the government had the ability to "restore law and order." We do not deny that organizations can become cautious and bureaucratic, but some form of organization nonetheless seems to us to be necessary for sustained protest and disruption. Organizations are both a blessing and a curse, not simply an impediment to strong actions that allegedly would be successful if leaders of organizations stayed out of the way.

At the conclusion of their most general discussion of protest-disruption theory, Piven and Cloward (2003, p. 52) note that "there is still a good deal that remains to be explained," an attitude we share. They then ask, "Why, in short, if all men and women are endowed with a capacity for politics, do they obey the rules of domination as much as they do?" (Piven and Cloward 2003, p. 53).

We do not pretend to have a complete answer to this question, but we think that it needs to be considered within a somewhat wider theoretical framework than protest-disruption theory provides. First, as sociologist Richard Flacks (1988, Chapters 1–2) emphasizes in his consideration of these issues, and as we just noted in our critique of Marxism, there is a compelling nature to the satisfactions and routines of everyday life even in onerous situations; people do not readily risk their lives when they have commitments and responsibilities concerning loved ones, children, and friends. They also find enjoyments in activities outside of work (such as sports, hobbies, and social groups), and many do gain some satisfaction from their work, even blue-collar work, especially if they have some degree of autonomy or have won secure benefits through collective action (see, for example, Blauner 1964; Hamilton and Wright 1986, Chapter 6). When looked at in this light, perhaps it is not as surprising that people stay within their everyday lives as much as they do.

Second, the general tendency to obey authority may be in part due to the long period of dependency everyone of necessity experiences from infancy to young adulthood within a family structure in which parents are clearly in charge and able to mete out rewards and punishments. Adults may have a propensity to exercise power and to resist domination, as Piven and Cloward (2003) and many other theorists assume, including us. But they also have experienced a long socialization that makes it difficult for most people to disobey authority. In a word, people are very ambivalent about resisting authority figures, which may be a key reason why the activists who lead social movements are such an essential part of the process (compare with Flacks 1973, for further discussion of these issues and several classic articles on obedience to authority, resistance, and self-determination).

Third, it seems useful to us to distinguish among types of social movements to understand their occasional rise and frequent decline. Using a classification suggested by Flacks (1988, Chapter 3), there are in theory three different types of social movements in developed capitalist democracies that are likely to have very different outcomes. Resistance movements, which can range from movements to protect a neighborhood from developers to strikes against wage cuts and other sudden changes at work, are frequent and fiercely fought. Their primary goal is to restore the terms of everyday life before the unexpected intrusions were forced upon them. Most members of these movements therefore return to their everyday interests and routines once the battle is over.

Liberation movements, on the other hand, are attempts by subjugated or disrespected people within a society to change the terms of their everyday lives to those enjoyed by other members of the society (the civil rights movement, women's liberation movement, and gay and lesbian rights movement are three good examples). Such movements usually arise against incredible odds when activists discover ways to take advantage of new power bases or slight shifts in the system of domination. They often meet with ferocious reactions by dominant groups, which are thereby resisting changes in their own everyday lives, and government leaders almost always side with the dominant groups at the outset. Once again, however, members of such movements tend to return to everyday lives if they are successful in their efforts.

Democratic movements, which are far more encompassing and problematic than the first two types, "envision the full participation of the people as a whole in decisions that affect them" (Flacks 1988, p. 85). Such movements are exemplified in the past two hundred years by efforts to create participatory democracy or socialism, either of which requires a "leap of the imagination" to envision because the degree of cooperation and participation they seek to institutionalize are rarely part of people's growing up or their adult experience (Flacks 1988, p. 87). These movements often begin within events and organizations created by resistance and liberation movements, as was the case for the many college students who joined socialist groups in the 1960s after taking part in the civil rights, anti-war, environmental, or feminist movements. It is these democratizing efforts that are the most difficult to sustain in the face of major resistance by the existent power structure.

Fourth, and finally, we agree with Mann's (1986, p. 7) point that for the most part ordinary people do not more often join into any form of protest movement because they are "organizationally outflanked;" in other words, "the masses comply because they lack collective organization to do otherwise, because they are embedded within collective and distributive power organizations controlled by others." Put another way, even when people overcome their ambivalence about challenging authority and take the step of abandoning their commitment to the pleasures and routines of everyday life, it is still very difficult to create the organizations that are needed if protest and disruption are to be successful. Thus we are once again arguing that the disruption of interdependent relations is usually not as spontaneous as it sometimes seems to protest-disruption theorists. Successful disruption requires a new organizational base that is able to grow larger within the gaps or openings created due to changes in the power dynamics among the four major networks of power.

A THEORETICAL MEETING GROUND

Our theory has general agreements with each of the three other theories even though we have stressed the disagreements concerning the New Deal in this book. In some sense, then, our analysis can be seen as an amalgam of the four rival theories. However, our general framework is more than an amalgam because it is informed by a wide-ranging and original theoretical synthesis on the sources of social power that in our view surpasses anything that has been offered by historical institutionalists, Marxists, or protest-disruption theorists. We refer to Mann's (1986) dynamic four-network theory of power, overviewed briefly in the Introduction. The theory starts with the idea that there are four major independent bases of power—the economic network, the political network, the military network, and the ideology (religious) network—that interact and intertwine in ways that are constantly changing due to newly created organizational forms, newly invented technologies, new methods of communication, military innovations, and new spiritual movements. There is an emergent and constantly changing quality to social organization that leads to continual changes in power relations, thereby providing openings for new challengers even though they nonetheless face the difficulty Mann stresses in explaining why rebellions and revolts are not more frequent: most people are embedded in power networks controlled by others.

We think this theory, which is far more complex and full of nuances than any brief overview could capture, is able to encompass the key insights of previous theories without incorporating their weaknesses. For example, it can explain the potential autonomy of the state due to its unique function of territorial regulation, while at the same time noting that there is great variation in the degree to which states are autonomous. It can agree that feudal lords and capitalists often have been dominant economic classes over the past several hundred years while at the same time documenting that earlier Western civilizations were empires of domination commanded by military leaders, and that states had a far less important role in Europe for the thousand years after the fall of the Roman Empire than before or since that epoch (Mann 1986). In the case of Europe from 1760 to 1914, it can demonstrate that capitalism developed in roughly the same pattern in several different countries, as Marxists might expect, while at the same time explaining why their power structures ended up being very different due to the way that the economic network was related to the other power networks, as historical institutionalists emphasize (Mann 1993). (For an original contribution to the understanding of the ways in which states developed in Europe during the sixteenth century and thereafter, which builds upon and adds to Mann's theory while at the same time providing insightful critiques of alternative theories, see Lachmann 2010).

When applied to the United States, and in keeping with the historical institutionalists' focus on why the United States is different in its welfare policy outcomes from its European counterparts, Mann's framework explains how and why the economic network has always had ascendancy over the other three power networks. It explains why the federal government was not very large until the 1940s and never very independent of those who dominated and benefited the most from the economic system. It explains what most Americans take for granted and that most social scientists agree upon: that the military has never had a large or independent role in important government decisions and that the religious network is too fragmented into constantly dividing Protestant churches to be the kind of power base that the Catholic Church provided in some European countries (Mann 1993, Chapters 5 and 18; 2011, Chapters 3 and 8).

If the dominance of economic networks in the United States is given its full due, and if the ownership class's desire to limit programs that might give government more independence and capacity is fully appreciated, then the country's weak union movement, the late arrival of its welfare state, and its provision of more social benefits through corporations than in other countries are all understandable as outcomes of corporate dominance. The claim about corporate dominance includes the conservative voting coalition's control of Congress on issues having to do with labor unions and business regulation throughout the twentieth century. Similarly, the prominence of economic networks, in conjunction with the somewhat conflicting needs of Northern business interests and Southern plantation capitalists in the eighteenth, nineteenth, and early twentieth centuries, helps account for the institutional impediments to majority rule that are stressed by historical institutionalists as independent causal factors, such as the nature of the Constitution, the fragmentation of government, the weakness of the federal bureaucracy, and the decentralization of power in Congress. The American federal government lacked "capacity" before and during the New Deal in good part because the corporate community and plantation capitalists did not want elected or appointed officials to have any potential bases of support outside government except organized capitalists and planters. Due to their dominance of the national government, they were unrestrained in their use of law enforcement and strikebreakers in the North to fend off the development of unions and in their use of terrorism and control of local government in the South to greatly limit the power and freedoms of the former slaves and low-income whites.

Because Mann's four-network theory transcends the theories that have been critiqued in this book, it provides a common ground that does not require rival theorists to abandon their key insights. We think our detailed study of the three most important policy legacies of the New Deal demonstrates that we all would benefit from having a new general starting point for creating a more detailed and accurate understanding of the American power structure, past and present.

BIBLIOGRAPHY

ARCHIVAL SOURCES

John B. Black Papers, Wisconsin Historical Society Archives, Madison, Wisconsin.
J. Douglas Brown Papers. Mudd Library, Princeton University, Princeton, New Jersey.
Marion Folsom Papers, University of Rochester Library, Rochester, New York.
Industrial Relations Counselors, Inc., Memorandums to Clients, IRC Library, 1211 Avenue of the Americas, New York.
Leon Keyserling Papers, Georgetown University Library, Washington, DC.
Murray Latimer Papers, Georgetown University Library, Washington, DC.
Rockefeller Family Archives, Rockefeller Archive Center, Sleepy Hollow, New York.
Rockefeller Foundation Collection, Rockefeller Archive Center, Sleepy Hollow, New York.
Laura Spelman Rockefeller Memorial Archives, Rockefeller Archive Center, Sleepy Hollow, New York.
Social Science Research Council Archives, Rockefeller Archive Center, Sleepy Hollow, New York.
Social Security Oral History Project, Columbia University Library, New York.
Gerard Swope Letters, Downs Collection, General Electric Archives, Schenectady Museum, Schenectady, New York.
Robert F. Wagner Papers, Georgetown University Library, Washington, DC.

REFERENCES

Adams, Graham. 1966. *The age of industrial violence, 1910–1915*. New York: Columbia University Press.
Albertson, Dean. 1961. *Roosevelt's farmer: Claude Wickard in the New Deal*. New York: Columbia University Press.
Albion, Robert. (1939) 1984. *The rise of New York Port, 1815–1860*. Boston: Northeastern University Press.
Alchon, Guy. 1985. *The invisible hand of planning: Capitalism, social science, and the state in the 1920s*. Princeton: Princeton University Press.
Alexander, Herbert E. 1992. *Financing politics: Money, elections, and political reform*. 4th ed. Washington, DC: CQ Press.
Allen, Michael Patrick. 1991. Capitalist response to state intervention: Theories of the state and political finance in the New Deal. *American Sociological Review* 56 (5):679–689.

Alston, Lee J., and Joseph P. Ferrie. 1999. *Southern paternalism and the American welfare state*. New York: Cambridge University Press.

Altman, Nancy. 2005. *The battle for Social Security: From FDR's vision to Bush's gamble*. New York: John Wiley & Sons.

Altmeyer, Arthur. 1968. *The formative years of Social Security*. Madison: University of Wisconsin Press.

Amenta, Edwin. 1998. *Bold relief: Institutional politics and the origins of modern American social policy*. Princeton: Princeton University Press.

———. 2005. State-centered and political institutional theory: Retrospect and prospect. In *The handbook of political sociology: States, civil societies and globalization*, edited by T. Janoski, R. Alford, A. Hicks, and M. Schwartz. New York: Cambridge University Press.

———. 2006. *When movements matter: The Townsend Plan and the rise of social security*. Princeton: Princeton University Press.

American Federation of Labor. 1901. *Report of the Proceedings of the Twentieth Annual Convention of the American Federation of Labor*. New York: AFL.

Anderson, Mary, and Mary Winslow. 1951. *Women at work*. Minneapolis: University of Minnesota Press.

Archer, Robin. 2007. *Why is there no Labor Party in the United States?* Princeton: Princeton University Press.

Armstrong, Barbara N. 1932. *Insuring the essentials: Minimum wage, plus social insurance—a living wage problem*. New York: Macmillan.

———. 1965. Oral history. In *Social Security Oral History Project*. New York: Columbia University Library.

Aronowitz, Stanley. 1973. *False promises: The shaping of American working class consciousness*. New York: McGraw-Hill.

———. 2003. *How class works: Power and social movement*. New Haven: Yale University Press.

Auerbach, Jerold S. 1966. *Labor and liberty: The LaFollette Committee and the New Deal*. Indianapolis: Bobbs-Merrill.

Baker, Dean. 2001. Defaulting on the Social Security Trust Fund bonds: Winner and losers. Washington, DC: Center for Economic and Political Research.

Baker, Dean, and Mark Weisbrot. 1999. *Social Security: The phony crisis*. Chicago: University of Chicago Press.

Bakke, E. Wight. 1940a. *Citizens without work: A study of the effects of unemployment upon the workers' social relations and practices*. New Haven: Yale University Press.

———. 1940b. *The unemployed worker: A study of the task of making a living without a job*. New Haven: Yale University Press.

Baldwin, Sidney. 1968. *Poverty and politics: The rise and decline of the Farm Security Administration*. Chapel Hill: University of North Carolina Press.

Baltzell, E. Digby. 1964. *The Protestant establishment: Aristocracy and caste in America*. New York: Random House.

Barnard, Chester. 1938. *The functions of the executive*. Cambridge: Harvard University Press.

Benedict, Murray. 1953. *Farm Policies in the United States, 1790–1950*. New York: Twentieth Century Fund.

Berkowitz, Edward. 1987. The first Advisory Council and the 1939 amendments. In *Social Security after fifty: Success and failures*, edited by E. Berkowitz. New York: Greenwood Press.

Bernstein, Irving. 1950. *New Deal collective bargaining policy*. Berkeley: University of California Press.

———. 1960. *The lean years: A history of the American worker, 1920–1933*. Boston: Houghton Mifflin.

———. 1969. *Turbulent years: A history of the American worker, 1933–1941*. Boston: Houghton Mifflin.

———. 1985. *A caring society: The New Deal, the worker, and the Great Depression*. Boston: Houghton Mifflin.

Biddle, Francis. 1962. *In brief authority*. New York: Doubleday.

Biles, Roger. 1994. *The South and the New Deal*. Lexington: University Press of Kentucky.

Billings, Dwight. 1979. *Planters and the making of a new South: Class, politics, and development in North Carolina, 1865–1900*. Chapel Hill: University of North Carolina Press.

Black, John D. 1928. Letter to Beardsley Ruml, November 28. In *Black Papers, Chronological Correspondence File*. Madison: Wisconsin State Historical Society Archives.

———. 1929a. *Agricultural reform in the United States*. New York: McGraw-Hill.

———. 1929b. Letter to Henry Taylor, March 19. In *Black Papers, Chronological Correspondence File*. Madison: Wisconsin State Historical Society Archive.

Blauner, Bob. 1964. *Alienation and freedom: The factory worker and his industry*. Chicago: University of Chicago Press.

Boone, Gladys. 1942. *The Women's Trade Union League in Great Britain and the United States of America*. New York: Columbia University Press.

Brand, Donald. 1988. *Corporatism and the rule of law: A study of the National Recovery Administration*. Ithaca, NY: Cornell University Press.

Brecher, Jeremy. 1997. *Strike!* 2nd ed. Cambridge, MA: South End Press.

Brents, Barbara. 1984. Capitalism, corporate liberalism and social policy: The origins of the Social Security Act of 1935. *Mid-American Review of Sociology* 9:23–40.

Brinkley, Alan. 1982. *Voices of protest: Huey Long, Father Coughlin, and the Great Depression*. New York: Vintage Books.

———. 1995. *The end of reform: New Deal liberalism in recession and war*. New York: Alfred A. Knopf.

Brody, David. 1980. *Workers in industrial America: Essays on the twentieth century struggle*. New York: Oxford University Press.

Brown, J. Douglas. 1935a. Letter to Edwin Witte, February 13. In *Brown Papers, Box 15, 1935 File*. Princeton, NJ: Mudd Library, Princeton University.

———. 1935b. Letter to Edwin Witte, February 23. In *Brown Papers, Box 15, 1935 File*. Princeton, NJ: Mudd Library, Princeton University.

———. 1935c. Letter to Murray Latimer, August 12. In *Latimer Papers, Box 1, Folder 2*. Washington, DC: Special Collections, George Washington University Library.

———. 1965. Oral history. In *Social Security Oral History Project*. New York: Columbia University Library.

———. 1972. *An American philosophy of social security: Evolution and issues*. Princeton, NJ: Princeton University Press.

Brown, Josephine. 1940. *Public relief, 1929–1939*. New York: Henry Holt.

Brownlee, W. Elliot. 2000. Historical perspective on U.S. tax policy toward the rich. In *Does Atlas shrug? The economic consequences of taxing the rich*, edited by J. Slemrod. Cambridge: Harvard University Press.

Brownlow, Louis. 1958. *A passion for anonymity: The autobiography of Louis Brownlow*. Vol. 2. Chicago: University of Chicago Press.

Bruce, Robert V. 1959. *1877: Year of violence*. Indianapolis: Bobbs-Merrill.

Bulmer, Martin, and Joan Bulmer. 1981. Philanthropy and social science in the 1920s: Beardsley Ruml and the Laura Spelman Rockefeller Memorial, 1922–29. *Minerva* 19:347–407.

Bunting, David. 1983. Origins of the American corporate network. *Social Science History* 7:129–142.

———. 1987. *The rise of large American corporations, 1889–1919*. New York: Garland.

Burch, Philip. 1973. The NAM as an interest group. *Politics and Society* 4:100–105.

———. 1980. *Elites in American history: The New Deal to the Carter Administration*. Vol. 3. New York: Holmes & Meier.

———. 1981a. *Elites in American history: The Federalist years to the Civil War*. Vol. 1. New York: Holmes & Meier.

———. 1981b. *Elites in American history: The Civil War to the New Deal*. Vol. 2. New York: Holmes & Meier.

Burk, Robert. 1990. *The corporate state and the broker state*. Cambridge, MA: Harvard University Press.

Burns, Eveline. 1966. Oral history. In *Social Security Oral History Project*. New York: Columbia University Library.

Campbell, Christina. 1962. *The Farm Bureau and the New Deal*. Urbana: University of Illinois Press.

Carmines, Edward G., and James A. Stimson. 1989. *Issue evolution: Race and the transformation of American politics*. Princeton, NJ: Princeton University Press.

Carosso, Vincent. 1970. *Investment banking in America*. Cambridge, MA: Harvard University Press.

Carp, Robert, and Ronald Stidham. 1998. *Judicial process in America*. Fourth ed. Washington, DC: CQ Press.

Carter, Dan. 2000. *The politics of rage: George Wallace, the origins of the new conservatism, and the transformation of American politics*. 2nd ed. Baton Rouge: Louisiana State University Press.

Carter, Franklin. 1934. *The New Dealers*. New York: Simon & Schuster.

Casebeer, Kenneth. 1987. Holder of the pen: An interview with Leon Keyserling on drafting the Wagner Act. *University of Miami Law Review* 42:285–363.

Chambers, Clarke. 1952. *A historical study of the Grange, the Farm Bureau, and the Associated Farmers, 1929–1941*. Berkeley: University of California Press.

———. 1963. *Seedtime of reform: American social service and social action, 1918–1933*. Minneapolis: University of Minnesota Press.

Chernow, Ron. 1998. *Titan: The life of John D. Rockefeller, Sr*. New York: Warner Books.

Cohen, Adam. 2009. *Nothing to fear: FDR's inner circle and the hundred days that created modern America*. New York: Penguin.

Collins, Robert M. 1981. *The business response to Keynes, 1929–1964*. New York: Columbia University Press.

Commons, John. 1934. *Myself*. New York: Macmillan.

Conner, Valerie. 1983. *The National War Labor Board*. Chapel Hill: University of North Carolina Press.

Conrad, David. 1965. *Forgotten farmers: The story of sharecroppers in the New Deal*. Urbana: University of Illinois Press.

Cooper, Jerry M. 1980. *The army and civil disorder: Federal military intervention in labor disputes, 1877–1900*. Westport, CT: Greenwood Press.

Cortner, Richard. 1964. *The Wagner Act cases*. Knoxville: University of Tennessee Press.

Cowdrick, Edward. 1928. *Pensions: A problem of management*. New York: American Management Association, Annual Convention Series, No. 75.

Critchlow, Donald. 1985. *The Brookings Institution, 1916–1952*. DeKalb: Northern Illinois University Press.

Crocker, Ruth. 2006. *Mrs. Russell Sage: Women's activism and philanthropy in Gilded Age and Progressive Era America*. Bloomington: Indiana University Press.

Cyphers, Christopher. 2002. *The National Civic Federation and the making of a new liberalism, 1900–1915*. New York: Praeger.

Dahl, Robert A. 1957. The concept of power. *Behavioral Science* 2:202–210.

———. 1958. A critique of the ruling elite model. *American Political Science Review* 52:463–469.

Danforth, Brian. 1974. The influence of soio-economic factors upon political behavior: A quantitative look at New York City merchants, 1828–1844. Ph.D. diss., Department of History, New York University.

Daniel, Pete. 1985. *Breaking the land: The transformation of cotton, tobacco, and rice cultures since 1880*. Urbana: University of Illinois Press.

Davies, Gareth. 1999. The unsuspected radicalism of the Social Security Act. In *The Roosevelt years: New perspectives on American history, 1933–1945*, edited by R. Garson and S. Kidd. Edinburgh, Scotland: Edinburgh University Press.

Davis, Allen. 1964. The Women's Trade Union League: Origins and organization. *Labor History* 5:3–17.

———. 1967. *Spearheads for reform*. New York: Oxford University Press.

Davis, Chester. 1929. Letter to John D. Black, March 22. In *Black Papers, Chronological Correspondence File*. Madison: Wisconsin State Historical Society Archives.

Davis, Kenneth. 1986. *FDR: The New Deal years, 1933–1937*. New York: Random House.

Davis, Mike. 1986. *Prisoners of the American dream: Politics and economy in the history of the U.S. working class*. London: Verso Press.

Day, Edmund. 1928. Letter to John Black, June 21. In *Laura Spelman Rockefeller Memorial, Box 48, Folder 495 (Agricultural Survey—Black 1928–1930)*. Sleepy Hollow, NY: Rockefeller Archive Center.

Dempsey, Joseph R. 1961. *The operation of right-to-work laws: A comparison between what the state legislatures say about the meaning of the laws and how state court judges have applied these laws*. Milwaukee: Marquette University Press.

Devine, Edward. 1939. *When social work was young*. New York: Macmillan.

Devine, Thomas. 2003. The Communists, Henry Wallace, and the Progressive Party of 1948. *Continuity: A Journal of History* 26:33–79.

Domhoff, G. William. 1967. *Who rules America?* Englewood Cliffs, NJ: Prentice-Hall.

———. 1970. *The higher circles*. New York: Random House.

———. 1978. *Who really rules? New Haven and community power re-examined.* New Brunswick, NJ: Transaction Books.

———. 1979. *The powers that be: Processes of ruling class domination in America.* New York: Random House.

———. 1987. Where do government experts come from? The CEA and the policy-planning network. In *Power elites and organizations*, edited by G. W. Domhoff and T. Dye. Beverly Hills: Sage.

———. 1990. *The power elite and the state: How policy is made in America.* Hawthorne, NY: Aldine de Gruyter.

———. 1996. *State autonomy or class dominance? Case studies on policy making in America.* Hawthorne, NY: Aldine de Gruyter.

———. 1998. *Who rules America? Power and politics in the year 2000.* Third ed. Mountain View, CA: Mayfield.

———. 2007. C. Wright Mills, Floyd Hunter, and fifty years of power structure research. *Michigan Sociological Review* 21:1–54.

———. 2010. *Who rules America? Challenges to corporate and class dominance.* Sixth ed. New York: McGraw-Hill.

Downey, Kristin. 2009. *The woman behind the New Deal: The life of Frances Perkins, FDR's Secretary of Labor and his moral conscience.* New York: Doubleday.

Dubofsky, Melvyn. 2000. *Hard work: The making of labor history.* Chicago: University of Illinois Press.

Dubofsky, Melvyn, and Foster Rhea Dulles. 2004. *Labor in America: Seventh edition.* Wheeling, IL: Harlan Davidson.

Dubofsky, Melvyn, and Warren R. Van Tine. 1977. *John L. Lewis: A biography.* New York: Quadrangle/New York Times Book Company.

Dyson, Lowell K. 1982. *Red harvest: The Communist Party and the American farmer.* Lincoln: University of Nebraska Press.

Eakins, David. 1966. The development of corporate liberal policy research in the United States, 1885–1965. Ph.D. diss., Department of History, University of Wisconsin, Madison.

Eden, Elizabeth. 1936. Letter to Thomas Devevoise, October 30. In *Rockefeller Family Archives, Record Group III 2H, Box 122, Folder 909.* Sleepy Hollow, NY: Rockefeller Archive Center.

Edsall, Thomas B., and Mary D. Edsall. 1992. *Chain reaction: The impact of race, rights, and taxes on American politics.* New York: Norton.

Eliot, Thomas. 1992. *Recollections of the New Deal: When the people mattered.* Boston: Northeastern University Press.

Farhang, Sean, and Ira Katznelson. 2005. The Southern imposition: Congress and labor in the New Deal and Fair Deal. *Studies in American Political Development* 19:1–30.

Farrell, John. 1967. *Beloved lady.* Baltimore: Johns Hopkins University Press.

Feigenbaum, Harvey. 1985. *The Politics of public enterprise: Oil and the French state.* Princeton, NJ: Princeton University Press.

Ferguson, Thomas. 1995. *Golden rule: The investment theory of party competition and the logic of money-driven poliical systems.* Chicago: University of Chicago Press.

Ferrell, Robert. 1998. *The presidency of Calvin Coolidge*. Lawrence: University Press of Kansas.

Fine, Sidney. 1969. *Sit-down: The General Motors strike of 1936–1937*. Ann Arbor: University of Michigan Press.

Finegold, Kenneth, and Theda Skocpol. 1995. *State and party in America's New Deal*. Madison: University of Wisconsin Press.

Fishback, Price V., and Shawn E. Kantor. 2000. *A prelude to the welfare state: The origins of workers' compensation*. Chicago: University of Chicago Press.

Fisher, Donald. 1993. *Fundamental development of the social sciences*. Ann Arbor: University of Michigan Press.

Fitch, Robert. 1993. *The assassination of New York*. New York: Verso.

Flacks, Richard. 1973. *Conformity, resistance, and self-determination: The individual and authority*. Boston: Little, Brown.

———. 1988. *Making history: The radical tradition in American life*. New York: Columbia University Press.

Folsom, Marion. 1934. Letter to Frank W. Lovejoy, December 12. In *Folsom Papers, Box 108, Folder 3*. Rochester, NY: University of Rochester Library.

———. 1935. Letter to Rainard Robbins, December 18. In *Folsom Papers, Box 108, Folder 3*. Rochester, NY: University of Rochester Library.

Foner, Eric. 2006. *Forever free: The story of Emancipation and Reconstruction*. New York: Alfred A. Knopf.

Foner, Philip. 1941. *Business and slavery: The New York merchants and the irrepressible conflict*. Chapel Hill: University of North Carolina Press.

———. 1955. *The history of the labor movement in the United States: From the founding of the American Federation of Labor to the emergence of American imperialism*. Vol. II. New York: International Publishers.

———. 1977. *The great labor uprising of 1877*. New York: Pathfinder Press.

Fosdick, Raymond. 1933. Letter to John D. Rockefeller, April 27. In *Rockefeller Family Archives, Record Group 2 (OMR), Economic Reform Interests, Box 16, Folder 127*. Sleepy Hollow, NY: Rockefeller Archive Center.

———. 1934. Letter to John D. Rockefeller, March 22. In *Rockefeller Family Archives, Record Group 2 (OMR), Economic Reform Interests, Box 16, Folder 127*. Sleepy Hollow, NY: Rockefeller Archive Center.

———. 1952. *The Story of the Rockefeller Foundation*. New York: Harper & Brothers.

———. 1956. *John D. Rockefeller, Jr.: A portrait*. New York: Harper & Brothers.

Fraser, Steven. 1989. The "labor question". In *The rise and fall of the New Deal order, 1930–1980*, edited by S. Fraser and G. Gerstle. Princeton, NJ: Princeton University Press.

———. 1991. *Labor will rule: Sidney Hillman and the rise of American labor*. New York: Free Press.

Freidel, Frank. 1973. *Franklin D. Roosevelt: Launching the New Deal*. Boston: Little, Brown.

Gable, Richard. 1953. NAM: Influential lobby or kiss of death? *Journal of Politics* 15:254–273.

General Education Board. 1930. *The General Education Board: An account of its activities, 1902–1914*. New York: GEB.

Genovese, Eugene. 1965. *The political economy of slavery*. New York: Pantheon.

Gibb, George, and Evelyn Knowlton. 1956. *History of Standard Oil Company (New Jersey): The resurgent years, 1911–1927.* Vol. 2. New York: Harper & Brothers.

Gitelman, H. M. 1984. Being of two minds: American employers confront the labor problem, 1915–1919. *Labor History* 25:189–216.

———. 1988. *Legacy of the Ludlow Massacre.* Philadelphia: University of Pennsylvania Press.

Glenn, John. 1947. *The Russell Sage Foundation, 1907–1946.* New York: Russell Sage Foundation.

Gold, David, Clarence Lo, and Erik Wright. 1975. Recent developments in Marxist theories of the capitalist state. *Monthly Review* 27:29–43.

Goldfield, Michael. 1987. *The decline of organized labor in the United States.* Chicago: University of Chicago Press.

———. 1989. Worker insurgency, radical organization, and New Deal labor legislation. *American Political Science Review* 83:1257–1282.

Goldmark, Josephine. 1953. *The impatient crusader.* Urbana: University of Illinois Press.

Goodman, Paul. 1964. *The Democratic-Republicans of Massachusetts.* Cambridge, MA: Harvard University Press.

Goodwyn, Lawrence. 1978. *The Populist moment: A short history of the agrarian revolt in America.* New York: Oxford University Press.

Gordon, Colin. 1994. *New deals: Business, labor, and politics in America, 1920–1935.* New York: Cambridge University Press.

Gordon, Linda. 1994. *Pitied but not entitled: Single mothers and the history of welfare, 1890–1935.* New York: Free Press.

Gotham, Kevin Fox. 2000. Racialization and the state: The Housing Act of 1934 and the creation of the Federal Housing Administration. *Sociological Perspectives* 43:291–317.

———. 2002. *Race, real estate, and uneven development.* Albany: State University of New York Press.

Graebner, William. 1980. *A history of retirement.* New Haven: Yale University Press.

Graham, Otis L. 1967. *Encore for reform: The old Progressives and the New Deal.* New York: Oxford University Press.

Grantham, Dewey. 1988. *The life and death of the Solid South: A political history.* Lexington: University of Kentucky Press.

Green, Marguerite. 1956. *The National Civic Federation and the American Federation of Labor, 1900–1925.* Washington, DC: Catholic University of America Press.

Greider, William. 2009. The looting of Social Security. *The Nation,* March 2, 12–15.

Griffith, Barbara. 1988. *The crisis of American labor: Operation Dixie and the defeat of the CIO.* Philadelphia: Temple University Press.

Gross, James A. 1974. *The making of the National Labor Relations Board.* Albany: State University of New York Press.

———. 1981. *The reshaping of the National Labor Relations Board.* Albany: State University of New York Press.

———. 1995. *Broken promise: The subversion of U.S. labor relations policy.* Philadelphia: Temple University Press.

Grubb, Donald. 1971. *Cry from the cotton*. Chapel Hill: University of North Carolina Press.

Guttsman, W. L. 1969. *The English ruling class*. London: Weidenfeld & Nicholson.

Hacker, Jacob. 2002. *The divided welfare state: The battle over public and private social benefits in the United States*. New York: Cambridge University Press.

Hacker, Jacob, and Paul Pierson. 2002. Business power and social policy: Employers and the formation of the American welfare state. *Politics & Society* 30:277–325.

———. 2004. Varieties of capitalist interests and capitalist power: A response to Swenson. *Studies in American Political Development* 18:186–195.

Hamilton, David. 1991. *From New Day to New Deal*. Chapel Hill: University of North Carolina Press.

Hamilton, Richard 1991. *The bourgeois epoch: Marx and Engels on Britain, France, and Germany*. Chapel Hill: University of North Carolina Press.

Hamilton, Richard, and James Wright. 1986. *State of the masses: Sources of discontent, change, and stability*. New York: Aldine de Gruyter.

Hammond, Bray. 1957. *Banks and politics in America*. Princeton: Princeton University Press.

Hansen, Alvin, Merrill Murray, Russell Stevenson, and Bryce Stewart. 1934. *A program for unemployment insurance and relief in the United States*. Minneapolis: University of Minnesota Press.

Harr, John, and Peter Johnson. 1988. *The Rockefeller century*. New York: Charles Scribner's Sons.

Harris, Carl. 1976. Right fork or left fork? The section-party alignments of southern Democrats in Congress, 1873–1897. *Journal of Southern History* 42:471–506.

Hawley, Ellis. 1966. *The New Deal and the problem of monopoly*. Princeton: Princeton University Press.

Hayes, Erving. 1936. *Activities of the President's Emergency Committee on Unemployment*. Concord, NH: Rumford Press.

Haynes, John, Harvey Klehr, and K. M. Anderson. 1998. *The Soviet world of American communism: Annals of communism*. New Haven: Yale University Press.

Heard, Alexander. 1960. *The costs of democracy*. Chapel Hill: University of North Carolina Press.

Heinz, John P., Edward O. Laumann, Robert L. Nelson, and Robert H. Salisbury. 1993. *The hollow core: Private interests in national policy making*. Cambridge, MA: Harvard University Press.

Hicks, Clarence. 1934a. Letter to Senator Robert F. Wagner, January 16. In *Wagner Papers, General Correspondence*. Washington, DC: George Washington University.

———. 1934b. Letter to Senator Robert F. Wagner, March 26. In *Wagner Papers, General Correspondence*. Washington, DC: Georgetown University.

———. 1941. *My life in industrial relations*. New York: Harper & Brothers.

Himmelberg, Robert. (1976) 1993. *The origins of the National Recovery Administration*. New York: Fordham University Press.

Hofstadter, Richard. 1969. *The idea of a party system: The rise of legitimate opposition in the United States, 1780–1840*. Berkeley: University of California Press.

Hoopes, James. 2003. *False prophets: The gurus who created modern management and why their ideas are bad for business today*. New York: Perseus Book Group.

Hough, Jerry. 2006. *Changing party coalitions: The mystery of the red state-blue state alignment*. New York: Agathon Press.

Huberman, Leo. 1937. *The labor spy racket*. New York: Modern Age Books.

Hunter, Floyd. 1953. *Community power structure: A study of decision makers*. Chapel Hill: University of North Carolina Press.

———. 1959. *Top leadership, U.S.A.* Chapel Hill: University of North Carolina Press.

Huthmacher, J. Joseph. 1968. *Senator Robert F. Wagner and the rise of urban liberalism*. New York: Atheneum.

———. 1973. *Trial by war and depression: 1917–1941*. Boston: Allyn & Bacon.

Industrial Relations Counselors, Inc. 1934a. *Memorandum to Clients*, No. 1, July 10. New York: IRC.

———. 1934b. *Memorandum to Clients*, No. 4, October 31. New York: IRC.

———. 1935a. *Memorandum to Clients*, No. 5, January 25. New York: IRC.

———. 1935b. *Memorandum to Clients*, No. 6, February 1. New York: IRC.

———. 1935c. *Memorandum to Clients*, No. 8, March 1. New York: IRC.

———. 1935d. *Memorandum to Clients*, No. 9, March 27. New York: IRC.

———. 1935e. *Memorandum to Clients*, No. 10, April 10. New York: IRC.

———. 1935f. *Memorandum to Clients*, No. 12, May 27. New York: IRC.

———. 1935g. *Memorandum to Clients*, No. 13, July 3. New York: IRC.

———. 1935h. *Memorandum to Clients*, No. 14, August 16. New York: IRC.

———. 1935i. *Memorandum to Clients*, No. 15, August 23. New York: IRC.

Irons, Peter. 1982. *The New Deal lawyers*. Princeton, NJ: Princeton University Press.

Jacoby, Sanford. 1993. Employers and the welfare state: The role of Marion B. Folsom. *The Journal of American History* 47:525–556.

———. 1997. *Modern manors: Welfare capitalism since the New Deal*. Princeton, NJ: Princeton University Press.

Jamieson, Stuart M. 1945. *Labor unionism in American agriculture*. Washington, DC: U.S. Government Printing Office.

Jenkins, J. Craig, and Barbara Brents. 1989. Social protest, hegemonic competition, and social reform. *American Sociological Review* 54:891–909.

Jensen, Gordon. 1956. The National Civic Federation: American business in the age of social change and social reform, 1900–1910. Ph.D. diss., Department of History, Princeton University, Princeton.

Jones, Alfred. 1941. *Life, liberty, and property: A story of conflict and a measurement of conflicting rights*. Philadelphia: J. B. Lippincott.

Jones, Jesse. 1951. *Fifty billion dollars: My thirteen years with the RFC, 1932–1945*. New York: Macmillan.

Kahn, Jonathan. 1997. *Budgeting democracy: State building and citizenship in America, 1890–1928*. Ithaca, NY: Cornell University Press.

Karl, Barry. 1963. *Executive reorganization and reform in the New Deal*. Cambridge, MA: Harvard University Press.

———. 1974. *Charles E. Merriam and the study of politics*. Chicago: University of Chicago Press.

Katz, Irving. 1968. *August Belmont: A political biography*. New York: Columbia University Press.

Kaufman, Bruce. 2003. Industrial Relations Counselors, Inc.: Its history and significance. In *Industrial relations to human resources and beyond: The evolving process of employee relations management*, edited by B. Kaufman, R. Beaumont, and R. Helfgott. Armonk, NY: M.E. Sharpe.

———. 2009. *Hired hands or human resources: Case studies of HRM practices and programs in early American industry*. Ithaca, NY: Cornell University Press.

Kelly, Laurence. 1987. *Industrial relations at Queen's: The first fifty years*. Kingston, Ontario, Canada: Industrial Relations Centre, Queen's University.

Kennedy, David. 1999. *Freedom from fear: The American people in depression and war, 1929–1945*. New York: Oxford University Press.

Kerbo, Harold, and Richard Shaffer. 1992. Lower class insurgency and the political process: The response of the U.S. unemployed, 1890–1940. *Social Problems* 39:139–154.

Key, V. O. 1949. *Southern politics in state and nation*. New York: Random House.

Kimeldorf, Howard. 1999. *Battling for American labor: Wobblies, craft workers, and the making of the union movement*. Berkeley: University of California Press.

———. 2010. When did early unionization efforts succeed? Unpublished manuscript, Ann Arbor: Department of Sociology, University of Michigan.

Kirkendall, Richard. 1964. Social science in the Central Valley of California: An episode. *California Historical Society Quarterly* 43:195–218.

———. 1966. *Social scientists and farm politics in the Age of Roosevelt*. Columbia: University of Missouri Press.

Kirstein, Louis. 1934. Letter to Gerard Swope, February 7. In *General Electric Archives, Downs Collection, 898.15.1, Series 5, Box A-19*. Schenectady, NY: Schenectady Museum Archive.

Klass, Bernard. 1969. John D. Black: Farm economist and political advisor, 1920–1942. Ph.D. diss., Department of History, University of California, Los Angeles.

Klehr, Harvey. 1984. *The heyday of American communism*. New York: Basic Books.

Klehr, Harvey, John Haynes, and Fridrikh Firsov. 1995. *The secret world of American communism: Annals of communism*. New Haven: Yale University Press.

Klein, Jennifer. 2003. *For all these rights: Business, labor, and the shaping of America's public-private welfare state*. Princeton, NJ: Princeton University Press.

Klepper, Michael, and Robert Gunther. 1996. *The wealthy 100: From Benjamin Franklin to Bill Gates—A ranking of the richest Americans, past and present*. New York: Carol Publication Group.

Kolko, Gabriel. 1963. *The triumph of conservatism: A re-interpretation of American history, 1900–1916*. New York: Free Press of Glencoe.

Kousser, J. Morgan. 1974. *The shaping of Southern politics: Suffrage restriction and the establishment of the one-party South, 1880–1910*. New Haven, CT: Yale University Press.

Lachmann, Richard. 2010. *States and power*. Cambridge, UK: Polity Press.

Lagemann, Ellen. 1989. *The politics of knowledge: The Carnegie Corporation, philanthropy, and public policy*. Middletown, CT: Wesleyan University Press.

Lambert, Josiah. 2005. *If the workers took a notion: The right to strike and American political development*. Ithaca, NY: Cornell University Press.

Laslett, John. 1970. *Labor and the left: A study of socialist and radical influences in the American labor movement, 1881–1924*. New York: Basic Books.

Latham, Earl. 1959. *The politics of railroad coordination, 1933–1936*. Cambridge, MA: Harvard University Press.

Latimer, Murray. 1933. Memorandum on work for federal government. In *Rockefeller Foundation Collection, Record Group 1.1, Series 200S, Box 348, Folder 4143*. Sleepy Hollow, NY: Rockefeller Archive Center.

———. 1934. Correspondence with Industrial Relations Counselors, Inc., on salary and taxes. In *Latimer Papers, Box 9, Folder 12*. Washington, DC: Special Collections, George Washington University Library.

———. 1935. Letter to Robert Gooch, March 20. In *Latimer Papers, Box 1, Folder 2*. Washington, DC: Special Collections, George Washington University Library.

———. 1936. Memorandum to members of the Social Security Board. In *Altmeyer Papers, Box 2, Folder on the Clark Amendment*. Madison: Wisconsin State Historical Archives.

Latimer, Murray, and Stephen Hawkins. 1938. Railroad retirement system in the United States. In *Latimer Papers*. Washington, DC: Special Collections, George Washington University Library.

Leuchtenburg, William. 1963. *Franklin D. Roosevelt and the New Deal, 1932–1940*. New York: Harper & Row.

———. 1995. *The Supreme Court reborn: The constitutional revolution in the age of Roosevelt*. New York: Oxford University Press.

Levine, Rhonda F. 1988. *Class struggle and the New Deal*. Lawrence: University of Kansas Press.

Levy, Philip. 1935. Letter to Senator Robert F. Wagner, May 20. In *Keyserling Papers, Labor Series, Box 1, Folder 10*. Washington, DC: Georgetown University Library.

Lichtman, Allan. 2008. *White Protestant nation: The rise of the American conservative movement*. New York: Grove Press.

Light, Paul. 1985. *Artful work*. New York: Random House.

Linn, James. 1935. *Jane Addams: A biography*. New York: D. Appleton Century.

Lipset, Seymour, and Gary Marks. 2000. *It didn't happen here: Why socialism failed in the United States*. New York: W.W. Norton & Co.

Loetta, Louis. 1975. Abraham Epstein and the movement for old age security. *Labor History* 16:359–377.

Loth, David. 1958. *Swope of G.E.: The story of Gerard Swope and General Electric in American business*. New York: Simon & Schuster.

Lowitt, Richard. 1979. Henry A. Wallace and the 1935 purge in the Department of Agriculture. *Agricultural History* 53:607–621.

———. 1984. *The New Deal and the West*. Bloomington: Indiana University Press.

Lubove, Roy C. 1968. *The struggle for Social Security, 1900–1935*. Cambridge, MA: Harvard University Press.

Lundberg, F. 1937. *America's sixty families*. New York: Vanguard.

Lynd, Robert S., and Helen Merrill Lynd. 1937. *Middletown in transition*. New York: Harcourt, Brace.

MacDougall, Curtis. 1965. *Gideon's army*. Vol. 3. New York: Marzani & Munsell.

Majka, Linda, and Theo Majka. 1982. *Farm workers, agribusiness and the state.* Philadelphia: Temple University Press.

Mann, Michael. 1986. *The sources of social power: A history of power from the beginning to A.D. 1760.* Vol. 1. New York: Cambridge University Press.

———. 1993. *The sources of social power: The rise of classes and nation-states, 1760–1914.* Vol. 2. New York: Cambridge University Press.

———. forthcoming. *The sources of social power: Globalization.* Vol. 3. New York: Cambridge University Press.

Manza, Jeff. 1995. Policy experts and political change during the New Deal. Ph.D. diss., Department of Sociology, University of California, Berkeley.

———. 2000. Political sociological models of the U.S. New Deal. *Annual Review of Sociology* 26:297–322.

Marx, Anthony. 1998. *Making race and nation: A comparison of the United States, South Africa, and Brazil.* New York: Cambridge University Press.

May, Stacy. 1936. Letter to Joseph P. Harris, February 1. In *Rockefeller Foundation Collection, Record Group 1.1, Series 200S, Box 397, Folder 4714.* Sleepy Hollow, NY: Rockefeller Archive Center.

Mayer, Arno. 1981. *The persistence of the old regime.* New York: Pantheon.

McCammon, Holly J. 1990. Legal limits on labor militancy: U.S. labor law and the right to strike since the New Deal. *Social Problems* 37 (2):206–229.

———. 1993. From repressive intervention to integrative prevention: The U.S. state's legal management of labor militancy, 1881–1978. *Social Forces* 71 (3):569–601.

———. 1994. Disorganizing and reorganizing conflict: Outcomes of the state's legal regulation of the strike since the Wagner Act. *Social Forces* 72 (4):1011–1049.

———. 1995. The politics of protection: State minimum wage and maximum hours laws for women in the United States, 1870–1930. *The Sociological Quarterly* 36 (2):217–249.

———. 1996. Protection for whom? Maximum hours laws and women's employment in the United States, 1880–1920. *Work and Occupations* 23 (2):132–164.

McConnell, Grant. 1953. *The decline of agrarian democracy.* Berkeley: University of California Press.

———. 1966. *Private power and American democracy.* New York: Alfred A. Knopf.

McCune, Wesley. 1956. *Who's behind our farm policy?* New York: Praeger.

McGann, James. 2007. *Think tanks and policy advice in the United States: Academics, advisors and advocates.* New York: Routledge.

McQuaid, Kim. 1976. The Business Advisory Council in the Department of Commerce, 1933–1961. *Research in Economic History* 1:171–197.

———. 1979. The frustration of corporate revival in the early New Deal. *Historian* 41:682–704.

———. 1982. *Big business and presidential power from FDR to Reagan.* New York: Morrow.

McWilliams, Carey. 1939. *Factories in the field.* Boston: Little, Brown.

———. 1942. *Ill fares the land: Migrants and migratory labor in the United States.* Boston: Little Brown.

Mertz, Paul. 1978. *New Deal policy and Southern rural poverty.* Baton Rouge: Louisiana State University Press.

Mettler, Suzanne. 2002. Social citizens of separate sovereignties: Governance in the New Deal welfare state. In *The New Deal and the triumph of liberalism*, edited by S. Milkis and J. Mileur. Amherst: University of Massachusetts Press.

Mills, C. Wright. 1956. *The power elite*. New York: Oxford University Press.

———. 1959. *The sociological imagination*. New York: Oxford University Press.

———. 1962. *The Marxists*. New York: Dell.

Mink, Gwendolyn. 1986. *Old labor and new immigrants in American political development, 1870–1925*. Ithaca, NY: Cornell University Press.

Mintz, Beth. 1975. The president's cabinet, 1897–1972: A contribution to the power structure debate. *The Insurgent Sociologist* 5:131–148.

Mizruchi, Mark. 1982. *The American corporate network, 1904–1974*. Beverly Hills, CA: Sage.

Mizruchi, Mark, and David Bunting. 1981. Influence in corporate networks: An examination of four measures. *Administrative Science Quarterly* 26 (3):475–489.

Mollenkopf, John. 1975. Theories of the state and power structure research. *The Insurgent Sociologist* 5:245–264.

Morgan, Ted. 2003. *Reds: McCarthyism in twentieth-century America*. New York: Random House.

Moss, David. 1996. *Socializing security: Progressive Era economists and the origins of American social policy*. Cambridge, MA: Harvard University Press.

National Industrial Conference Board. 1931. *Elements of industrial pension plans*. New York: NICB.

Nelson, Daniel. 1969. *Unemployment insurance: The American experience, 1915–1935*. Madison: University of Wisconsin Press.

———. 1982. The company union movement, 1900–1937: A reexamination. *Business History Review* 56:335–357.

———. 1997. *Shifting fortunes: The rise and decline of American labor from the 1820s to the present*. Chicago: Ivan R. Dee.

———. 2001. The other New Deal and labor: The regulatory state and the unions, 1933–1940. *Journal of Policy History* 13:367–390.

New York Times. 1935. Rather go to jail than accept Wagner Bill, says U.S. Steel executive, getting medal. *New York Times*, May 25, 1.

Norwood, Stephen H. 2002. *Strikebreaking and intimidation: Mercenaries and masculinity in twentieth century America*. Chapel Hill: University of North Carolina Press.

O'Brien, Ruth. 1998. *Worker's paradox: The Republican origins of New Deal labor policy, 1886–1935*. Chapel Hill: University of North Carolina Press.

Ohl, John. 1985. *Hugh S. Johnson and the New Deal*. DeKalb: Northern Illinois University Press.

Okrent, Daniel. 2003. *Great fortune: The epic of Rockefeller Center*. New York: Viking.

———. 2010. *Last call: The rise and fall of Prohibition*. New York: Scribner.

Olson, James. 1988. *Saving capitalism: The Reconstruction Finance Corporation and the New Deal, 1933–1940* Princeton, NJ: Princeton University Press.

Orloff, Ann. 1993. *The politics of pensions: A comparative analysis of Britain, Canada, and the United States, 1880–1940*. Madison: University of Wisconsin Press.

Orloff, Ann, and Eric Parker. 1990. Business and social policy in Canada and the United States, 1920–1940. *Comparative Social Research* 12:295–339.

Overacker, Louise. 1932. *Money in elections*. New York: Macmillan.

———. 1933. Campaign funds in a depression year. *American Political Science Review* 27:769–783.

———. 1937. Campaign funds in the presidential election of 1936. *American Political Science Review* 31:473–498.

Parrish, Michael E. 1970. *Securities regulation and the New Deal*. New Haven, CT: Yale University Press.

Patterson, James T. (1967) 1981. *Congressional conservatism and the New Deal: The growth of the conservative coalition in Congress, 1933–1939*. Lexington: University of Kentucky Press.

Peck, Darius. 1934. Letter to Gerard Swope, March 5. In *General Electric Archive, Downs Collection, 898.15.1, Series 5, Box A-19a*. Schnectady, NY: Schenectady Museum Archive.

Perkins, Frances. 1930. Letter to Beardsley Ruml, November 5. In *Spelman Fund, Series 4, Box 9, Folder 275*. Sleepy Hollow, NY: Rockefeller Archive Center.

———. 1946. *The Roosevelt I knew*. New York: Harper & Row.

Perman, Michael. 2001. *Struggle for mastery: Disfranchisement in the South, 1888–1908*. Chapel Hill: University of North Carolina Press.

Perrow, Charles. 2002. *Organizing America: Wealth, power, and the origin of corporate capitalism*. Princeton, NJ: Princeton University Press.

Pierce, Lloyd. 1953. The activities of the American Association for Labor Legislation in behalf of social security and protective labor legislation. Ph.D. diss., Department of Economics, University of Wisconsin, Madison.

Piven, Frances. 2006. *Challenging authority: How ordinary people change America*. Lanham, MD: Rowman and Littlefield.

———. 2008. Can power from below change the world? *American Sociological Review* 73:1–14.

Piven, Frances, and Richard Cloward. 1977. *Poor people's movements: Why they succeed, how they fail*. New York: Random House.

———. 2003. Rule making, rule breaking, and power. In *The handbook of sociology: States, civil society, and globalization*, edited by T. Janoski, R. Alford, A. Hicks, and M. Schwartz. New York: Cambridge University Press.

———. (1971) 1993. *Regulating the poor: The functions of public welfare*. Updated ed. New York: Vintage Books.

———. 1982. *The new class war: Reagan's attack on the welfare state and its consequences*. New York: Pantheon Books.

Polakoff, Keith. 1973. *The politics of inertia: The election of 1876 and the end of Reconstruction*. Baton Rouge: Louisiana State University Press.

Polenberg, Richard. 1966. *Reorganizing Roosevelt's government, 1936–1939: The controversy over executive reorganization*. Cambridge: Harvard University Press.

Poole, Mary. 2006. *The segregated origins of Social Security: African Americans and the welfare state*. Chapel Hill: University of North Carolina Press.

Potter, David. 1972. *The South and the concurrent majority*. Baton Rouge: Louisiana State University Press.

Poulantzas, Nicos. 1969. The problem of the capitalist state. *New Left Review* 58:67–78.

————. 1973. *Political power and social classes*. London: New Left Books.

Powell, Walter, and Paul DiMaggio. 1991. *The new institutionalism in organizational analysis*. Chicago: University of Chicago Press.

Quadagno, Jill S. 1988. *The transformation of old age security: Class and politics in the American welfare state*. Chicago: University of Chicago Press.

Rae, Douglas. 1971. *The political consequences of electoral laws*. New Haven, CT: Yale University Press.

Rae, Nicol. 1994. *Southern Democrats*. New York: Oxford University Press.

Ramirez, Bruno. 1978. *When workers fight*. Westport, CT: Greenwood.

Reagan, Patrick. 1999. *Designing a new America: The origins of New Deal planning, 1890–1943*. Amherst: University of Massachusetts Press.

Rich, Andrew. 2004. *Think tanks, public policy, and the politics of expertise*. New York: Cambridge University Press.

Robbins, Rainard. 1935. Letter to Marion Folsom, December 16. In *Folsom Papers, Box 108, Folder 3*. Rochester, NY: University of Rochester Library.

————. 1936. Preliminary report on the status of industrial pension plans as affected by old age benefits sections of the Social Security Act. In *Social Science Research Council Archives, Record Group 1.1., Box 261*. Sleepy Hollow, NY: Rockefeller Archive Center.

Roberts, Alasdair. 1994. Demonstrating neutrality: The Rockefeller philanthropies and the evolution of public administration, 1927–1936. *Public Administration Review*, 221–228.

Robertson, David. 1994. *Sly and able: A political biography of James F. Byrnes*. New York: Norton.

Rockefeller, John D. 1934. Letter to Arthur Young, February 10. In *Rockefeller Family Archives, Record Group 2F, Box 16, Folder 127*. Sleepy Hollow, NY: Rockefeller Archive Center.

————. 1936. Letter to T.H.A. Tiedemann. In *Rockefeller Family Archives, Record Group 2F, Box 16, Folder 127*. Sleepy Hollow, NY: Rockefeller Archive Center.

————. 1937. Letter to Mackenzie King, April 30. In *Rockefeller Family Archives, Record Group III, 2H, Box 72, Folder 557*. Sleepy Hollow, NY: Rockefeller Archive Center.

Rockefeller, John D. III. 1934. Letter to John D. Rockefeller, March 22. In *Rockefeller Family Archives, Record Group 2F, Box 16, Folder 127*. Sleepy Hollow, NY: Rockefeller Archive Center.

————. 1936. Letter to John D. Rockefeller, June 8. In *Rockefeller Family Archives, Record Group 2F, Box 16, Folder 127*. Sleepy Hollow, NY: Rockefeller Archive Center.

Rogne, Leah, Carroll L. Estes, Brian R. Grossman, Brooke A. Hollister, and Erica S. Solway. 2009. *Social insurance and social justice: Social Security, Medicare, and the campaign against entitlements*. New York: Springer.

Roosevelt, Eleanor, and Lorena Hickok. 1954. *Ladies of courage*. New York: G.P. Putnam's Sons.

Roosevelt, Franklin. 1938. *The public papers and addresses of Franklin D. Roosevelt: The people approve, 1936*. New York: Random House.

Rosen, Elliott. 1977. *Hoover, Roosevelt and the Brains Trust*. New York: Columbia University Press.

Rosenstone, Steven J., Roy L. Behr, and Edward H. Lazarus. 1996. *Third parties in America: Citizen response to major party failure.* 2nd ed. Princeton, NJ: Princeton University Press.

Rowley, William. 1970. *M. L. Wilson and the campaign for the domestic allotment.* Lincoln: University of Nebraska Press.

Roy, William G. 1983. Interlocking directorates and the corporate revolution. *Social Science History* 7:143–164.

———. 1997. *Socializing capital: The rise of the large industrial corporation in America.* Princeton, NJ: Princeton University Press.

Ruml, Beardsley. 1928a. Letter to John D. Black, November 30. In *Black Papers, Chronological Correspondence File.* Madison: Wisconsin State Historical Society Archives.

———. 1928b. Memo to Arthur Woods, November 30. In *Laura Spelman Rockefeller Memorial Collection.* Sleepy Hollow, NY: Rockefeller Archive Center.

———. 1929. Letter to John D. Black, March 6. In *Black Papers, Chronological Correspondence File.* Madison: Wisconsin State Historical Society Archives.

Russell, Bertrand. 1938. *Power: A new social analysis.* London: Allen and Unwin.

Saloutos, Theodore. 1960. *Farmer movements in the South.* Berkeley: University of California Press.

———. 1982. *The American farmer and the New Deal.* Ames: The Iowa State University Press.

Salzman, Harold, and G. William Domhoff. 1980. The corporate community and government: Do they interlock? In *Power structure research*, edited by G. W. Domhoff. Beverly Hills, CA: Sage.

Sargent, James E. 1981. *Roosevelt and the hundred days: Struggle for the early New Deal.* New York: Garland.

Sass, Steven A. 1997. *The promise of private pensions: The first hundred years.* Cambridge: Harvard University Press.

Saunders, Charles B. 1966. *The Brookings Institution: A fifty-year history.* Washington, DC: Brookings Institution.

Scheinberg, Stephen. 1986. *Employers and reformers: The development of corporation labor policy, 1900–1940.* New York: Taylor and Francis.

Schenkel, Albert. 1995. *The rich man and the kingdom: John D. Rockefeller, Jr., and the Protestant Establishment.* Minneapolis: Fortress Press.

Schlabach, Theron F. 1969. *Edwin E. Witte: Cautious reformer.* Madison: State Historical Society of Wisconsin.

Schlesinger, Arthur. 1957. *The decline of the old order.* Boston: Houghton Mifflin.

———. 1958. *The coming of the New Deal.* Boston: Houghton Mifflin.

———. 1960. *The politics of upheaval.* Boston: Houghton Mifflin.

Schulman, Bruce. 1994. *From Cotton Belt to Sunbelt: Federal policy, economic development, and the transformation of the South, 1938–1980.* Durham, NC: Duke University Press.

Schwartz, Michael. 1976. *Radical protest and social structure: The Southern Farmers' Alliance and cotton tenancy, 1880–1890.* New York: Academic Press.

Shamir, Ronen. 1995. *Managing legal uncertainty: Elite lawyers in the New Deal.* Durham, NC: Duke University Press.

Shefter, Martin. 1994. *Political parties and the state: The American historical experience.* Princeton, NJ: Princeton University Press.

Shesol, Jeff. 2010. *Supreme power: Franklin D. Roosevelt vs. the Supreme Court*. New York: W.W. Norton.

Shostak, Arthur. (1962) 1973. *America's forgotten labor organization: A survey of the role of the single-firm independent union in American industry*. Westport, CT: Greenwood Press.

Shover, John. 1965. *Cornbelt rebellion: The Farmers' Holiday Association*. Urbana: University of Illinois Press.

Simkhovitch, Mary. 1938. *Neighborhood*. New York: W. W. Norton.

Skocpol, Theda. 1979. *States and social revolutions: A comparative analysis of France, Russia, and China*. New York: Cambridge University Press.

———. 1980. Political responses to capitalist crisis: Neo-Marxist theories of the state and the case of the New Deal. *Politics and Society* 10:155–202.

———. 1992. *Protecting soldiers and mothers: The political origins of social policy in the United States*. Cambridge, MA: Harvard University Press.

Skocpol, Theda, and John Ikenberry. 1983. The political formation of the American welfare state in historical and comparative perspective. In *Comparative Social Research*, edited by R. Tomasson. Greenwich, CT: JAI.

Smith, Jason. 2006. *Building New Deal liberalism: The political economy of public works, 1933–1956*. New York: Cambridge University Press.

Smith, Jean. 2007. *FDR*. New York: Random House.

Smith, Robert M. 2003. *From blackjacks to briefcases: A history of commercialized strikebreaking and unionbusting in the United States*. Athens: Ohio University Press.

Soule, George. 1935. Sidney Hillman turns architect. *The Nation*, April 3, 383–384.

Stark, Louis. 1934. Steel men assail "vicious" labor bill. *New York Times*, April 5, 1.

Starr, Paul. 2007. *Freedom's power: The true force of liberalism*. New York: Basic Books.

Stepan-Norris, Judith, and Maurice Zeitlin. 2003. *Left out: Reds and America's industrial unions*. New York: Cambridge University Press.

Stewart, Bryce. 1925. An American experiment in unemployment insurance in industry. *International Labor Review* 11:319–323.

———. 1928. *Financial aspects of industrial pensions*. New York: American Management Association.

———. 1930. *Unemployment benefits in the United States: The plans and their setting*. New York: Industrial Relations Counselors, Inc.

———. 1933. Memorandum: Government work of Bryce M. Stewart. In *Rockefeller Foundation Collection, Record Group 1.1, Series 200S, Folder 4143*. Sleepy Hollow, NY: Rockefeller Archive Center.

Stewart, Bryce, and Meredith Givens. 1934a. Planned protection against unemployment and dependency: Report on a tentative plan for a proposed investigation. In *Rockefeller Foundation Collection, Record Group 1.1, Series 200, Box 398, Folder 4723*. Sleepy Hollow, NY: Rockefeller Archive Center.

———. 1934b. Project report: Exploratory study of unemployment reserves and relief (economic security). In *Rockefeller Foundation Collection, Record Group 1.1, Series 200S, Box 408, Folder 4824*. Sleepy Hollow, NY: Rockefeller Archive Center.

Stillman, William J. 1927. *Balancing the farm output: A statement of the present deplorable conditions of farming, its causes, and suggested remedies*. New York: Orange Judd.

———. 1929. Memorandum to H. C. Tolley, April 8. In *Black Papers, Chronological Correspondence File*. Madison: Wisconsin State Historical Society Archives.

Storrs, Landon. 2000. *Civilizing capitalism: The National Consumers' League, women's activism, and labor standards in the New Deal era*. Chapel Hill: University of North Carolina Press.

Stowell, David. 1999. *Streets, railroads and the Great Strike of 1877*. Chicago: University of Chicago Press.

Sugrue, Thomas. 2008. *Sweet land of liberty: The forgotten struggle for civil rights in the North*. New York: Random House.

Swenson, Peter. 2002. *Capitalists against markets: The making of labor markets and welfare states in the United States and Sweden*. New York: Oxford University Press.

———. 2004. Varieties of capitalist interests: Power, institutions, and the regulatory welfare state in the United States and Sweden. *Studies in American Political Development* 18:1–29.

Swope, Gerard. 1934a. Letter to Darius Peck, March 2. In *General Electric Archives, Downs Collection, 898.15.1, Series 5, Box A-19a*. Schenectady, NY: Schenectady Museum Archive.

———. 1934b. Letter to Pierre du Pont, February 26. In *General Electric Archives, Downs Collection, 898.15.1, Series 5, Box A-19a*. Schenectady, NY: Schenectady Museum Archive.

———. 1934c. Telegram to Senator Robert F. Wagner, March 12. In *General Electric Archives, Downs Collection, 898.15.1, Series 5, Box A-19a*. Schenectady, NY: Schenectady Museum Archive.

———. 1935. Letter to Senator Robert F. Wagner, March 28. In *Wagner Papers, General Correspondence*. Washington, DC: Georgetown University.

Tarrow, Sidney. 1994. *Power in movement: Social movements, collective action and politics*. New York: Cambridge University Press.

Taylor, Henry. 1928. Letter to John Black, July 5. In *Black Papers, Chronological Correspondence File*. Madison: Wisconsin State Historical Society Archives.

Taylor, Nick. 2008. *American-made: The enduring legacy of the WPA*. New York: Bantam Books.

Teagle, Walter. 1934a. Letter to Gerard Swope, March 15. In *General Electric Archives, Downs Collection, 898.15.1, Series 5, Box A-19a*. Schenectady, NY: Schenectady Museum Archive.

———. 1934b. Memorandum to Senator Robert F. Wagner, March 14. In *General Electric Archives, Downs Collection, 898.15.1, Series 5, Box A-19a*. Schenectady, NY: Schenectady Museum Archive.

———. 1935. Letter to Gerard Swope, October 1. In *General Electric Archives, Downs Collection, 898.15.1, Series 5, Box A-19a*. Schenectady, NY: Schenectady Museum Archive.

Thorndike, Joseph. 2009. "The unfair advantage of the few": The New Deal regime of "soak the rich" taxation. In *The new fiscal sociology: Taxation in comparative and historical perspective*, edited by W. M. Martin, A. Mehrotra, and M. Prasad. New York: Cambridge University Press.

Tomlins, Christopher. 1985. *The state and the unions: Labor relations, law and the organized labor movement in America, 1880–1960*. New York: Cambridge University Press.

Troy, Leo. 1965. *Trade union membership, 1897–1962.* New York: National Bureau of Economic Research.

U.S Bureau of the Budget, *Government Budget, 1938.* Washington: U.S. Government Printing Office.

U.S. Senate. 1939. *Violations of free speech and rights of labor, Part 45: The Special Conference Committee.* Washington, DC: U.S. Government Printing Office.

Valocchi, Steve. 1990. The unemployed workers movement of the 1930s: A reexamination of the Piven and Cloward thesis. *Social Problems* 37:191–205.

———. 1993. External resources and the Unemployed Councils of the 1930s: Evaluating six propositions from social movement theory. *Sociological Forum* 8:451–469.

Van Sickle, John. 1936. Memorandum on interview with Bryce Stewart, March 24. In *Rockefeller Foundation Collection, Record Group 1.1, Series 200S, Box 348, Folder 4146.* Sleepy Hollow, NY: Rockefeller Archive Center.

Vittoz, Stanley. 1987. *New Deal labor policy and the American industrial economy.* Chapel Hill: University of North Carolina Press.

Voss, Kim. 1993. *The making of American exceptionalism: The Knights of Labor and class formation in the nineteenth century.* Ithaca, NY: Cornell University Press.

Waddell, Brian. 2001. *The war against the New Deal: World War II and American democracy.* DeKalb: Northern Illinois University Press.

Wagner, Robert F. 1935a. Letter to Norman Thomas, April 2. In *Wagner Papers, General Correspondence.* Washington, DC: George Washington University.

———. 1935b. Letter to Walter Teagle, February 23. In *Wagner Papers, General Correspondence.* Washington, DC: Georgetown University.

Wald, Lillian. 1934. *Window on Henry Street.* Boston: Little, Brown.

Wall, Bennett, and George Gibb. 1974. *Teagle of Jersey Standard.* New Orleans: Tulane University Press.

Webber, Michael. 2000. *New Deal fat cats: Business, labor, and campaign finance in the 1936 presidential election.* New York: Fordham University Press.

Weiner, Merle. 1978. Cheap labor and the repression of farm workers. *The Insurgent Sociologist* 8:181–190.

Weinstein, James. 1967. *The decline of socialism in America, 1912–1925.* New York: Monthly Review Press.

———. 1968. *The corporate ideal in the liberal state.* Boston: Beacon Press.

Weir, Margaret, Ann Orloff, and Theda Skocpol. 1988. Understanding American social politics. In *The politics of social policy in the United States*, edited by M. Weir, A. Orloff, and T. Skocpol. Princeton: Princeton University Press.

Werner, M. R. 1939. *Julius Rosenwald: The life of a practical humanitarian.* New York: Harper & Brothers.

Winders, Bill. 2005. Maintaining the coalition: Class coalitions and policy trajectories. *Politics and Society* 33:387–423.

Witte, Edwin E. 1963. *The development of the Social Security Act.* Madison: University of Wisconsin Press.

Wolfskill, George. 1962. The revolt of the conservatives. Boston: Houghton Mifflin.

Woodward, C. Vann. 1951. *Origins of the new South, 1877–1913.* Baton Rouge: Louisiana State University Press.

————. 1960. *The burden of Southern history*. Baton Rouge: Louisiana State University Press.

————. 1966. *Reunion and reaction: The compromise of 1877 and the end of Reconstruction*. Boston: Little, Brown.

————. 1973. Yes, there was a Compromise of 1877. *Journal of American History* 60:215–223.

Wright, Gavin. 1978. *The political economy of the cotton South: Households, markets, and wealth in the nineteenth century*. New York: W.W. Norton.

————. 1986. *Old South, new South*. New York: Basic Books.

Wrong, Dennis. 1995. *Power: Its forms, bases, and uses*. Second ed. New Brunswick, NJ: Transaction Publishers.

Young, Alfred. 1967. *The Democratic Republicans of New York*. Chapel Hill: University of North Carolina Press.

Young, Arthur. 1933. Grant from Rockefeller Foundation to cover expense of cooperation with government agencies, December 22. In *Rockefeller Foundation Collection, Record Group 1.1, Series 200S, Box 348, Folder 4143*. Sleepy Hollow, NY: Rockefeller Archive Center.

Zieger, Robert. 1986. *American workers, American unions, 1920–1985*. Baltimore: Johns Hopkins University Press.

————. 1995. *The CIO, 1935–1955*. Chapel Hill: University of North Carolina Press.

Zieger, Robert, and Gilbert Gall. 2002. *American workers, American unions: Third edition*. Baltimore: Johns Hopkins University Press.

Zilg, Gerald. 1974. *DuPont: Behind the nylon curtain*. Englewood Cliffs, NJ: Prentice-Hall.

After the Fall of the Wall: Life Courses in the Transformation of East Germany
EDITED BY MARTIN DIEWALD, ANNE GOEDICKE, AND KARL ULRICH MAYER
2006

The Moral Economy of Class: Class and Attitudes in Comparative Perspective
BY STEFAN SVALLFORS
2006

The Global Dynamics of Racial and Ethnic Mobilization
BY SUSAN OLZAK
2006

Poverty and Inequality
EDITED BY DAVID B. GRUSKY AND RAVI KANBUR
2006

Mobility and Inequality: Frontiers of Research in Sociology and Economics
EDITED BY STEPHEN L. MORGAN, DAVID B. GRUSKY, AND GARY S. FIELDS
2006

Analyzing Inequality: Life Chances and Social Mobility in Comparative Perspective
EDITED BY STEFAN SVALLFORS
2005

*On the Edge of Commitment: Educational Attainment and Race
in the United States*
BY STEPHEN L. MORGAN
2005

Occupational Ghettos: The Worldwide Segregation of Women and Men
BY MARIA CHARLES AND DAVID B. GRUSKY
2004

Home Ownership and Social Inequality in Comparative Perspective
EDITED BY KARIN KURZ AND HANS-PETER BLOSSFELD
2004

Reconfigurations of Class and Gender
EDITED BY JANEEN BAXTER AND MARK WESTERN
2001

Women's Working Lives in East Asia
EDITED BY MARY C. BRINTON
2001

The Classless Society
BY PAUL W. KINGSTON
2000